Wilderness Trails
of Tennessee's
Cherokee National Forest

Wilderness Trails of Tennessee's Cherokee National Forest

Edited by William H. Skelton

Written by the Harvey Broome Group
of the Tennessee Chapter of the Sierra Club

Foreword by Lamar Alexander

Outdoor Tennessee Series
Jim Casada, Series Editor

THE UNIVERSITY OF TENNESSEE PRESS / KNOXVILLE

To celebrate Tennessee's bicentennial in 1996, the Outdoor Tennessee Series covers a wide range of topics of interest to the general reader, including titles on the flora and fauna, the varied recreational activities, and the rich history of outdoor Tennessee. With a keen appreciation of the importance of protecting our state's natural resources and beauty, the University of Tennessee Press intends the series to emphasize environmental awareness and conservation.

 Printed on recycled paper.

The paper in this book meets the minimum requirements of the American National Standard for Permanence of Paper for Printed Library Materials. ∞   The binding materials have been chosen for strength and durability.

Frontispiece: South Holston Lake from Flint Mill Scenic Area. Photo by Roger Jenkins

Library of Congress Cataloging in Publication Data

Sierra Club. Tennessee Chapter. Harvey Broome Group.
    Wilderness trails of Tennessee's Cherokee National Forest / edited by William H. Skelton; written by the Harvey Broome Group of the Tennessee Chapter of the Sierra Club.—1st ed.
        p.   cm. — (Outdoor Tennessee series)
    Includes bibliographical references and index.
    ISBN 0-87049-771-5 (cloth: alk. paper).
    ISBN 0-87049-772-3 (pbk.: alk. paper).
    1. Hiking—Tennessee—Cherokee National Forest—Guidebooks.
    2. Cherokee National Forest (Tenn.) —Guidebooks.
I. Skelton, William H., 1942-   II. Title.   III. Series.
GV 199.42.T22C447   1992
917.688—dc20   92-18726
                                                        CIP

To the thousands of people who worked for passage of Tennessee's Cherokee National Forest Wilderness Acts

This book is intended only as a general guide for the Cherokee National Forest's natural areas and trails and is not a substitute for individual outdoor skills, including survival and route finding. Each user of the Cherokee National Forest should possess those outdoor skills, or be accompanied by an individual who does, since the specific information provided herein has been compiled from a variety of sources and is subject to the ever-changing natural and human-made environment.

Contents

Foreword

Near our cabin in West Miller's Cove outside Maryville, Tennessee, there are three trails. Walk back of the cabin and you will find a hunter's trail. It leads up the ridge to some coonhunter's shack. There are plenty of places to lie down and watch leaves float and see clouds through branches and listen to the wind making trees creak and smell air so clean that you know for sure that you are a long way away.

To the north of our cabin, another trail runs along Trunk Branch through two miles of land that the National Park Service wanted in the 1930s but couldn't afford even at ten dollars per acre. Walk those two miles—including the steep horse-slide at the end (so named because horses slide when they try to walk down it)—and you come to the Boundary Trail along the edge of the Great Smoky Mountains National Park. This Boundary Trail was once so overgrown that it was too rough to travel; today it is so well used that not many sprouts in the trail survive.

Go south from our cabin and you can find a network of old trails that will take you back through early history in East Tennessee—trails that run across the mountain to Maryville, or to the mouth of Abrams Creek or over to Cades Cove. A century ago mountaineers ran these ridges to the city to swap honey for salt and pepper; now the trails are busy again with refugees from the city looking for quiet.

The problem is, the quiet is getting hard to find. Too many people know these trails in and around the Great Smoky Mountains. When I was a boy it was different. We could walk the Appalachian Trail from Davenport Gap to Newfound Gap and rarely see a soul, never giving a thought to the possibility that there might not be a vacancy at the trail shelters. Now hikers must have permits to use the shelters, and once you are there the surrounding area can be as busy as an RV campground. Some trails are so worn that they might as well be paved. Some trails are paved.

Congestion in the Smokies is one reason why this guidebook about trails in the Cherokee National Forest is so welcome. Think of the CNF this way: the border of Tennessee and North Carolina meanders along the crest of the highest and most magnificent mountains in the eastern United States. The Great Smoky Mountains are a slice from the middle of this border. The Cherokee National Forest is everything else—larger than the Smokies, not nearly as well known and, as a result, as untrampeled as the Smokies were when I was a boy.

They are part of God's same quilt, but there are parts of the CNF that even the Smokies cannot match. Have you ever walked the Highlands of Roan Mountain in June, at 6,000 feet, the wind blowing so that wearing a poncho invites flying, the grasses bent to the ground, old yellow birches bending, the rhododendron in display? These are the most beautiful views along the entire Appalachian Trail. They are a part of the Cherokee National Forest. So is the John Muir National Recreation Trail along the Hiwassee, of which Muir in 1814 wrote: ". . . a most impressive mountain river . . . with its surface broken to a thousand sparkling gems, and its forest walls vinedraped and flowery as Eden."

This guidebook's dedication to the "thousands of people who worked for passage of Tennessee's Cherokee National Forest Wilderness Acts" should alert you: this is more than a guidebook. It is a political statement—and why should it not be? It is hard to discover the back country of these mountains without wanting to save them. In a nation this diverse it is important for those who know these mountains best to make their case.

I recall how in 1984 I thought the United States Congress would unanimously want to make most of the Great Smoky Mountain National Park a wilderness as a part of the park's fiftieth birthday celebration. The Smokies already were being managed like a wilderness in order to absorb the visits from nine million people each year. A permanent wilderness designation made sense.

Western U.S. senators had a different perspective. The federal government owns most of the West, and many westerners see more wilderness as a threat, the government owning too much more. But the government owns very little land in the East. Protecting the mountains along the border of North Carolina and Tennessee is a case that must be made.

Through this guidebook runs the enthusiasm of thousands of hikers who have discovered the Cherokee National Forest and who have worked to protect it. These friends of the CNF give us plenty of advice. About what to wear and how to camp. About rock formations. About what trees and flowers and plants grow in the CNF and what flies or moves at daybreak and at dusk. About speckled trout and where the rainbows hide. About the recent arrival of humans. And, of course, about how you can join their efforts to make certain that some of this wilderness remains as civilization encroaches.

One hundred years from now when my great-great-grandchildren will be as old as I am today, the main trails of Cherokee National Forest will be at least as populated as are today's trails through the Smoky Mountains. Campsites in the CNF will be crowded. There may even be, perish the thought, paved trails.

What there will not be, one hundred years from now, is still another Cherokee National Forest to explore and save. In Tennessee there are no more high mountains, grassy balds, rushing creeks. All there will be more of one hundred years from now are people and the residue of people.

This guidebook is welcome, first, because it is a road map to enjoyment, up Rattlesnake Ridge, down Stony Creek, over Pond Mountain, through the Doe River Gorge. (Let us not become so preoccupied with saving the forest that we forget to enjoy it!) And, second, it is welcome because it will multiply the thousands who have worked to protect the CNF into the larger army of tens of thousands who love walking a trail to some resting place where the noises are trees creaking, the smells of wet moss and leaves, the colors pure, and the world at peace.

A couple of salutes are in order. First, to Will Skelton and the members of the Harvey Broome Group of the Tennessee Chapter of the Sierra Club, not only for their work on this guidebook but because no Tennesseans have been more consistent and effective in reminding us that the outdoors surrounding us are worth saving.

A second salute goes to the University of Tennessee. *Wilderness Trails of Tennessee's Cherokee National Forest* is the first book in the Outdoor Tennessee Series, which the University of Tennessee Press plans in connection with the state's two-hundredth birthday in 1996. This is another one of those UT Press guidebooks that everyone who cares about our mountains will want two of—one for the bookshelf, one for the backpack.

Lamar Alexander
West Miller's Cove
June 1, 1992

Preface

Today we typically find material sustenance in the cities, but it is the high, remote hills that offer food for the soul. The Cherokee National Forest (CNF) is such a place—one where solitude beckons those who find solace amidst nature's splendor. This is not primeval wilderness, for earlier generations cut the region's virgin hardwood forests and eked out a precarious existence in its secluded coves and hollows. The healing hand of time has worked wonders, though, and today extensive portions of the CNF appear much as they did before pioneering settlers first began to fell trees and till soil along the west-facing spine of the Appalachians. Only the knowing, discerning eye detects the vestiges of human presence even though, just a few generations back, surprising numbers of hardy mountain folk wrested a hardscrabble existence over much of the CNF.

Here a pair of boxwoods, bright green where the gray of mid-winter dominates, mark the path leading to an old home place. Piles of stones, the occasional rock wall, and house foundations recall back-breaking labor of proud, self-sufficient men and women who lived close to the earth. The springtime pilgrim in the high country may find rambling roses, tiger lilies, or ancient fruit trees abloom. In isolated spots, usually atop a hill with a breathtaking view, one sometimes encounters slabs of stone marking long-forgotten grave sites. As a rule these crude stones are mute, for rarely could the hill folk afford the luxury of an engraved marker. Still, for those of a reflective nature, they bear poignant, powerful testament to a world we have lost. For the most part, though, the scars left by man are well hidden, with only isolated pockets of recent timber cutting striking a discordant note in this world of visual harmony.

Those who lived here in yesteryear saw it as a land full of hope and promise, and today we can look on the CNF in similar fashion. Those who once lived here sought fulfillment of basic physical needs; as visitors we look for mental peace and escape from the madding crowd. There are other differences as well. The regal monarch that once dominated Appalachian hardwood forests, the American chestnut, is gone, the victim of a virulent imported blight. With its passage we lost much, for the tree and its myriad benefits—rich nuts to feed man and beast, tannic acid unexcelled for leatherworking, virtually rot-proof fenceposts, shingles sure to stand the test of the most adverse weather conditions, and the wood to make beautiful furniture—loomed large in the lifestyles of southern highlanders. Today the American chestnut is almost gone from living memory. Sadly, the inhabitant of cold, pristine streams, the brook trout, may be traveling the same road, albeit at a slower pace. Siltation, acid rain, competition from rainbow and brown trout, and a host of other factors threaten this sprightly, strikingly beautiful fish. For now, though, "speckled trout," as they are known throughout the mountains, still survive in the laurel-shaded headwaters of the CNF, a lovely linchpin joining us to bygone days. For every species lost or threatened, however, there are dozens of survivors. Pink lady slippers blooming on a dry pinewoods ridge; a dozen different species of trilliums thriving in the moist, acid-rich soil; showy orchis catching the springtime wayfarer's eye; or a regiment of mayapples in their lime-green uniforms, standing shoulder-to-shoulder as they savor the warmth of earth's annual rebirth. These and countless other sights offer a visual feast no matter what the season, and the other senses of those who traverse the CNF encounter similar delights. Keen ears detect the raucous cry of the raven about the high ridges; the startling sound of a pileated woodpecker readily explains why it is known as the "Lord God bird" in some regions of the South; and always there are gray squirrels chirring and chipmunks squealing. Along with sound and sight, smell is accorded its due. Spring means the alluring fragrance of azaleas and the heady aroma of sweetshrub; summer brings the rank odor of rotting fungi blended with the tempting smell of ripening blackberries; autumn is characterized by the tangy essence of ripening persimmons and the pungency of pawpaws; and even in the dead of winter one can savor the sweetness of honey locust pods or the pleasingly acrid odor of spruce.

These sensations are all a part of the CNF's complex character, and the only real way to know this world of wonder is to walk through it. Roads do not reach its more remote fastnesses, and even if they did the automobile is ill suited to knowing the forest in intimate fashion. The CNF demands ample quantities of that priceless quality, time, but those who do tread its hidden footpaths and beckoning byways are richly rewarded. This is something the members of the Harvey Broome Group of the Tennessee Chapter of the Sierra Club have long recognized, and now, in a collective labor of love, they have seen fit to share their treasured experiences with others.

The result, *Wilderness Trails of Tennessee's Cherokee National Forest*, is a work eminently suited to the Outdoor Tennessee series. From the outset, one intent of this series has been to make Tennesseans, as well as others, more fully aware of the variegated offerings the Volunteer State presents to those who cherish the outdoor experience. Until now, there has been no truly suitable guide to the CNF, although the nearby Great Smoky Mountains National Park, along with that portion of the Appalachian Trail that traces its way along the North Carolina-Tennessee border, has attracted considerable attention. Works such as Carson Brewer's *Hiking in the Great Smokies* (1962), Dick Murlless and Constance Stallings's *Hiker's Guide to the Smokies*

(1973), Rodney and Priscilla Albright's *Walks in the Great Smokies* (1979, 1990), and the Appalachian Trail Conference's *Appalachian Trail Guide to Tennessee-North Carolina* (9th ed., 1989), among others, come to mind. Yet we have had no work focusing solely on the CNF's trails, and only a handful of books, such as Evan Means's *Tennessee Trails* (3rd ed., 1989) and Robert Brandt's *Tennessee Hiking Guide* (1982), have touched on the region at all.

With the appearance of *Wilderness Trails*, we have a work that fills a gap in the literature of hiking and constitutes a model for this genre. Featuring well over a score of contributors, the volume draws on literally hundreds of years and untold thousands of miles of hiking experience. Often efforts of this type are disjointed or of uneven quality, but thanks to Will Skelton's solid grip on the editorial tiller, the present work steers well clear of such shoals.

Instead, what we have is a guide that bids fair to serve hikers in the CNF, and serve them exceptionally well, for many years to come. That being said, let me hasten to add that the book is much more than just another handy reference tool to be stowed away in one's backpack for occasional consultation. *Wilderness Trails* is a truly comprehensive work. It not only gives the reader details on intended routes but also provides a solid overview of the CNF's natural and human history. A number of appendices add to the book's usefulness; novices will find a helpful chapter on the "dos and don'ts" of safe hiking; detailed maps, which are essential to a guide of this sort, are present. In sum, this easily understood work is "reader friendly."

Wilderness Trails will appeal to a wide audience. Hikers will find it indispensable, as will bird watchers, wildlife photographers, and those who find joy in the simple act of communing closely with nature. Sportsmen too, especially those of a more adventurous nature, will discover grist for their mills here. For example, any angler worth his salt is always looking for forgotten creeks, for trout-filled waters that are, as that consummate outdoorsman, Horace Kephart, put it, "back of beyond." These pages suggest avenues to such treasure troves for fisherman (and hunters), as indeed they open up enticing vistas for all who appreciate what oneness with the natural world can mean.

Finally, and perhaps most importantly, devotion to keeping the CNF forever wild runs as a bright ribbon of hope throughout the work. As a volume forming part of a series devoted to environmental awareness and conservation, that is only as it should be. With that in mind, as you use this book remember that the good earth, properly treated, will never, ever, let mankind down.

Jim Casada
Series Editor
Rock Hill, South Carolina

Acknowledgments

We would like to acknowledge, first, a gift that helped make this book possible. The Lana S. Lombardo Wilderness Trust Fund was established by Mrs. Lombardo's husband, Thomas G. Lombardo, family, and friends in her memory after her death in an automobile accident in 1985 at the age of forty-one. The trust was established to help maintain, expand, and preserve wilderness and hiking areas in east and middle Tennessee and western North Carolina. Lana Lombardo was an avid hiker and a lover of wilderness trails. Her legacy has helped to provide funding both to support the passage of the 1986 Tennessee Wilderness Act and the publication of this book. We are thankful, as will be many future generations of Cherokee National Forest hikers.

Second, we would like to acknowledge the efforts of all the people who worked on this book, many of whose names are indicated as contributors in a separate section. Hugh Irwin deserves special thanks for his extraordinary contributions. Several people helped with editing portions of the manuscript, including Barbara Muhlbeier, Hartwell Herring, James Wedekind, Samantha Pack, Martha Ketelle, Janet Goodwin, and Janice Irwin. The most time-consuming editing was by Cata Folks, Emily Ellis, and Jo Wetherall, who each reviewed the entire manuscript. Margaret Olson, Susie McDonald, and Janice McMillan were invaluable; they typed the original manuscript, often from a variety of difficult-to-read sources, and Janice McMillan retyped the manuscript numerous times. Several members of the State of Franklin Group of the Tennessee Chapter of the Sierra Club worked on various sections of the book. The Cherokee National Forest provided valuable information; particularly helpful were Sam Brocato and Reese Scull. Expertise on wildlife and botany was also provided by, respectively, Andrew Schiller and Paul Somers. Retired Cherokee National Forest Recreation Staff Officer Russ Griffith provided a substantial amount of factual information and read the entire manuscript. Will Fontanez, at the University of Tennessee Cartography Laboratory, prepared the maps on very short notice. Although Roger Jenkins provided most of the photographs, Lance McCold, E. Kenneth McDonald, William H. Skelton, Suzanne McDonald, and Russ Manning also provided photographs. And there were many others who helped in both large and small ways.

Third, we would like to thank the public officials and elected representatives who made possible the protection of the areas described in this guidebook; many are listed in the Political History section. Senators James Sasser and Al Gore have consistently supported the protection of wilderness in the Cherokee National Forest and deserve special thanks. Former Governor Lamar Alexander, former Senator Howard Baker, Congressman James Quillen, and the late Congressman John Duncan also deserve special thanks for introducing and/or supporting the acts that designated the Cherokee National Forest's wilderness areas. Finally, the Cherokee National Forest staff, including then-Supervisor Don Rollens, deserve our thanks for supporting such wilderness acts.

Finally, we thank the University of Tennessee Press and especially its managing editor, Stan Ivester. Their contributions resulted in many improvements in this book.

Statement of Purpose

Members of the Harvey Broome Group of the Sierra Club's Tennessee Chapter have roamed the world in search of wilderness places and experiences, from the world's highest mountains in Nepal to the canyons of Utah, to the summit of Mt. Kilimanjaro, to Alaska's Brooks Range. But they always come home to the southern Appalachians and especially the mountains, ridges, and valleys in Tennessee's Cherokee National Forest along the eastern Tennessee-western North Carolina state line. Here are spectacular vistas, looking west over the broad, gentle, and green Tennessee Valley or east to a succession of misty high blue mountaintops; crystal-clear mountain streams cascading over mountain rocks and waterfalls; a veritable cornucopia of wildflowers that match any artist's palette; historical echoes of long-gone Cherokee Indians and pioneer settlers as well as extinct species like the cougar, bison, elk, and gray wolf; and one of the few remaining refuges of the black bear and other species that have suffered from encroachments of our modern society.

The Cherokee National Forest is an asset to present and future generations because a small portion has been protected, we hope for all time, in a variety of land-use categories that generally prohibit clear-cutting, road building, motor vehicles, and development. Hiking and backpacking in these natural areas are truly experiences to be treasured, experiences that will not be marred by our society's seemingly endless need to destroy natural areas.

There is no existing comprehensive guidebook to the protected natural areas of the Cherokee National Forest. The present guidebook to the forest's wilderness trails provides such a comprehensive guide and was prepared for two interrelated reasons: first, to encourage and help people visit, hike, backpack, hunt, fish, bird-watch, and otherwise enjoy these natural areas; second, and most important, to encourage the public to insist, to our elected United States representatives and senators and the United States Forest Service, that the trails and natural areas described in this book be kept forever wild and natural. They are protected only by statutes or administrative decision, both of which can be changed or modified by, respectively, the United States Congress and the United States Forest Service. Indeed, the United States Forest Service reviews its administrative protection of natural areas approximately every ten years. It is now up to the public to see that the natural areas included in this guidebook continue to be protected from timber harvesting, road building, and development that would destroy the very attributes that resulted in their protection. That is our goal, and we seek your help in ensuring that it is realized.

The benefits of protecting the natural areas of the Cherokee National Forest are numerous and include the following:

1. Watershed protection. Stable soil found in natural areas is a source of clean water for streams and rivers.

2. Baseline information. Natural areas provide places where human influences have not drastically modified natural processes, thus allowing comparison from time to time to see how the other areas are faring.

3. Education and research. Natural areas provide opportunities for numerous Tennessee and southeastern United States educational institutions, ranging from elementary-school field trips to university researchers.

4. Diversity of forest trees. The United States Forest Service proposes substantial clear-cutting of much of the Cherokee National Forest within the next fifty years. Natural areas will ensure that a significant portion of the Cherokee National Forest continues to be covered with large trees—"late successional species" in the United States Forest Service's terminology—that many people want to see when they visit a national forest.

5. Diversity of wildlife habitat. Different animal species have different habitat requirements. Some species—and especially the black bear, bobcat, and cougar—require large roadless tracts, which natural areas provide. Other species, such as brook trout, squirrel, raccoon, and ruffed grouse, will also do well in natural areas.

6. Diversity of plant species. Different species of plants also require different habitats, and some plant species will survive better in natural habitats.

7. Recreation. Purely and simply, hiking in a natural area is a pleasure for many people for many reasons—adventure, exploration, exercise, and solitude. The assurance that there will be no off-road vehicle traffic and noise, no clear-cuts and no roads, makes for a special experience. These attributes also improve the recreational aspects of many other uses of natural areas, from horseback riding to hunting, fishing, bird-watching, and backpacking.

8. Living museum. An almost endless forest once covered most of the southern Appalachian Mountains and, indeed, most of the eastern United States. We have been steadily reducing that forest, year by year, to a bare remnant of what once existed. Although the natural areas in this book contain only traces of that virgin forest, they are primarily covered with older trees. Protecting those areas will provide a living museum of what once existed for our study and enjoyment.

How to Use This Guidebook

This guidebook is both a resource for general information on the Cherokee National Forest and a source of detailed descriptions of areas and trails and their access. General information on the Cherokee National Forest is presented in Section A, including the natural, human, and political environments that have made the Cherokee National Forest what it is today. Section B provides detailed area and trail descriptions for areas in the northern Cherokee National Forest (presented in geographical order from north to south). Section C presents descriptions of the areas and trails in the southern portion of the Cherokee National Forest (also in geographical order from north to south).

This guidebook is not intended to be a how-to-hike or backpack book and does not provide the information and skills necessary for those activities. If you lack the necessary skills, you should, before striking out on your own, obtain such skills through a variety of sources: several excellent how-to books are listed in the bibliography; many colleges and universities, including the University of Tennessee, offer noncredit courses in hiking and backpacking; numerous environmental and hiking groups have an active outings program, often featuring one or more beginner backpacks; several backpacking and outfitter shops located near the Cherokee National Forest are listed in Appendix 4 and are a good source of practical information and, in some cases, backpacking courses; and friends and acquaintances who know something about backpacking and hiking are invaluable. The Tennessee Chapter of the Sierra Club and, particularly, its east Tennessee groups in Knoxville, Chattanooga, and the Tri-Cities probably have the greatest concentration of outings to the Cherokee National Forest. These groups and other environmental and outing clubs in the area are listed in Appendix 3.

Once you have the necessary skills, your principal problem will be the smorgasbord of outstanding areas and trails from which to choose. This guidebook will help in that respect by giving you a general idea of the attributes of the various areas and trails. You may want to scan the various descriptions to determine whether a particular area or trail appeals to you. Note that alternate Trail names are sometimes shown in parenthesis. Or you may choose an area based on proximity to your residence **(see the Cherokee National Forest Location Map)** or a friend's recommendation. Once you have focused on a particular area—because of location, attributes, or a recommendation—you may want to buy a US Geological Survey topographic map of the area. The maps in this book were prepared from topographic maps but do not show all topographic features, such as elevation contours. Sources for topographic maps are identified in Appendix 1. Before actually getting started, many people choose to make photocopies of the relevant pages from guidebooks (and perhaps even the topographic maps) rather than lugging along the book itself; most of the book will usually relate to trails you are not hiking on a specific day.

This guidebook also contains a wealth of information on aspects of the Cherokee National Forest other than trails which many people will want to read before or after visiting an area. For example, if you saw a rock outcrop and wondered what it meant geologically, there is a section on geology. Other sections cover history, both political and human, and the wildlife and vegetation of the Cherokee National Forest. With your topographical map and this guidebook, you can get to the trailhead and have a pretty good idea of where to go and what to expect.

At this point we want to say a word about the difficulty of trails. After much debate we have chosen not to assign a difficulty rating to each trail. This decision comes from the authors' years of experience with other guidebooks which assign difficulty ratings that are often so inconsistent when applied to specific hikers that they are worthless, if not dangerous. One person's easy trail is often another person's hard trail. Sometimes we have mentioned particularly steep and difficult trail sections. We also provide starting and ending elevations. With that and other information in this book and topographical maps, you can get a general idea as to the difficulty of a trail for you. However, the advice must always be to know your limitations and, if a trail seems too difficult, turn back.

It is particularly important to remember, when using this guidebook and topographical maps, that the Cherokee National Forest trail system is a "living" system with both human and environmental changes each and every year. Most of the trails included herein were hiked during 1989 through 1991. It is therefore certain that some of the trails will have changed by this book's publication date. Human changes may have resulted from official relocation of trails in order to correct trail erosion; changes in permitted uses, such as from hiker use only to horse and hiker use; changes in trail blazes, names, and numbers; and changes by hikers who sometimes find what they think is a better route and move the trail location by use. (Under current plans, the USFS may reduce the number of trail blazes, and the CNF's wilderness management plans specify axe, rather than painted, blazes in the future.) Environmental changes may include bridges that are washed out, trees that are blown down over the trail, and trails that are overgrown due to lack of maintenance. In addition to dating the information in this guidebook, such changes can be even more pronounced with regard to roads, trails, and developments shown on the topographical maps. Most of the topographical maps you will use are not really current; some date back to the 1950s.

Hikers and backpackers will find this book of invaluable benefit. However, we want to make it clear that numerous other related users of the Cherokee National Forest will also find valuable information in this guidebook. Anglers looking for trail access to a trout stream, hunters looking for a back-country campsite near a favorite hunting area, horseback riders looking for a good trail ride, bird-watchers looking for a particular species, and botanists looking for a particularly beautiful flower will all benefit from this guidebook. Hunting and fishing are legitimate uses of our national forests, provided there is compliance with applicable state game and fish laws and seasons. Horseback riding is also a legitimate use on designated horse trails, some of which are identified in this guidebook. All users can enjoy and benefit from the Cherokee National Forest's wilderness trails, and all we ask is that they respect the natural beauty of the forest and leave it just as natural and beautiful when they leave.

We would appreciate your letting us know of any significant changes in the trails and areas included herein, any errors you feel may have slipped through our editing process, and any other comments to help us in connection with future editions of this guidebook. Send your comments to:

William H. Skelton, Editor
Wilderness Trails of the Cherokee National Forest
c/o Baker, Worthington, Crossley, Stansberry & Woolf
Suite 2200, Riverview Tower
900 Gay Street, SW, Knoxville, TN 37902

We hope to see you on one of the many Cherokee National Forest trails.

Abbreviations

We will use the following abbreviations throughout this book.

AT	Appalachian Trail
CNF	Cherokee National Forest
FS	Forest Service Road
GA	Georgia
GSMNP	Great Smoky Mountains National Park
I-	Interstate Highway
NC	North Carolina, North Carolina Highway Number
NPS	National Park Service
ORV	Off-Road Vehicle
Primitive Area	Semiprimitive Nonmotorized Recreation Opportunity Area
TN	Tennessee, Tennessee Highway Number
Trail No.	United States Forest Service Trail Number
TVA	Tennessee Valley Authority
TWRA	Tennessee Wildlife Resources Agency
US	United States, United States Highway Number
USFS	United States Forest Service, United States Forest Service Road Number
USGS	United States Geological Survey
USNF	United States National Forest
VA	Virginia
WMA	Wildlife Management Area

"Area(s)" will be used to refer to Wildernesses, Scenic Areas, and/or Primitive Areas that are the subject of specific sections; if "area" is not capitalized, it refers to the general geographic area.

SYMBOL GUIDE TO TRAIL MAPS

75 Interstate Highway		Paved Road
411 US Highway		Gravel Road
68 State Primary Route		ORV Road
165 State Secondary Route		Trail
▲ Mountain		State Line
● Landmark Site		Railroad
AT Shelter		Primitive Area
152 Trail Number		Scenic Area
Ⓐ Trail Head		Wilderness Area

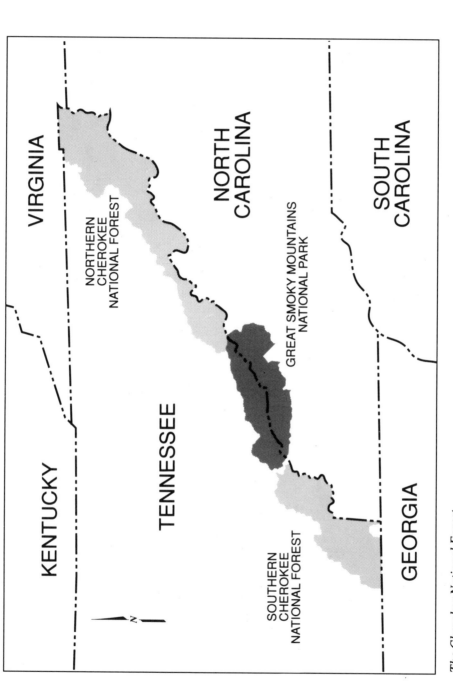

The Cherokee National Forest.

Section A

General Information

1. THE CHEROKEE NATIONAL FOREST

The CNF consists of approximately 626,420 acres of forested federal lands generally located along the TN-NC state line, extending from GA to VA. The GSMNP also lies on the TN-NC state line and divides the CNF into two portions. The northern CNF (see map, page 45) extends north from the GSMNP to the VA-TN state line and includes 327,470 acres. There are three ranger districts on the northern CNF, with the Watauga District on the north, the Unaka District in the center, and the Nolichucky District on the south (see Appendix 2 for addresses). The southern CNF (see map, page 166) includes 298,997 acres and extends south from the GSMNP and the Little Tennessee River to the GA-TN state line. Three ranger districts are also located on the southern CNF, with the Tellico District on the north, the Hiwassee District in the center, and the Ocoee District on the south (addresses in Appendix 2).

The CNF is part of the national forest system managed by the USFS. As a national forest, the CNF is managed according to different statutory guidelines from national parks. National parks, pursuant to the National Park Service Organic Act of 1916, are managed so as to "conserve the scenery and the natural and historic objects and the wildlife therein" but, at the same time, the management must "provide for the enjoyment of the same in such a manner and by such means as will leave them unimpaired for the enjoyment of future generations." Preservation is therefore the principal requirement of national park management. On the other hand, national forests are managed for a variety of multiple uses pursuant to the National Forest Management Act of 1976 and related statutes. Such uses include a variety of benefits including water, forage, wildlife, wood, minerals, and recreation. Timber production, often by the use of clear-cutting of forest tracts of up to 40 acres, is an important part of the USFS's legislative mission.

Although much of the CNF is therefore not managed as a park, significant portions have, under the multiple-use concept, been recognized by the USFS as having outstanding scenic, wildlife, and recreation qualities. Such acres are protected in a variety of management categories by the USFS, including *wilderness areas, scenic areas,* and *primitive areas.* We have generally included in this guidebook only those trails located in or providing access to such protected areas. In a few cases individual trails that have a protected corridor are included. By describing only such protected areas and trails, your outdoor experience should therefore avoid those activities that can quickly ruin one's wilderness experience: clear-cuts, motorized vehicles, roads, and development.

Following is a description of the various management categories used by the CNF.

WILDERNESS AREAS

Wilderness designation of federal lands by Congress under the 1964 Wilderness Act is the best protection and the most secure in that only Congress can change it. The 1964 Wilderness Act defines *wilderness* as a natural environment where "the earth and its community of life are untrammeled by man, where man himself is a visitor who does not remain." Further, it should be "an area of undeveloped Federal land retaining its primeval character and influence, without permanent improvements or human habitation." Commercial and other timber harvesting, motorized vehicles (including ORVs), development, and construction (other than trails) are prohibited, leaving these areas as natural as possible. Hiking, backpacking, hunting (in national forests but not national parks), fishing, horseback riding (but only on trails designated for horse use), nature study—these are all allowed. The use of vehicles and timber cutting are allowed, with proper approval, for fighting forest fires, search and rescue, and treating insect infestation. The USFS's wilderness management guidelines are as follows: "The physical and biological components are managed so that natural processes, excluding naturally occurring wildfire, proceed unrestricted by human activities. . . . Visitor use will be managed to a level compatible with the wilderness resource to prevent loss of solitude or unacceptable depreciation of wilderness qualities."

SCENIC AREAS

The term *scenic area* is a USFS designation for a block of land that has outstanding scenic characteristics. Scenic areas are only administratively protected, and such designation may be changed by the USFS pursuant to Forest Management Plans, which are revised every 10 to 15 years (the current plan was adopted on August 4, 1988). The protection is also of a lesser degree than for wilderness although it is significant since logging is generally prohibited. The guidelines state simply: "Timber will not be managed," although limited cutting is allowed for hazard prevention, vista enhancement, and pest-infested tree removal. Roads and vehicles are allowed under strict guidelines, and practically this should mean that vehicle use will be limited to a very few existing roads. The overall management criteria are to "provide an environment for a high quality dispersed recreation opportunity and . . . maintain and protect the ecological, scenic, and botanical attributes of the areas."

PRIMITIVE AREAS

These areas are designated by the USFS to maintain the resources and attributes most desirable for those types of outdoor recreation practiced in a semiprimitive environment. Although these are called *semiprimitive,* nonmotorized recreation areas by the USFS (also known as "management category 14 areas"), we will refer to these areas as *primitive areas* for brevity's sake. Primitive areas are also protected only by the current CNF Management Plan; pending any change, they will generally not have timber harvesting, road construction/reconstruction, or ORV use. Within this category are several subcategories. Most will not have any timber harvesting or motor vehicle use. However, a few indicated areas may have limited timber harvesting, but with less than 20-acre clear-cuts and with road access being closed after any timber operation. Two areas will also allow motor vehicles, but only on specific roads. All of these primitive areas are at risk, and continued efforts by conservationists will be necessary to protect them under the USFS's future forest plans.

As to the trails themselves, hiking is a legal use of all the routes covered by this guidebook. In some cases trails are designated by the USFS as horse trails; both hikers and horses may use those trails. Horses are otherwise prohibited on the trails in this book, often because of steep terrain or a trail that was not constructed to horse use standards. Trails will therefore be specified as *hiking,* meaning foot travel only, or *horse,* meaning horse or foot travel. In a few cases primitive roads that either provide access to or enter an area will be described. Those roads are specified as *road,* and motor vehicle, horse and foot travel are allowed. Motor vehicles are otherwise prohibited on all trails described in this guidebook.

2. SOME WARNINGS AND ADVICE

Hiking in the southern Appalachians brings one into intimate contact with nature. These encounters should be a delight to the senses and should not be threatening. It is important to act as responsible hikers. If you are just getting started in hiking, there are a number of fine books to help you on your way, some of which are listed in the Bibliography. *Backpacking, One Step at a Time,* by Harvey Manning, *Walk Softly in the Wilderness,* by John Hart, and *The New Complete Walker III,* by Colin Fletcher, are all excellent guides, with much more detail than would be appropriate for this book. Nevertheless, we will provide some specific advice for the CNF.

Because of hunting pressure, CNF black bears tend to be more wary than their counterparts in the GSMNP. So consider yourself fortunate if you see a bear, but be careful. Small cubs are usually within earshot of their mothers, and mama bears often act unpredictably if they sense that their cubs are threatened. Give bears, wild boars, and any other wild animals plenty of distance. Relax, enjoy your experience, but remember: it's *their* home; *you* are just a visitor.

As much as you may enjoy wild animals, don't ever feed them, intentionally or otherwise. The "otherwise" is usually the major problem. Protect your food, and never underestimate the cleverness or resourcefulness of a panhandling bear. Remember that if a bear is of the panhandling type, it sees that brightly colored stuff sack hanging in the tree much as a human might see the Golden Arches—an announcement of food availability. Hang your food well off the ground, at least 6 feet from any trunk or branch big enough to support a small bear, and several feet below the branch on which it is hanging. Little animals, such as mice and squirrels, also get hungry and cold, and they can ruin a pack or stuff sack if they try to get to food or a nesting place. So here's a tip. If you leave your pack out overnight, don't leave any food in it, and open up all the pockets before you put your rain cover over it. It's better to have a mouse actually make a nest out of your wool hat than to have it first chew through your pack to get to the wool hat.

Copperheads and timber rattlesnakes are present in the CNF, although rarely seen. They are beautiful and are important to nature's balance. Do not even think of doing them harm. Show them the same respect that you would want. After all, would you like to be stepped on? Also, be careful where you put your hands and feet. Always look on the other side of a log before you step over it. The chance of a careful hiker's being bitten is extremely small, but you should be prepared with first aid knowledge and equipment. Indeed, a rudimentary knowledge of first aid should be a prerequisite for wilderness travel. *Medicine for Mountaineering*, published by the Mountaineers, is excellent (see Bibliography). More likely than snake bites are stinging insects. The biggest problem seems to be in early September and the fall when yellow jackets become particularly ornery. Know before you start hiking whether you might be susceptible to allergic reactions. It's usually a long way to medical help. And with the growing spread of Lyme disease, it's always a good idea to inspect for ticks at least twice a day.

The perception of weather in the southern Appalachians can be deceiving. It can be 88 degrees and sweltering in the TN Valley while a thunderstorm rages on the high peaks with the thermometer reading 45 degrees. Or it can be raining in Knoxville and partly cloudy on top of Fodderstack. The point is that the mountains can often create their own weather, and it is best to be prepared for anything nature might throw at you. A good rule of thumb is that for every 1,000 feet of elevation increase, the temperature will drop about 3 degrees Fahrenheit. It can often be windier in the mountains. And wind, combined with rain, can really accelerate the loss of body heat. That's why smart hikers in the CNF never leave home without rain gear (see list of Ten Essentials, below). The tops of the mountains around here are within a couple of inches of rainfall from being officially classified as a rain forest. Keep that in mind.

Lightning is something with which all sensible hikers concern themselves. Many people advise not waiting out a thunderstorm in a metal-roofed or gated trail shelter. People have perished in the GSMNP in such structures. Instead, get off the high ground. If you are hiking on a long ridgecrest, drop down in the woods a hundred yards or so, the lower the better. If you are caught out in the open and cannot get to lower ground, many advise to keep moving; do not stand still. If you do, you run the risk of allowing static charges to accumulate on your body, and acting as your own lightning rod.

The streams of the Cherokee can be delightful, especially in the summertime. But after a good rain, the water levels can rise very quickly and turn a babbling brook into a treacherous or impassable torrent. If you have any doubt in your ability to negotiate a stream safely, have one of the more sure-footed members of your party test the waters—without a pack. Stay away from large rocks in the stream, as currents near them can be especially hazardous. A rope tied across the stream can restore the confidence of the more timid party members and can be helpful in an emergency. If anyone ends up taking an unscheduled swim, watch out for the early signs of hypothermia (shivering, slow speech, loss of coordination). Many streams can feel like an ice bath in any season. The CNF is also blessed with a number of lovely waterfalls; do not be tempted to climb on them. Moss or algae-covered rocks can be unbelievably slippery and can be very unforgiving if your head or knee hits them at the right angle.

In most cases, the direction from which the trail is described in this book is from the trailhead that provides the easiest access. However, it should be obvious, but deserves stating explicitly, that all of the trails can be hiked in either direction, often giving quite different views, experiences, and impressions. When necessary, we hope, the descriptions can be deciphered in the reverse direction. An additional point regarding trails: trail mileage measurement is something of an art, and you may find the mileage in this guidebook sometimes differing from other sources, including posted mileage. Although each trail was walked with a measuring wheel, you should not rely absolutely on specific distances.

TEN ESSENTIALS

With all the excitement that the wilderness can throw at you, it seems to be only common sense that the hiker should be ready to meet it with at least the bare minimum of equipment. This minimum is usually referred to in hiking guides as the

Ten Essentials. (The exact number and composition of such a list can often consume hours of debate around the campfire, or anyplace else where hikers congregate.) Briefly, the Ten Essentials are those items that you should never leave the trailhead without. And that means NEVER! EVER! It is absolutely amazing how many hikers have heard this and yet fail to heed the advice. Why not? Laziness. Stupidity. The old "It can't happen to me" syndrome. Well, maybe not. But are you willing to bet your life on it? Some folks have and have either lost or come dangerously close to losing. The couple of pounds that the essentials represent are not "extra." They are absolutely critical. There is no way to emphasize this point too much. "OK, OK," you say. "I'll carry them—but what are they?" Again, the list will vary depending on whom you talk to, but the following are some that almost everyone can agree on.

First Aid Kit. The casual hiker can purchase ready-made kits, or you can fabricate your own. You don't have to be prepared for cardiac bypass surgery on the trail. Keep it simple: a few Band-Aids, some gauze and adhesive tape, an elastic bandage for twisted knees or ankles, some butterfly bandages for deep cuts, a few antihistamines for bee stings, and some painkillers are most of what is needed for day hiking. For extended backpacking trips, you might want to add a few more things. Talk to your family doctor about which prescription medications you might want to have.

Maps. At least carry copies of the relevant pages of this guidebook with you. Better yet, also carry topographic maps. You say you don't know how to read the maps? Learn. It is easy, and anyone intelligent enough to read a highway map and get to the trailhead is intelligent enough to read a topographic map. The complexity of the terrain in the CNF is almost unbelievable. Unless you are on a very well-maintained trail, it is easy to get onto a less well-maintained spur, and before you know it, you are in the next valley. You can purchase topographic maps from a number of sources (see Appendix 1).

Compass. Do not assume you can find north on a cloudy day without instrument assistance. Yes, moss does grow on the north side of a tree. But in the near-rain forests of the CNF, it also grows on the south side, on the east side, etc. You probably spent five or ten bucks' worth of gas getting to your hike; you do not have to spend much more on a good compass. And invest ten minutes' worth of your valuable time reading the material that came with it. It can be really amazing to learn how many people carry compasses and do not know how to use them.

Rain Gear. The comments above should have convinced you to take rain gear, even on a bright, sunny day. But do not feel that you cannot leave the trailhead without a $250 Gore-Tex rain suit. Sure, they are great, but so is anything that will keep you dry: garbage sacks, ponchos, coated nylon rain suits. Some hikers even carry umbrellas. And you backpackers, do not forget a cover for your pack. Even the coated nylon pack bags will let water seep in and dampen your sleeping bag or extra clothes.

Extra Clothes, including a Wool Hat. You lose 35 percent of your total body heat through your head. That 35 percent can make a tremendous difference in cool weather. It may be the thing that keeps you alive through an unscheduled night out. But most of all, it keeps the brain warm so that you can think your way out of any predicament in which you find yourself.

Matches. Get the waterproof variety, or put the regular ones in a waterproof container. Cigarette lighters are very convenient, especially for starting backpacking stoves. But try to use them after the flint has gotten wet, and you'll see why people who carry them also carry matches. And remember that starting a fire in the CNF can sometimes be a nontrivial matter, especially when it has been raining for a few days—or even a few hours. Don't be afraid to assist the start-up with a little toilet paper or a few pine cones.

Knife. We are not talking here about the forty-tool, everything-including-the-kitchen-sink Swiss Army variety. Just a simple, one- or two-bladed type will do. To cut fabric, shave kindling, cut some cord, etc.

Flashlight. This one seems to raise the most eyebrows among novice hikers. "Why do I have to take a flashlight for a day hike?" Of course, the answer is because it's only light about half of the time. Sometimes it's difficult to judge the amount of time it will take to complete a hike. Or maybe you just want to watch the sunset from an overlook 4 miles up the trail. There are any number of reasons why you might be out after dark. But walking in the dark on a trail, without a light, can be a terrifying experience, especially after the fourth fall. Just make sure that the batteries are reasonably fresh or that you're carrying spares. For extended trips, always carry a spare bulb or two.

Extra Food. "Extra" implies that you have some food with you to begin with. We know that no one is likely to starve to death even going without food for a week or two. But that extra snack bar will give your body a little charge to help keep warm on a cold day and may help you think straight. And relax. Do not worry about nutrition. Anything that is high in carbohydrates will be fine. This is your one chance to justify all of those things that you do not eat the rest of the time because you want to stay healthy. So go ahead, pour in the Twinkies and the M&Ms. This is not the time to be dieting.

The Tenth Essential. This is your call. *Think* about what might be important to you. For some it might be strong insect repellent or water purification tablets; for others, toilet paper, a hairbrush, make-up, or the latest Tom Clancy novel. Everyone should try to take along a good load of common sense.

In addition to these essentials, it is advisable to leave your trip itinerary with family, friends, and/or the USFS. Sometimes problems do arise, and even experienced backpackers can be unavoidably delayed. If the USFS is contacted to look for someone, it is a big help to know the lost party's location rather than simply "somewhere in the CNF." And with regard to getting lost, remember the common advice for the southern Appalachian mountains: you can usually follow any creek downstream and along a succession of larger streams to a road or other source of help. This advice does not necessarily apply in other parts of the United States or the world, but the relatively small size of most natural areas and population density make it appropriate for the southern Appalachians.

A lot of people seem to shy away from hiking during hunting season. That is too bad since that is often when the mountains are in their finest colors. Incidents of hikers being shot by accident are very rare in TN. Nevertheless, it's probably a good idea to wear bright colors (preferably hunter or international orange) during that time of year. Remember that probably the most dangerous thing you will do on your entire journey is to *drive* to the trailhead. Wear your seat belt when you do.

One final note of caution: the maintenance level of the trails in this book varies greatly, from well-marked, cleared, and graded trails to those receiving almost no maintenance. The USFS's record in such matters is spotty at best, and they should be encouraged to maintain all of the designated trails. Pending better upkeep, hikers should watch their maps and the trails carefully. Of course, there are always those who prefer the more adventurous course: off-trail. This can be an exciting experience, but it is not for beginners. Hiking off-trail in this part of the country can require anywhere from two to ten times the energy expenditure per mile as on-trail hiking. Good compass and map skills are absolutely critical to a successful off-trail trip, and an altimeter—and the knowledge to use it properly—can really help. If you are hiking off-trail in the foothills, there is always the risk that you will stumble onto a still or a marijuana patch. If you do, and it is during growing season, beat a hasty and quiet retreat.

3. GEOLOGY

When the Cherokee referred to the mountain ranges that partly divided their nation, they called them the *unica*—the white mountains—a curious name for the
spines of sinuous ridges, clothed by a rich green forest and often shrouded in a bluish
mist. It is doubtful they named them for the fleeting winter snowcover, which rarely
lasts into spring. Perhaps the Cherokee were most impressed by what made up the
mountains, rock faces protruding through the dense forest and gleaming white
against the prevailing green, brown, and blue-gray.

The Unaka Mountains, as they are now called, form the eastern boundary of
TN and comprise the bulk of the CNF. The Unakas and their sister range to the east,
the Blue Ridge, comprise much of the southern Appalachians.

When viewed from the TN Valley, the Unakas typically appear as a rampart of
rugged cliffs. These cliffs were formed by resistant layers of rock composed of nearly
1-billion-year-old sand and pebbles, fused by the natural forces of the Earth. In contrast, the Blue Ridge is characterized by smooth-faced peaks made up of even older
rocks that display crystals of quartz, feldspar, garnet, and mica. These dissimilar
mountain ranges formed the ultimate foundation of the Cherokee world. The geologic history of the CNF explores the story told from the rocks of the Unaka Mountains, a steadfast fixture in a constantly changing environment.

The history of the southern Appalachians began about 800 million years ago
during Late Precambrian time. Most of the rock in the Unakas consists of sedimentary material (sand, silt, and mud) that was shed off the early North American continent (Laurentia) and an offshore volcanic archipelago. Deposition of these sediments continued for about 100 million years; then the region experienced a relatively
minor mountain-building event, the Avalonian orogeny. This was accompanied by
150 to 200 million years of deposition as thousands of feet of sediment were eroded
off the early mountains. Then the major mountain-building event, called the Appalachian (or Alleghanian) orogeny, began about 250 to 300 million years ago and continued for almost 100 million years. This event spawned a lofty, wide mountain
range that stretched from the southern US to Newfoundland and beyond. While the
dinosaurs flourished, the young Appalachians were being eroded by the Earth's per-
vasive responses to climate and gravity. The entire range may have been reduced to
a sloping plain by the time the dinosaurs disappeared, about 65 million years ago.
However, a gentle uplift, accompanied by increased erosion during subsequent glacial periods, eroded the less resistant shale and limestone, leaving the present-day
topography. Sandstone, more resistant to erosion, forms the high ranges in the Unakas
as well as many of the low ridges in the TN Valley.

Many of the major rivers of today in this region originated during the onset of this latest erosive period. That is why the Little Tennessee, Pigeon, and French Broad rivers have impressive gorges cut through the Unakas rather than snaking between them. These ancient rivers originally meandered across a rather flat plain, then retained their original configuration as they cut into the harder rock below. The slopes of the present-day Unakas are often mantled with a veneer of boulder fields, talus-like colluvial deposits, and streambeds of well-rounded stones, sand, and gravel. These geologically young features are the latest phase of a continuing history. They are the product of intensive erosion, much of which resulted from extremely cold temperatures associated with several glacial episodes, the last of which ended some 17,000 years ago.

Although snowfields may have existed year-round during Pleistocene time, no true glaciers existed in the southern Appalachians. Much of the southern Appalachians during the periods of continental glaciations show geologic evidence of being periglacial, or "near glacial." The Unakas were sparsely vegetated in tundra and taiga reminiscent of the northern portions of modern-day Alaska and Canada. As the climate warmed and the continental glaciers receded, the Unakas were again covered, this time not by thousands of feet of sediment but by a diverse forest retaining much of its northern character. The boulder fields and talus were stabilized by one of the richest forests on Earth, which remained relatively unchanged until the Europeans arrived about 250 years ago.

Anyone who has hiked both ranges will notice that the rock structure of the TN Unakas is very different from that found in the eastern Blue Ridge. The Unakas are composed mostly of folded and faulted sedimentary strata, while the rocks of the eastern Blue Ridge are metamorphic and igneous in origin, attesting to intense deformation by extreme heat and pressure deep within the earth.

Within the Unakas themselves, the rocks differ from north to south in age and composition. The Unakas north of the French Broad River are composed primarily of Cambrian-period sandstone, conglomerate, dolostone, and shale, with Precambrian-era granite and gneiss. The Cambrian rock forms the impressive white cliffs seen on Bald Mountain, Holston Mountain, and Iron Mountain at the western rim of the Unakas. The Precambrian igneous and metamorphic rock is found primarily in the vicinity of Roan Mountain and Flag Pond, TN, which form the core of the range.

South of the French Broad River, the Unakas (often referred to as the *Unicoi* Mountains south of the Smokies) are primarily made up of massive units of Precambrian sandstone, slate, and conglomerate. Unlike the Cambrian rocks composed of similar material, these rocks have been more intensely deformed by heat and pressure, altering many of their original characteristics. The Cambrian rocks comprising much of the northern Unakas are found only in the long ridges that form the foothills in the southern part. Chilhowee Mountain, Starr Mountain (part of which is in the Gee Creek Wilderness), and much of English Mountain are all composed of rocks similar to those found throughout the northern section of the CNF.

The oldest rocks of the CNF are found in the northeastern part of the state, in easternmost Johnson, Unicoi, and Carter counties. These rocks are referred to as the basement complex since they comprise the most ancient rocks upon which all later sediments were deposited. These metamorphic rocks are composed of schist and gneiss and include some igneous rocks such as granite and gabbro. Much of the schist and gneiss originated as sandstone and shale deposited nearly 1 billion years ago. These rocks were deformed and intruded by molten rock (magma), which cooled to form granite (a pink, white, or light gray rock, rich in silica) and gabbro (a darker, iron-rich type). The rocks were then further altered by heat and pressure, destroying much of their original character. The basement complex is not very common in the CNF, although it comprises most of the eastern Blue Ridge in NC and GA. The best place to observe the ancient basement rocks in the CNF are in road cuts along US 19E near the town of Roan Mountain, where the pink and white granite is very common. On the bald summits around Roan Mountain itself, look for the dark green or black gabbro and banded gneiss and schist.

The basement rocks probably represent an ancestral chain of mountains and volcanic islands that once fringed the edge of the young North American continent. Precambrian sediment eroding off this ancient range covered the continental shelf with enormous amounts of sand, gravel, and mud. This massive wedge of sediment was slowly compressed and provided the materials for another rock formation called the Ocoee Supergroup, which is believed to have been up to 8 miles thick! This massif of metamorphosed sandstone, conglomerate, and slate makes up the bulk of the Great Smokies and the southern Unakas.

The Ocoee Supergroup itself is subdivided into three groups: the Snowbird Group (named for rock exposures on Snowbird Mountain in the CNF), the Great Smoky Group, and the Walden Creek Group. The Snowbird Group is well exposed along I-40 near the TN-NC border. Cleavage (the realignment of mineral orientation in response to stress) is quite evident along that interstate section. Construction of the highway undercut the smooth cleavage planes, causing massive rocks to slide catastrophically onto the roadway and into the adjacent Pigeon River. The cost of efforts to remedy these continuing rock slides since completion of the roadway has been substantial.

The Great Smoky Group and Walden Creek Group form the backbone of the Unicoi. The Great Smoky Group is composed mainly of massive, coarse-grained sandstone, with thin units of shale. The Great Smoky Group forms the high summits along the state line from Mount Cammerer in the GSMNP, south to Copperhill, TN, and into GA. The Walden Creek Group is characteristically composed of thick beds of conglomerate sandwiched between contorted shale and siltstone. The Walden Creek Group is believed to have been deposited at the edge of the continental shelf, where ancient submarine canyons avalanched great masses of sediment deep onto the ocean floor.

The Great Smoky and Walden Creek groups are well exposed along road cuts throughout the transmountain highways in the CNF. The massive sandstone of the Great Smoky Group can be seen on the Tellico Plains-Robbinsville Road located on the spine of Sassafras Ridge above the Jeffery Hell portion of the Citico Creek Wilderness. Farther along the road near the state line, a particularly conspicuous roadcut exposes reddish brown and black slate on both sides of the road. This is the Anakeesta Formation, noted for its highly acidic rock. Disturbance of this rock type has been blamed for numerous fish kills in creeks below the construction of the Tellico Plains-Robbinsville Road and the rerouting of the NC portion of US 441 through the GSMNP. Close examination of this rock reveals small cubes of golden-colored pyrite (fool's gold), which is an iron sulfide mineral. When surface water reacts with these sulfides, it creates a weak sulfuric acid, which lowers the pH of the streams, killing the fish. Another place to view the Walden Creek and Great Smoky groups is along US 64 above Parksville Dam on the Ocoee River, through the gorge, and into Ducktown. Due to the extreme defoliation associated with sulfuric acid production in Ducktown, the Great Smoky Group (known as the Copperhill Formation in the Ducktown area) is well exposed, affording excellent observation of the highly deformed bedrock. Generally, the Great Smoky Group in the southeastern part of the state is composed of more shale and siltstone and a type of muddy sandstone rich in feldspar and rock fragments called "greywacke." These finer-grained rocks more readily show evidence of being squeezed into folds and sheared by faults.

The Walden Creek Group is clearly exposed in road cuts at two locations in the CNF and vicinity. One is just outside the CNF boundary along US 129 as it runs beside Chilhowee Lake and the GSMNP. Just past Chilhowee Dam are coarse-grained sandstones and conglomerate with pebbles of white quartz and other minerals. Further up the road, past the Foothills Parkway, a road cut on the left reveals numerous tight folds in the shale and siltstone, testament to the forces required to transport these massive deposits of rock from deep beneath the earth to the high mountains that once stood here. Impressive folding in the Walden Creek Group is also seen along the recently widened section of the Tellico Plains-Robbinsville Road (TN 165) paralleling the Tellico River. To the right of the road before the first new bridge, thick sandstone units are bent into several large folds with smaller folds within the larger ones. A mile or so farther, where a vertical face was blasted into the rock, are hundreds of small folds of pink quartzite between thin layers of shiny, blue-green rock called *phyllite*.

Much as the rock of the Precambrian Ocoee Supergroup forms the peaks of the

Great Smokies and southern Unakas, Cambrian strata comprise the rugged ridgetops of the northern Unaka range. The Cambrian rocks in the CNF are, for the most part, members of the Chilhowee Group. The Chilhowee Group is composed of about 3,000 to 6,000 feet of brown, white, and gray sandstone and shale. The Chilhowee can be further subdivided into several smaller units, with names that indicate places where they are found: the Erwin Formation, Hesse Sandstone, Hampton Formation, and Unicoi Formation are named for various east-TN towns, creeks, and counties where these rocks were first described. The most striking difference between the sandstone of the Chilhowee and the Ocoee Supergroup has traditionally been the presence of fossils and animal burrows in the former. The Chilhowee, being Cambrian in age, was deposited about 550 million years ago, as complex multicellular marine organisms (worms, trilobites, jellyfish) began to inhabit the shallow sea floor. Another distinguishing feature of the Chilhowee sandstones is their tendency to display impressive cliffs visible from the TN Valley, with gentler slopes inclined towards the east. These features reflect the tilted strata, which moved up to 70 miles along thrust faults during the collision of North America and Africa some 250 to 300 million years ago, when the Appalachians were formed. The oldest Chilhowee rocks (Unicoi Formation) were deposited directly on top of the Precambrian Ocoee rocks and on the basement rocks as well. The sediments that were to become the Chilhowee Group were deposited in shallow seas which experienced a gradual environmental change. As the seas became clearer and sediment loads lessened, marine organisms flourished and thick deposits of lime accumulated on the sea floor. The carbonate rock that resulted is now exposed in many of the valleys in the northeastern CNF, such as Shady Valley, where the Shady Dolomite is exposed. Deposition of lime by marine organisms generally continued for nearly 200 million years thereafter, resulting in the extensive limestone deposits found throughout the TN Valley.

The Chilhowee Group can be viewed in numerous locations throughout the CNF, especially in the northeastern Unakas along US 19E, 19W, and 321. Holston and Iron mountains, incidentally, are composed of the same units as the Chilhowee, bent into a broad U or syncline. The excavation for Watauga Dam, near the Big Laurel Branch Wilderness, affords spectacular exposure of the Chilhowee, and the associated Iron Mountain Fault. A particularly scenic exposure of the Chilhowee Group occurs in the southern Unicois where the Hiwassee River gorge has cut through a ridge of Chilhowee and into the Ocoee Supergroup below. The impressive cliffs on Chestnut Mountain (to the northeast) and Bean Mountain (on the opposite bank) contain an almost complete representation of the Chilhowee.

From a geological standpoint, the mountains of the CNF consist mainly of the long ridges of the Unaka Mountains. The rocks of the Unakas are the result of a complex history of past mountain ranges, coastlines, dawning organisms, and climatic change. However, the visitor will be most impressed by the present beauty of these mountains and can only reflect on their past. Perhaps the geologist James Safford, describing the geology of the Unakas in the 1860s, summarized these feelings best when he wrote: "when the great and magnificent views of the world below and around them are associated, they become in truth, sublime. They must be visited to be appreciated. There is a fascination about them which cannot be told."

4. VEGETATION

The CNF supports a great diversity of plant species. Although there have been no botanical surveys of the forest as a whole, a measure of its diversity can be gleaned from surveys of portions of the forest and adjacent areas. The vascular plants, which include flowering plants, conifers, ferns, fern allies, and club mosses, have been most extensively studied. A total of 536 species and varieties of vascular plants are found in the Citico Creek Wilderness; 70 species of these are trees. A total of 476 species and varieties of vascular plants are found in the Big Frog Mountain Area, consisting of Big Frog Mountain Wilderness and a small section of Cohutta Wilderness.

The most thoroughly studied area of the region in terms of its biological richness is the GSMNP, where approximately 1,350 species of vascular plants have been found, including 130 species of native trees. No absolute conclusions about the species diversity of the CNF can be drawn from what is known about GSMNP since the park contains the highest portion of the Unaka Mountains and was left with more old-growth forest than the CNF. However, most or all of the habitat types found in the GSMNP can be found in the CNF. In addition, the CNF extends both further north and south than the GSMNP. Perhaps the most significant indicator of plant species diversity in the CNF is the fact that there are 2,391 species and varieties of plants known to inhabit the Blue Ridge Province, of which the CNF is a part.

The nonvascular plants of the CNF have been studied even less than the vascular plants. However, species of fungi, algae, lichens, liverworts, and mosses are very diverse in the CNF. Fungi, mosses, and lichens in particular are diverse and make notable contributions to the forest environment. The neighboring GSMNP is known to have 1,800 species of fungi, 330 species of mosses and liverworts, and 230 species of lichens.

VEGETATION HISTORY
OF THE BLUE RIDGE PROVINCE

The CNF lies in the Unaka Mountains of the Blue Ridge Province, a physiographic province in eastern North America, consisting of mountains of great antiquity (see Geology section). Mountains have been present in what is now eastern North America since the end of the Paleozoic era (230 million years ago), and they have gone through several cycles of uplift and erosion. The southern portion of the Blue Ridge has also been continuously vegetated for about the same time. The Blue Ridge has thus played a crucial role in the vegetational history of North America and the world. While other areas have been submerged under seas, covered by glaciers, or subjected to great climatic change, the southern Blue Ridge has remained as a refuge for plants.

The ancestral forests of the Blue Ridge Province actually developed during the Tertiary period, 65 or more million years ago. These composed a broad-leaved forest with a diverse herbaceous layer known as the Arcto-Tertiary forest. It extended over much of the northern portion of present-day North America and Eurasia and is thought to have extended south along high-elevation chains such as the Blue Ridge while subtropical flora dominated nearer sea level in the south. This ancient forest is thought to closely resemble in structure and types of species the present-day mixed mesophytic or cove hardwood forests of the Blue Ridge and Cumberland mountains.

Climatic changes in the later Tertiary period led to more temperate conditions and an expansion of the Arcto-Tertiary forest at the expense of more tropical species. Essentially all the elements of the modern forest were present by 34 million years ago in the Arcto-Tertiary forest, the dominant forest in eastern North America. The gradual rise of mountains in western North America resulted in increasing dryness in the western interior. The Arcto-Tertiary forest retreated eastward, to be replaced with grassland. The oak-hickory forest also developed during this period, in response to dry conditions. The mixed mesophytic forest was retained in the cove and uplands of the Blue Ridge. An oak-chestnut forest began to dominate the Ridge and Valley Province around the Blue Ridge and the drier ridges of the mountains, and an oak-pine forest began to develop in the Piedmont Region.

The Pleistocene epoch (1 to 3 million years ago) of the Quaternary period was characterized by periods of cold lasting about 100,000 years, during which glaciers moved south. These periods were interrupted by periods of relative warmth, lasting 10,000 to 30,000 years, during which the glaciers receded. From four to ten such periods occurred. The southern Blue Ridge was south of the ice sheets but was nevertheless greatly affected by them. Periods of cooling were associated with southward migrations of plant species; interglacial warming was associated with northward migrations as the ice sheet receded. The migration to the south as the climate cooled is thought to have occurred much more slowly than the northward migration following warming of the climate. The northward migration would have been into bare or sparsely occupied land; southern plant migrants would have had to compete with plants in relatively closed communities. The faster northward migration has been estimated at 48 miles per century.

There is evidence that climatic cooling produced a timberline on the higher mountains of GSMNP and displaced vegetation to lower elevations. During interglacial periods vegetation would have been displaced upward again. It has been estimated that vegetation may have been displaced upward 1,000 to 1,300 feet above even present levels during the dry warm period following glaciation.

The importance of the Blue Ridge in preserving species during this period cannot be overemphasized. The mountain ranges in the Blue Ridge run generally south to north, allowing plants to migrate up or down the chain. In contrast, the mountains of Europe run east to west and formed a barrier to plant migration, resulting in the elimination of most species of plants north of the mountains. In addition, the mountains of the Blue Ridge are deeply cut by stream valleys and side ridges, creating a diversity of local climates varying in elevation (temperature), moisture, and aspect. These local climates provided a continuum of conditions that allowed plants to migrate, not only north and south along the mountain chains but up and down and around the mountains to find suitable habitat.

Another important marker of the major climatic changes and plant migrations in the Blue Ridge Province are disjunct populations of plants. As plants migrated in response to climatic change, some populations were able to adapt to conditions in particular areas, such as mountaintops, but were not able to survive in the surrounding areas. When the main population of the species reached an equilibrium in far-away places, the disjunct population was left isolated from the main population. Such isolated species of plants occur frequently in the Blue Ridge.

DYNAMICS IN THE OLD-GROWTH FOREST

Characteristic of all life, individual trees and plants in an old-growth forest become established, mature, reproduce, age, die, and decay. In general, these milestones will be different for each species of plant. The trees, being the largest living structures, will tend to dominate the forest. Each species of tree has different requirements for light, moisture, soil, temperature, and other conditions. Some species of trees will tend to be more "dominant" than others. A number of tree species will tend to share dominance.

Gaps in the canopy of the forest, which allow light to penetrate to the forest floor, occur for many reasons. Old age may cause the death of a giant old tree; lightning may strike a tree standing higher than its neighbors; fire may burn an area; ice may strip the limbs from one or more trees; wind may blow over one weakened tree or a group of trees. They vary in size, but gaps are usually relatively small in comparison to the forest. All of these disturbances open up gaps that allow light to penetrate to the floor of the forest. Saplings in the understory of the forest take advantage of the light and compete to fill the gap. Some of the saplings will win the struggle and become larger; others will die or grow very little. Another tree that falls may give some of the trees a spurt of growth. Through the creation of a series of adjacent gaps over the years, some of the trees will eventually become dominant or subdominant in the forest, while most will die. The tree species that thrive and grow in this cycle will depend on the amount of light created in these gaps, the moisture in the area, the trees producing seeds in the area, and the seed and seedling characteristics. Through this process, a characteristic canopy of dominant and subdominant tree species will form. Distinctive layers of vines, shrubs, and herbaceous plants will form under the canopy.

FOREST VEGETATION TYPES

Forest vegetation types have been classified in various ways. The ecologist R. H. Whittaker in 1956 studied species distribution with variations in elevation and moisture. Although this study was for the GSMNP in particular, the vegetation types would seem to have a broader application, and they will be used to describe the natural vegetation of the CNF.

Cove Hardwood Forest. These beautiful and very diverse forests occupy the valleys (coves) below 4,500 feet. In old-growth cove hardwood forests the canopy trees are 3 to 4 feet in diameter, with occasional tulip trees reaching 6 to 7 feet in diameter. The crowns of the trees are 75 to 100 feet above the forest floor, with the tops of the trees reaching 100 to 150 feet and occasionally 200 feet. Below the canopy, smaller trees form a broad foliage layer. Ferns and herbs cover the floor of the forest. The forest has an open, park-like appearance. Eastern hemlock, silverbell, buckeye, basswood, sugar maple, and yellow birch are usually the dominant trees. Often tulip tree and American beech share dominance of the canopy. A number of other trees share dominance with these eight trees in dispersed quantities. These species, which are widespread but never numerous, include white ash, green ash, northern red oak, cucumber tree, bitternut hickory, red maple, and wild black cherry.

Trees of small and medium stature that form another layer below the canopy trees include umbrella magnolia, blue beech, Fraser magnolia, yellowwood, holly, and hop hornbeam; mountain maple and serviceberry occur at high elevations.

A shrub layer, although frequently absent or poorly developed, may include strawberry bush and spicebush at low elevations; alternate leaf dogwood, hobblebush, and dogberry occur at higher elevations. Wild hydrangea occurs at all elevations. Rhododendron occurs along streams and, with doghobble, under hemlock and in other sites.

The herbaceous species development is the richest in the mountains, with over a hundred different species represented in this vegetation type. The herbaceous layer itself is stratified with canopy herbs and an undergrowth of prostrate herbs. A large variety of spring wildflowers is very well represented in the cove hardwood forests. A few of the spring herbs of the cove hardwood forests include blue cohosh, squirrelcorn, dutchman's breeches, bleeding heart, umbrella-leaf, trout lily, wild geranium, sharp-lobed hepatica, dwarf crested iris, bishop's cap, showy orchis, mayapple, Solomon's seal, bloodroot, black snakeroot, false Solomon's seal, giant chickweed, foamflower, several species of trillium, and numerous species of violets.

The foliage of some of the spring wildflowers persists through the summer. Others die back, and herbs characteristic of the summer come to dominate. Herbaceous cover during the summer is as high as 80 percent. The most abundant herbs during the summer are white snakeroot, black cohosh, blue cohosh, jewel weed, wood-nettle, heart-leaved aster, wood fern, and silvery glade fern. Underneath these herbs are smaller species, such as giant chickweed, foamflower, bedstraw, and strawberry bush.

Eastern Hemlock Forest. Hemlock forests commonly form dense, shaded stands along streams, on north-facing slopes, and on ridgetops. Tree stems of 3 and 4 feet diameter are common in the hemlock forest, and the canopy crowns reach over 100 feet. At higher elevations these stands may be almost entirely hemlock; at lower elevations, mesic tree species characteristic of the cove forest are increasingly represented. Below 2,500 feet the hemlock forest gradually blends into the cove forests. Hemlock is a large tree and grows very densely. It can thus dominate a forest that contains a number of other species.

Hemlock forests tend to have a dense, dark appearance. This impression is often heightened by a dense shrub layer of rhododendron that at high elevations may cover 60 to 80 percent of the ground. The understory and shrub layer species include rosebay rhododendron, mountain rosebay, dog hobble, wild hydrangea, and mountain laurel.

The herbaceous layer is usually nonexistent or sparse in a well-developed hemlock forest. The already dark conditions are exacerbated by a thick heath shrub layer. The superficial root systems of the heaths result in drying of the soil. In addition, the bed of hemlock needles and heath leaves on the floor of the forest tends to promote very acid conditions unfavorable to herbaceous plants. Where heath coverage is low, a herbaceous coverage may occur with wood fern, partridge berry, rattlesnake plantain, and foamflower being the most represented. Rock cap fern can be found on many exposed rocks and roots.

Gray Beech Forest. High-elevation beech forests occur above 4,500 feet. The American beech trees are gray from lichens and appear stunted with rounded crowns. These forests on north-facing slopes could be considered a continuation of the upper cove hardwoods and may contain yellow birch, buckeye, and a low tree layer of mountain maple, striped maple, and serviceberry. Witch hobble, alternate-leaf dogwood, and wild hydrangea occur in the shrub layer. The herb layer is similar to that of higher elevation cove forests, but with the addition of sedges, coneflower, and twisted stalk.

The south-facing beech forests are characterized by a preponderance of beech, with silverbell as a second species. The small tree and shrub layer is largely absent; wild hydrangea appears only sporadically. The south-facing beech forests are distinctive in their herb layer of sedges which cover up to 80 to 90 percent of the forest floor. Scattered plants of most of the herb species of the upper coves and north slopes occur with the sedges.

Oak-Hickory Forest. At elevations of 2,500 to 3,000 feet, oak-hickory forests occupy areas slightly more dry than the cove hardwoods. These forests are dominated by northern red oak, pignut hickory, white oak, and mockernut hickory. Stands usually include black oak, sweet pignut hickory, chestnut oak, American chestnut, black gum, and tulip tree. Red maple, flowering dogwood, and sourwood are important understory trees. Huckleberry and mountain laurel are most prevalent in the shrub layer, with rosebay rhododendron, flame azalea, buffalo nut, and other shrubs also present.

Herb coverage is generally low (1 to 10 percent). Christmas fern, goldenrod, false foxglove, and galax are the most frequent herbs. Spear-leaved violet, pipsissewa, beggar lice, downy rattlesnake plantain, gall-of-the-earth, false Soloman's seal, and bellwort also occur.

Chestnut Oak-Chestnut Forest. This forest, which has drastically changed since the chestnut blight, is the most extensive of the lower and middle elevations. It is now dominated by chestnut oak, formerly by American chestnut. Chestnut made up probably 30 to 70 percent of this forest type, with chestnut oak making up much of the rest. Components of northern red oak, white oak, black oak, black gum, red maple, tulip tree, and small percentages of hickories and cove species also occur. Oak-chestnut forests and oak-chestnut heaths (described below) occur on almost all slopes except those facing south and southwest. Before settlement and the blight, forests of large chestnut trees are believed to have grown in the lower coves and in the broad open valleys away from the streams. Chestnut trees on the slopes probably reached 4 to 5 feet in diameter. Chestnut oak, northern red oak, and red maple make up almost half the replacement for the dead chestnut. Other replacement trees are hemlock, silverbell, sourwood, black locust, scarlet oak, tulip tree, sweet birch, white oak, beech, and flowering dogwood.

Shrub coverage is high, especially above 2,500 feet. Mountain laurel, flame azalea, rosebay, and huckleberry are the most important shrubs. Buffalo nut, sweet pepperbush, sweet-shrub, and highbush blueberry are also usually present.

The herb layer is similar to that of the oak-hickory forest. The dominant species are false foxglove, gall-of-the-earth, wood betony, beggar lice, downy rattlesnake plantain, hellebore, and galax. Herb coverage ranges from a low of about 1 percent up to about 30 percent in higher elevations and more moist sites.

Chestnut Oak-Chestnut Heath. The oak-chestnut heath occurs on the drier slopes. Tree canopy coverage can fall below 40 to 50 percent. Large chestnut oak and chestnut were widely scattered; under the open forest, the shrub layer is closed, being covered by continuous evergreen heath made up of mountain laurel, with sweet pepperbush, male-blueberry, rosebay, buffalo nut, and highbush blueberry. A low shrub layer of huckleberry is usually below the higher shrub layer. Galax is the dominant herbaceous plant, with other minor components. Herbaceous cover is only about 1 to 5 percent.

Red Oak-Chestnut Forest. This vegetation is submesic (somewhat moist) in species composition and is the high-altitude equivalent of the chestnut oak-chestnut forest. Northern red oak and chestnut formed 70 to 80 percent of the canopy. Red maple, basswood, black cherry, yellow birch, buckeye, and white ash are important associates below 4,500 feet. Red maple and American beech are important associates above 4,500 feet and silverbell has come in thickly since the chestnut blight above 4,500 feet.

Shrub coverage above 4,500 feet is sparse, with flame azalea and highbush blueberry being the major species. The herbaceous layer above 4,500 feet resembles that of the south-slope beech stands, but with less coverage. Sedges and ferns predominate. Below 4,500 feet the herb layer is essentially the same as in the chestnut oak-chestnut forests; only the subalpine species painted trillium, goldenrod, and umbrella leaf distinguish it from the chestnut oak-chestnut forest. Herb coverage is from 10 to 40 percent at lower elevations and 20 to 60 percent above 4,500 feet.

White Oak-Chestnut Forest. Below 4,500 feet, the white oak-chestnut forests are not distinguishable from the red oak-chestnut. Above 4,500 feet, white oak becomes strongly dominant on some exposed southwest ridges, with an open growth of rather small trees and a diverse herbaceous layer of grasses, ferns, and herbs. American chestnut formerly shared dominance with white oak. Northern red oak is almost always present. Pignut hickory and chestnut oak occupy the canopy at lower elevations. Subdominant trees of red maple, sourwood, and black locust also occur.

Shrubs are predominantly flame azalea, highbush blueberry, and mountain laurel, with coverage from 20 to 60 percent. Herb coverage is 10 to 50 percent. New York fern, southern lady fern, bracken fern, and a variety of other herbs and grasses are represented.

Virginia Pine Forest. In low elevations Virginia pine is dominant in stands on south-facing slopes and in old fields. Shrub coverage is 10 to 40 percent with mountain laurel and lowbush blueberry usually dominant. Herb coverage is from 2 to 10 percent and includes such species as little bluestem, broomstraw, panic grass, bracken fern, goat's rue, wild indigo, tickseed sunflower, asters, and goldenrod.

Pitch Pine Forest. Pitch pine dominates pine stands in the elevation range of 2,200 feet to 3,200 feet. Scarlet oak sometimes shares dominance. Also present are chestnut oak and American chestnut. Shrub coverage is 40 to 50 percent and consists of mountain laurel, lowbush blueberry, and blueberry. Herb coverage is 5 to 20 percent and consists of little bluestem, bracken fern, trailing arbutus, and wintergreen.

Table Mountain Pine Heath. At higher elevations table mountain pine becomes more and more dominant. At the upper end of the pine heaths it is strongly dominant. The stands are usually small, low, and open. The shrub layer is usually dominated by blueberry or huckleberry, with 60 to 90 percent coverage. Herb coverage is 5 to 20 percent, with little bluestem, galax, trailing arbutus, and wintergreen.

Grassy Balds. Grassy balds are distinctive meadows covered with grass and herbs. The transition from forest to bald is quite abrupt, except for a gradual decrease in tree stature. However, the trees end in a distinct tree line of dwarfed trees of the surrounding forest. Usually these forests are beech and oak-chestnut. Shrubs in this tree line include highbush blueberry, flame azalea, and male-blueberry. Mountain oak grass is strongly dominant on the balds. Some introduced grasses are also important. Sedges also occur and various herbs are scattered throughout the grass. Five fingers is the most abundant herb, with hedge nettle, goldenrod, rattlesnake root, catbriar, bluets, coneflower, gentian, and giant chickweed also present, as well as a number of introduced weeds. Scattered shrubs of flame azalea, highbush blueberry, and blackberry may occur over the balds.

The origin of the balds and the means of their prehistoric maintenance are subject to much controversy. Everything from Indian fires to parasitic insects and large grazing animals has been used to explain the balds. Many of the bald areas were grazed by early settlers. Other areas were cleared by settlers for grazing purposes and are not true balds. Reinvasion by trees on the human-made balds seems to be faster than on the natural balds.

Heath Balds. The heath balds occur throughout the elevations of the subalpine forest down to 4,000 feet. These balds are composed of blueberry and other heath shrubs, the particular species depending on the elevation. The shrubs approach full coverage and are often impenetrable, forming dense thickets 3 to 10 feet high that are sometimes known as "hells." Herbal coverage is low, being well below 5 percent. Wintergreen, galax, cow wheat, Indian cucumber root, and painted trillium are the main herbal species. Tree seedlings that may be present at high altitudes are Fraser's fir, red spruce, mountain ash, and fire cherry. At lower elevations, seedlings of cherry birch, red maple, American chestnut, sourwood, sassafras, table mountain pine, black locust, and witch-hazel can be found.

Spruce-Fir Forest. The spruce-fir forests are generally above 5,000 feet in elevation. These dense, moist forests of red spruce and Fraser fir are characteristic of much more northerly forests. Associated species include yellow birch, mountain maple, striped maple, serviceberry, and mountain ash. The canopy is dominated by spruce and, to a lesser extent, yellow birch. The shrub and herbal layers are highly variable. In their most developed form, they show a characteristic five-tier layering. Mosses form the lowest layer. A low herb layer of wood sorrel is overtopped by a high herb layer of woodfern, bluebead-lily, aster, Rugel's ragwort, wake robin, and twisted stalk. A low shrub layer of bearberry is followed by a high shrub layer of hobblebush. Mountain maple and the other small trees form a low tree layer.

HUMAN IMPACT ON VEGETATION

There is a long history of human use of the southern Appalachian forests, including the CNF. It is probable that prehistoric native Americans used the mountains for hunting. There is also some evidence that they used fire as a tool to shape the forest. American Indians used the forested mountains for hunting, fishing, and other purposes. The coming of European settlers gradually meant the clearing of the more accessible portions of the CNF. Such settlers also intensified the use of fire to create better livestock browse and to clear the forest. Later, in the early 20th century, large timber companies moved in with massive logging operations. The end result of settlement and timber operations was a forest left ravaged by huge timber cuts, wildfires, and erosion. The land was to some extent rendered undesirable, and much of it was bought by the US government for incorporation into the new national forest system.

Little logging took place under early USFS management. The forests were protected from fires and were allowed to recover. This stewardship, coupled with the remarkable recuperative power of southern Appalachian forests, resulted in recovery of much of the botanical diversity in the CNF. Such diversity continues to recover and will improve as sections of the forest approach old-growth conditions.

However, biological diversity is not synonymous with timber productivity. As the forest has aged, the USFS has increased timbering activities. Conservation organizations, while acknowledging that timber harvesting is one valid use of our national forests, have pressed for greater emphasis on other uses of the national forests, including recreation, wildlife habitat, watershed and wilderness preservation, and nature study. In addition, they have supported the continued biological recovery of the national forests through wilderness and other special-area designations, longer rotation ages, and alternative methods of harvesting timber.

One of the greatest impacts on the vegetation of the CNF and on the forests of eastern North America in general has been the introduction of exotic organisms. Examples are legion, but none has had the impact nor has so changed the character of the forests as the inadvertent introduction of the chestnut blight. The blight, which is caused by the fungus *Endothia parasitica*, is fatal to trees of American chestnut. The fungus was brought to America from Asia on Asiatic chestnut trees, which have resistance to the fungus. The blight was discovered in New York City in 1904. Over the next few decades it slowly spread throughout the natural range of the American chestnut, frustrating efforts to eradicate it.

The American chestnut was one of the largest and most important trees of the southern Appalachian forests. Heights of 120 feet and stem diameters of 8 feet were reached. The nut of the chestnut was a very important wildlife food; it was much more reliable than the oaks, which are subject to major fluctuations in production from year to year. The American chestnut was a shade-tolerant tree and could regenerate well in mature forest; it was thus a dominant species of the old-growth forest and helped determine the environment of the forest. It was also a major component of many of the forest types. Its demise affected the whole forest ecosystem. Other trees have replaced it in the forest, but they fall short of filling its place in the ecosystem. Stump sprouts from the tree's root systems, which are not affected by the fungus, can still be seen in the CNF. There is ongoing research attempting to genetically breed the fungal resistance of the Asiatic species into the American chestnut. Other research indicates that forms of the fungus that are harmless may protect against the virulent forms. We can only hope that this great tree will some day grow once again throughout our forests.

EDIBLE AND MEDICINAL PLANTS

A large number of the plants found in CNF have been used for food and medicine. Native Americans were dependent on many of the berries, nuts, fruits, and roots of the forest for food and used many herbs for treatment of their medical conditions and as tonics. The pioneers helped preserve much of this knowledge. Science has shown the value of many of these remedies, and some of the herbs are used as the basis for modern medicines. Others have not been fully investigated.

You should definitely know what you are doing before ingesting anything found in the wild. The possibility of poisoning is very real. There is a large number of poisonous plants, and many of the plants used as herbs or medicines have the potential for poisoning if the wrong plant part or the wrong dose is taken. This guidebook does not cover the identification and preparation of the edible plants; there are knowledgeable people and excellent guides to edible and medicinal plants.

A few of the more tasty treats to be found in the CNF are blueberries, huckle-berries, blackberries, pawpaw (the pioneer's banana), persimmon, common greenbriar, wild grapes, hickory nuts, common elderberry, wood sorrel, violets, ramps, and wild strawberries. Native Americans used acorns (especially from the white oak) for a flour, but this required special preparation to remove the tannins. Before being eliminated by blight, the American chestnut was one of the most im-portant sources of food found in the CNF.

RARE, ENDANGERED, AND THREATENED PLANTS

You will have to be lucky and informed to see these plants—there are very few of them, and for obvious reasons their exact location is not publicized. They have per-sisted through centuries of change in the CNF; we hope that favorable management practices will allow them to continue. An endangered species is in danger of extinc-tion; a threatened species is likely to become endangered in the future. Three spe-cies listed as endangered and two listed as threatened by the US Fish and Wildlife Service are found in the CNF. Another twelve species are candidates for listing. TN also lists threatened and endangered species under the Rare Plant Protection Act of 1985; these plants are evaluated only for TN so many of them are more abundant in other parts of their range. TN also lists plants that are of special concern; these plants are uncommon in TN or have specific or unique habitat requirements. One hun-dred-twenty-two species of plants are listed on the Tennessee State List of Threat-ened, Endangered, and Special Concern Plants as of April 7, 1992 (prepared by Dr. Paul Sommers of the Department of Environment and Conservation's Ecological Services Division). A complete catalog of the threatened and endangered species that are listed, or are candidates for listing, on the federal list for the CNF is included in Appendix 6.

The hiker of the CNF's wilderness trails will leave with many impressions. One of the strongest and most memorable and pleasant will be of diverse and beautiful vegetation, ranging from vistas of soft green-blanketed ridges and valleys, to giant oak trees, to the smallest of bluet flowers. The land, the wildlife, but also the vegeta-tion, make these areas special and worthy of efforts to preserve and protect them.

5. WILDLIFE

The typical CNF hiker will see little wildlife—a few birds, a snake or lizard in the summer, or occasionally a deer. However, a little patience and knowledge will reveal a variety of wildlife in the diverse habitats provided by the CNF. Since the CNF is managed for multiple uses, including timber harvesting, its wildlife habitats range from protected wilderness to clear-cuts. Each habitat is important to different species of wildlife. The areas described in this guidebook will often feature what are called "late successional" habitats by foresters; "big, old trees" to laymen. This section will emphasize wildlife species dependent on such late successional habitats that are rare in TN.

BIRDS

Over 120 bird species may be found in the CNF, including wild turkey, 7 species of woodpecker, ruffed grouse, 5 kinds of owl, hawks, vultures, ravens, warblers, and much more. Birds are often difficult to see, so to see more than an occasional few you will need to learn where and when to look. A good bird guidebook, knowledge of the songs of birds, and a pair of binoculars are essential. Those who make the effort may be rewarded by the sight of some rare and interesting birds, possibly a red-cockaded woodpecker, a hooded warbler, a wild turkey, a golden eagle, or a peregrine falcon.

The red-cockaded woodpecker is the size of a cardinal, about 8.5 inches long. The cockade, for which it is named, is a small red patch behind the male's eye that is very difficult to see in the field. The best field mark is the bird's white cheek, which no other North American woodpecker has. The red-cockaded woodpecker is in trouble all over the southeastern US. There are only a few areas where the population is stable; everywhere else they are declining. The red-cockaded was once a common bird in the Southeast, including TN, extending as far north as NJ and PA. However, habitat changes have caused it to decline in numbers. The red-cockaded requires both large live pine trees, usually 70 to over 100 years old, in which to build their nest cavities, and sparse understory. Red-cockadeds build their cavities below the lowest branches on a tree, usually about 15 feet above the ground. When nearby vegetation gets as high as the cavity, they abandon it. Originally, the sparse understory required by the red-cockaded was naturally maintained by wildfire. Fire suppression has generally eliminated this aspect of their habitat even where old-growth pine forests persist.

Red-cockaded woodpeckers were not known to exist in the CNF until a single colony was found in 1987. With help and encouragement from conservationists, the USFS has been searching for other colonies. The USFS has also modified its timber-harvesting practices to avoid adverse impacts, but it remains to be seen whether the red-cockaded will survive in the CNF.

The hooded warbler is another of the fascinating birds that may be found in the CNF's special areas. It is named for the male's black hood that covers the top of the head, the throat, and chin. The underparts and face are bright yellow, and the wings, back, and tail are olive green. The female looks like a faded version of the male without the hood. The hooded warbler breeds in the mature deciduous forests with well-developed understories. They glean insects from trees and understory vegetation and seldom forage more than 15 feet above the ground.

Hooded warblers are characterized as forest-interior species because they avoid edge habitats and need relatively large uninterrupted tracts of forest for successful breeding. Hooded warblers have disappeared from forest fragments as large as 1,200 acres. Why they need such large forest tracts is not completely clear, but it appears to be related to their susceptibility to nest predators (e.g., bluejays) and nest parasites (brown-hooded cowbirds) that frequent forest edges.

Because of the decline and fragmentation of mature deciduous forests in eastern North America, large expanses of forest like the CNF are important for survival of the hooded warbler and other birds that are dependent on the interior of a forest. The CNF's protected areas that are the subject of this book, especially the larger ones, are important refuges for the hooded warbler and may be crucial to its long-term survival. Listen for its song as you hike and enjoy the wilderness even more by knowing wilderness helps to preserve this and other parts of our natural heritage.

The wild turkey is a wildlife success story. The turkey was eliminated from east TN by overhunting and habitat loss as the virgin forests were removed. However, they are now plentiful due to their reintroduction and management by the TWRA and the regrowth of the forests under supervision of the USFS. Wild turkeys are much more intelligent than their barnyard cousins, and only the lucky or persistent hiker is likely to see them. Those who do will have no trouble identifying them—except for eagles, no North American bird approaches their size.

In recent years, the USFS and the TWRA have been reintroducing bald eagles and peregrine falcons in the CNF. The ultimate result of these efforts is not yet clear; however, if these birds return to live and breed again in the CNF, they will be an invaluable addition to Tennessee's natural heritage.

MAMMALS

The USFS lists 47 species of mammals that may be found in the CNF. Among the most interesting are black bears, flying squirrels, red and gray fox, and bobcats. Red and gray fox are particularly elusive while flying squirrels and bobcats are nocturnal. Of these mammals, you are therefore most likely to see bears. However, because they are hunted in some areas of the CNF during season and often poached at other times, you are less likely to see them than in the nearby GSMNP. Other mammals you may see include raccoons, opossums, cottontail rabbits, and river otters. And of course there are the mice, shrews, voles, moles, bats, and many other important small-animal citizens of the CNF. Small and large, there are many fascinating mammals to observe and enjoy.

The larger protected areas of the CNF discussed in this guidebook constitute, with the GSMNP, the principal habitats of the black bear in TN. The historic range of the eastern black bear has declined significantly in the wake of deforestation and heavy exploitation, and the species now exists on less than 10 percent of its former range in the Southeast. Increasing human populations and developments continue to fragment the black bear population. As a result the bear now exists primarily on federal lands containing designated or de facto wilderness.

The survival of the black bear in the Southeast depends on the abundance of a diversity of late-successional trees (especially oaks over 100 years old), availability of seed and berry plant species, an adequate supply of old-growth forest distributed throughout its range, limitations on future road developments, greatly increased educational and enforcement activities by responsible resource agencies, and regular and systematic population monitoring. Of these requirements, food is obviously very important. Although black bears are omnivores, they primarily eat berries and nuts. Berries are the predominant food in the summer. In the fall, bears begin to make physiological and behavioral changes that allow them to accumulate body fat. They must accumulate enough body fat to carry them through three to four months of winter denning (during which they eat nothing) and another month of scarce early spring foods. For bears to accumulate body fat, they often abandon their typical summer range and feed almost continuously over extensive areas. It is not uncommon for bears to gain 1 or 2 pounds per day during the peak of this "feeding frenzy" period. In the Southeast, nuts are their predominant fall food. In the CNF, acorns provide almost all of their fall and winter energy needs.

Black bears also require high-quality denning sites. Bears are adaptable enough to den in a number of different kinds of sites. However, adult females need highly protected sites for their newborn cubs. The best sites occur in old-growth forests under the root mass or in cavities in large trees. Males are less demanding and can often take advantage of thickets created by fallen trees or timber-cutting activities.

As more and more of the private lands near the CNF come under intensive management, the bear becomes more dependent on the national forest. The protected areas described in this guidebook are therefore essential to the black bear's future.

Bobcats are nocturnal and hunt by stealth. Alert hikers may find evidence of the bobcat's presence in scats or their scrapes, piles of dirt, or duff which they sometimes use to mark their territories. Large rodents and rabbits are bobcats' dominant foods, but they also eat birds, mice, eggs, reptiles, and squirrels. Bobcats are capable of killing deer but seldom do so.

The white-tail deer is another of TN's wildlife success stories. After being hunted nearly out of existence, regulated hunts and reintroductions have made the deer one of the most plentiful animals in the state. The deer's high fecundity and preference for edge habitat created by clear-cuts have allowed them to support remarkably high hunting pressures. Hikers may see them, especially at dawn and dusk, and especially in the northern CNF; they are less numerous in the southern CNF.

Coyotes are moving into the CNF from the west, including western TN, where their numbers are higher. Coyotes are highly omnivorous with principal items in the diet being rodents (mice, rats, and rabbits), squirrels, insects, berries, fruit, birds, and carrion. Rabbits are the largest part of the diet overall, but carrion may be largest in the winter. Berries and fruits are important in the fall, whereas insects are consumed chiefly in the spring and early summer. Occasionally a group of coyotes will gang up on a larger animal, usually the young of deer, sheep, or cows. However, these larger animals make up a small portion of the coyote's diet. Coyotes breed rapidly and at a young age, are extremely adaptable, and will den almost anywhere. Although the coyote's original habitat is the dry and open intermountain basin areas in the American West, it has successfully colonized nearly every habitat on the continent, including urban areas. Its numbers are expected to grow in the entire Southeast, including in the CNF.

Some of the most exciting wildlife news for the southern Appalachians is the planned reintroduction of the red wolf in the GSMNP. If this reintroduction is successful, the CNF may also once again support this fascinating animal. The red wolf interbreeds with the coyote, which may prove a problem for the red wolf's reintroduction. Adult red wolves weigh up to 60 pounds and prey primarily on birds, rabbits, and large rodents; they also eat insects and berries. They generally do not kill deer as do their larger cousins, the gray wolf.

Two top predators that have disappeared from the southern Appalachians, but which may someday be reintroduced, are the gray wolf and cougar. With the addition of these species to the southern Appalachians, our wilderness areas would again be truly wild. Restoration of these and other extirpated species is a principal goal of many TN conservationists.

A discussion of CNF mammals would not be complete without mention of the European wild boar. This exotic game animal causes serious damage to plants of the forest by rooting for tubers. It also competes with native wildlife for food. A typical adult boar can consume 1,300 pounds per year of acorns, the most important wildlife food in the southern Appalachians. Many conservationists support elimination of this nonnative animal from the forests of the state while some hunters value it as a game animal in spite of its adverse impact on native species.

The wild boar was introduced to the mountains of NC in 1912 by an entrepreneur named George Moore. Moore's intention was to build a hunting preserve for wealthy businessmen on approximately 1,500 acres of fenced Hooper Bald land. By 1920, when financial difficulties caused him to abandon his venture and release the boars, his original 14 boars had increased to over 100. Those few boars have prospered, multiplied, and caused unending damage in the mountains of east TN and western NC.

The NPS requires about $200,000 each year for trapping and hunting to keep the population of wild boar in the GSMNP at acceptable levels. Many of the boars trapped in the GSMNP are released in TN and NC national forests, where the principal controls on boar numbers are hunters and starvation in years with mast crop failures. They are managed as a game species in the national forests. The boar has therefore grown in numbers and remains a problem today.

REPTILES, AMPHIBIANS, AND FISH

The USFS recognizes 30 reptiles as residents of the CNF, including eastern and three-toed box turtles, 9 lizard species, and 19 snake species. The snake species include northern copperheads and timber rattlesnakes which were once common in the region but now are more likely to be found in remote areas like the CNF. They are not especially common in the CNF, but care should be taken to avoid them. Snakes are a part of the mountains; admire them but do not harm them.

The USFS recognizes 46 amphibians as residents of the CNF. Thirty-two of these are salamanders, many of which are found only in the southern Appalachians. Salamanders are most commonly found in moist areas near streams. In such places, lifting large stones and fallen logs may give you the pleasure of finding one of these interesting reptiles. Salamanders eat insects and worms, making them the top predators of the leaf litter on the forest floor.

The habitat needs of many of these reptiles and amphibians are not well known. There is a considerable amount of uncertainty about the effects of clear-cuts on the amphibians, particularly salamanders. Most salamanders live near streams, which receive protection from clear-cuts; however, some species live a considerable distance from streams and may not survive in clear-cut areas. Further, because they move slowly and do not migrate, it is uncertain whether they will recolonize cut-over areas before they are clear-cut again.

As trout fishermen know, the CNF contains the most important cold-water fishing in TN, especially in places like the Citico Creek Wilderness. Good rainbow trout fishing in the mountains is a tribute to the cold, clean water that comes off the forested mountains. Unfortunately, much of the rainbow fishing exists at the expense of the native brook trout. Competition from rainbow trout, a native of the Pacific Northwest which was introduced to the southern Appalachians, has driven the brook trout to the brink of extinction on many streams. Trout Unlimited and the USFS are restoring brook trout to some of the streams in the CNF. Conservationists support these efforts and look forward to restoration of the brook trout throughout the CNF, especially in wilderness areas.

THREATENED AND ENDANGERED SPECIES

A remote and relatively undisturbed area, the CNF is the last refuge of many animal species that were once common in TN. The U.S. Fish and Wildlife Service has identified a number of species that are listed or proposed for listing as threatened or endangered and either live in the CNF or have habitat in it. The federal list of the CNF's endangered and threatened wildlife species is included in Appendix 6. Endangered species are defined as species in danger of becoming extinct while threatened species are likely to become endangered. As you look this list over, realize that these species, without careful management or, in most cases, lack of human interference with their habitat, can soon be lost forever. There are probably many other species in the CNF that either have not yet been found or are in much worse condition than is presently known. The protected areas described in this guidebook are therefore important refuges for much of the wildlife discussed in this chapter.

While walking the trails of the CNF, take some time to search for the wildlife that is there but not easy to see. Remember that hiking is not only a means of transportation but a pilgrimage to our roots. When the hour gets late or you get tired of walking, let your mind wander to an earlier time when the cougar, the wolf, and the elk walked the forest. Ask yourself if it is not time to begin to put the pieces back into the wilderness. Think how thrilling it would be to hear the wolf's song, to glimpse a cougar on a rock outcrop, or to hear the clashing antlers of bull elk in rut. These visions and sounds could be within our grasp if we work to put the wild back in the wilderness. The future of the CNF is in our hands.

6. HUMAN HISTORY

The wilderness trails of the CNF often provide solitude, a momentary respite from the cares of the world. And yet even on the most remote forest trail one cannot escape the human imprint, for the history of the area is long and filled with many different peoples.

No one knows when the first Indians hunted in these forested mountains and valleys, but archaeological evidence suggests it was perhaps 12,000 years ago. Hundreds of generations later, local Indians adopted a diversified economy featuring a corn-based agriculture, settled in semipermanent communities, and developed complex cultural patterns. When the Spanish conquistador Hernando De Soto arrived in 1540, he encountered well-established tribal groups, although it is not clear to what extent these correspond to later tribes. For more than 100 years after De Soto this area remained a mystery to whites. Not until the late 1600s did English traders operating out of VA and SC establish contact with the Cherokees, who occupied a number of scattered villages in the southern Appalachians. Maps of the 1720s and 1730s show Cherokee towns along the Little Tennessee, Hiwassee, and Tellico rivers in the southern part of today's CNF. For a time Chota, on the Little Tennessee, was the "principal town" of the Cherokees and the center of tribal diplomacy and ceremonies.

Because of their strategic location, the Cherokees assumed great importance in the colonial wars between Britain and France. Near Chota, in 1756-57, the British built Fort Loudon, their first major fortification west of the Appalachians. Fort Loudon was the scene of a memorable siege and massacre in 1760 when the long-suffering Cherokees vented their frustration on the garrison. British troops retaliated by destroying many Cherokee towns. A restored version of the fort, near Vonore, TN, makes a nice side trip for a visitor to the CNF. Sequoyah, the famous inventor of the Cherokee alphabet, was born in the area and is honored by a modern museum near the restored fort.

Despite the absence of permanent Cherokee habitations in the northern part of the CNF, the tribe still claimed the area and hunted there frequently. A few white adventurers also visited periodically, including famous "long hunters" like Daniel Boone. The first white residents settled along the Watauga, Holston, and Nolichucky rivers in the early 1770s (in defiance of British law) and quickly aroused resentment among the Cherokees, resulting in widespread Indian raids during the American Revolution. The frontiersmen responded with brutal efficiency, laying waste to Cherokee villages. In 1780 these same backwoodsmen, the so-called "Over-the-Mountain Boys," marched eastward across the mountains and helped defeat British troops at the battle of King's Mountain. The Overmountain Victory National Historic Trail (No. 193) through the Highlands of Roan Scenic Area commemorates the Overmountain trek. The frontier soldiers began their march at Sycamore Shoals, a famous gathering place on the Watauga and today the site of the Sycamore Shoals State Historic Park in Elizabethton. Visitors may also want to see nearby Jonesborough, the state's oldest white settlement.

Following the Revolutionary War, American settlers quickly spread across the Appalachians into the Ohio, Mississippi, and TN river valleys. During the 1830s most of the indigenous tribes were forced to leave their homelands and migrate westward to present-day Oklahoma. For the Cherokees it literally became a "Trail of Tears," with thousands perishing during the ordeal. Red Clay State Historic Park, near the CNF headquarters in Cleveland, is the site of the last tribal council held before removal. A few Indians in the more isolated mountain areas were able to avoid eviction and became the ancestors of today's Eastern Band of Cherokees, a federally recognized tribe occupying a reservation on the NC side of the GSMNP.

With the vast interior of the continent offering readily accessible fertile lands, most whites chose to bypass the valleys, coves, and highlands of today's CNF. It became predominantly an isolated region of subsistence farming, although a few areas—like Cades Cove in the GSMNP—remained surprisingly dynamic and cosmopolitan. The people of these mountains were a mixture of Scotch-Irish, German, English, and other ethnic stock, all melding together into a fiercely independent yet pious people. Francis Asbury, America's first Methodist bishop and circuit rider, regularly crossed the mountains in the northern part of what is now the CNF as he conducted his ministerial duties in a growing America.

Because the mountainous part of east Tennessee was a region of small farms, few whites owned any slaves and, indeed, some resented the social and economic influence of slaveholders. Among many there was also a deep attachment to the Union, explaining why Confederate leaders viewed the area as a nest of subversion during the Civil War. Escaped Union prisoners-of-war often found safety there, amid a society of divided loyalties. "Bushwhacking" and other forms of violence were common as old scores were settled and animosities lingered for years afterwards.

Not until the late 19th and early 20th centuries did the area begin to develop economically, as northern mining and lumber interests moved in. Once geographically isolated, the region opened up as railroads spanned the mountains and reached into remote valleys to make exploitation easier; these ranged from temporary narrow-gauge lines to standard-gauge track still in use. Especially attractive to entrepreneurs were the virgin forests, and before long, large corporations were logging hundreds of thousand of acres. In the extreme southern part of the CNF, at Copperhill and Ducktown, the railroads opened up mining operations that proved ecologically disastrous, creating an eerie, barren landscape that astronauts have seen from space. Such considerations were secondary, however, as times were good and jobs plentiful in a region that had been economically depressed. The Ducktown Basin Museum has displays telling this story well. Even though the heyday of mining, milling, and railroading is long past, locomotives are occasionally dusted off and polished for excursions of sightseers who wish to enjoy a few hours amid the forest's autumn colors.

Even in the boom days, some people had a grander vision for the forest. They were interested in protecting watersheds, managing forests for sustained yields, and preserving a portion of these mountains through the creation of a new national park. The allure of money was also a part of this new concern. Prominent citizens of east TN and western NC, envisioning a possible tourist bonanza, organized a campaign during the 1920s that finally led to creation of the GSMNP, which was formally dedicated in 1934.

The genesis of the CNF was different. In 1911, Congress authorized the federal government to acquire lands for protecting the headwaters of navigable streams, and the following year the US began purchasing units in the extreme southeastern part of TN as well as in GA. In 1920 President Woodrow Wilson officially proclaimed these combined lands to be "Cherokee National Forest." On July 8, 1936, President Franklin D. Roosevelt issued another proclamation, enlarging the CNF and redrawing its boundaries so that it was exclusively within TN. The southern part, the Cherokee Division, consisted mostly of earlier-acquired forest lands while the portion north of the national park, the Unaka Division, consisted of new acquisitions and cessions from the Unaka and Pisgah national forests.

Roosevelt's New Deal had other important consequences for the CNF. The TVA, established in 1933, built a series of dams throughout the region, impounding reservoirs like Watauga and South Holston lakes in the north; in the south, reservoirs earlier impounded by ALCOA, a private corporation, were joined by TVA projects like Ocoee and, most recently, Tellico lake. TVA brought jobs, flood control, and electric power to a desperately needy region—and it brought controversy over environmental issues. Whatever its merits, TVA has provided a different kind of recreation for visitors, from boating on reservoirs to whitewater rafting, canoeing, and kayaking on dam-controlled streams.

Today the visitor taking any major highway in the CNF will inevitably confront the powerful presence of the federal government. Paradoxically, this same presence has created avenues of escape. The CNF is latticed by a network of paved and gravel roads offering access to remote trailheads where it is possible to escape for a time most of life's pressures, to find solace amid the trees and rushing streams; in a few areas one can even find small stands of virgin timber. But even along the most isolated pathway one is still brought back to the forest's human history by encountering the unexpected: some crumbling foundations, perhaps, or a meandering stone wall—mute, lichen-covered mementos linking past with present.

7. POLITICAL HISTORY

The CNF's protected natural areas are outstanding botanical, wildlife, and recreation preserves, but they are and will remain wild because, quite simply, of politics. Such protection resulted from literally thousands of people-hours during the 1970s and 1980s, leading finally to the passage of wilderness bills by Congress in 1984 and 1986 and resolution of an appeal of the Forest Management Plan in August of 1988. Much of that effort was directed toward the most difficult task—designation of a portion of the CNF as wilderness under the 1964 Wilderness Act.

The earliest mention of formal protection for a portion of the CNF occurred in 1935 when the USFS proposed designating a primitive area in the Citico Creek watershed to be called "Citico-Cheoah Primitive Area." No action, however, was taken on the proposal.

The road to wilderness in the CNF must therefore begin with the passage of the Wilderness Act, which authorized wilderness protection for federal lands. It was enacted by Congress in 1964 and provided for protection of only three small wildernesses in the eastern US while a substantial amount of wilderness was designated in the western US. No areas were designated in TN's CNF. The correction of this imbalance was a priority of national environmental groups, particularly the Sierra Club and the Wilderness Society, in the subsequent years.

The first formal recognition of wilderness for the CNF was in 1974 when the Eastern Wilderness Areas Act was passed by Congress (and signed by President Gerald Ford on January 3, 1975), designating three small wilderness areas (only 1.3 percent of the total CNF acreage) and two large wilderness study areas in TN. The wildernesses were an extension of the Cohutta Wilderness from GA into TN, an extension of the Joyce Kilmer-Slickrock Wilderness from NC into TN, and the small Gee Creek Wilderness located wholly within TN. The wilderness study areas were Big Frog Mountain and Citico Creek. The 1974 effort was coordinated by Citizens for Eastern Wilderness, of which Dave Sayor (Washington, DC) was coordinator, Felix Montgomery (Chattanooga) was southeastern-US coordinator, and Ray Payne (Knoxville) was TN coordinator. TN's Third District congressman, Lamar Baker, cosponsored the Eastern Wilderness Areas Act in the House of Representatives and deserves much of the credit for the act, as does Ernie Dickerman of the Wilderness Society. Ernie spent untold hours and lobbied for enactment of the bill during the waning hours of the 93rd Congress.

The principal obstacle to the TN-NC portions of the Eastern Wilderness Areas Act was a proposed road between Tellico Plains, TN, and Robbinsville, NC. The route for the road ran directly through the most scenic portion of the proposed Joyce Kilmer-Slickrock Wilderness (along the Hangover, Naked Ground, and Bob's Bald mountain crest). Accordingly, the proroad forces, headed by Mayor Charles Hall of Tellico Plains, were squarely faced off against Ted Snyder and the Joyce Kilmer Wilderness Advocates. A compromise was thus in order, and the parties were brought together by the efforts of Dr. Houston Lowry of Madisonville. The proroad people agreed to reroute the road across the less scenic Beech Gap while the Wilderness Advocates agreed not to oppose the road along its new route.

After passage of the 1974 act, TN conservationists began looking toward additional TN areas to be protected as wilderness. A principal candidate was the Bald River watershed. Ray Payne and Will Skelton met with CNF Supervisor Bob Lusk and various interested parties to discuss its protection but were pretty much stonewalled. Supervisor Lusk maintained, as did official USFS policy then, that there were no lands that qualified for wilderness in the East. So there was much work to be done.

Conservationists throughout the nation worked on an unprecedented scale for the election of Jimmy Carter as president in 1976. President Carter ran as a candidate sympathetic to the idea of wilderness and, once elected, implemented a formal procedure for correcting the eastern-western wilderness designation imbalance. The procedure was called RARE II (Roadless Areas Review and Evaluation; the "II" reflects that a previous review had been conducted only in the western US).

The first RARE II function in TN was a meeting conducted by the USFS in Knoxville on July 29, 1977. Areas possessing some potential for wilderness designation were to be identified by participants. The meeting seemed to go very well, as conservationists took maps of the CNF and generally were able to agree with the other interest groups on areas that "might" possess some potential for wilderness. However, much later, environmentalists were told that this innocuous meeting was at least part of the beginning of vehement wilderness opposition in eastern TN. The meeting was conducted in small subgroups, and apparently a wilderness proponent in one of the subgroups was overly eager and came across as somewhat of a fanatic, urging that the entire CNF be designated wilderness. This scared other members of that subgroup, and they promptly went home and began organizing against wilderness, particularly in the Elizabethton and Tellico Plains areas. The opposition in Elizabethton was led by the Carter County Sportsmen's Club, a hunting and fishing group, while the opposition in Tellico Plains was led by Save Our Recreational Environment ("SORE") organized by Mayor Hall of Tellico Plains. SORE subsequently produced the most active opposition.

There was a variety of reasons given by opponents of wilderness for their position. Deer are a principal large-game species in east TN, and hunters were concerned with loss of their habitat. Many hunters feel that deer thrive in a forest that is managed for timber harvesting, which wilderness designation would not allow. Wilderness proponents responded that, aside from disagreement by other hunters on the need for managed habitat, other important species such as black bear clearly need the nonmanaged habitat provided by wilderness. Individuals involved with the timber industry were concerned that wilderness areas would be taken out of the CNF timber base. Wilderness proponents responded that the amount of commercial timber in the proposed areas was small, especially in view of the rugged topography that made much timber difficult to harvest. Motor vehicle interests were concerned that wilderness areas would be closed to ORVs. Wilderness proponents responded with lists of the negligible mileage involved in road closures and the need to have a few areas off-limits to ORVs. The USFS was a reluctant wilderness supporter in the beginning, largely because many USFS employees felt timber harvesting was a necessary part of good forest management. However, they gradually came to accept wilderness as a legitimate use of the national forests within a multiple-use context. Other reasons given for opposition to wilderness often resulted from misunderstandings of the Wilderness Act. The most common was the false belief that hunting would be banned in wilderness areas. Some wilderness opposition was also based on deliberate misinformation, as discussed below.

The RARE II process continued with the USFS identifying 21 possible wilderness areas in a draft Environmental Impact Statement released on June 15, 1978. Written comments were then solicited on the areas during the summer of 1978, but no hearings were scheduled. The USFS advised conservationists, both orally and in writing, that their comments should be site-specific and substantive to help the USFS make a professional decision. They further advised that form letters and petitions would not be considered. The Cherokee National Forest Wilderness Coalition was formed to coordinate the preparation of these comments by conservationists. Will Skelton served as coordinator of the coalition, which was initially composed of the Tennessee Chapter of the Sierra Club, Great Smoky Mountains Hiking Club, Tennessee Citizens for Wilderness Planning, Trout Unlimited, and Tennessee Council of the Audubon Society. Other groups were subsequently added. John Thomas of Knoxville served for some time as assistant coordinator.

Meanwhile, on the other side of the issue, SORE was producing input in a totally different way. SORE essentially collected petitions and form letters, contrary to the USFS's request. There were also reports of false information being disseminated by unknown parties with regard to wilderness, e.g., "They are going to close all of the roads in the National Forest"; "They are closing the campgrounds"; "If you own land outside the National Forest, it will also be managed as wilderness"; and "You will not be able to hunt in the National Forest anymore." When the coalition learned what was happening, it was too late. The antiwilderness people submitted 12,586 petitions and form letters opposing wilderness (and 7,492 supporting multiple use) but almost no substantive, site-specific letters opposing wilderness. The coalition submitted, in addition to detailed area reports, 724 site-specific substantive letters supporting wilderness, but submitted few form letters. The coalition's comments to the USFS were, without question, the most detailed and substantive public comments on wilderness ever received by the CNF. The coalition won the site-specific battle 87.6 to 12.4 percent but lost the petition and form-letter battle. Who was to win the war itself was still unclear.

With this input, CNF Supervisor Marvin Laurisen obviously had a problem. He elected to change horses in the middle of the stream, accepted the antiwilderness petitions and form letters, and made his decision based on them. The result was a devastating defeat in terms of numbers for wilderness designation. The USFS announced their final RARE II recommendations at a press conference held in the

Howard Johnson's West in Knoxville on January 4, 1979. The wilderness recommendations were few. Only Bald River Gorge was recommended for wilderness designation while Little Frog Mountain, Citico Creek, Big Frog Mountain, Flint Mill, and Pond Mountain were recommended for further planning. Pond Mountain Addition and Unaka Mountain were later added as further planning areas, after numerous protests by environmentalists.

The Wilderness Coalition vowed not to be a victim of the USFS's misrepresentation again. Accordingly, shortly after the RARE II process was over, it began collecting petition signatures with the aim of fighting fire with fire in the event other hearings were held. Since the process is essentially political, the coalition also began obtaining letters to east TN Congressmen John Duncan and James Quillen and TN Senators Howard Baker and James Sasser. Finally, in an effort to combat the misinformation about wilderness during RARE II, Ken McDonald and Susie McDonald, with the help of other members of the Harvey Broome Group of the Sierra Club's TN Chapter, produced and subsequently began presenting a multimedia slide show entitled "Wilderness for Tomorrow." The format was essentially beautiful pictures of the CNF, together with answers to the most frequently asked questions about wilderness.

Various efforts at compromise over the years helped to humanize the people on both sides of the issue. Ray Payne, Will Skelton, and Sandy Hodge met with SORE's president, Mayor Charles Hall of Tellico Plains, on several occasions, all friendly and helpful, but inconclusive. In northeast TN the Carter County Club and the Greene County Hunting and Fishing Club in Greeneville were the principal sources of opposition to wilderness. The Greene County Club refused to meet with the coalition. The coalition did meet with the Carter County Club on two occasions in the late 1970s, but without success. The initial meeting was in Elizabethton on June 6, 1978, and, in spite of being fairly friendly, resulted in a letter which stated, after a vote by their club, "It is now a matter of record that our Club will oppose your Coalition in every way we can." However, after some passage of time, the coalition tried again in October of 1979 and, although another vote of the Carter County Club was close, it was again antiwilderness. These failed compromise efforts made it clear that, if the coalition wanted wilderness, an easy compromise was not possible.

The first opportunity to test whether the coalition's activities after RARE II were having any effect was the USFS's hearings on Citico Creek and Big Frog Mountain. The USFS was required by the 1974 Eastern Wilderness Areas Act to study these two areas for wilderness by December 31, 1979. They did not make that deadline, but on June 10, 1982, the USFS distributed its draft Environmental Impact Statement on the areas and conducted public hearings. From the substantive, site-specific standpoint, Lance McCold, of Knoxville, organized a committee to critique the draft statement in detail and produce a written analysis. A massive petition effort coordinated by Will Skelton resulted in 20,642 petition signatures versus only 10,313 antiwilderness signatures. A change in public opinion was also reflected at the public hearings in Chatsworth, GA, and Athens, TN, with 67 witnesses for wilderness and only 16 against.

After the Citico Creek and Big Frog hearings, the next logical step was to convince Congressman John Duncan, in whose district all of the areas in the southern CNF were located, that he should introduce a wilderness bill. Such effort included forwarding Congressman Duncan copies of the 20,642 petition signatures (plus additional signatures obtained after 1982), meeting with him in Sweetwater and showing him the slide show, and soliciting additional letters supporting wilderness from a wide variety of people. On November 1, 1983, Congressman Duncan introduced H.R. 4263, the Southern CNF Wilderness Act. The bill provided for the designation of Citico Creek, Bald River Gorge, and Big Frog Mountain as wilderness, while Little Frog Mountain would be a wilderness study area. The real suspense with regard to H.R. 4263 was the USFS's attitude, since they had not released the final Environmental Impact Statement on Citico Creek and Big Frog Mountain. However, about this time the wilderness cause was fortunate to gain a new supervisor of the CNF, Don Rollens. His experience with western national forest wilderness resulted in a greater willingness to view wilderness as a legitimate use of the CNF.

The US House of Representatives moved quickly on the bill as public hearings were held by the Public Lands Subcommittee of the Interior Committee on March 29, 1984, by Congressman John Seiberling. Max Petterson, the chief of the USFS, testified and supported the bill, as did Charles Howell, the commissioner of the Tennessee Department of Conservation. Congressman Duncan also testified in favor of the bill. Their testimony was followed by Will Skelton on behalf of the coalition, and Dr. Houston Lowry of Madisonville, who testified for wilderness as a local resident. S. 590, the Senate version of H.R. 4263, was introduced on April 25, 1984, by both Tennessee senators, Howard Baker and James Sasser. Hearings were held before the Forestry Subcommittee of the Senate's Agriculture Committee on May 24, 1984, and were chaired by Iowa Senator Roger Jepsen. The USFS representative, Lamar Beasley, again supported the bill. Walter Criley, director of planning of the Tennessee Department of Conservation, likewise supported the bill. Will Skelton also testified on behalf of the coalition, and Ralston Bailey, of Benton, testified for the bill as a local resident and as president of the Cherokee Sportsmen's Association.

The Senate passed the bill on October 2, 1984, just before adjournment. The House thereafter acted promptly and repassed the Senate version of the bill. President Ronald Reagan then signed the act into law on October 30, 1984.

After the passage of the Southern CNF Wilderness Act, the coalition's efforts were directed toward the northern CNF and Congressman James Quillen, who was not willing to introduce a bill in 1984. The legal requirement of the National Forest

Management Practices Act that the USFS prepare a Management Plan for the CNF provided the first real opportunity to influence the USFS toward a wilderness recommendation for the northern CNF. The draft Forest Management Plan was released in mid-January of 1985, with wilderness recommendations that were an improvement over RARE II but still considered inadequate by the coalition. The coalition prepared comments on wilderness while the Tennessee Chapter of the Sierra Club, Tennessee Citizens for Wilderness Planning, and Smoky Mountains Hiking Club prepared comments on the management aspects of the Forest Plan. Both sets of comments were thorough and comprehensive, and presented factual arguments. The coalition also, remembering past lessons, ensured that they had the "numbers," and 4,387 petition signatures were delivered to the USFS ; 1,384 of those were from Congressman Quillen's First Congressional District.

One of the problems facing the legislation was the largest RARE II area in the Northern CNF, the Jennings Creek area located near Greeneville. Jennings Creek is a large, unique, and beautiful area located on the western slopes of the Bald Mountain Ridge; the area contains everything from large waterfalls to grassy balds and the AT. It was also the source of perhaps the toughest site-specific controversy in the northern CNF. District Ranger Bill Sweet encouraged the various parties to work out a compromise, and efforts in that regard were subsequently led by Tony Campbell and the Tennessee Conservation League. A public meeting on January 25, 1985, was followed by a more productive meeting and hike among the leaders. The final compromise had something for everyone: a new Bald Ridge Mountain Scenic Area that encompassed most of the old Jennings Creek area, with two dead-end roads left open, and an adjacent Sampson Mountain Wilderness.

The final Management Plan was released on April 1, 1986, and contained a much improved wilderness recommendation for additional CNF wilderness: four wilderness areas in upper east Tennessee (Pond Mountain, Unaka Mountain, Sampson Mountain, and Big Laurel Branch) and the Little Frog and Big Frog Mountain Addition in southeast TN. These recommendations left open the prospect that Congressman Quillen would go along with the wilderness designation. Ed Williams and Will Skelton met with Congressman Quillen on June 27, 1986, and asked him to introduce a bill. The State of Franklin Sierra Club Group and the Watauga Audubon Society also met with Congressman Quillen shortly afterward and presented him with additional petitions and showed him the wilderness slide show. Congressman Quillen then gave his aides the go-ahead on the bill, leaving primarily a problem of logistics in completing passage during the remainder of the legislative year.

The bill was introduced as H.R. 5166 in the House of Representatives by Congressmen Duncan and Quillen on July 15, 1986, and in the US Senate as S. 2685 by Senators James Sasser and Al Gore on July 24, 1986.

Hearings were promptly held in the House of Representatives on July 31, 1986.

Dan Lady and Will Skelton testified from TN and worked, with the USFS, on resolving several problems that had arisen. These included the discovery of a rare mineral, niobium, in the proposed Big Laurel Branch Wilderness (the USFS overcame this one by continuing to recommend wilderness designation because of plentiful existing supplies in Canada and Brazil); the concern over whether boaters could continue to dock their boats on the Big Laurel Branch/Watauga Lake shoreline (resolved by the conclusion that such was allowed under the Wilderness Act); the desire by some residents for a road from Butler to Blue Springs across the proposed Big Laurel Branch Wilderness; and the demand of Unicoi County that approximately 100 acres of USFS land be given to the county. The last two were bigger problems and required some negotiations and work. The road issue was settled by a USFS report reflecting that, if the road were built, the most practical location would be outside the wilderness (and even then very expensive and environmentally questionable). The Unicoi issue was resolved by a committee report encouraging the parties to settle the land transfer issue.

With those issues out of the way, Senate hearings were thereafter held on September 25, 1986. The noncontroversial nature of the bill, and the lack of time in view of the pending end of the session, meant only Senators Gore and Sasser presented "live" testimony. Thereafter, with the support of Senators Sasser and Gore as well as Congressmen Quillen and Duncan, the Tennessee Wilderness Act of 1986 was passed by the US House of Representatives on September 22, 1986, and by the Senate on October 3, 1986, with President Ronald Reagan signing it on October 16, 1986.

With wilderness designation being settled by the 1984 and 1986 acts, environmentalists turned to an appeal of the CNF Management Plan to obtain administrative protection for areas left out of the wilderness acts. A formal appeal of the Management Plan was filed by the Sierra Club, Wilderness Society, Smoky Mountain Hiking Club, Tennessee Citizens for Wilderness Planning, and Tennessee Audubon Council soon after the plan was released in 1986. The initial phase of the appeal was to the USFS Regional Forester in Atlanta under USFS rules. Shortly thereafter, settlement negotiations commenced and were consummated in July of 1988. Those who filed the appeal were represented in the negotiations by Bill Bumpers, a Washington, DC, attorney. The Wilderness Society's Ron Tipton and Peter Kirby coordinated the appeal from a national standpoint while Ray Payne coordinated the TN efforts. Other individuals participating in the appeal negotiations for TN conservation groups were Hugh Irwin, Lance McCold, Roger Jenkins, Will Skelton, Dana Eglinton, Arthur Smith, John Doyal, and Kirk Johnson. Both timber harvesting practices and special area protection were considered and were the subject of many negotiating sessions. The last roadblock to a settlement was the Upper Bald River area, which had persistently defied final agreement. Finally, in July of 1988 discussions between Mike Murphy of the USFS, Ken Arney of TWRA, and Will Skelton of the Sierra Club forged a resolution that allowed an overall settlement. The agreement protected a significant number of additional scenic and primitive areas, reduced the amount of future clear-cutting, and contained provisions designed to help the CNF's black bear population.

The settlement was announced in Knoxville on August 4, 1988, at a joint press conference by the USFS, the appellants, and the intervenors (Tennessee Conservation League, TWRA, Tennessee Valley Sportsmen's Club, Appalachian Chapter of Trout Unlimited, Tennessee Forestry Association, Tennessee Forestry Commission, Kentucky-Tennessee Society of American Foresters, and Multi-Use Council of the Southeast). At the time the settlement was signed, the USFS issued an amendment to the CNF Management Plan that incorporated the settlement items (except for changes in timber harvest methods and volumes that required a supplemental Environmental Impact Statement and certain issues of national scope that were forwarded to the chief of the USFS for decision). Finally resolved for the duration of the Management Plan was the fate of numerous wild areas that are now protected under various management categories.

A new coalition, Cherokee Forest Voices, was subsequently organized by the appellants with Hugh Irwin as coordinator. The organization's principal purpose was monitoring future compliance by the CNF with the Management Plan.

This political history of the CNF's wild areas has, for now, a happy result. However, politics is if anything a changeable process, and continued vigilance will be necessary to keep these areas wild.

8. MAINTAINING AND PROTECTING THE TRAILS

As you visit the natural areas included in this guidebook, remember that all of these areas have been lived on, logged, or otherwise used within the past hundred years; they have recovered immensely from those times and will continue to recover if we allow them to do so.

Such recovery will be ensured if everyone practices no-trace camping. The idea is to leave no significant evidence of your having hiked or camped in an area. This can be a challenge, but every effort to maintain natural conditions will reward you and others on future hikes. A littered campsite and trail versus a campsite and trail that appear to be part of the natural environment will make a difference in your wilderness experience. John Hart's *Walk Softly in the Wilderness* (see Bibliography) is one of the best guidebooks on no-trace camping. The key phrase is: "pack it in, pack it out." Some other specific suggestions include the following:

Campfires. If you can avoid a campfire by using a backpacking stove, you've made a huge contribution to your campsite's environment. Campfires, together with litter, create the most adverse visual and ecological impacts of back-country camping. The fire ring detracts from the naturalness of the area by introducing blackened rocks and piles of ash, charcoal, and unburned wood. The wood for the fire also removes dead wood critical to a healthy forest's ecosystem. If you do choose to build a campfire, remember several guidelines. Use an existing fire ring or, if none exists, choose a site with little or no vegetation and do not build an unnecessary fire ring. Keep the fire small and burn only dead and down wood that can be broken by hand; leave saws and axes at home. Never leave the fire unattended. Afterward, completely erase the campfire. Make sure it is dead out, remove unburned foil, plastic, or other foreign materials, scatter the ashes, and camouflage the burned area with organic matter. If there was an existing fire ring, you may want to scatter the rocks and erase the fire ring unless it is in a popular area where it is likely to be rebuilt. Scatter any unused firewood in the forest.

Campsites. Many people hope for a "virgin" campsite and avoid the "used" campsite. Actually, it is preferable to use existing campsites that are in acceptable condition (where understory vegetation is worn away on some or most of the site but humus, litter, leaves, or needles cover most of the ground). If everyone develops a "new" campsite, the area will soon be littered with campsites. However, you should avoid overused sites that need to rest (where the entire area is bare ground with eroding soil, damaged trees, tree stumps, and exposed roots). Also avoid lightly used campsites that are near an established site. When in camp, minimize your impact. Avoid "site engineering" by digging, cutting, and moving the natural environment. Also avoid spreading out and expanding the area. Prepare and eat meals in one location.

When leaving camp, pack out *all* trash and garbage and make a conscious effort to leave the site in as good, if not better, condition than when you arrived. The littered and overused sites will not improve by themselves; give nature a helping hand.

Sanitation. Proper disposal of human waste is a critical part of no-trace camping (everything else should be burned or carried out). A cat-hole should *always* be used for human excrement; no exceptions. It should be located at least 100 feet from water sources and campsites. Dig the hole at least 6 to 8 inches deep. After using it, burn your toilet paper (carry a matchbook with your toilet paper) and then refill the hole with soil. Scatter organic matter on top to camouflage the site. A group cat-hole can be used, in which case it should be larger and deeper, with only a light layer of soil placed in the hole after each use.

Horse Use. If you are riding horses, make a particular effort to see that horse manure does not foul campsites, streams, and trails. Keep the horses well away from campsites and trails during stops and at night. Remember that horses can do a tremendous amount of damage to dirt trails.

As you visit these areas, remember that their protection as wilderness, scenic, and primitive areas did not come easily—many people worked many hours for their protection. You can thank those people by taking care of our natural areas and reporting to the CNF any abuse you observe (the most likely abuse will be ORVs; they are absolutely prohibited in wilderness areas and should not be present; they are allowed in scenic and primitive areas only on existing roads where specifically authorized). Call or write the CNF district ranger or supervisor (see Appendix 2 for addresses and telephone numbers).

You can also help these areas and trails by volunteering to maintain trails or work for the future protection of the natural areas in this guidebook; in either case, contact the Sierra Club Group nearest you or the CNF (see Appendix 2 for addresses). Finally, you can help by simply writing your congressperson (US House of Representatives, Washington, DC 20515) or senator (US Senate, Washington, DC 20510) and the CNF supervisor (see Appendix 2 for address) and telling them that areas you have hiked should continue to be protected from timber harvesting, road building, vehicle use, and development.

Section B

The Cherokee National Forest's Wilderness Trails—North

1. ROGERS RIDGE SCENIC AREA AND PRIMITIVE AREA

The Rogers Ridge Scenic Area and the Rogers Ridge Primitive Area are located in the extreme northeastern corner of TN in Johnson County and the Watauga Ranger District. They border the Tri-State Corner where TN, NC, and VA meet. Of the total 5,255 acres, 3,865 are a Scenic Area and 1,390 a Primitive Area (the Primitive Area is on the TN-VA state line, north of the Scenic Area). The outstanding feature of the Areas is the high grassy ridges that provide truly spectacular vistas to range after range of mountain highlands, including Mt. Rogers and Whitetop to the north and Roan Mountain and Grandfather Mountain to the south. The balds on Rogers Ridge are among the most beautiful and extensive in the southern Appalachians. They were severely damaged by ORV traffic prior to designation of the Scenic Area in 1988, but ORV use is now prohibited in much of the Areas, and the balds are recovering. Perhaps the finest "up-close" scenery is on Gentry Creek where two beautiful 30-foot waterfalls tumble over high rock walls into clear pools.

In addition to the marvelous views, the Areas contain a variety of wildflowers, including the rare silverling, Robbins ragwort, Rock skullcap, Roan rattlesnake root, Fraser's sedge, mountain bitter cress, Appalachian twayblade, rosy twisted-stalk, and Minnie bush. Some of the gaps contain high mountain bogs, which are important biological ecosystems. Wildlife in the Areas include abundant deer and turkey populations. Of special note is that one of the last authenticated sightings of the eastern panther in TN was in the Rogers Ridge area.

HISTORY

The Areas include the former 1,297-acre Gentry Creek Scenic Area, plus acreage added to the Scenic Area, and the contiguous Primitive Area designated in the CNF's final Management Plan in 1988. Most of the Areas were logged within the past century, but only traces of this activity can still be found. Logging and fires may be partially responsible for the extensive grassy balds in the Areas. However, the balds' exact origin is still a mystery, with fires set by Indians and pioneers being

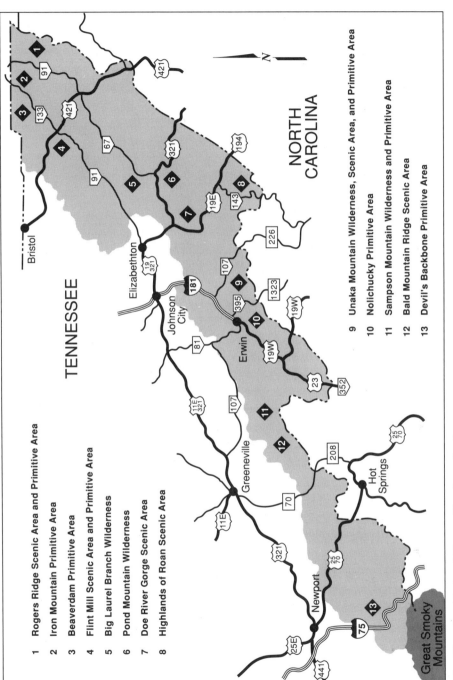

1   Rogers Ridge Scenic Area and Primitive Area
2   Iron Mountain Primitive Area
3   Beaverdam Primitive Area
4   Flint Mill Scenic Area and Primitive Area
5   Big Laurel Branch Wilderness
6   Pond Mountain Wilderness
7   Doe River Gorge Scenic Area
8   Highlands of Roan Scenic Area

9   Unaka Mountain Wilderness, Scenic Area, and Primitive Area
10 Nolichucky Primitive Area
11 Sampson Mountain Wilderness and Primitive Area
12 Bald Mountain Ridge Scenic Area
13 Devil's Backbone Primitive Area

The Cherokee National Forest, Northern Section.

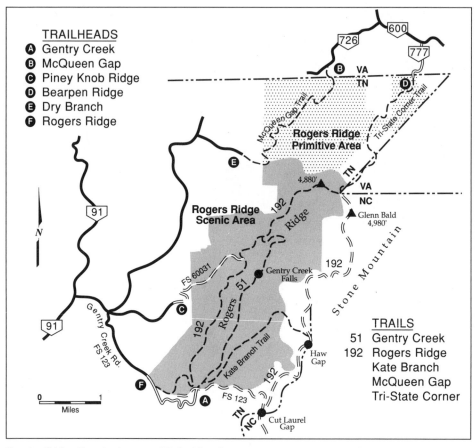

Rogers Ridge Scenic Area and Primitive Area.

a frequently mentioned possibility. ORV use, particularly in areas accessed from private land in NC east of the Areas, has traditionally been a management problem. Primitive and Scenic Area designations have brought some improvement.

TRAILHEADS AND MAPS

Most of the trailheads are located just east of Laurel Bloomery, TN. Laurel Bloomery is reached by taking TN 91 7.6 miles north from the US 421, TN 91, and TN 67 intersection in Mountain City, TN. Directions from Laurel Bloomery to nearby trailheads are described below. Although the Scenic Area is in TN, it is also very accessible from VA. From I-81 at Abingdon, VA, take US 58 12 miles to Damascus, VA. Directions from Damascus to the McQueen Gap Trailhead and Laurel Bloomery area trailheads are described below.

Rime covers the trees following a mid-winter storm in Rogers Ridge Scenic Area. Photo by Roger Jenkins.

Laurel Bloomery Area Trailheads

Gentry Creek Road (FS 123) turns east off TN 91 in Laurel Bloomery but is not marked. When approaching from the south, the road turns right at 7.6 miles just before crossing the bridge over Gentry Creek; note the flag and volunteer fire department on the other side of the bridge. There is a very small sign on the right at this point stating "Gentry Creek—3 miles." When approaching from Damascus, VA, it is 7.0 miles south to Laurel Bloomery. Take US 58 south 1.0 mile; turn right on VA 91, which becomes TN 91 at the state line. Note a volunteer fire department building on the left, usually with a flag out front. Immediately cross a bridge (over Gentry Creek) and turn left on FS 123. Whether approaching from north or south, drive up the paved Gentry Creek Road 0.8 mile, past two churches, to an intersection. Four trailheads are reached from this intersection ("Gentry Creek Intersection") and will be described separately. At the Gentry Creek Intersection is a small "Gentry Creek Falls—3 miles" sign pointing right and a sign pointing left for the State Line Church.

*Winter backpackers pause for a break atop the scenic balds of Rogers Ridge.
Photo by Roger Jenkins.*

Rogers Ridge and Gentry Creek Trailheads

Turn right at the Gentry Creek Intersection on a paved road and drive past two
ponds on the left. At 1.1 miles from the Gentry Creek Intersection the pavement
turns to gravel. At 1.3 miles a spur road turns left into a gravel parking lot. The
Rogers Ridge Trail starts at the back side of the parking lot. For the Gentry Creek
Trailhead, continue on up the Gentry Creek Road to the right, past the parking area.
The road becomes difficult but not usually impassable for two-wheel-drive automobiles. At 1.6 miles a small car camping area is on the left and a side trail turns left
at 2.3 miles. At 2.4 miles the road ends in an oval parking area. The Gentry Creek Trail
angles off into the woods at the back-left side of the parking area. Note a rough road
angling up at the back-right of the parking area. This is the Gentry Creek ORV road
(FS 123), which climbs up to Cut Laurel Gap and then north to Winnie Knob and Haw
Gap. It provides a means of making a large loop hike in the Rogers Ridge Area (see
Rogers Ridge Trail).

Piney Knob Ridge Road Trailhead

From the Gentry Creek Intersection described above, turn left (toward State Line
Church) on a paved road. Drive only 0.1 mile and turn right onto another paved

Winter backpackers establish camp in the Rogers Ridge Scenic Area. Photo by Roger Jenkins.

road that proceeds up Dry Branch. Continue up the Dry Branch Road for 1.1 miles from the Gentry Creek Intersection. The paved road will dead-end at a log fence with a house to the left and another house behind the fence. Permission of the local homeowners should be obtained to park vehicles at this trailhead. Between the two houses a narrow, rocky road will lead off to the left. This is the USFS Piney Knob Ridge ORV road, which is badly rutted and leads 2.5 miles to a clearing on Rogers Ridge and, at the far side of the clearing, a junction with the Rogers Ridge Trail. To the right the Rogers Ridge Trail is marked with a horse-trail sign, and straight ahead it is a continuation of the ORV road.

Dry Branch Trailhead

At the Gentry Creek Intersection described above, turn left on the paved road and follow signs for the State Line Church. At 0.1 mile take the left fork. At 0.85 mile turn right onto Greer Branch Road. At 3.4 miles reach the Sugar Creek Community and, at a fork just past the State Line Church, turn right up Dry Creek. At 3.85 miles turn right off the main road and continue up Dry Creek. The road dead-ends at about 4.55 miles, and the McQueen Gap Trail proceeds up the Dry Creek Valley toward McQueen Gap.

Snow and rime cover trees following winter storm at Rogers Ridge Scenic Area. Photo by Lance McCold.

McQueen Gap Trailhead

Follow US 58 south from Damascus, VA, for 1.0 mile. Turn right on VA 91, which becomes TN 91 at 2.7 miles. At 3.4 miles turn left on the paved Dellanville Road (no sign but it is the only paved side road nearby). The road crosses back into VA, becoming the Taylor Valley Road (VA 725), and enters the village of Taylor Valley at 6.1 miles. Turn right in Taylor Valley onto VA 726.The pavement ends at 7.1 miles on VA 726 but resumes after 1.8 miles of good gravel road. Near the top of a rise in the road you will reach the trailhead at 9.2 miles. Park on the right near the entrance to a barricaded USFS road, which is the trailhead.

Bearpen Ridge Trailhead

A little over 28 miles east of Abingdon, VA on US 58, turn right on VA 600 at the Green Cove Church. Go about 1.1 miles, take a hard left turn off VA 600 onto a gravel road (VA 777) that runs up the valley of Buckeye Branch. Follow this road for about 0.5 mile until the first obvious fork in the road. Take the fork to the right, which is a very narrow one lane gravel and rock road. It will look rough, and like someone's driveway, but it is usually passable to normal passenger cars. Go about 0.4 mile, until the road deteriorates into a jeep track. On your right, across the road from a house, is a small parking area. This is the trailhead.

Topographic Maps: Grayson, TN-NC-VA; Laurel Bloomery, TN-VA.

TRAIL DESCRIPTIONS

Gentry Creek (Gentry Creek Falls) (Trail No. 51)
Length: 4.0 miles
Elevation Change: Start 2,800 feet, end 4,020 feet (high point 4,020 feet)
Trailheads: Gentry Creek Trail (start) and Rogers Ridge Trail (end)
Type: Hiking

Comments: The good-quality Gentry Creek Trail leads to Gentry Creek Falls, one of the Scenic Area's most outstanding sights. Above the falls the trail degenerates into no trail at all and, although an official USFS trail, requires off-trail hiking. Continuing on up Gentry Creek provides opportunities for loop trips. A small white metal sign sometimes marks the trail. This is also known as Gentry Creek Falls Trail.

Details: The trail begins in a shady grove of white pine and rhododendron that bloom in early to mid-July. It immediately crosses a small creek and follows an old logging-railroad bed. At 0.1 mile, Kate Branch Trail (barricaded by an earth mound) splits off to the right. Gentry Creek Trail continues along Gentry Creek, through a carpet of wildflowers in the early spring. The trail is generally dirt but quite rocky in some places. The predominant tree along the creek is the yellow birch, with its characteristic peeling bark. A high canopy of second-growth hardwoods—poplar and maple—provides dense shade and leaves the forest floor remarkably open except for the mounds of rhododendrons. In early morning, shafts of sunlight pierce the canopy and create an inspiring pattern of light in the morning mist.

At 0.26 mile the trail appears to cross Gentry Creek; do not cross but instead go up a small rise to the right. The trail proceeds on the right bank, crossing a small side stream, and finally at 0.56 mile crosses to the west side of the creek. This is the beginning of numerous crossings, all of which require rock-hopping or fording as there are no bridges. At 0.8 mile note a USFS property sign and yellow "bearing tree" sign on the left. At 0.85 mile there is an interesting low rock cliff on the left displaying cubic fractures. Even in the thick growth of summer, the character of the gorge is influenced by the rock faces that outcrop, revealing thick and thin bands of sediment laid down in basins that preceded today's mountain ridges. Piles of talus from the gorge walls accumulate on the otherwise broad, flat valley bottom. At 1.02 miles an old logging railroad grade on the left side of the creek goes back and up to the left of the trail.

The trail ascends very gradually through the steep-sided gorge, crossing and recrossing the creek about 15 times before reaching Gentry Falls. At 1.36 miles go straight up a usually dry rocky streambed instead of taking an obvious trail across the streambed to an island area; a small white trail sign marks the route. At 1.4 miles the rock changes to quartzite, which in places forms the stream bottom, channeling the water into slides and small cascades. The gorge in this area features prolific ferns and nettles. In mid-summer mountain hydrangea and crimson bee balm (oswego tea) bloom along the creek.

A logging cable and old railroad grade back to the left of the trail are passed at 1.86 miles. At 2.36 miles the trail drops down to the creek but then makes a hard left back up the bank. Look upstream at this point for your first view of Gentry Creek Falls in the distance. Follow a rocky trail on upstream.

At 2.4 miles, the approach to Gentry Falls is heralded as the trail goes around the left side of a huge, high boulder covered with leathery lichen. Go down to the creek once around the boulder. From this beautiful vantage point below the falls, both an upper and lower cascade are visible, each 30 feet high. The water spills over two broad rock ledges that span the width of the gorge. To the right a fern-covered slope ascends from the pool beneath the falls.

Beyond the lower falls the ascent steepens and becomes more challenging. Do not continue unless you have off-trail hiking experience. To continue the hike to the upper falls, climb the steep talus pile beside the left wall of the lower falls and scramble up a stack of rocks. Then traverse over to the right; the trail crosses the stream between the upper and lower falls. The pool between the two is more delightful than the one below, with deep water under a jutting rock face sprouting rhododendrons. The falls are a logical destination for a day hike, including a swim in the heat of summer.

The ascent continues up the right side of the upper falls; there is no trail at this point, and caution is advised. An optional route is to continue climbing very steeply up to the left side of the falls instead of traversing to the right between the upper and lower falls. Once on top of the ridge, descend to the right down to the creek and trail above the falls. From the top of the falls at 2.5 miles the trail levels out and the character of the woods changes. The stream is quieter and the understory increasingly dense. The trail is well defined just above the falls but later virtually disappears. At 2.7 miles you will pass two pieces of metal from the railroad logging days; one has printed on it "Built By Meadow Mill Co., N. Wilkesboro, N.C." A short distance on, you will see the remnants of an old stove and an obvious fork in the trail. This is the Gilbert Branch and Gentry Creek junction. At one time a trail came down from Stone Mountain on the right following a logging railroad grade and then went up the mountain to the left to Rogers Ridge. It is not shown on topographical maps, but an experienced off-trail hiker could follow the route either way. Just up the railroad grade to the right are the remains of an old cabin, including bedsprings.

To follow the Gentry Creek Trail, continue by crossing the creek and proceeding upstream. At 3.0 miles a railroad grade descends from the right. At 3.25 miles is an almost impenetrable series of blow-downs across the trail. The trail has, in any event, generally disappeared at this point and, once past the blow-downs, you will be walking mainly in the creek. You may choose to stay on the left side of the creek in winter and early spring. However, in summer chest-high nettles discourage this route and proceeding straight up the creek may be easier.

At around 3.4 miles you should leave the creek and angle back up to the left on an old ORV road. The route is shown on the USGS map but is difficult to find. Perhaps the best advice is to begin looking at about 3.0 miles and, if you do not find the trail in another 0.5 mile, start going up cross-country to the left, in a northwest direction. The trail leads up to join the Rogers Ridge Trail in a clearing at 4.0 miles. It will switchback to the right just before reaching the clearing. At the clearing the Rogers Ridge Trail leads along Rogers Ridge left to the Gentry Creek watershed. To the right it goes up to acres of grassy balds. Straight across the clearing an ORV road leads down into Seng Cove.

The USFS has proposed a new horse trail that would come down into Gentry Creek from the Rogers Ridge Trail at Tri-State Corner and connect with the Gentry Creek Trail where it leaves Gentry Creek. The trail had not been constructed by the early 1990s.

McQueen Gap (No USFS Number)
Length: 2.2 miles
Elevation Change: Start 3,320 feet, end 3,200 feet (high point 3,920 feet)
Trailheads: McQueen Gap (start) and Dry Branch (end)
Type: Hiking

Comments: This trail is entirely in the Primitive Area, mostly just south of the TN-VA state line. It provides access to the intimate beauty of Whetstone Branch. Although it is possible to begin or end the trail at the Dry Branch Trailhead, permission of the owners of the private property at that trailhead must be obtained. Such owners may not be cooperative; ordinarily it is preferable to hike in and out from the McQueen Gap Trailhead. This trail is not presently included in the CNF trail system.
Details: The trail starts on the south side of McQueen Gap and follows an old jeep road surrounded by rhododendron blooming in the early summer months. At about 0.3 mile, the trail crosses Richardson Branch at its confluence with Valley Creek. The USGS map shows a side trail heading up Richardson Branch to Flat Springs Ridge, which affords excellent views. The trailhead to this side trail is barricaded with a small earthen mound, and the trail quickly disappears along the creek. Proceeding on up Richardson Branch is possible but moderately difficult and should only be attempted with the aid of a topographic map.

Continue along McQueen Gap Trail up Whetstone Branch, a small but beautiful portion of the Primitive Area. At 1.0 mile the trail crosses Whetstone Branch. Immediately after the crossing, tempting blueberries are within reach in season. The USFS boundary is posted at about 2.2 miles. Just on the other side of the boundary, the trail climbs moderately to its highest elevation at about 3,920 feet and begins to narrow as it descends along Dry Branch to the Dry Branch trailhead, about 1.0 mile further.

Rogers Ridge (Rogers Ridge Horse Trail) (Trail No. 192)

Length: 6.75 miles
Elevation Change: Start 2,680 feet, end 4,640 feet (high point 4,880 feet)
Trailheads: Rogers Ridge Trail (start) and Tri-State Corner Trail (end)
Trail Connections: Gentry Creek Trail and Kate Branch Trail
Type: Horse

Comments: The Rogers Ridge Trail is the major trail in the Rogers Ridge Scenic Area. Two major trailheads and several branch trails make this trail easily accessible. Much of the trail runs along bald ridgetops offering beautiful views all year long. There is a good campsite at the highest spot along the trail, complete with a freshwater spring that runs most of the year. However, the spring may be dry during very dry seasons or periods of drought. The first 6.7 miles of the trail up Rogers Ridge from the Rogers Ridge Trail Trailhead to Tri-State Corner is the official USFS trail. However, we have described an extension, mainly on private land, which allows a large loop trip. This extension proceeds south from Tri-State Corner along the TN-NC state line to Haw Gap. There either the Gentry Creek ORV road (FS 123) or the Kate Branch Trail can be used to get back to the starting trailhead. Topographical maps are essential for following such a route.

The trail is sometimes well blazed, sometimes not. The blazes vary but are usually a vertical yellow slash and/or a metal horse-and-rider logo. This is also known as Rogers Ridge Horse Trail.

Details: The Rogers Ridge Trail starts at the far end of the parking area. You will immediately see two wooden structures directing hikers to the left. The trail generally follows an old ORV road up Gentry Creek. At 0.08 mile a littered campsite is passed, after which you cross the creek to the north side. At 0.27 mile cross the creek back to the south side. At 0.41 mile an old road comes in from the right. Continue straight ahead until 0.49 mile at which point the road continues straight ahead to the Gentry Creek Trail Trailhead. However, the Rogers Ridge Trail makes a 90-degree turn to the left and crosses Gentry Creek. Note yellow horse-and-rider metal trail markers and a yellow blaze at the point where the trail turns and again on the other side of the creek. Once across the creek, which requires fording, the trail heads up an old logging road toward Rogers Ridge and is quite steep at times. There are several earth mounds near the creek to discourage ORV use. The trail is initially quite rocky but becomes a nice dirt trail. Higher up, it will be grassy.

At 0.67 mile cross a creek and continue up a valley through a deciduous forest to the creek's headwaters, then circle around to the right. A huge boulder will be passed in the middle of the trail at 0.87 mile. At 1.14 miles the trail reaches and circles around the head of Rogers Ridge, from the west to the east, then up onto the ridgetop itself. The trail continues climbing, sometimes very steeply, as it crosses from side to side or stays on top of the ridge. Wintertime views out over Gentry Creek are outstanding as you proceed upward.

The trail reaches a level area at 1.81 miles. The upward incline is more gradual from this point on, and the trail is usually grassy. The trail often leads up and over small knolls and down to gaps. It continues to pass through a deciduous forest, often with fern understory. At 2.59 miles an old road goes left downhill at a gap. Continue straight up along a ridge and note a trail sign indicating the correct direction. At 3.46 miles, in a gap, an old road goes left down the side of the ridge. Do not leave the ridge; continue straight along it. Note USFS property signs here. At 3.54 miles cross over a high knoll at around 4,000 feet and descend to a level area where you will pass an old cinder-block shack on the right. Garbage generally litters this area.

At 3.87 miles the trail comes out into a small clearing along an ORV road. To the left the ORV road descends along Piney Knob Ridge to the Piney Knob Ridge Trailhead. Within sight a spur splits off that road to the right. The Rogers Ridge Trail turns right and follows the ORV road up and across a 4,080-foot wooded knoll and down to a meadow.

At 4.32 miles enter the 2-acre meadow surrounded by large white pine and shagbark hickory trees. This is an important junction area. ORVs sometimes come to this clearing but should not go beyond it on the Rogers Ridge Trail. At the clearing the Gentry Creek Trail (No. 51) comes in at 90 degrees from the right (east). An ORV road comes in from the left, having ascended from Seng Cove. The Rogers Ridge Trail proceeds straight through the clearing into the woods on the old ORV road.

At 4.77 miles the trail comes out onto a huge grassy bald, with the route up to a high grassy ridge in the distance being marked by an opening in the forest. This is the beginning of the high, open Rogers Ridge country. Pass over a grassy knoll and down to a gap at 5.08 miles. Then climb up toward the ridgetop on a trail that is steep and rocky toward the end.

At 5.57 miles reach the ridgetop you have been walking toward. Just over and below the crest in the woods is a great campsite located in the forested saddle where Catface Ridge joins Rogers Ridge. To the left a short distance several rock outcrops provide outstanding views. To the right the grassy balds lead up to an evergreen forest and all around you is green grass in the summer. Turn right to follow the Rogers Ridge Trail and proceed toward the evergreens covering the high point of the official trail.

Following the ridge trail, the peak of Rogers Ridge at 4,880 feet is reached at 6.17 miles. Although the USGS map shows this peak as Mt. Rogers, the actual Mt. Rogers is to the north in VA. On the east side of this knob is a lovely open meadow with nearly unlimited campsites. Water can be found about 200 yards south-south-east of the campsites, at a small spring that feeds the headwaters of Gentry Creek. This spot offers superb panoramic views throughout the year. Grandfather Mountain in NC can be seen to the southeast.

To continue on the Rogers Ridge Trail, walk east along the ridge trail for a little over 0.25 mile. From this point, it is advisable to use the topographic map to follow the trail description. The trail continues to follow the ridgeline and affords many lovely views but is marred by the condition of the roads, which are severely eroded into deep ruts.

At 6.5 miles, the trail meets a jeep trail coming up from Big Horse Creek to the east. Big Horse Creek road/trail is on private land but may be hiked with the permission of the owner. It is about a 0.25-mile walk down this side trail to the point where TN, VA, and NC converge. This Tri-State Corner is the official end of the Rogers Ridge Trail. However, we describe an unofficial continuation along the TN-NC state line, making a large loop trip possible. Most of the continuation is on private land, so respect any use limitation signs. To continue on this portion of the trail, walk east along the grassy ridge instead of down to the Tri-State Corner. You will walk toward and then to the south below a huge house that has been constructed, at great expense, on a high grassy ridge. Access to the house is by the ORV road from Big Horse Creek. Continue south. At 6.8 miles, the Rogers Ridge Trail reaches a high point on Glenn Bald (4,980 feet), from which Mt. Rogers (5,729 feet) and White Top Mountain (5,520 feet) are clearly visible to the north.

As the trail heads south down the ridge, it weaves in and out of the USFS boundary. At 7.3 miles, the trail veers west, then south, past an old corral. Turn onto the road and enter a wooded area. At 9.2 miles turn west and ascend a hill to Haw Gap (4,237 feet). At this point you can descend Kate Branch Trail 2.9 miles to the Gentry Creek Trail Trailhead. An alternate is to follow the ORV road that leads to Cut Laurel Gap (about 1.5 miles). At Cut Laurel Gap turn right at a magnificent 4-foot-diameter black oak and proceed 1.4 miles west on the Gentry Creek ORV road (FS 123), which leads to the Gentry Creek Trail Trailhead.

Kate Branch (No USFS Number)
Length: 2.9 miles
Elevation Change: Start 2,840 feet, end 4,237 feet (high point 4,237 feet)
Trailheads: Rogers Ridge Trail (start) and Gentry Creek Trail (end)
Type: Hiking

Comments: Much of this trail is overgrown and difficult to follow. It is included because it and the Gentry Creek jeep road (FS 123) allow a good loop hike in conjunction with the Gentry Creek and Rogers Ridge trails. Fortunately the trail stays along Kate Branch Creek, making it somewhat easier to follow. This trail is not presently included in the CNF trail system. The trail is described from Haw Gap down to its junction with Gentry Creek Trail, 0.1 mile above the Gentry Creek Trailhead.

Details: The trail starts out from the west side of Haw Gap (see Rogers Ridge Trail) and descends from the jeep road into the Kate Branch drainage. Kate Branch begins with a spring that flows into two small artificial ponds. The trail stays on the west side of the creek to about 0.5 mile where it begins several crossings. A major stream comes in from the west at about 1.2 miles. The trail improves at about 2.0 miles and begins to stay along the hillside above and moving to the east of Kate Branch until it joins the Gentry Creek Trail at 2.9 miles. Follow the Gentry Creek Trail left for 0.1 mile to the Gentry Creek Trail Trailhead.

Tri-State Corner (No USFS Number)
Length: 2.3 miles
Elevation Change: Start 3,246 feet, end 4,640 feet (high point 4,640 feet)
Trailheads: Bearpen Ridge (start) and Tri-State Corner (end)
Trail Connections: Rogers Ridge Trail
Type: Part ORV and part hiking

Comments: This is more of a route than a trail and provides the shortest access to Tri-State Corner and the grassy balds just beyond. It can be beautiful in winter when snow keeps ORVs out, but at other times ORVs will intrude. Topographic map use is advised. The trail is not marked.

Details: Proceed straight up the narrow valley on the ORV road. At the head of the valley the trail will circle around an old logging operation as it gradually gains elevation. Some views are outstanding, and portions of the route are not used by ORVs. After ascending to Flat Spring Ridge at about 1.2 miles the trail makes a very sharp turn to the left; other trails go right toward a grassy bald. Proceed southeast and at around 1.6 miles you will come to the ridgecrest, where a picturesque cabin is located. The trail turns right at the cabin and leads up the ridge to the Tri-State Corner at 2.3 miles. TN, VA, and NC meet here, and this is the official end of the Rogers Ridge Trail, which comes from the south. Walk on up the ridge, on the Rogers Ridge Trail, for 0.25 mile, and you will have the option of turning right (west) and hiking over the scenic balds of the Scenic Area or turning left (southeast) and proceeding along the Rogers Ridge Trail's unofficial extension to Haw Gap described above. Most of the extension is on private land.

2. IRON MOUNTAIN PRIMITIVE AREA

The Iron Mountain Primitive Area protects the steep, forested slopes on the northern end of Iron Mountain. The Area is in Johnson County, TN, next to the VA state line between Mountain City, TN, and Damascus, VA. It is approximately 2,568 acres in size and is in the Watauga Ranger District. The Iron Mountain Trail extends through the Area and on to the south along Iron Mountain for a total of 17.8 miles. This Area and the Iron Mountain Trail provide one of the best long-distance hiking opportunities, other than the AT, in the CNF. The Iron Mountain Trail is relatively flat along a long ridge and features wildflowers, large high-elevation hemlock trees, and outstanding views of the valleys on both sides of the ridge.

HISTORY

This corner of northeast TN was supposed to be in VA; however, when it was surveyed in 1749, the surveyor made a mistake in the rough mountain topography. When the mistake was later discovered, an aide was sent back to correct the mistake, but he left the original lines through this area (probably wanting to avoid again walking the difficult terrain). Originally a part of NC, it was ceded to TN when TN later became a state. If you look closely, you may find one of the old survey markers by the stream at the TN-VA state line.

The Iron Mountain Trail formerly extended further north and south. The section described in this guidebook is between Camp AHISTADI and US 421. Sections of the old trail to the north into VA and to the south (between US 421 and FS 53) are unmaintained and overgrown. In the case of the portion just south of US 421, the trail is the site of a large clear-cut. The possibility of rerouting that portion and constructing additional trail to connect the Iron Mountain Trail with the AT on both north and south would provide a huge loop-backpacking opportunity.

This Area was designated as a Primitive Area (Managed) in 1988 by the CNF's Management Plan. Unlike most primitive areas, limited timber harvesting may be allowed in this Area (see Section A). There are three small clear-cuts in the Area that have almost completely regrown. Outside the Area, the Iron Mountain Trail is protected by a 200-foot corridor.

TRAILHEADS AND MAPS

Sandy Gap Trailhead
From Shady Valley, TN, and the US 421, TN 91, and TN 133 junction, drive southeast on US 421 4.2 miles to Sandy Gap. From Mountain City, TN, and the US 421, TN 67, and TN 91 junction, drive northwest on US 421 6.8 miles to Sandy Gap. The Iron Mountain Trailhead is on the north side of the road in the gap; stone steps lead up the side of the bank. A small parking area is on the south side of the road.

Camp AHISTADI and Corinth Church Trailheads
To reach Iron Mountain Primitive Area from Damascus, VA, take VA 91 south at the intersection of US 58, 1.0 mile outside of Damascus. It is 3.1 miles from the intersection to a Methodist church camp, Camp AHISTADI, and parking is available outside the metal gate. Go through the gate or fence, cross a bridge, and turn right to reach the Trailhead. It is 10.2 miles further to a sign for the Corinth Church (turn right), and then 1.7 miles to the church. From Mountain City, TN, at the junction of US 421 and TN 91, it is 9.4 miles north on TN 91 to a sign for the Corinth Church (turn left), and then 1.7 miles to the church. It is 19.6 miles north on TN 91 from the junction of US 421 and TN 91 to Camp AHISTADI. The parking and entrance to the camp are on the left.
Topographic Map: Laurel Bloomery, TN-VA.

TRAIL DESCRIPTION

Iron Mountain (Trail No. 54)
Length: 12.4 Miles
Elevation Change: Start 3,862 feet, end 2,220 feet (high point 4,200 feet)
Trailheads: Sandy Gap (start) and Camp AHISTADI (end)
Type: Hiking

Comments: Although public camping is not allowed at Camp AHISTADI, the land is part of the CNF and access is available through it. Part of the Iron Mountain Trail passes through the Area and provides an opportunity for a long backpack. This is a very little-used trail except during hunting season. Extreme caution should then be used, and wearing international orange is advised. A shorter loop trail of about 4.9 miles can be made through the Iron Mountain Primitive Area by hiking the Iron Mountain Trail from the Camp AHISTADI Trailhead to the Corinth Church Trailhead.

Details: For the first 0.4 mile, the trail climbs moderately through stands of rhododendron, laurel, and blueberries. At 0.4 mile, the trail levels off and provides views to the south and Doe Valley. Coreopsis and false foxglove bloom here in mid-summer. The trail skirts the south side of Grindstone Knob, which is the high point of the trail at approximately 4,200 feet.

At 0.5 mile, the trail turns right and descends, following the ridgetop. False Solomon's seal and teaberry grow here and bloom in the spring. The trail then levels where wild strawberries grow. At 0.7 mile, the forest opens some, and a field, which would make a good campsite, is on the left side. The trail climbs moderately, then levels off among black cohosh, which blooms in the summer. At 1.0 mile, the trail climbs moderately into a sugar maple forest and then begins a long descent through some tall oaks. The ridge narrows with views to the south as the trail descends moderately through hickory trees. At 1.4 miles, a huge oak log lies across the trail with steps cut in the sides to allow hikers to climb over it.

At 1.7 miles, there is a fork in the trail. Use caution here, and take the trail to the right. The trail to the left follows Grindstone Ridge to the north of Iron Mountain. Descend to the right, following the Iron Mountain Trail through mayapples. At 1.9 miles the trail passes through a small gap lined with ferns. About 250 feet further, the trail crosses a small drainage. At 2.0 miles the trail enters a second drainage and follows it for about 0.1 mile. The trail then levels off with a hollow on the right.

At 2.2 miles, a second fork in the trail is encountered. Use caution and take the trail to the left. The right fork goes downhill and south into Doe Valley. Follow the level trail through ground cedar, cross a small stream, and then enter a hollow with tall maples. Late in the evening barred owls hunt here, and their distinctive calls may be heard. At 2.4 miles a level saddle and potential campsite are reached. Two more saddles follow, the first having many Frasier magnolias. The trail then ascends gradually to the ridgetop among striped maples at 3.0 miles and skirts the rocky ridgetop, first to the left, then to the right.

At 3.2 miles the trail enters a large thicket of blackberries and blueberries and shortly thereafter crosses through rocks. At 3.5 miles there are some small chestnut trees trying to make a comeback from the blight that eliminated them sixty years earlier. Now pines and oaks have replaced them in the thin rocky soil along these dry ridgetops. The trail continues to ascend and descend as it follows the ridgetop, sometimes skirting to one side or the other. Bladderwort, oswego tea, and Carolina lilies, all summer-blooming flowers, are found on this section. Large rock outcrops are located to the right of the trail at 3.8 miles and 4.3 miles. At 5.7 miles the trail descends through large rocks. Alternately climb and descend gradually for the next 0.5 mile. At 6.2 miles, skirt the right side of the ridge where a steep drop-off is on the right.

The ridgetop and a small clearing and level area are reached at 6.3 miles, after which the trail descends sharply and then levels off. At 6.7 miles, skirt the left side

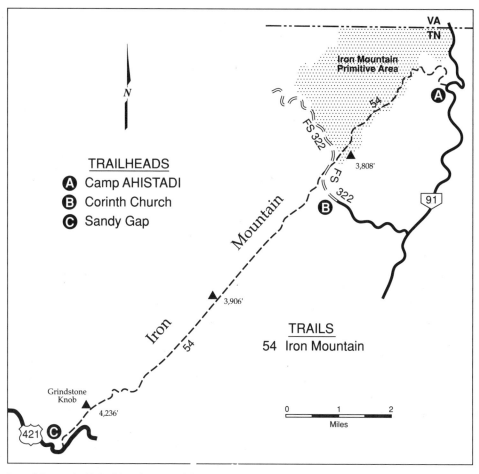

Iron Mountain Primitive Area and Trail.

of the ridge among rue anemone and continue straight where a faint trail comes in from the left. The trail returns to the ridgetop and skirts the right side of the ridge among large hemlock and oak trees. At 7.1 miles weave through some large rock outcrops, and then enter a small grove of pine trees. The trail begins a steep descent at 7.7 miles, and a faint trail comes in from the left. Continue straight, and after 0.3 mile the trail levels off among some cherry trees. At 7.9 miles the trail widens as it encounters heavier use, primarily from hunters in season. Deer tracks can often be seen here. At 8.0 miles the trail climbs, and several of the parasitic pine sap flowers can be seen.

At 8.1 miles a power line crosses Iron Mountain, and good views of Doe Valley and Doe Mountain can be seen to the south. Some small antennas are erected here. At 8.2 miles a jeep road crosses the trail from north to south. This is FS 322, and 0.7 mile to the right (south) on FS 322 is Corinth Church Trailhead at the intersection of Waters Road and Deer Run Road. To the left (north) the road goes approximately 3 miles to TN 133, near Backbone Rock Recreation Area. Careful planning with topographical maps should be done if traveling FS 322 to the north.

To continue on the Iron Mountain Trail, cross the jeep road and climb moderately past the rock outcrops and flame azaleas. At 8.4 miles the trail levels out and enters the Iron Mountain Primitive Area. At 8.7 miles the trail reaches the ridgetop, then descends steeply for 0.2 mile. Here the trail levels off and widens. There are springs on either side of the ridge, and a good campsite can be made.

At 9.1 miles the trail enters a large stand of tall pine trees. The trail follows the ridgecrest of Iron Mountain for approximately 0.5 mile, gently climbing and descending. The trail avoids some ups and downs throughout its length by skirting around the rocky peaks, making hiking easier and pleasant. At 9.6 miles, skirt the ridge to the right side; then at 9.7 miles the trail leaves the crest. At 10.0 miles, there is a large rock outcrop to the right, and good views of Mt. Rogers, White Top, and Doe Valley are available. For the next 0.9 mile the trail is fairly level with moderate rises and drops. Dwarf iris and wild lily of the valley bloom here in early spring.

At 10.9 miles the trail forks, with the trail to the left going to Damascus, VA. Careful planning with topographical maps should be done before taking the trail to the left, which is not maintained. Take the right fork and descend from the ridgetop. At 11.1 miles, there are rock outcroppings and rock slides to the east, opening up good views of the valley and mountains. Flame azaleas bloom here in late spring. At 11.3 miles the trail descends sharply for approximately 0.5 mile. Yellow star grass blooms here in late spring. At 11.8 miles the trail levels off among Fraser magnolias and striped maples and then turns east.

At 12.0 miles, the trail begins a very sharp descent of Butt Mountain as it leaves Iron Mountain; the first of several switchbacks is reached. Deer tracks may be seen, and an occasional grouse. At 12.1 miles the trail comes to a small stream and follows it down the valley. Crested dwarf iris and fire pinks grow here as the trail leaves the pine-oak forest and enters the cove hardwoods. At 12.3 miles, the trail levels out and abandons the small stream, which continues into Laurel Creek. At 12.4 miles a side road, used by the Methodist church's Camp AHISTADI, enters from the right. Continue straight for 200 feet and come to a gravel road and turn left. Cross the bridge and 100 yards ahead are the gate at Camp AHISTADI and the parking area by TN 91.

3. BEAVERDAM CREEK PRIMITIVE AREA

The Primitive Area consists of 710 acres, stretching from the Beaverdam Creek Scenic Road Corridor to the crest of Holston Mountain; the Area borders the TN-VA state line and is southwest of Damascus, VA. The Scenic Road Corridor stretches along Beaverdam Creek and TN 133 for approximately 6.0 miles, just before the creek flows northeasterly into VA. The Area is in Johnson County, TN, and the Watauga Ranger District.

Parking, camping, and picnic facilities are located along the Scenic Road Corridor and include Backbone Rock Campground. Two outstanding features make the corridor worth a visit. The "backbone" rock for which the campground is named consists of a natural wall of sandstone several hundred feet high and of similar length, and approximately 50 feet wide, which protrudes from a ridge off of Holston Mountain. Beaverdam Creek is forced to make a detour around the eastern end of the rock, adjacent to the foot of Iron Mountain. An old railroad tunnel has been blasted in the vertical-sided rock ridge through which TN 133 now passes. The tunnel was constructed by the logging company that cut the virgin forest of the Area. Evidence of an early steam engine is still visible in the form of soot on the roof of the tunnel. The other outstanding feature of this area is Beaverdam Creek itself, a beautiful whitewater trout stream bordered by lush forest and liberally decorated with rhododendron.

The Primitive Area consists of second-growth forest reaching up the side of Holston Mountain. The Area is used for deer hunting, trout fishing, and hiking. While not excessively steep, the trail up Holston Mountain climbs continuously to meet the AT and offers quiet solitude rather than scenic vistas.

In the bottomland along the stream, a variety of wildflowers abound. The rare Carolina saxifrage grows on the lower portions of the backbone rock. In August one may find the beautiful grass-of-parnassus in bloom on a low wet cliff just across Beaverdam Creek from the eastern end of the rock. The upper portion of the Primitive Area contains scattered specimens of Carolina hemlock—a fuller, richer tree than the more common eastern hemlock.

The major trail in the Area is the Backbone Rock Trail. Another very short trail, Backbone Falls Trail (No. 198) starts on the north side of the Tunnel and proceeds about 0.1 mile to the small Backbone Falls on Backbone Branch; a spur Trail goes up and over the top of Backbone Rock, using stairs, railings, and boardwalks, and intersects the Backbone Rock Trail.

HISTORY

The entire area has been logged, and some sections have been planted in white pine. Much of the second-growth oak-hickory forest is approximately 70 to 100 years old. Traces of old roads are present, but the Area does not appear to have been used for residences. There are extensive ruins of recreational facilities along the creek near Backbone Rock, attesting to early tourist fascination with the rock and the area.

The Area was designated as a Primitive Area (Managed) in the CNF's Management Plan in 1988. Unlike most primitive areas, limited timber harvesting may be allowed in this Area (see Section A).

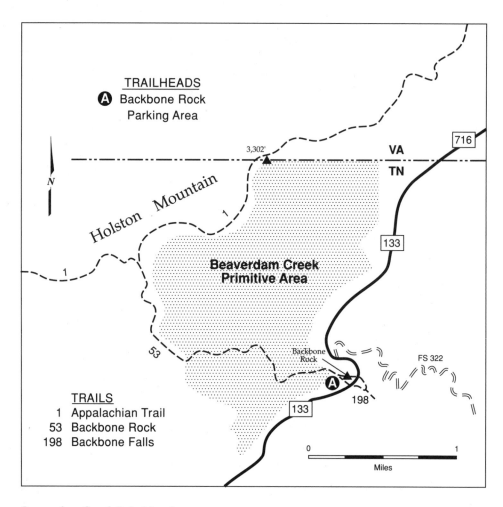

TRAILHEADS
A Backbone Rock
Parking Area

3,302'

VA
TN
716

N

Holston Mountain

1

133

**Beaverdam Creek
Primitive Area**

1

53

Backbone
Rock

FS 322

TRAILS
 1 Appalachian Trail
53 Backbone Rock
198 Backbone Falls

A

198

133

0   1
Miles

Beaverdam Creek Primitive Area.

TRAILHEADS AND MAPS

Backbone Rock Recreation Area Trailhead

The approach is via either US 421 or VA 716. From the US 421-TN 133 intersection in Shady Valley, TN, go north on TN 133, 9.5 miles to the Backbone Rock parking area (on the left before going through the Tunnel). Alternatively, proceed south 3.7 miles from the intersection with US 58 in downtown Damascus, VA, on VA 716, which becomes TN 133, to the Backbone Rock parking lot (on the right after going through the tunnel).

Topographic Map: Laurel Bloomery, TN-VA.

TRAIL DESCRIPTIONS

Backbone Rock (Trail No. 53)

Length: 2.1 miles
Elevation Change: Start 2,200 feet, end 3,480 feet (high point 3,480 feet)
Trailheads: Backbone Rock (start) and AT (end)
Type: Hiking

Comments: The trail goes from Backbone Rock to the AT on the crest of Holston Mountain, following a ridge between Stillhouse Branch and Backbone Branch. Find the trail on the south side of the paved parking lot at Backbone Rock. Ascend the stone stairs at the west end of the rock and keep left at the top of the stairs up a 10-foot rocky scramble to a well-defined blue-blazed trail; the trail over Backbone Rock joins from the right near the top.

Details: The trail climbs steadily. At 0.8 mile it levels off, and again at 1.1 miles and at 1.3 miles. At 1.7 miles and at 2.0 miles, you will think you have reached the top of the ridge, but not yet. Go down, then up some more. The crest of the mountain is reached at 2.1 miles, where the trail intersects the AT. Just 250 feet before the junction with the AT is a colony of shinleaf, a rare plant, beautiful in bloom in June. The AT at the intersection proceeds 4.2 miles north to Damascus, VA, and 10.4 miles south to US 421 in TN.4. Flint Mill Scenic Area and Primitive Area

4. FLINT MILL SCENIC AREA AND PRIMITIVE AREA

The Flint Mill Primitive and Flint Mill Scenic Areas are comprised of 6,540 acres of protected land straddling the middle of Holston Mountain. This 30-mile-long ridge stretching from the town of Damascus, VA, to Elizabethton, TN, forms the southeastern backdrop to upper east TN's pastoral Holston Valley. Elevations in the Flint Mill Areas range from 2,600 feet at the base of the mountain to over 4,200 feet at Rich Knob. The northwest slopes of the mountain are very steep and dominated by short spur ridges clothed in table mountain pine and other fire-dependent pine species. There are numerous rock outcroppings on these ridges that offer outstanding views of the Holston Valley, the best-known being Flint Rock. The main ridge and southeastern slopes of the mountain are more gradual and covered with cove and upland hardwoods. The Areas are located in Carter and Sullivan counties, TN, and the Watauga Ranger District.

Many small streams drain the Areas, creating scenic waterfalls and providing

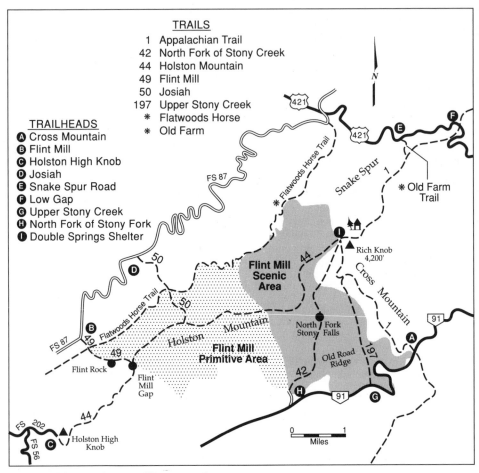

Flint Mill Scenic Area and Primitive Area.

habitat for brook trout and many species of wildflowers. The two most scenic of these are Fishdam Creek and North Fork Stony Creek. Large mammals inhabiting the area include deer, bear, and bobcat. Turkeys are common, as are many other woodland bird species. Four rare plants are found in the Areas: round-leaved orchis, kidney-leaved twayblade, large purple-fringed orchis, and Frazier's sedge.

A hiker following the trails gets a good taste of the Area, but many outstanding scenic features—including waterfalls, overlooks, rare plants, and old-growth timber—reveal themselves only to those willing to hike off-trail.

HISTORY

The Flint Mill Areas are presently protected in two land-use categories. 3,920 acres on the northeast end form the Flint Mill Scenic Area, while 2,620 acres on the southwest end are presently protected as the Flint Mill Primitive Area. A portion of such Areas was included in the CNF's RARE II process in the late 1970s (see Section A) as the Flint Mill Area, which portion protected only the southeast slopes of the mountain. The Areas currently protected have given up land from both ends of the previous RARE II tract but have added the northwest slopes of the mountain. Most important is the protection given to the scenic Fishdam Creek Gorge.

The Scenic Area was designated in 1988 in the CNF's Management Plan. The Primitive Area was designated in the same plan, with no timber harvesting to be allowed. Most of the Areas were destructively logged after the turn of the century, and old logging grades are abundant. The top of Rich Knob was a bald used for pasture and still shows signs of old field conditions, with blackberries and locusts. There are also prehistoric sites in the Areas.

TRAILHEADS AND MAPS

Josiah and Flint Mill Trailheads

Start at the US 421 bridge over South Holston Lake east of Bristol. Note the mileage at the far (southeast) end of the bridge; continue southeast to mile 3.9 and turn right onto Camp Tom Howard Road at a USFS sign to Little Oak Campground. Camp Tom Howard Road begins as a paved road but becomes the gravel Flatwoods Road (FS 87). It is usually in good shape for passenger cars from June to December but deteriorates through the winter and by spring is heavily rutted and best left to four-wheel-drive vehicles. At mile 4.9 there is a gated road to the left (it is the second gated road on the left), which connects to a horse trail. At mile 5.8 stay left at the fork. Sulphur Spring Branch is crossed at mile 7.8 and Fishdam Creek at mile 8.8. At mile 10.6 the road to Little Oak Campground turns right. Stay left and continue to the Josiah Trailhead on the left along an unusually straight stretch of road at mile 12.0. There may be a small sign back from the road, but it is difficult to see unless you are looking for it. Park along the roadside. To reach the Flint Mill Trailhead continue up the road;

at mile 14.0 cross the old Flatwoods Road and at mile 14.2 reach the Flint Mill Trailhead. The trail begins as an old road on the left. Park along the roadside.

Snake Spur Road and Low Gap Trailheads

These trailheads are reached from the southeast end of the bridge over South Holston Lake (as above). At mile 6.4, Snake Spur Road, a gated, gravel USFS road, is on your right. The Old Farm Trail begins on the uphill side of Snake Spur Road. Park without blocking the gate. For the Low Gap Trailhead proceed on up US 421 to mile 7.8, where the trailhead and parking are on the right just before you reach Low Gap at the top of the mountain. These trailheads can also be reached by driving 2.8 miles west of Shady Valley, TN, to Low Gap and 1.4 miles further to Snake Spur Road.

Holston High Knob Trailhead

The Holston Mountain Trail begins at the fire tower on Holston High Knob. To reach the trailhead begin from the intersection of the new US 19E and TN 91 (this is 0.4 miles north of the US 321, US 19E, and TN 91 intersection) in Elizabethton. Follow TN 91 north and turn left onto Panhandle Road (FS 56) at mile 10.2. At mile 11.0 the road becomes gravel (the road stays in good shape year round, although snow and ice can be a problem in winter). At the ridgetop take the right fork (FS 202 turns left) at mile 14.5 and continue on to the gate at mile 14.9. Park without blocking the gate. Continue on foot up the road for 0.4 mile. The trailhead is on the right at the last switchback before the fire tower. There is no sign.

Double Springs Shelter Trailhead

Double Springs is an AT shelter located just to the northwest of Rich Knob, the high point of the Area at 4,247 feet and just outside the Scenic Area. It accommodates six and is built of concrete blocks. The shelter is on the AT 3.4 miles from TN 91 and 3.4 miles from US 321. The Rich Knob Area is a converging point for several trails in the Areas; AT, North Fork of Stony Creek Trail, and Holston Mountain Trail. See descriptions of those trails for access to Double Springs Shelter.

North Fork of Stony Creek, Upper Stony Creek, and Cross Mountain Trailheads

Beginning at the new intersection US 19E, TN 37, and TN 91 (this is 0.4 miles north of the US 321, US 19E, and TN 91 intersection) in Elizabethton, TN, go north on paved TN 91. At 14.6 miles from the intersection a dirt road turns left (west); there is a "keep out" sign on a tree on the left as you turn onto this road. Drive 0.2 mile to a fork, take the right fork, and go 0.1 mile to where it dead-ends at the unmarked trailhead for the North Fork of Stony Creek Trail. This is private property; permission must be secured from an adjacent landowner to park at the trailhead. If you continue on TN 91 to 16.2 miles from the TN 19E and TN 91 junction in Elizabethton, you will reach a small unmarked parking area on the right (east) side of the road. The Upper Stony Creek Trailhead is on the opposite (west) side of the road. If you continue further on TN 91 from the TN 19E and TN 91 junction in Elizabethton, at 18.7 miles the AT crosses the road just below the top of Cross Mountain. However, continue on to the gap at mile 18.8 and a gravel parking lot for the AT on the right. These trails can also be approached from the north and the US 421, TN 91, and TN 133 junction in Shady Valley. Follow TN 91 3.6 miles south to the gap just above where the AT crosses TN 91; the Upper Stony Creek Trailhead is 2.5 miles from the gap, and the North Fork of Stony Creek Trailhead is 4.1 miles from the gap.

Topographic Maps: Doe, TN; Carter, TN; Holston Valley, TN-VA; Shady Valley, TN-VA.

TRAIL DESCRIPTIONS

AT (US 421 to Holston Mountain Trail Section) (Trail No. 1)
Length: 3.4 miles
Elevation Change: Start 3,384 feet, end 4,080 feet (high point 4,080 feet)
Trailheads: Low Gap (start) and Double Springs Shelter (end)
Trail Connections: Holston Mountain Trail, North Fork of Stony Creek Trail, and Old Farm Trail
Type: Hiking

Comments: This section of the AT is not in the Flint Mill Area but provides access to the northeast end of Holston Mountain Trail. The parking lot on US 421 is a gathering spot for local teenagers and motorcycle groups in the warm months. An alternate trailhead is the Snake Spur Road Trailhead, also on US 421. The trail has vertical white blazes.

Details: From the parking area on US 421 below Low Gap, head southwest on the AT, which follows the crest of Holston Mountain, beginning at an elevation of 3,380 feet. At 1.3 miles the trail comes to the edge of an old farm and at 1.4 miles is joined by an old road, known as the Old Farm Trail, which comes up from Snake Spur Road Trailhead and US 421. At 1.9 miles the trail turns left out into an old field. There are excellent views of Shady Valley and Iron Mountain, with Whitetop and Rogers Ridge in the background. The trail reenters the woods at 2.0 miles and goes over a knoll. After descending the trail climbs and passes over Locust Knob (4,200 feet) at 3.0 miles. It then curves to the right around Rich Knob and at 3.4 miles, in a small opening, the AT turns left with Holston Mountain Trail going straight ahead near a half-completed, roofless, log shelter. On the AT just past Holston Mountain Trail on the right is the Double Springs AT Shelter, with a spring several hundred feet behind it. The shelter is constructed of concrete blocks and accommodates six. See description below of the AT from TN 91 for the trail details on the rest of the AT within the Areas.

AT (TN 91 to Holston Mountain Trail Section) (Trail No. 1)
Length: 3.4 miles
Elevation Change: Start 3,450 feet, end 4,080 feet (high point 4,080 feet)
Trailheads: Cross Mountain (start) and Double Springs Shelter (end)
Trail Connections: Upper Stony Creek Trail, North Fork of Stony Creek Trail, and Holston Mountain Trail
Type: Hiking

Comments: This section of the AT follows the northeast boundary of the Flint Mill Area and provides access to the northeast end of Holston Mountain Trail. It generally follows the crest of Cross Mountain, constantly gaining in elevation up to Rich Knob and the junction with Holston Mountain Trail. The trail has vertical white blazes.

Details: The trail is entirely within deciduous forest and begins 0.1 mile to the west of the crest of Cross Mountain on TN 91. After dipping down to a small creek the trail ascends. At 2.0 miles the trail turns left onto a dirt road and at 2.4 miles passes several small springs and campsites. These springs are the headwaters of Stony Creek. At 2.6 miles the trail turns sharply right (to the left is Old Road Ridge). At 3.4 miles are the Double Springs Shelter and spring on the left. The junction with the Holston Mountain Trail, also on the left, is several hundred feet beyond the shelter near a half-completed, roofless, log shelter.

Old Farm Trail (No USFS Number)
Length: 0.7 mile
Elevation Change: Start 3,000 feet, end 3,440 feet (high point 3,440 feet)
Trailheads: Snake Spur Road (start) and AT (end)
Trail Connections: AT
Type: Hiking

Comments: This short trail provides access to the AT from US 421.

Details: The trail is an old road and is not maintained as a trail but is available for hiking. The route begins at the junction of US 421 and the USFS Snake Spur logging road. The trail begins at the top of the bank on the uphill side of the road junction. It is difficult to see once parked, but easy to see from US 421. For the first 0.2 mile the trail parallels US 421 heading east; then it curves around to the south and continues up the mountain. At 0.7 mile the trail joins the AT (at mile 1.4 from US 421).

Holston Mountain (Holston) (Trail No. 44)

Length: 7.7 miles
Elevation Change: Start 4,150 feet, end 4,080 feet (high point 4,200 feet)
Trailheads: Holston High Knob (start) and Double Springs Shelter (end)
Trail Connections: Josiah Trail, AT, North Fork of Stony Creek Trail, and Flint Mill Trail
Type: Hiking

Comments: Holston Mountain Trail begins outside the Flint Mill Areas at Holston High Knob fire tower and follows the main ridgeline northeast into the Areas to its junction with the AT on Rich Knob. The trail is in hardwood forest for its entire length, with occasional views through the trees of Iron Mountain to the southeast and the Holston Valley to the northwest. The view from the fire tower is excellent. Holston Mountain Trail connects several other trails in the Areas and provides a jumping-off point for off-trail exploration. The trail has yellow blazes and some old blue blazes. This is also known as Holston Trail.

Details: The trail begins in the last switchback of the road to the fire tower. The trail descends through hardwoods to a messy junction with Flint Mill Trail at 2.1 miles (3,380 feet). First you will encounter a dirt road on the right, blocked with an earth mound (this is an unmaintained extension of the Flint Mill Trail). Go left on the dirt road and you will immediately come into a small opening. To the left is a USFS dirt logging road. Flint Mill Trail is straight ahead (blue blazes). Go right on a dirt road that immediately forks. Take the left fork and continue on your way (the right fork is an unused logging road that parallels the trail for several miles). At this point you enter the protected Primitive Area. At 2.5 miles there is a view of South Holston Lake to the left through a blow-down. This section of trail occasionally follows the logging road for short distances. The Josiah Trail enters on the left at 3.4 miles. The trail then intersects and crosses the logging road at 3.5 miles. There is a spring in the cove to the left. From here the trail climbs steeply to the top of a small knob at 3.7 miles. From this point Red Eye Ridge extends off-trail to the southeast (right); 0.25 mile off-trail to the north (left) is a grove of large old-growth poplars and oaks that apparently escaped the loggers' axes. In a dip at 4.4 miles are a campsite and spring to the left of the trail in a small cove. This area is at times used as a hunter's camp. At 4.8 miles Fishdam Creek Gorge can be seen off to the left. The trail begins a large curve to the left at 6.0 miles and descends to a saddle at 6.3 miles. This is a good jumping-off point for off-trail hiking to Fishdam Creek on the left and North Fork Stony Creek on the right. The trail begins to climb at this point and reaches the ridgetop again at 6.6 miles. You are now on Rich Knob, and the trail gradually ascends to the top of the knob (4,200 feet) at 7.6 miles. A short descent brings you to the junction with the AT and Double Springs Shelter at 7.7 miles.

Flint Mill (Trail No. 49)
Length: 1.4 miles
Elevation Change: Start 2,120 feet, end 3,380 feet (high point 3,380)
Trailheads: Flint Mill (start) and Holston Mountain Trail (end)
Trail Connections: Holston Mountain Trail
Type: Hiking

Comments: Flint Mill Trail is a short, very steep trail beginning on Flatwoods Road (2,120 feet), climbing the northwest slope of the mountain and ending at Holston Mountain Trail (3,380 feet) on the main ridge. It begins outside of the protected areas but forms the southwestern boundary of the Primitive Area for most of its length. Flint Rock provides outstanding views of the Holston Valley, and a small bog near the top of the mountain offers some unusual vegetation. The trail has blue blazes.

Details: The trail begins as an old logging road. At 0.1 mile a horse trail goes to the left in a wildlife food plot. The horse trail goes to the right at 0.15 mile. The trail turns steeply upwards, enters the protected Areas, and leaves logging scars behind at 0.5 mile. For the next half mile the trail is very steep and eroded. At 0.6 mile the trail passes out of the upland hardwood forest and into dry ridge vegetation dominated by table mountain and other pines, with an understory of laurel. This section of the trail is beautiful when the laurel are in bloom in June. At 1.0 mile the trail climbs up and around Flint Rock. In clear weather the rock provides an exceptional view of South Holston Lake and the Holston Valley, with VA's Clinch Mountain as a backdrop. At this point the trail levels out through pine woods until it crosses a small stream and bog at 1.3 miles. A little exploration will turn up quite a list of orchids blooming at various times during the spring and summer. The bog and surrounding area provide habitat for pink and yellow lady slippers, whorled pogonia, Adder's mouth, yellow fringed orchis, pale green orchis, dwarf rattlesnake plantain, and the rare kidneyleaf twayblade. The bog is also a good place to catch a glimpse of a hooded warbler. There is a littered campsite beside the stream. The trail continues on through hardwoods to its junction with the Holston Mountain Trail at 1.4 miles. The topographic map shows the trail continuing down the other side of the mountain, which it does as an overgrown logging road. It disappears into a maze of old roads from a long-abandoned mine on the edge of USFS property.

Josiah (Trail No. 50)
Length: 2.2 miles
Elevation Change: Start 1,800 feet, end 3,520 feet (high point 3,520 feet)
Trailheads: Josiah (start) and Holston Mountain Trail (end)
Trail Connections: Holston Mountain Trail
Type: Hiking

Comments: Josiah Trail provides a moderate climb from Flatwoods Road up the
northwest slopes of the mountain to the ridgetop and Holston Mountain Trail. It
begins outside the protected Area and can be used to make a loop via Holston
Mountain Trail, Flint Mill Trail, and the Flatwoods Horse Trail (see Additional
Trails, below). The trail has blue blazes.

Details: The trail begins on Flatwoods Road and climbs gradually to the Flatwood
Horse Trail (a gravel logging road) at 0.6 mile. Turn left onto the gravel road, go 50
feet, and turn right back onto Josiah Trail. At 0.7 mile go left at the fork. The trail
becomes steeper at 1.2 miles and soon passes into the protected Areas. At 1.4 miles
a short, steep section is encountered that formerly had steps. After this point the
trail begins a series of switchbacks between oak, pine, and laurel dry ridge vegetation and cove hardwoods. At 2.0 miles the switchbacks end as the top of the mountain
is approached. At 2.2 miles the trail dead-ends into Holston Mountain Trail. There is a
small spring 0.1 mile to the left down Holston Mountain Trail. The spring is in the
cove to the left of the trail. At the end of May the vicinity of the trail junction has
quite a variety of azaleas.

North Fork of Stony Creek (Trail No. 42)
Length: 3.2 miles
Elevation Change: Start 4,080 feet, end 2,420 feet (high point 4,080 feet)
Trailheads: Double Springs Shelter (start) and North Fork of Stony
Creek (end)
Trail Connections: AT and Holston Mountain Trail
Type: Hiking

Comments: This trail is not well maintained and, except for the lower portion from
the private property trailhead to the waterfall, should be considered off-trail hiking.
The North Fork of Stony Creek Trailhead, off TN 91, is on private property; parking
and crossing permission must be secured. The trail generally follows old logging
grades.

Details: North Fork of Stony Creek has its beginnings in the springs next to the Double Creek AT Shelter. If you are very fond of rhododendron thickets, start here and head downstream about 1.6 miles to the falls. An easier way to reach the most scenic part of the watershed is to begin at the junction of the AT and Holston Mountain Trail and head southwest on Holston Mountain Trail. 1.4 miles out you will be at the low point in the saddle between North Fork Stony and Fishdam Creeks (this is the same place used as a jump off for Fishdam Creek and is described coming from the other direction in the Fishdam Creek Gorge section below). Turn left (east) off the trail and follow the drainage 0.4 mile down to the creek. Head downstream and in another 0.4 mile you will come to the falls of North Fork Stony, the premier falls in the Areas. The stream drops 30 feet over a semicircular cliff into a beautiful rock amphitheater. Scramble down on the right side. If you continue down the stream there are nice wildflowers in the spring, but you will eventually come out, after about 1.6 miles from the falls, on private property that you need permission to cross.

Upper Stony Creek (Trail No. 197)
Length: 2.2 miles
Elevation Change: Start 2,759 feet, end 3,880 feet (high point 3,880 feet)
Trailheads: Upper Stony Creek (start) and Double Springs Shelter (end)
Trail Connections: AT
Type: Hiking

Comments: This trail is not maintained and should be considered an off-trail hike. The lower portion from the TN 91 trailhead off TN 91 is used by fishermen and can easily be followed. However, after a mile the trail disappears. Essentially the route is directly up Stony Creek. Take the left fork at 0.7 mile when Water Hollow comes in from the right. Otherwise, follow the creek to a junction with the AT at about 2.2 miles. The trail generally follows old logging grades.

Additional Trails and Off-Trail Hiking
In addition to the trails described above, there is a horse trail created by joining several logging roads with short sections of trail. Called the Flatwoods Horse Trail, it is outside of the Flint Mill Areas but parallels the entire northwest boundary. It generally follows the old Flatwoods Trail, marked on USGS topographical maps. The horse trail is not great hiking, as it is mainly gravel road with lots of views of timber cuts, but it provides connections at the base of the mountain between Flint Mill Trail, Josiah Trail, Fishdam Creek, and Sulphur Spring Branch.

Of the top scenic attractions in the Flint Mill Areas only two are directly accessible by the trail system: Flint Mill Trail with its overlook and bog and the North

Fork Stony Creek drainage with its wildflowers and outstanding waterfall. The others all require off-trail exploration and are: Fishdam Creek Gorge with its many small waterfalls and view providing rock outcroppings; the north fork of Sulphur Spring Branch with its waterfall and outstanding view; and the grove of old-growth poplars and oaks on the main ridge of the mountain opposite Red Eye Ridge.

Direction finding is generally not too difficult in the Areas as there is only one main ridge with small drainages dropping off to either side. If you get oriented to the proper drainage with a topographical map, you can experience these other areas. The terrain, however, can be challenging. Slopes are often steep and there are plenty of rhododendron thickets. Patience and a pace suited to the terrain are the key; the rewards in wildlife, solitude, and scenery are well worth the effort. Brief descriptions of the off-trail routes are provided below.

Fishdam Creek Gorge is accessed via Holston Mountain Trail or Flatwoods Road (FS 87). Traveling northeast on the Holston Mountain Trail from Holston High Knob Trailhead, look for the saddle at 6.3 miles where the main ridge is offset and, at the low point of the saddle, turn left (west) and follow the drainage down the mountain. It is approximately 2.0 miles to the horse trail at the base of the mountain. As you descend, gradually at first, keep alert for three rare plants: Frazier's sedge, round leaf orchid, and large purple fringed orchid. At the point where the gorge begins to drop steeply, Vulture Rock rises above the creek on the left. It is a bit of a scramble, but the view is excellent. The purple rhododendron, mountain laurel, and white rhododendron are beautiful from the end of May to the beginning of July. Also at this point there is an old logging grade to the right (described below) which offers a short hike out to another overlook and an alternative exit from the gorge. Below this point the stream is very steep and rocky with many small waterfalls and pools.

To approach the gorge from Flatwoods Road, park at Fishdam Creek (see Josiah Trail Trailhead) and head up the creek. It is approximately 1.0 mile to the horse trail and the mouth of the gorge. A longer but easier entrance to the gorge from Flatwoods Road involves parking your car at Sulphur Spring Branch (see trailhead for Josiah Trail). Follow the modern logging roads up the mountain for 1.25 miles until you cross the horse trail. At this point continue up the mountain into the woods. After several hundred yards you will hit an old logging grade. Turn right and follow it southwest up and across the face of the mountain. It is about 1.0 mile to the gorge. There are several places where the grade has been washed out, and one where it makes a double switchback. As the grade wraps around into the gorge it passes a large rock offering an outstanding view of the mountain, the gorge, and the Holston Valley. Another 0.25 mile and the grade reaches the creek just above the steepest part of the gorge.

Sulphur Spring Branch (North Fork). To reach the falls and overlook on Sulphur

Spring Branch, begin where the Sulphur Spring Branch crosses Flatwoods Road (FS 87) (see Josiah Trail Trailhead, above). Head southeast toward Holston Mountain on the logging road to the right of the creek. The upper part of this area has been recently logged, and there are several road choices, but keep heading at the mountain and remember that all logging roads lead to bigger roads. You will soon arrive on the Flatwoods Horse Trail. It is approximately 1.25 miles from Flatwoods Road to the horse trail, and you should emerge on it between the two forks of Sulphur Spring Branch. Turn left (northeast), and the first stream you cross will be the north fork. The best tactic here is to head right up the streambed. In several hundred yards you will enter the Scenic Area, and in 0.25 mile you will reach the falls. Follow the cliff line that creates the falls up through the woods to the left (north). Climb up to the ridgeline through one of the breaks in the cliff and come down the nose of the ridge to the best vantage point on Holston Mountain. The view down the mountain over the Flatwoods is great; you can also see back up the watershed and out over the Holston Valley. Unfortunately this is also rattlesnake heaven, and the best ledge to sit on is one of their favorite sunning spots. Remember this if you visit the area in the warm months.

Grove of Old Growth. There are several coves near the main ridgeline on the northwest slope of the Holston Mountain that contain some very large trees. The largest are poplars, but there are also oak and ash. Many have fallen in recent years, but some are still standing. The trees are along a shoulder of the mountain below the main ridgeline but before the steep drop-off. On the USGS topographical map this area is across the main ridgeline from Red Eye Ridge. To reach the area, hike northeast on Holston Mountain Trail from the Holston High Knob Trailhead. At 3.5 miles the trail crosses a logging road. Leave the trail and follow the logging road several hundred yards till it dead-ends. At this point continue out onto the shoulder of the mountain, and within 0.5 mile you should find the trees. Backtrack or head up the slope to the trail.

5. BIG LAUREL BRANCH WILDERNESS

This 6,251-acre Wilderness is approximately 10 miles east of Elizabethton, TN, at the southern end of Iron Mountain between TN 91 and Watauga Lake. The Area is in Carter and Johnson counties, TN, and the Watauga Ranger District.

The Wilderness includes the completely forested southern end of Iron Mountain, where Iron Mountain consists of double parallel crests that enclose the secluded Big Laurel Branch and Little Laurel Branch valleys. A unique sense of isolation and solitude is thus provided to those willing to travel cross-country (no maintained trails lead into the Big Laurel Valley). The southeast side of the Area rises steeply 1,100 to 1,400 feet from Watauga Lake to the crest of the mountain. The AT follows the crest, sometimes at the base of high and lengthy outcroppings of rock, with several spectacular views from the tops of cliffs up to 40 feet high. Numerous creeks cut deep, steep-sided ravines in the beautiful northwest side of the mountain, including Big Laurel Branch itself. Wilbur Lake resembles a fjord because of the mountain wall, which rises precipitously over 600 feet from the water's edge at the southwest end of the Wilderness; a graceful 50-foot waterfall tumbles over the cliffs. The Area includes thriving stands of the Carolina hemlock and specimens of the rare Fraser's sedge.

HISTORY

In 1963 the Area was the site of the severe and extensive Blue Springs Fire, which burned approximately 2,800 acres along the mountain crest. Both the north and south slopes were burned in places, and bulldozers were used to create fire breaks. The forest has regenerated itself very well. Old logging and wagon roads penetrated the Area but have generally become overgrown, with the exception of the Bowers Branch and Vandeventer Branch jeep roads which, now being closed, will revert to trails. The AT through the Area was preceded by a hunter's trail; a section of it was known as the Iron Mountain Trail. The Laurel Branch Wilderness was designated by the US Congress in 1986.

TRAILHEADS AND MAPS

Watauga Dam Road Trailhead

The principal trail in the Area is the AT, and the principal access to its trailhead is near Watauga Dam. From Elizabethton, TN, and the east end of Broad Street (junction of TN 91, US 19E, US 321, and TN 67) go south on US 321 for 0.5 mile. Turn left (east) on Siam Road and follow it to the Watauga River. At the river turn right (no signs) on Watauga Dam Road without crossing the river, and follow the Watauga Dam signs up the river and past Wilbur Dam and Wilbur Lake (the Wilderness is on the other side of the lake) and across Wilbur Lake. After crossing the lake, Watauga Dam Road goes up to the crest of the ridge where the AT crosses. From the Elizabethton junction, it is 8.6 miles to this crossing. AT signs are clearly visible, and parking areas are provided nearby, with the largest parking area being 0.7 mile down the road on Watauga Lake.

Cross Mountain Trailhead

The Area can also be reached by hiking 9.8 miles down the AT from the north, starting at TN 91 on Cross Mountain. From the east end of Broad Street (junction of TN

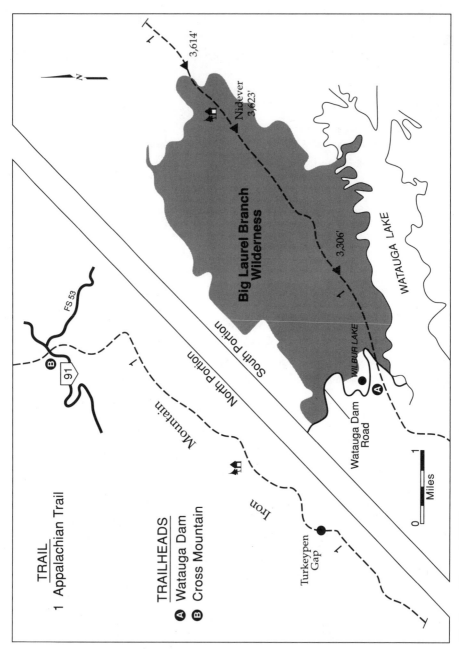

TRAIL
1 Appalachian Trail

TRAILHEADS
Ⓐ Watauga Dam
Ⓑ Cross Mountain

N

FS 53

91

Iron Mountain

Turkeypen Gap

North Portion

South Portion

Big Laurel Branch
Wilderness

3,614'

Nidever
3,623'

3,306'

WATAUGA LAKE

WILBUR LAKE

Watauga Dam
Road

Ⓐ

Ⓑ

0   1
Miles

Big Laurel Branch Wilderness.

91 with US 19E, US 321, and TN 67) in Elizabethton, TN, follow TN 91 north 18.7 miles. The AT crosses TN 91 about 100 feet south of the Carter County-Johnson County line. A parking area is 0.1 mile farther on the right. From the AT crossing it is 6.8 miles north on TN 91 to the junction with US 421 in Shady Valley, TN. The AT crossing of the road is well signed. Proceed south on the AT.

Most of the northwest side of the Wilderness can be reached from farther south on TN 91, particularly along the former jeep roads that proceed up Bowers Branch, Vandeventer Branch, and Lower Nidifer Branch, from the Blue Spring Community. To reach the Blue Spring Community take the Blue Spring Road south from mile post 9 on TN 91. However, topographical maps are necessary to locate these old roads.

Topographic Maps: Watauga Dam, TN; Carter, TN; Doe, TN.

TRAIL DESCRIPTION

AT (Watauga Dam Road to TN 91 Section) (Trail No. 1)
Length: 15.6 miles
Elevation Change: Start 2,240 feet, end 3,450 feet (high point within Wilderness 3,560 feet)
Trailheads: Watauga Dam Road (start) and Cross Mountain (end)
Type: Hiking

Comments: The principal trail in the Wilderness is the AT, with the trailhead beginning at the Watauga Dam access road and continuing northward through the Area for about 5.8 miles.

Details: The trail initially climbs very steeply to the Iron Mountain ridgetop, then follows the crest northeast. From mile 1.0 to 4.4 the trail passes through an area partially burned by a 1963 fire, with mile 1.0 to mile 2.8 being completely burned. This area is amazingly revived now, although there is some evidence of bulldozer firefighting and the AT sometimes follows the old bulldozer road. At the 2.8 mile point, an old grown-over jeep road (formerly a spur of the Iron Mountain Trail) leads left (west) down the mountain about 3.5 miles to the Blue Spring Community, accessible from TN 91 via Blue Spring Road. Along this road about 0.25 mile from the AT, an unmaintained and grown-over side trail to the right (north) leads down into the headwaters of Face Camp Branch and continues northwest along Bowers Branch on an old jeep road that continues into the Blue Spring Community.

At 3.6 miles is one of the most outstanding rock formations along the crest, pro-

Blooming rhododendrons in Big Laurel Branch Wilderness.
Photo by Suzanne McDonald.

viding great views; another is at 4.0 miles. At 4.4 miles the old unmaintained and overgrown Vandeventer Trail leads left off the mountain and along Vandeventer Branch to the Blue Spring Community. The Bowers Branch and Vandeventer Branch trails are connected by an old unmaintained and overgrown jeep road in the valleys between the north and south parallel crests of Iron Mountain. The Vandeventer Appalachian Trail Shelter, a concrete block shelter, which accommodates six, is at 4.4 miles. Cliffs behind the shelter provide splendid views of the mountains to the east and south, and of Watauga Lake below. At 5.8 miles, where the AT skirts to the right of a round knoll, at the division between Lower Nidifer Branch and Peters Branch, a USFS sign marks the boundary of the Wilderness. The AT continues 9.8 miles, northeast, along the crest of Iron Mountain to TN 91 on Cross Mountain.

The trail is relatively easy, except for very short sections, as it continues to follow the ridge. At 8.1 miles an unmaintained trail to the left leads to TN 91 by way of a ridge between Stover Branch and Grindstaff Branch. At around 8.6 miles the trail begins following an old jeep road that is reverting to a trail. At 9.0 miles and later at 9.6 miles trails lead off to the left, also unmaintained, and proceed to TN 91 via Hurley Hollow. At 10.3 miles a clearing under a TVA power line provides clear views to the large valleys on both sides of the mountain. Otherwise, the views on the trail outside the Wilderness are mainly limited to clifftops, all facing southeast.

At 10.9 miles water is available in a small hollow on the left or 100 yards to the right on a blue-blazed trail. This is the water supply for the Iron Mountain AT Shelter just up the trail at 11.1 miles. The shelter is constructed of concrete blocks and accommodates six. The old road ends beyond the shelter at 11.2 miles.

At 12.4 miles a monument to, and grave of, Uncle Nick Grindstaff are located to the left of the trail. The monument states: "Uncle Nick Grindstaff—born Dec. 26, 1851—died July 22, 1923—lived alone, suffered alone, and died alone." He was an orphan who returned from a trip out west at age 26, became a hermit, and lived for 46 years on Iron Mountain. The 4,135-foot-high point of the trail outside the Wilderness is reached on a knoll at 12.7 miles. At 14.4 miles the trail begins to descend from the crest of Iron Mountain and leads down to TN 91 at 15.6 miles. The parking area is just north of the point where the AT crosses the road.

Off-Trail Hiking

The Big Laurel Branch and Little Laurel Branch watersheds provide an outstanding and remote off-trail hiking area. No trails lead into the watersheds, which are completely enclosed and protected by the Wilderness. High ridges also enclose and protect the watersheds on three sides, with Wilbur Lake forming the other boundary. A USGS topographical map will provide the experienced off-trail hiker with access to this secluded and beautiful portion of the Area.

6. POND MOUNTAIN WILDERNESS

The 6,195-acre Pond Mountain Wilderness is in Carter County, TN, and lies within both the Unaka and Watauga ranger districts. The Area is characterized by rugged terrain with elevations ranging from about 1,900 feet along Laurel Fork Creek to 4,329 feet at the summit of Pond Mountain. The majority of Pond Mountain is in stands of upland hardwoods, with some small stands of cove hardwoods. The Area also contains some stands of virgin timber that were inaccessible to loggers. Perhaps the major attraction of the wilderness is the spectacular Laurel Fork Gorge. Sheer rock cliffs rise 100 to 200 feet from the banks of the stream, and wooded slopes rise over 1,000 feet from the streambed to the top of Black Mountain at 3,231 feet. Laurel Falls is big, 40 feet high and 50 feet wide, and is quite picturesque, with a deep, wide pool at its base. Above and back of the falls are rock promontories crowned with evergreens. The nearby slopes of Black Mountain contain some virgin timber. The gorge also features Potato Top and Buckled Rock. Potato Top is a large rocky promontory shaped much like a potato hill, with a forest cover. Laurel Fork makes a loop around Potato Top. Buckled Rock is a vertical cliff rising from the creek. About 150 feet high, it derives its name from the pattern of bends in the strata.

Vegetation found in the Area includes flame azalea, mountain laurel, rhododendron, Carolina hemlock, Fraser's sedge, mountain mint, and Allegheny cliff fern. There are several trails in the Area, with the AT being the best maintained. There is an AT shelter along the AT as well as good campsites on Pond Mountain and in the gorge. Laurel Fork Creek is a popular trout-fishing stream, and the Area is also used by deer and grouse hunters.

HISTORY

The Laurel Fork Valley was timbered from 1911 to 1925, with a railroad being constructed from Braemar (adjacent to Hampton) up the gorge and into the Dennis Cove Valley above. This railroad bed now provides the location for the AT through much of the gorge. The Wilderness was designated by the US Congress in 1986.

TRAILHEADS AND MAPS

All trailheads are reached by taking US 19E south out of Elizabethton, TN, for about 5 miles and turning left onto US 321-TN 67 at Hampton, TN. Or you can drive north on 19E from NC and Roan Mountain, TN, to the junction and turn right. There is a convenience market at this road junction. All directions and distances are given from this intersection of US 19E, US 321, and TN 67 in Hampton. Turn east on US 321 and TN 67.

Dennis Cove Trailhead

Drive through Hampton on US 321 0.8 mile to Dennis Cove Road (County 50). Turn right on County 50, which is not marked. Continue for 3.9 miles on a narrow, steep, winding paved road to the USFS parking lot for the AT on the left.

Laurel Fork Creek Trailhead

Drive 1.3 miles east on US 321 from the junction in Hampton, TN. The parking area is on the right immediately after you cross the second of two bridges (the first is over Laurel Creek and the second is over a tributary). The trail goes up the creek at the back of the parking area. Vandalism of cars left overnight has been a problem at this trailhead.

Shook Branch Recreation Area Trailhead

Drive 3.2 miles east on US 321 from the US 19E junction in Hampton, TN. The Shook Branch Recreation Area is on the left, and a gravel road leads through a grassy area.

Park in the recreation area. Walk up to US 321 from the parking area and watch for trail blazes on the other side of the highway.

Rat Branch Launching Site Trailhead

Drive 3.7 miles east on US 321 from the US 19E junction in Hampton, TN. The Rat Branch Launching Site is on the left, and a gravel road leads down to Watauga Lake. Park in the parking area. Cross the highway, turn left along US 321, and look for trail blazes.

Watauga Shooting Range Trailhead

Drive 4.8 miles east on US 321 from the US 19E junction in Hampton, TN. A short gravel road, FS 344, is on the right and is signed "Rifle Range-Pond Mountain." Follow the gravel road 0.1 mile into the woods. At its end the shooting range is on the right, and the trailhead is straight ahead at several earth mounds that block ORVs. Be careful because of shooting activities in the area.

Watauga Point Recreation Area Trailhead

Drive 6.85 miles east on US 321 from the US 19E junction in Hampton, TN. Just past the Watauga Point Recreation Area is a gravel pull-off on the left with a picnic table down by the lake. Cross the highway and look for the post marking the trail. Yellow blazes mark the Pond Mountain Trail.

Pond Mountain Trailhead

Drive 0.8 mile east on US 321 from the US 19E junction in Hampton, TN. Turn right onto the Dennis Cove Road (County 50). Follow County 50 past the parking lot for the AT (at 3.9 miles) described above, past USFS Dennis Cove Campground (5.3 miles), past some private homes, and onto FS 50, which is gravel. Continue up the mountain to the Pond Mountain Trail Trailhead on the left at 7.3 miles. This trailhead can also be reached by continuing on US 321 past the Watauga Point Recreation Area Trailhead and turning right onto Little Stony Creek Road (FS 39). Follow it until it forms a T with FS 50, turn right (west), and go another 2.5 miles to the trailhead on the right (north).

Topographic Maps: Elizabethton, TN; Watauga Dam, TN.

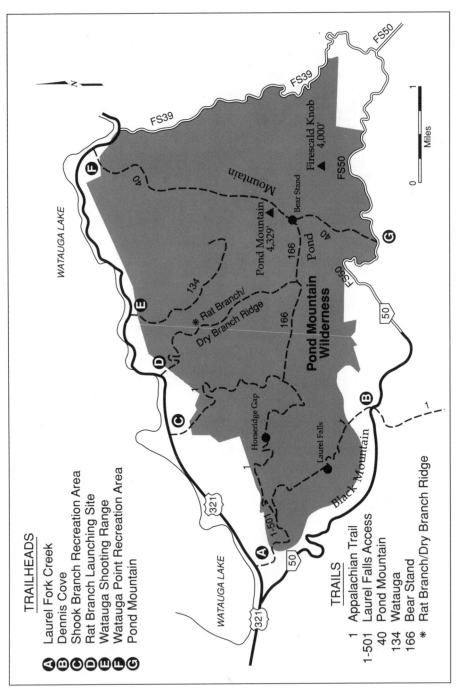

TRAILHEADS

Ⓐ Laurel Fork Creek
Ⓑ Dennis Cove
Ⓒ Shook Branch Recreation Area
Ⓓ Rat Branch Launching Site
Ⓔ Watauga Shooting Range
Ⓕ Watauga Point Recreation Area
Ⓖ Pond Mountain

TRAILS

1 Appalachian Trail
1-501 Laurel Falls Access
40 Pond Mountain
134 Watauga
166 Bear Stand
∗ Rat Branch/Dry Branch Ridge

Pond Mountain Wilderness.

TRAIL DESCRIPTIONS

AT (Dennis Cove to US 321 Section) (Trail No. 1)

Length: 6.8 miles
Elevation Change: Start 2,533 feet, end 1,900 feet (high point 3,760 feet)
Trailheads: Dennis Cove (start) and Shook Branch Recreation Area (end)
Trail Connections: Bear Stand and Laurel Falls Access
Type: Hiking

Comments: This section of the AT is maintained by the Tennessee Eastman Hiking Club and includes a trail shelter in Laurel Fork Gorge. This section has a lot of climbing to it, no matter which direction you hike, because of the climb over Pond Mountain. If you want an easy day hike, you can hike the AT from Dennis Cove Trailhead and take the blue-blazed Laurel Falls Access Trail off the AT below the falls back to US 321 at the Laurel Creek Trailhead. This route is downhill the whole way, but a car shuttle is necessary.

Please note that this section of the AT is undergoing a major relocation during the early 1990s which is expected to be completed during 1993. The AT is described herein as it will be relocated, which relocation was not, however, completed at the time we hiked the trail. You might want to check with the USFS as to the status of the relocation if you hike the trail prior to 1993.

Details: From the Dennis Cove USFS parking lot walk through a rustic fence and continue straight ahead on an old railroad grade through rhododendron and forest of hemlocks, beech, and maple with Laurel Creek on your right. At 0.5 mile there are some Carolina hemlocks. The trail turns right and descends to the creek. There are nice views of rock cliffs as you descend. Cross a creek at 0.7 mile on a footbridge. Follow along the river for a short distance and then ascend back onto an old railroad grade passing through cuts in the rocks. Continue along the rim of the gorge. At 0.9 mile there is a rough 0.2-mile trail to the summit of Potato Top. You are likely to walk right past this if you do not look for it. The hike is worthwhile for the spectacular views of the gorge. Back on the AT, continue to the trail junction at 1.1 miles. Here the AT turns back sharply left and descends into the gorge to Laurel Falls. (The blue-blazed trail straight ahead follows the railroad grade about 0.5 mile to Laurel Fork AT Shelter and reconnects with the AT. This blue-blazed trail is intended to be used when high water floods the AT below the falls. The shelter is constructed of native stone and accommodates six. Water is found 150 feet north of the shelter.) Reach the base of the falls at 1.3 miles. Turn right and follow the creek along the rocks. The

Backpacker prepares dinner in the Pond Mountain Wilderness. Photo by Will Skelton.

trail widens to an old roadbed at 1.5 miles. At 1.7 miles the AT bears right and ascends a narrow trail to the ridgecrest. At 1.8 miles the blue-blazed shelter trail rejoins the AT. Continue on the AT down the ridge and rejoin the wide trail close to the creek at 2.0 miles. Waycaster Spring is reached at 2.2 miles. This is the last dependable water before the crest of Pond Mountain, where the spring may not be flowing in summer. Cross the stream on a footbridge at 2.3 miles and then again at 2.5 miles. At 2.7 miles the AT turns sharply right. Straight ahead the blue-blazed Laurel Falls Access Trail (No. 1-501) goes about 1 mile to US 321 and the Laurel Creek Trailhead. About 0.4 mile down this trail is the very impressive Buckled Rock, a high cliff across the creek.

Ascend the AT steeply and turn right onto an old railroad grade, climbing high above the creek. At 3.0 miles, turn left from the railroad grade and keep climbing. At 3.5 miles, reach the crest of a ridge, turn sharply right on an old road and ascend (straight ahead is posted property). Pass a rock ledge at 3.8 miles and then two more ledges. Along here are good views of White Rocks and the Highlands of Roan to the south and Hampton to the west. At 4.0 miles the trail narrows and climbs steeply for 0.3 mile. A trail junction is at 4.3 miles; continue straight (east) along the ridge, still climbing. At 4.8 miles descend into Pond Flats, which is a good camping spot. There is a spring here, but in dry weather you may have to go further down the drainage to find it.

Laurel Falls in Pond Mountain Wilderness Area. Photo by Will Skelton.

The AT formerly, prior to the relocation mentioned above in the Comments, continued straight ahead at 5.1 miles as it left Pond Flats. However, after relocation it will turn left to the north and head down the wide ridge of Pond Flats. When the relocation is completed the trail straight ahead will be blue-blazed and the AT will be white-blazed; the trail straight ahead will be the Bear Stand Trail. Because the AT relocation was not complete when this guidebook was written, we cannot provide details for the balance of the AT. Upon completion it will be well marked with white blazes and will generally follow the ridgetop between Rat Branch and Shook Branch down to the trailhead at Shook Branch Recreation Area on US 321. From about 3,760 feet the gradual descent will be to 1,900 feet. Outstanding views will be visible out over Watauga Lake and to the Big Laurel Branch Wilderness on the far side of the lake. Near the trailhead the trail will pass under a power line and end at 6.8 miles at the Shook Branch Recreation Area.

Laurel Falls Access (Trail No. 1-501)
Length: 1.0 mile
Elevation Change: Start 1,880 feet, end 1,960 feet (high point 2,040 feet)
Trailheads: Laurel Fork Creek (start) and AT (end)
Type: Hiking

Comments: This trail provides a short access into the Laurel Fork Gorge and the AT.

Details: The trail essentially follows the east bank of Laurel Fork Creek along the route of the old logging railroad in the Area. Follow the obvious trail with blue blazes. You will notice evidence of mining in the Area and will walk near a power line for the first 0.3 mile. At 0.6 mile pass Buckled Rock, a high, scenic cliff, across the creek. Numerous campsites can be found along the creek, most of which are well used. At 1.0 mile the AT junction is reached with the left fork going up to Pond Mountain on to US 321 and the right fork going up Laurel Fork Creek to Dennis Cove.

Pond Mountain (Trail No. 40)
Length: 4.5 miles
Elevation Change: Start 1,968 feet, end 3,280 feet (high point 4,040 feet)
Trailheads: Watauga Point Recreation Area (start) and Pond Mountain
Trail Connections: Bear Stand
Type: Hiking

Comments: This trail is a rugged 4.5-mile hike. The trail is not well maintained and in many places goes straight up the fall line. With much use severe erosion will take place. There is no reliable water on the trail. The yellow blazes that mark the trail are often obscure.

Details: Cross US 321 and you will see a treated post marked "Pond Mountain Trail." The trail proceeds to the left. Straight ahead is a metal gate behind which is private property. Follow the yellow blazes. The trail ascends very steeply, very quickly. At 0.1 mile pass under power lines, and beyond the power lines lies the Wilderness. At 0.2 mile an old road intersects with the trail. Go left on the road for 30 feet, then turn right onto the trail. Look for yellow blazes, which are faint in many places. At 0.3 mile the trail bends to the right and continues a steep ascent through hardwood forest and rhododendrons. As you stop to rest, you can look back and get some good views of Watauga Lake. You reach the ridgecrest at 0.4 mile. Descend from the ridge into a small gap and then back up another ridge. At 0.5 mile the trail turns right and begins another steep ascent. At 0.7 mile you reach the ridgeline and continue along the ridge. This area is scarred by fire and blow-downs. As you scramble to the next high point along the ridge, there are nice views of the lake and surrounding valleys. At 1.0 mile the trail turns left and descends into another small gap. For the next 0.5 mile walk along the ridge, climbing gently. At 1.5

miles climb steeply again and reach the top of the ridge at 2.0 miles. The next 0.4 mile is gentle ridge walking. At 2.4 miles you enter a broad open wooded area with a number of large old oak trees. The yellow blazes are a little obscure in this area, but they are there. Continue straight ahead and ascend, with the trail bending left up the ridge for 0.2 mile to the ridgetop. Continue along the ridge. At 2.8 miles the trail turns left and leaves the ridge with a steep descent. At this point the Bear Stand Trail proceeds straight ahead to the AT but is not marked in any way. At 2.9 miles the trail intersects with an old skid road. Turn left and continue downhill. The trail intersects with a closed USFS road at 3.2 miles. Turn left and follow the road for 1.3 miles to the FS 50 Trailhead.

Bear Stand (Trail No. 166)
Length: 1.8 mile
Elevation Change: Start 3,760 feet, end 4,200 feet (high point 4,200 feet)
Trailheads: 5.1 miles on AT (from Dennis Cove) (start) and 2.8 miles on Pond Mountain Trail (from US 321) (end)
Trail Connections: Old AT
Type: Hiking

Comments: This trail connects the AT to the Pond Mountain Trail. The first 1.0 mile was formerly the AT and is in good shape, but the last 0.8 mile has not been maintained for years and is very obscure and difficult to follow. Occasionally you will see old faded yellow blazes on trees. It may be cleared and maintained in the future. The trailhead from the Pond Mountain Trail is difficult to find. At 2.8 miles on the Pond Mountain Trail (from US 321), that trail turns left and leaves the ridge while the Bear Stand Trail continues straight ahead. There is no sign nor clear evidence of a trailhead; you must simply follow the ridge.

Details: The Bear Stand Trail leaves Pond Flats and heads southeast, to the left of the knoll, with a quite level trail. At 0.3 mile the trail ascends along a narrow crest. At 0.9 mile, veer left off the crest and skirt left, descending gently. At 1.0 mile the trail ascends to the right and proceeds along the ridge while the former AT (called Rat Branch/Dry Branch Trail in this guidebook) goes straight and begins descending steeply. This junction can be a problem, so be careful. From this point the Bear Stand Trail is difficult to follow, as it leads 0.8 mile on to the Pond Mountain Trail. In places it is obvious; in others it is very obscure. Perhaps the best advice for hiking this trail is to attempt to stay on the ridgecrest for the entire length of the trail and use a topo-

graphical map. Although forested, the trail features occasional outstanding views of
the surrounding mountains. The trail ends at 1.8 miles at the Pond Mountain Trail.

Watauga (Watauga Scenic Area) (Trail No. 134)

Length: 2.2 miles
Elevation Change: Start 1,800 feet, end 3,280 feet (high point 3,280 feet)
Trailheads: Watauga Shooting Range (start and dead-end)
Type: Hiking

Comments: This trail leads you into the heart of the former Watauga Scenic Area,
which formed the core of the subsequently designated Pond Mountain Wilderness.
This is also known as Watauga Scenic Area Trail. The trailhead is at the Watauga
Shooting Range on US 321, and the end is on a 3,280-foot knoll overlooking much of
the Wilderness. However, as of the early 1990s, this is more of an off-trail route than
a trail; it has not been maintained and is very difficult to follow. Accordingly, it cannot be described in detail. With a topographical map and the map in this book, however, you can follow the route up Dry Branch, proceeding generally southeast. At
about the 3,000-foot contour, the route turns sharply to the left and to the northeast;
you will almost be heading back toward the direction you came from earlier. The
knoll is less than 0.5 mile ahead on the horizon.

Rat Branch/Dry Branch Ridge AT (No USFS Number)

Length: 3.7 miles
Elevation Change: Start 4,040 feet, end 2,000 feet (high point 4,040 feet)
Trailheads: Bear Stand Trail (start) and Rat Branch Launching Area (end)
Type: Hiking

Comments: This trail was formerly the location of the AT, which is to be relocated
to the ridge on the west side of Rat Branch from the AT (see AT description above).
The name of the trail may also be changed.

Details: At 1.0 mile on the Bear Stand Trail, the Rat Branch/Dry Branch Ridge Trail
proceeds straight, beginning a descent, while the Bear Stand Trail leads up along a
ridge. Finding this trailhead can be a problem, so be careful. The Trail gradually
descends along the crest of the ridge. At 0.6 mile the trail leaves the crest and descends very steeply to the left (west) for 2.9 miles over several summits and through
small gaps. At 3.5 miles you pass under a power line and leave the Wilderness. At
3.7 miles the trail ends on US 321 across from the Rat Branch Launching Area.

7. DOE RIVER GORGE SCENIC AREA

The Doe River Gorge Scenic Area, located in Carter County just southeast of Eliza-bethton, is in the Unaka Ranger District. The Area contains 1,783 acres and is a hid-den treasure of the CNF. The Area can be entered by USFS roads on the east and west boundaries or through an abandoned hand-dug railroad tunnel, a unique key-hole entry into the gorge. The tunnel entrance, which allows access to a trail along the river, is perhaps the most spectacular access to the Scenic Area, although it is entirely on private land. The trail follows a section of abandoned railroad right-of-way passing through three tunnels as it leads you into this secluded pocket of pris-tine beauty.

The Doe River is a steeply dropping mountain stream with numerous swimming holes between boulder-strewn rapids. The trail, which follows the abandoned railroad right-of-way, is very gradual and easy walking. Spectacular views down to the river and up to the exposed rock cliffs and ridges make the 5.0-mile-roundtrip hike inter-esting and not strenuous. The rocks exposed by the river's downcutting are early Cambrian quartzite which has been metamorphosed, leaving the original bedding lines folded in interesting configurations. The vegetation is mixed hardwoods with abundant common wildflowers and a number of rare plant species.

Two hikes can be taken into the Scenic Area. One is on USFS land and follows an old USFS road to the top of Fork Mountain. The other starts at the Christian Con-ference Center and follows the old railroad grade along the Doe River and is en-tirely on private land.

HISTORY

The principal cultural feature of the gorge is the East Tennessee and Western North Carolina (ETWNC) Railroad, on which construction began in 1868. From its rather early history, the line has been referred to as the Tweetsie Railroad. This affection-ate name is thought to have been given to the line by young girls riding as passen-gers on their way to the exclusive camps of western NC; they referred to the train as the *tweetsie* from the sound of its whistle.

Unlike most of the rail lines in the CNF, which were built for lumber hauling, the ETWNC served the iron industry first, connecting the Cranberry Iron Works near Elk Park, NC, with blast furnaces in Johnson City.

After a false start in 1868, construction of the narrow-gauge rail line was begun in 1880 and finished in 1882, from Johnson City to Cranberry, a distance of 34 miles. The five tunnels on the line were manually dug and pass through the rocky spurs that extend from the high ridges to the valley bottom. To speed construction on the line, the tunnels were dug from both ends, with the assistance of many small mules.

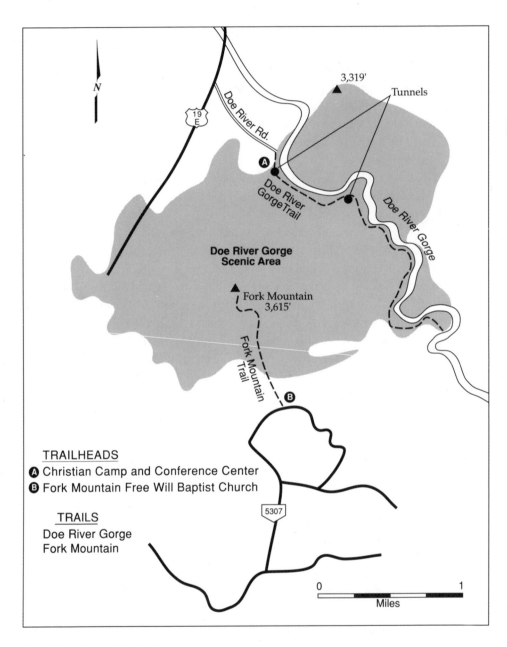

Doe River Gorge Scenic Area.

The animals were lifted over the ridges with block and tackle, the cliffs on the side of the gorge being too sheer to risk the loss of the mules.

In addition to hauling iron ore, the line also offered passenger service and general freight, including timber, supplied by the numerous small branch lines in the area. The railroad opened a very remote area isolated from the developing communities in the valley, delivering social liberation to its inhabitants through numerous personal services offered by the train crew. From the early years, the line ran excursion trains to picnics, church socials, reunions, baptisms, and other events of importance to the local people.

Operation of the Tweetsie line was extremely informal; there was always time for the train to stop for a visit with the crew. For many years the crew consisted of the same four men, serving as engineer, brakeman, fireman, and conductor, who knew every family along the line and were known to occasionally provide such service as accompanying children to their door while the train waited. Conductor Cy Crumley reminisced, "I guess I've carried everything from a spool of thread to a kitchen range, and stopped at the house to take them in. I liked doing it. The biggest trouble was buying something that didn't suit, then having to take it back and exchange it!"

Heavy rains and flooding were a periodic menace to the lines. In 1901 a cloudburst washed the line out in 39 locations. In August 1904 sections of the track in NC were lost, this time precipitating the abandonment proceedings.

The creation in 1927 of the ETWNC Motor Transportation Company, at first operating in areas not served by the train, was a hint of things to come. Abandonment of the lines in the ETWNC network began about 1944, with closure of the Linville River Railway Company. Service on the line through the gorge declined in the early 1940s, down to three round-trips a week from the heyday when trains ran daily, including Sunday. By 1950 a request to abandon the gorge section was filed and granted. Subsequently, the lower part of the line through the gorge was rebuilt and operated by the Doe River Railroad Company as a tourist attraction. However, use was discontinued in 1975. The tracks remain in place, but the old bridge trestles have largely been destroyed or barricaded because of their hazardous conditions.

The Scenic Area was designated in 1988 by the CNF's Management Plan.

TRAILHEADS AND MAPS

Christian Camp and Conference Center Trailhead

This trailhead is reached by driving southeast from Elizabethton on US 19E toward Roan Mountain. At the junction of US 19E and US 321 with TN 67 and TN 91, check the mileage and go 5 miles to the split of US 19E and US 321 in Hampton, TN. Continue on US 19E another 1.1 miles to Doe River Road; on the left is a house with a "Ole

House Crafts" sign. Note the huge man-made hill on the left; it is built from dirt removed in widening the highway between Hampton and Elizabethton. Turn left onto Doe River Road, which dead-ends after 0.5 mile at the Doe River Christian Camp and Conference Center. Parking is available in an open area between the center buildings and the caretaker's trailer. It is necessary to request permission and sign a release form before entering the gorge on this trail, which is privately owned by the camp and conference center. See the caretakers, Hugh and Louise Slemp (615) 725-2212; or contact the Center at P.O. Box 791, Elizabethton, TN 37643 (615) 928-8936. The gorge is surrounded by USFS land that starts at approximately the 2,000-foot contour in the lower gorge.

Fork Mountain Free Will Baptist Church Trailhead

This trailhead is reached by driving southeast of Elizabethton on US 19E toward Roan Mountain. Note the mileage at the intersection of US 19E with TN 91N, on the east side of Elizabethton. At 10.9 miles, turn left onto paved Bear Cage Road (County 5307) and follow signs to the Fork Mountain Free Will Baptist Church. Proceed 0.6 mile on Bear Cage Road to the intersection with Fork Mountain Road. Take the left fork onto paved Fork Mountain Road toward the church. Another 0.8 mile brings you to the church parking lot and the trailhead, which is directly across the road to the north. The dirt USFS road up Fork Mountain has been barricaded, but vehicles sometimes travel the road, bypassing the barricade.

Topographic Maps: Elizabethton, TN; Iron Mountain Gap, TN.

TRAIL DESCRIPTIONS

Doe River Gorge (No USFS Number)

Length: 2.4 miles
Elevation Change: Start 1,960 feet, end 2,200 feet (high point 2,200 feet)
Trailhead: Christian Conference Center (start and dead-end)
Type: Hiking

Comments: This Trail is not on USFS land and is not included in the CNF trail system. In the late spring (mid-May) the gorge is abloom with dogwood, Carolina rhododendron, purple facelia, fire pink, Solomon's seal, wild iris, jack-in-the-pulpit, and bleeding heart. The blooming season is considerably delayed due to the lack of sunshine in the steep-sided gorge. In the summer, the stream offers numerous trout-filled fishing and swimming holes. Turtle head, wild grapes, and wild raspberries persist into the fall with the display of colors offered by the mixed hardwoods.

Details: The trail begins behind the pool and an abandoned water tower. It immediately enters a rock tunnel (marked "Second Tunnel" on topographical maps), emerging 200 feet later in the Doe River Gorge. At 0.5 mile a side stream enters from the right into a rhododendron-filled depression. At 0.7 mile a side trail on the left gives easy access to the river at a spot used for camping. An old railroad structure stands at the junction. The river trail is 0.2 mile each way.

The main trail proceeds through a second rock tunnel (marked "Third Tunnel" on topographical maps), emerging at 0.9 mile to a spectacular viewpoint. A scramble over the rocks at the left puts you atop a cliff overlooking the Doe River, with a view up several hundred feet to the ridgeline atop an impressive exposure of folded rock strata. It is in this area that some of the more unusual plant species in the gorge occur on the cliff base to the right of the tracks.

At 1.6 miles a small trail goes off steeply to the left to the water's edge. A collapsed building, partially hidden by wild raspberries, is on the right at 1.7 miles. A side stream enters here from the right as well. At 2.3 miles the river diverges from the track at a broad open clearing. The trail continues through a narrow cut another 0.1 mile, ending at 2.4 miles at a bridge trestle crossing of the Doe River. Visible on the other side of the trestle is a third rock tunnel, which is followed immediately by a second and less sound bridge crossing of the river. Crossing of either bridge is prohibited by posted signs and is inadvisable due to the hazardous condition of both the structures and the trackbed.

Fork Mountain (No USFS Number)
Length: 1.5 miles
Elevation Change: Start 2,600 feet, end 3,615 feet (high point 3,615 feet)
Trailhead: Fork Mountain Free Will Baptist Church (start and dead-end)
Type: Hiking

Comments: This trail is not included in the CNF trail system.

Details: The dirt road heads north and passes behind a small house as it enters USFS land. At a little less than 0.1 mile, bear right at a fork. At 0.3 mile another fork to the right takes you alongside an area that was clear-cut in the late 1970s and is now regenerating in maple and sourwood. The road winds upward for almost a mile through an older forested area, which was likely last harvested in the 1930s. At 1.2 miles the top of the first peak is reached, at an elevation of 3,560 feet, with a vehicle turnaround on the left. Proceeding on the road, which is now more of a trail, as fallen trees have not been removed, you descend gradually to a point at 1.3 miles which is directly below the saddle between the two peaks of Fork Mountain. A narrow foot trail takes off to the left at this point and rises steeply into the saddle at 1.4 miles. A right turn onto the ridge trail ascends steeply again through mountain laurel and rock outcrops to the top of Fork Mountain at 1.5 miles and an elevation of

3,615 feet. From the top there are views in all directions during the winter when the leaves are down. To the north, the lip of the Doe River Gorge is seen, and to the south Strawberry Mountain dominates.

8. HIGHLANDS OF ROAN SCENIC AREA

The Highlands of Roan is the range of mountains along the TN-NC state line from US 19E on the east to near NC 226/TN 107 on the west, located in Carter County, TN, and Avery and Mitchell counties, NC, southeast of the city of Roan Mountain, TN. Above approximately the 4,000-foot elevation, about 12,000 acres are located in the Unaka Ranger District of the CNF and NC's Pisgah National Forest. About 11,000 additional acres are owned by private owners and are at risk of development.

For over 17 of its 2,100 miles, the AT traverses the Highlands of Roan, which many consider to be one of the most rewarding portions of the entire AT. The USFS in its 1974 Composite Plan for the Highlands of Roan states:

> The Highlands of Roan present an exceptional recreational opportunity for the Appalachian Trail hiker to experience the most extensive area of mountain balds on the entire 2,000 miles of the Trail. . . . There is no other area . . . that offers such extensive panoramic views of the high mountain country of the southern Appalachians. Unique is not, at least in this sense, misleading.

The Highlands of Roan is a vast high country with great balds that roll and undulate in every direction and which are the most extensive in the southern Appalachians. The balds are treeless areas of sedges, grasses, and wildflowers covering several hundred acres along rounded ridges and peaks from 5,400 feet to 6,100 feet above sea level. Wild yet tranquil, rugged yet fragile, this place is unlike any other. Winds, averaging 25 miles per hour year-round, ripple the sedges and hair grass like seaweed in a great tide. Great rocks, weathered and timeworn into strange and fascinating shapes, jut from the knee-deep grasses. Wind-wracked, rocky crags edge the balds. Ancient many-colored lichens, centuries old, creep across the rocks at the rate of only 1/16 of an inch every 25 years.

In season, wildflowers carpet the trails. Acres of white fringed phacelia cover the ground in May, accented with splotches of mayapples, with white and purple violets, trout lilies, and many other early spring flowers. A month later the balds streak yellow and red with hawkweed, ragwort, and other sun-loving flowers.

Scattered along the edges of the meadows, the heath shrubs produce great bursts of color: flame azaleas, in colors ranging from pale lemon yellow to a deep brilliant sunburst orange, and the Catawba rhododendron, with its purplish-pink

Highlands of Roan Scenic Area.

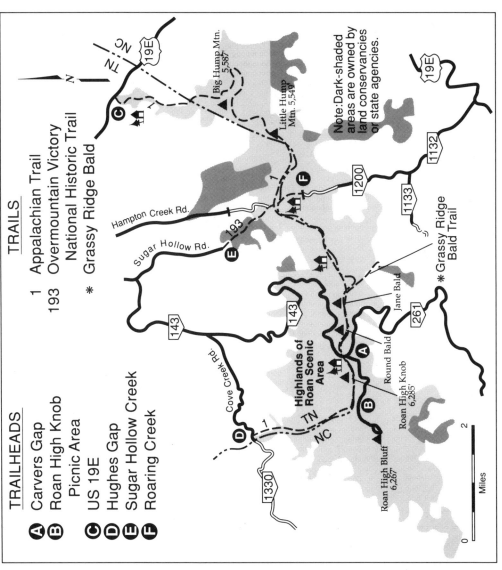

TRAILHEADS

Ⓐ Carvers Gap
Ⓑ Roan High Knob
     Picnic Area
Ⓒ US 19E
Ⓓ Hughes Gap
Ⓔ Sugar Hollow Creek
Ⓕ Roaring Creek

TRAILS

1   Appalachian Trail
193   Overmountain Victory
        National Historic Trail
*   Grassy Ridge Bald

Note: Dark-shaded areas are owned by land conservancies or state agencies.

Big Hump Mtn. 5,587'

Little Hump Mtn. 5,549'

Hampton Creek Rd.

Sugar Hollow Rd.

Cove Creek Rd.

Highlands of Roan Scenic Area

Jane Bald

Round Bald

Roan High Knob 6,285'

Roan High Bluff 6,267'

* Grassy Ridge Bald Trail

TN
NC

19E

1132

1133

1200

143

261

1330

0   1   2
Miles

color, lighting up 600 acres along the mountain each June. These natural but gar-
den-like displays occur throughout the Area but especially at its western end, where
they provide the best displays of Catawba rhododendron in the world.

The Highlands of Roan are notable for such biotic diversity. Over 300 species of
plants are found there, including the rare Gray's lily. From a botanist's perspective,
the Roan Mountain massif is superlative because of the outstanding diversity of
plant species and the exceptional quality and variety of plant communities found
there. In an ecological evaluation of the area for the NPS in 1981, L. L. Gaddy, con-
sulting biologist, wrote: "The Roan Mountain massif is, without doubt, nationally
significant."

Gaddy reported that there are more nationally or regionally ranked rare species
on the Roan massif than at any other site in the high mountains of the southern Appalachians, which would include the GSMNP, an area noted for its ecological diversity.
An updated version of Gaddy's listing of the rare plants of Roan shows that there are
54 currently recognized rare plant species on the massif, including the Blue Ridge goldenrod, Roan Mountain bluet, and spreading avens.

The northern hardwood forests surrounding the balds are among the best examples of this community type anywhere in the Blue Ridge. One yellow birch tree
in this forest was determined to be 385 years old. At the edge of the balds, dwarf
beeches, only 12 inches in diameter, are as old as 250 years. A mature stand of table-
mountain pine, a southern Appalachian endemic, and the dwarfed yellow buckeye,
an "orchard" of which is in one of the gaps, are other unique forest species there.

The Highlands also has varied and abundant wildlife, which can be attributed
to its exceptional habitat diversity, a product of latitude, altitude, physiography,
vegetation, and even history. The Roan massif is a vast, high-altitude island surrounded and isolated by low and narrow valleys and rolling hills. Because its slopes
vary in steepness, soils, orientation, and drainage, it supports a mosaic of vegetation types and microhabitats, and these are of sufficient total area to sustain substantial animal populations. The Area's ice-age history transformed the 18-mile
ridge into a faunal melting pot of northern, southern, and local animals. These factors, helped by the low level of human activities, have created the living space for a
wide array of animal species.

A few species, such as the New England cottontail and bog lemming, are at or
near their southern limits and may be relics of a past ice age. Others, like the opos-
sum and southern flying squirrel, are warm-climate species that periodically invade
the upper slopes. Some species are confined to one type of habitat on a permanent
or seasonal basis. For example, meadow mice inhabit the grass balds, a habitat used
by the rare snow bunting only in winter. Other species occupy the adjacent parts of
two vegetation zones; the threatened northern flying squirrel frequents the lower

Gnarled tree on the open balds of the Highlands of Roan. Photo by Roger Jenkins.

spruce-fir and upper northern hardwood forests. Still other animals (shrews, jumping mice, salamanders, and many invertebrates) require certain microhabitats within a zone to provide special foods or refuges. Finally, active carnivores (least weasels, spotted skunks), large species (bear, bobcats, and foxes), and fliers with special needs (owls, bats, hummingbirds) must range widely over the mountain and, in fact, would probably not survive if confined to a single area.

HISTORY
Recorded history of the Area goes back to at least 1770, when the Overmountain Men mustered at Sycamore Shoals (presently Elizabethton, TN) and marched across the Highlands through Yellow Mountain Gap to help the North Carolinians defeat the British at King's Mountain, a turning point of the Revolutionary War. The Overmountain Victory National Historic Trail has been designated along this route, crossing the Highlands of Roan near its center.

Throughout the 19th century, botanists from around the world visited the Highlands in their studies of Appalachian flora. Elisha Mitchell, for whom the East's highest mountain is named, worked in the Area. In the early part of the present century Roan High Knob became a resort area, with visitors reaching the hotel in horse-

*Blooming rhododendrons frame a distant view of Big Hump Mountain in the
Highlands of Roan. Photo by Roger Jenkins.*

drawn carriages. The hotel is now gone; in recent decades the Area has been increasingly patronized by day visitors who enjoy the rhododendron and views.

In the mid-1960s the USFS, cooperating with the Appalachian Trail Conference,
initiated an acquisition program in the Area. A central core has to date been protected as public lands, especially along the AT corridor, but significant acres remain
unprotected.

The Southern Appalachian Highlands Conservancy, a regional private land
trust, is leading current efforts to complete the mountain's protection and to assure
management excellence. The USFS has created special management categories for
the Highlands in both TN and NC, essentially creating a scenic/scientific area that
will be free from timber harvesting. The CNF states in its 1988 Management Plan
for the Area:

> This management area on Roan Mountain contains some of the most unique
> flora and fauna in the Eastern United States. Much national attention has been
> directed to identifying and classifying these unique features as well as being
> recognized for its outstanding scenic qualities of high mountain balds, rhododen-
> dron gardens, and spruce-fir timber types. . . . This area is unsuitable for timber
> production.

TRAILHEADS AND MAPS

Carvers Gap and Roan High Knob Picnic Area Trailheads

Follow TN 143 south from the intersection of US 19E and TN 143 in Roan Mountain, TN, for 12.7 miles to an obvious gap. At that point there will be "NC State Line" and "Mitchell County" signs on TN 143 and a USFS sign pointing to the right for the Roan Mountain Gardens. There is a small parking lot, picnic area, and primitive rest-rooms. The paved road to the right leads to the natural concentrations of Catawba rhododendron on the mountains to the west and Roan High Knob Picnic Area, another trailhead for this section of the AT. The AT crosses TN 143 in the gap. To the west the trail to Hughes Gap enters the forest while to the east the AT ascends the huge grassy Round Bald. Carvers Gap may also be approached from the NC side by following NC 261 14.0 miles north of Bakersville, NC.

US 19E Trailhead

Follow US 19E 3.85 miles east from the junction of US 19E and TN 143 in Roan Mountain, TN. The trailhead, which is easily missed, is located shortly after a highway passing lane begins, on the right in a break in the metal guardrail. Several white blazes mark the small parking area. Recurring vandalism of vehicles is a problem at this trailhead and, indeed, in the general area (an AT shelter was burned nearby in the late 1980s). Cars can instead be left with permission at a package beer store 0.5 mile further south on US 19E. Note that this store is open seven days a week, and the owner allows hikers to park on the premises, with permission, in the hope that they will purchase some liquid refreshment when the hike is over. From NC the trailhead is on the left 3.0 miles west from the junction of US 19E and NC 194 north in Elk Park, NC; it is also 0.9 mile west of the TN-NC state line.

Hughes Gap Trailhead

From Roan Mountain, TN, follow TN 143 south from the junction of TN 143 and US 19E for 5.3 miles. Turn right (west) on County 2680, Cove Creek Road (no sign), at signs for Calvary Baptist and Cove Creek Presbyterian churches. Immediately cross a bridge and follow a paved road upward for 3.1 miles to an obvious gap marked by "NC State Line" and "Mitchell County" signs. The AT trailhead is on the left. Parking is limited, and overnight parking not recommended. Hughes Gap may also be approached from Bakersville, NC. Drive north from Bakersville on NC 226 for 12.1 miles to Buladean, NC. Turn right on paved NC 1330 (Hughes Gap Road) and drive 4.4 miles to Hughes Gap (the uppermost 1.1 miles is gravel but in good shape).

Sugar Hollow Trailhead

From the junction of US 19E and TN 143 in Roan Mountain, TN, follow TN 143 south for 2.3 miles. Turn left on paved and narrow Sugar Hollow Road; this road is not signed, but there is a sign for Sugar Hollow F. W. B. Church. Caution: a *second* road turns left off TN 143 just 0.1 mile further and is Heaton Creek Road. Proceed 2.3 miles on Sugar Hollow Road to the trailhead at its upper end, opposite the Shell residence. If possible, please check at the house for suggestions as to where to park as space is limited. Avoid taking up all of the turning space to the right of the pavement and below a garage; a school bus needs this space for turning. Also do not block the gravel private road extending beyond the pavement; other residences use this road for access. The trail proceeds up this gravel road.

Roaring Creek Trailhead

Find the junction of paved NC 1132 (Roaring Creek Road) and US 19E 3.0 miles north of Plumtree, NC, and 4.5 miles south of Minneapolis, NC, on US 19E. At the intersection are McCoury's Rock F. W. Baptist Church and a historical marker commemorating the Overmountain Men's march. Follow narrow and winding NC 1132 for 2.2 miles to its end at a Y intersection where NC 1200 (Old Roaring Creek Road) turns right and NC 1133 (Jerry's Creek Road) turns left. Turn right and follow NC 1200 up the valley. At 3.5 miles NC 1200 ends and the gravel, unsigned FS 5545 continues. Both NC 1200 and FS 5545 are narrow. Notice at 3.95 miles, on the left, a vandalized metal plaque on a boulder commemorating the Overmountain Men. The trailhead is reached at 4.6 miles at a USFS gate on FS 5545. There is parking for several vehicles, and the trail proceeds up the road behind the gate.

Topographic Maps: Elk Park, NC-TN; White Rocks Mountain, TN-NC; Carvers Gap, NC-TN; Bakersville, NC; Iron Mountain Gap, TN-NC.

TRAIL DESCRIPTIONS

AT (Carvers Gap to Hughes Gap Section) (Trail No. 1)

Length: 4.9 miles
Elevation Change: Start 5,512 feet, end 4,040 feet (high point 6,150 feet)
Trailheads: Carvers Gap (start), Hughes Gap (end), and Roan High Knob Picnic Area
Type: Hiking

Comments: The AT is well marked with white blazes. This section of the AT is also accessible from two parking lots near the Cloudland Hotel site on the Roan Mountain Gardens Road.

Details: The trail begins at the southeast corner of the Carvers Gap parking lot, beside an information shelter. It proceeds inside a log fence, with the Roan Mountain Gardens Road on the other side. After a short distance the trail passes an AT mileage sign. The trail then enters a dense fir and spruce forest and climbs steeply on an eroded trail. At 0.15 mile the trail turns right on an old road, now grassy, that comes up from the left. The trail proceeds up an easy incline on a trail that is wide and clear and has a good surface. At 0.25 mile the first of several wet-weather streams is crossed. Such streams sometimes run in the trail. At 0.3 mile is the first of six switchbacks, which provide the easy grade up the mountain. Ferns are frequent beside the trail. The trees are mainly evergreens, predominantly Fraser or balsam fir and some red spruce (the last spruce and fir between this area and New England except for Mt. Rogers National Recreation Area and Shenandoah National Park). A fair number of dead trees reflects possible acid rain problems.

At 1.1 miles the trail reaches the top of a ridge and then proceeds along the southeast and then northeast sides of the ridge. A partially clear opening to the right at 1.17 miles allows views out over the valley below. The side-trail to the Roan High Knob AT Shelter, reflected by a wooden sign, is reached at 1.3 miles; the shelter is 0.1 mile to the left. The shelter is an old fire warden's cabin with a large downstairs room and upstairs sleeping loft. Water from a pipe can be found 50 feet below the shelter on a blue-blazed trail. The shelter is the highest on the entire AT at 6,285 feet.

Past the shelter the trail inclines down the north side of the ridge. A series of rock outcrops is passed at 1.55 miles, and the trail goes through a small open grassy area at 1.6 miles. At this point the Roan Mountain Gardens Road is just below the trail and cars can be heard. The trail passes to the right of a small gravel parking lot at 1.7 miles; simply go by the lot and reenter the forest. Just behind the lot at 1.8 miles the trail goes around a sturdy 14-foot chimney that remains from an old cabin. The trail then proceeds up a ridge and is quite open.

At 1.9 miles the trail reaches a large, open grassy area and turns sharply to the right. A short walk to the left across the grassy area leads to the Roan High Knob Picnic Area, an alternate trailhead. At the edge of the grassy area is a historical marker for the site of the former Cloudland Hotel at 6,150 feet. The three-story hotel was built in 1885 and abandoned around 1910. It had 166 rooms but only four baths and cost $2.00 per day or $10.00 per week, three meals included. The hotel was built by Union Army General John Thomas Wilder. An interesting method was used to get materials to this high mountain site. Railroad tracks were laid from the valleys in NC and TN up to the hotel site; railroad cars were then connected by cable and one car filled to act as a counterbalance to pull the other car up to the site; the process was then reversed.

The trail proceeds to the right of the hotel site, past a series of campfire rings, and at 1.93 miles climbs steeply up to the hotel site and then to the right across its back side. At 1.96 miles the trail begins a long descent toward Hughes Gap. This less-used section of the trail is more narrow and closed-in by vegetation. It passes through a principally deciduous, rather than evergreen, forest. The route is often steep and is generally down a ridge where lush grass often appears, possibly indicating the location of a former bald.

At 2.1 miles the trail passes around several rugged outcrops and continues the descent. Several slick rocks are crossed at 2.28 miles. A one-tent campsite, no water, is at 2.6 miles. Many ferns and blackberries are located in this section. The trail levels off in Ash Gap at 2.8 miles, providing a good large campsite, with open grassy forest. Water is located a short distance to the left. The trail continues along the ridgetop, inclining slightly upward at first, then more level. After passing around a large rounded rock at 3.2 miles the trail reaches the top of a knoll known as Beartown Mountain offering good views when the leaves are off the trees. The trail then continues to descend along a narrow ridge to a possible small campsite in a grassy area at 3.27 miles. A steep descent follows.

Several large rocks are passed at 3.3 miles, and at 3.5 miles a short trail to the left leads to a large, picturesque beech tree and views of the valley below. The trail then continues steeply down through second-growth beech forest with a few level areas and several large beech trees. At 4.0 miles the trail turns left to the side of the ridge and begins a series of switchbacks. The forest changes to predominant oak at around 4.1 miles and levels off several times. At 4.4 miles the trail has returned to the ridge and cuts to the right side through an open oak forest. Several switchbacks follow; at 4.7 miles the trail continues the switchbacks on an old road. At 4.9 miles the trail ends at a paved road at Hughes Gap. Note that, if reversing the route described, an ORV track goes straight up the mountainside at Hughes Gap, while the AT angles off to the left and upward.

AT (Carvers Gap to US 19E Section) (Trail No. 1)

Length: 13.3 miles
Elevation Change: Start 5,512 feet, end 2,900 feet (high point 5,900 feet)
Trailheads: Carvers Gap (start) and US 19E (end)
Trail Connections: Grassy Ridge Bald Trail and Overmountain
Victory National Historic Trail
Type: Hiking

Comments: This trail is one of the most spectacular hikes described in this guidebook. The combination of magnificent vistas, open grassy balds, unusual vegetation, and marvelous campsites makes this traverse of the spine of the Appalachians from Carvers Gap to US 19E a classic. However, the steep ascents and descents, combined with sometimes difficult footing, make this not a trip for the novice backpacker. The trip is described from south to north, the easier direction, and is often done as a two-day backpack. The one-way trip requires a shuttle; several local businesses provide such service.

Details: The trail starts by going through a wooden fence at the western base of Round Bald, entering and climbing through some magnificent rhododendron gardens. At 0.35 mile, a patch of lovely high-altitude fir trees is passed near the summit of Round Bald (5,826 feet), and another 0.1 mile of level walking provides superb views of Grassy Ridge Bald and Big Hump Mountain, the latter being a day's walk away. For the next 1.3 miles, the vistas are nearly overwhelming. At 0.57 mile, begin a moderate descent and notice the interesting moss and lichen growing in patches, with pink rounded tops. Huckleberry bushes can be seen nearby. At 0.72 mile, end the descent at Engine Gap, amidst carpets of wildflowers. A minor relocation of the trail from Round Bald down to Engine Gap in the early 1990s will add up to 0.1 mile to the trail distance. At 0.88 mile is a spectacular flame azalea. At 0.92 mile, begin the ascent of Jane Bald, topping out at 1.02 miles at a large rock formation. The trail starts another descent at 1.08 miles, arriving at a low saddle at 1.22 miles. A moderate ascent starts at 1.34 miles, and the junction with the Grassy Ridge Bald Trail is reached at 1.57 miles. This side trip is separately described and is well worth the short climb.

At its junction with the Grassy Ridge Bald Trail, the AT forks left and traverses around the north side of Grassy Ridge Bald, encountering the first of many springs at 1.66 miles. At 1.79 miles, the trail passes through a tunnel of rhododendrons, ferns, and beech trees. Following a very slight uphill stretch, the trail begins a steep descent of the northeast spur of Grassy Ridge Bald at 2.01 miles through deep woods. There is a small sheltered campsite at 2.14 miles, but you would have to carry water from the springs previously described. The trail levels out briefly at 2.33 miles and passes a large rock on the right at a knoll at 2.54 miles. The descent moderates somewhat at 2.62 miles, arriving at the Roan Highlands AT Trail Shelter (5,050 feet) at 3.0 miles. This wooden shelter accommodates six. There is water down a small side trail to the south. At 3.1 miles, following a moderate ascent through somewhat open terrain, there is a classic view of the east face of Grassy Ridge. Around mid-June this is seen as being pink from the blooming rhododendron. But do not miss the wild strawberries growing at your feet. And keep an eye out for the rare Gray's Lily. As this Area has become more protected, this 30-inch-high, deep orange flower is making a strong comeback. The trail tops out at 3.21 miles, and there is a small (two tents) campsite. The trail enters woods and begins a moderate descent. At 3.82 miles, the trail flattens out. Over the next 0.8 mile, the trail undulates, until reaching a small knoll with space for three tents at 4.66 miles. At times, the cow parsnip can be well over the tallest hiker's head. After a short descent, Yellow Mountain Gap is reached at 4.9 miles. The Overmountain Victory National Historical Trail crosses the AT at this gap and is separately described. There is a small campsite, with water about 300 yards down a side trail to the left (north). There is also usually water at 0.1 mile on a side trail to the right (south). To the immediate south and west is a barn-like structure used as a trail shelter. Known as the Overmountain Shelter or Yellow Mountain Barn, it accommodates twenty or more. It is not visible from the trail unless you get out into the field to the south.

At 4.95 miles the trail leaves the woods, enters an open meadow, and begins a steep ascent. At 5.31 miles, the climb becomes more moderate, entering woods. At 5.93 miles, an old fence stile is reached. Note that the trail turns left, crosses the fence line, and leaves the old roadbed. After passing by some woods on the left, the trail breaks out into the open. There are only 150 feet of climbing left to the summit of Little Hump Mountain. At 6.5 miles the summit, one of the most spectacular campsites on the TN-NC state line, is reached. There is room for numerous tents, the sunsets are magnificent, and the views in every direction make you feel like you are flying. But be mindful of the exposure. With wind-driven rain and fog, it can be an intimidating place. There are some more sheltered spots on the south side of the bald near some small beech trees. The easiest route to water is to follow the path that parallels the tree line on the south side of the bald. It descends about 130 feet, curls around to the north, enters the woods, and follows an old road grade as it descends some more, before crossing a nice spring. The total distance amounts to a 15-minute stroll. Water can be found also near the AT, further along the trail.

At 6.55 miles, the trail begins a very steep and somewhat difficult descent in woods, passing a small clearing at 6.68 miles. Descending more moderately, the trail enters woods at 6.73 miles. Here is a small campsite, and water can be found on the old road grade to the south about 200 yards. At 6.91 miles, there is a small side trail to some water (sign on the tree) to the right. At 6.96 miles, the trail enters open meadows with trees, and Bradley Gap is reached at 7.29 miles. For the next 1.75 miles, the views are even more outstanding. Take a deep breath, and begin the steep, 600-foot climb of Big Hump Mountain. Frequent rest stops can be easily justified on the basis of the increasingly grander views. Note, however, that dense fog is frequently encountered on this stretch, and very close attention to the white blazes marking the AT is critical. It is quite easy to lose your way. Near the summit of Big Hump Mountain (8.14 miles), the trail takes a very sharp right-hand turn, reaching the summit at 8.18 miles (5,587 feet). Relax and pretend you are Julie Andrews in *The Sound of Music*. The settlements nestled in the valleys have a postcard quality.

As the trail begins a moderate descent of the southeast spine of Big Hump Mountain, carpets of yellow wildflowers in June make this an unforgettable experience. Pay attention in fog at 8.94 miles, as the trail leaves the main ridge, turns left, and crosses open fields before entering woods at 9.06 miles. Here the trail begins a shallow traversing descent of the northeast face of Big Hump Mountain on a frustratingly rocky section of trail. At 9.96 miles, the trail crosses a spring, the first high-quality water actually crossing the trail for the last 8 miles. At 10.43 miles, the edge of a steep meadow is reached, and the trail arrives at Doll Flats at 10.59 miles. Here is good camping among shade trees and large rocks, with a spring nearby. At 10.62 miles, the AT crosses an old fence line. The aforementioned spring can be found by turning left, going about 50 yards, turning right, and following the old roadbed about 200 yards. A small side trail leaves the roadbed to the right, and a spring can be heard gurgling in the woods. The AT bears slightly right at the fence line and begins a descent which at times can be very steep and slippery. At 10.97 miles, there is a side trail leading 75 feet to the left to a fine, unobstructed view of the valley. At 11.09 miles, the first of many switchbacks is reached as the trail zigzags down to lose elevation as fast as possible. At 11.59 miles, cross a fence line. There is an "emergency" campsite here (no water). At 11.78 miles, cross a small field. At 12.08 miles, the trail merges with an old roadbed and turns very sharply left. After a sharp turn to the right, the roadbed narrows to the width of a path (12.18 miles). At 12.4 miles, the trail takes a sharp left near a small streambed, passes a side trail (12.62 miles) on the right to the site of an old mine, and reaches the Apple House AT Trail Shelter at 12.74 miles. This shelter was originally used to store explosives for a quarry in the hollow below as well as tools for nearby orchards. At 13.13 miles, the trail enters a small field, crosses a small bridge at 13.17 miles, and reaches the US 19E Trailhead at 13.3 miles.

Overmountain Victory National Historic Trail (No. 193)

Length: 2.66 miles
Elevation Change: Start 3,250 feet, end 4,200 feet (high point 4,660 feet)
Trailheads: Sugar Hollow Creek (start) and Roaring Creek (end)
Trail Connections: AT
Type: Hiking

Comments: Only the portion of this trail that passes through the Area is described. It is described from the north (TN) to the south (NC). The entire trail extends for approximately 315 miles from Craig's Meadow in Abingdon, VA, to the King's Mountain National Battlefield in SC and is, for most of its distance, a motor vehicle route. About 12 miles are hiking trail, including the portion through the Highlands. The frontiersmen who answered the call to battle camped in the Highlands on the way to King's Mountain. The Battle of King's Mountain resulted in the death of British Major Patrick Ferguson on October 7, 1780, and the defeat of his army, a turning point in the Revolutionary War. The trail through the Highlands is blazed with light blue vertical rectangles. However, two portions on USFS roads are not blazed.

Details: Proceed up the private gravel road from the trailhead. At 0.12 mile there is water at a spring box overflow on the left and a picnic table/shelter that the Shells welcome hikers to use, although permission should be requested. Proceed through a road-width gate in a white board fence and pass a small pond on the right. At 0.19 mile go through another trail-width gate in a woven wire fence. At this point the trail leaves private land and enters protected lands, first owned by the Southern Appalachian Highlands Conservancy and then the USFS. The trail continues up an old farm road, generally near the right side of an overgrown field where there are wildflowers and blackberries in season. At 0.35 mile the trail leaves the field and enters the woods, after which a stream is crossed. At 0.39 mile another stream is crossed at a large boulder on the left. The trail then leaves the woods and enters a small open area. At 0.43 mile leave the open area and reenter the woods, with a stream on the right.

At 0.74 mile the trail exits the woods and enters the lowest corner of another old field. At this point the trail leaves the old farm road and stream and continues approximately east-southeast steeply up across the field on a less well-established and sparsely blazed trail. Care should be taken here as the trail may not be obvious. Wildflowers and apples may be found in season, and there are views down Sugar Hollow toward the White Rocks Mountains.

At 0.8 mile the trail leaves the upper side of the old field and enters the woods, continuing approximately east-northeast. The blazing improves, and at 0.83 mile there is an intersection with an unmarked side trail leading left down the ridgeline. Care should be taken here. At this point the trail turns sharply right to continue up the ridge with a woven wire fence on the left. This is Hampton Creek Ridge. At 0.88 mile the trail crosses to the left through a break in an old fence line. A faint unmarked side trail continues straight up the ridgeline; care should be taken not to continue on it. The trail continues along the left (east) side of the ridge and is fairly level. The trail is now in the watershed of the westernmost fork of Hampton Creek. There are traces of an old road or trail a short way down the ridge, roughly paralleling the trail.

At 1.23 miles the trail enters an interesting "rock garden" and seepage area as it curves left across a cove drainage system. There is poor footing at this point, and the rocks can be slippery. A local resident believes that the jumble of rocks at this point was caused by the tremendous flood of May 20-23, 1901. At 1.34 miles leave the rock garden and seepage area and continue steeply uphill.

At 1.4 miles, on the ridgeline, the trail joins the old cross-mountain Yellow Mountain Road at its uppermost switchback. This was formerly a public road but is now a gated USFS road. There are potentially good campsites here and in the level wooded expanse to the left on the ridge, which was known by old-time residents as "Pig Pen Flats." The trail turns right and continues up the old road, with the road section not being blazed.

At 1.62 miles, there is usually water on the left at the lower end of a steel culvert pipe under the road. Further up, an earth mound across the road was constructed by the USFS to discourage motorized vehicles. Almost immediately thereafter at 1.74 miles the trail leaves the road, bearing slightly left into the woods. Again the trail becomes blazed, with the trail being relocated through the woods to avoid a series of trees felled across the road to block motorized vehicles. At 1.8 miles leave the woods and reenter the road, continuing upward.

At 1.82 miles, the trail reaches historic Yellow Mountain Gap and intersects with the AT. This is the high point of the trail, and there is an excellent campsite just to the left on the AT. Water may usually be found 0.1 mile south on the trail. The Overmountain Men on their march to King's Mountain are said to have camped around this gap on September 27, 1780. That night was cold, and the ground was covered with snow that was "shoemouth deep." One militiaman is said to have frozen to death; his grave may be nearby. The Yellow Mountain Road originally crossed the mountain at this point but is no longer maintained as a road. This was also the location of an early migration route from western NC to eastern TN known as "Bright's Trace."

A few paces beyond the AT the trail turns right through an old fence row to follow a blue-blazed AT side trail in a road trace across a small meadow. At 1.87 miles the trail leaves the meadow and enters the woods. The road the trail is following becomes obvious. At 1.92 miles there is water on the left from a small pipe below the road; this source can fail in droughts. At 1.96 miles the trail intersects with the gravel FS 5545. The road is gated further down the mountain. By turning right on the road and proceeding 0.11 mile you will reach the AT Overmountain Shelter (Yellow Mountain Barn), a converted barn with sleeping space for 20 or more. The loft is for sleeping, with cooking and fires on the ground floor. Outstanding views may be seen from the area of the shelter, with the upper Roaring Creek Valley below, the Big Yellow Mountain Bald (partially protected by the Nature Conservancy) to the left, and Elk Hollow Ridge to the right. The trail turns sharply left onto FS 5545 and continues down the road through the woods. This road segment is not blazed. At 2.66 miles the trail reaches a gate across FS 5545, which is the Roaring Creek Trailhead.

Grassy Ridge Bald (No USFS Trail Number)
Length: 0.8 mile
Elevation Change: Start 5,900 feet, end 6,070 feet (high point 6,200 feet)
Trailhead: AT (1.57 miles east of Carvers Gap) (start and dead-end)
Type: Hiking

Comments: This delightful little spur trail is a great way to extend a day hike across the high balds of the Roan Highlands. Note that it is dead-end trail, ending in a saddle on the ridge. Experienced cross-country hikers may want to explore further but should note that much of Grassy Ridge is privately owned.

Details: The beginning of the trail is reached by hiking east (northbound) on the AT, 1.57 miles from the Carvers Gap Trailhead. The trail begins in a nice, grassy area but quickly becomes narrow and rutted, with many rocks underfoot. The views are so distracting that it is hard to pay attention to the placement of your feet. At 0.21 mile, there are dense rhododendron on both sides of the trail. At 0.3 mile, the trail reaches a false summit in open, nearly tundra-like surroundings at about 6,100 feet. The true summit (6,200 feet) of Grassy Ridge is reached at 0.53 mile. Stop for a moment, look around, and savor the 360-degree views. You will truly feel like you are on top of the world. At 0.61 mile, the trail begins an easy descent to a saddle at 0.79 mile (6,070 feet). Here is a very good, albeit exposed and sometimes windy, campsite. Water can be found about 100 yards down a path on the east side of the saddle. Consider this a stoves-only camp, as dead vegetation is quite sparse. There are some interesting rocks to scramble around to the south, and a path leads to and beyond them, but for the purposes of this guidebook, the trail can be considered to end.

9. UNAKA MOUNTAIN WILDERNESS, SCENIC AREA, AND PRIMITIVE AREA

Unaka Mountain is in Unicoi County, southeast of Erwin, TN, in the Unaka Ranger District. The Wilderness consists of 4,700 acres on the north slope of Unaka Mountain (5,180 feet), with steep slopes and numerous waterfalls. An additional 910 acres are included in a Scenic Area designation and 1,248 acres in a Primitive Area designation. Two of the most outstanding falls are Red Fork Falls (about 60 feet high at the top of a series of five falls beside a steep, rhododendron-covered cliff) and Rock Creek Falls (about 50 feet high in a shady glen framed by overhanging cliffs). Complementing the waterfalls are virgin timber stands, including huge eastern hemlocks, heath balds, cliffs, and ridges that provide panoramas of the TN Valley, and a dense forest cover, consisting of about 60 percent upland hardwoods. Along the higher elevations red spruce are found.

Flora of both the eastern US and Canadian life zones are present in the Area. Several rare plants have been found, including Fraser's sedge, rattlesnake root, gentian, mountain mint, and Mitchell's St. John's wort. Unaka Mountain provides good black bear habitat, although whitetail deer and ruffed grouse are the primary game species. Many other mammals and birds inhabit the Areas as well. A 10.8-mile section of the AT borders the Areas on the north, traversing the crest of Unaka Mountain. A gravel road, FS 230, runs between the Areas and the AT.

HISTORY

Unaka Mountain is part of the Appalachian Mountain chain, and its geology is similar to the rest of the area, reflecting a history of mountain building, including uplifting, folding, and faulting of the strata. The Unaka Mountain Quartzite takes its name from this prominent peak in the northern CNF.

Much of the area was logged prior to acquisition by the USFS. Those logging activities during extremely dry weather resulted in a major fire on the mountain in 1925. Hiking in the Areas provides a good opportunity to see how nature has healed the land after some 60 years and allows for comparison with areas not touched by the fire. A fire in 1978 also burned 180 acres, which are now recovering. Silver and copper exploration is reported to have occurred in the Areas years ago, but no silver was found and the copper proved too expensive to mine. Because of the steepness of the slopes, little logging was carried out by the USFS except for a large clearcut on Stamping Ground Ridge over 20 years ago and two very small clear-cuts in the 1970s.

The Wilderness was designated by the US Congress in 1986 while the Scenic Area and Primitive Area were designated in the CNF Management Plan in 1988. The Wilderness incorporated a previously designated Unaka Mountain Scenic Area.

TRAILHEADS AND MAPS

Rock Creek Recreation Area Trailhead

From Erwin, TN, take TN 395 (Tenth Street, Rock Creek Road) east toward NC. Rock Creek Recreation Area is 3.2 miles from the traffic light in Erwin. Two trailheads, Rock Creek Falls Trail and Rattlesnake Ridge Trail, are located at the end of the road into the Recreation Area.

Unaka Mountain Road Trailheads: Pleasant Garden Overlook and Stamping Ground Ridge Trail Parking Area

From Erwin, TN, take TN 395 (Tenth Street, Rock Creek Road) east toward NC for 6.3 miles and a gap known as Indian Grave Gap. At that point, and at the obvious high point on the road, the AT crosses TN 395 and a gravel road turns left (TN 395 continues 4.0 miles to Poplar, NC, and is known as NC 230). The road to the left is Unaka Mountain Road, FS 230 (no signs identify this road). Turn left onto Unaka Mountain Road and continue 3.1 miles from Indian Grave Gap to the Beauty Spot area, an area of scenic grassy balds. Continue to signs on the left for the Pleasant Garden Overlook Trailhead and the Stamping Ground Ridge Parking Area Trailhead.

Limestone Cove Recreation Area Trailhead

From Unicoi, TN, take paved TN 107 east toward Buladean, NC. The Limestone Cove Recreation Area is on the right about 3.0 miles from Unicoi.

Limestone Cove Church and Red Fork Falls Trailheads

The low-elevation access road to the Stamping Ground Ridge Trail is about 5.6 miles east of Unicoi on TN 107 at the Limestone Cove First United Methodist Church. The Unaka Mountain gravel road (FS 230) turns right off TN 107 8.0 miles east of Unicoi and proceeds to the Red Fork Falls Trailhead on the right. The high-elevation Stamping Ground Ridge Parking Area Trailhead, Pleasant Garden Overlook Trailhead, and Beauty Spot can be reached by continuing on FS 230.

Topographic Maps: Unicoi, TN-NC; Erwin, TN; Huntdale, NC-TN.

TRAIL DESCRIPTIONS

Rattlesnake Ridge (Trail No. 26)

Length: 3.0 miles
Elevation Change: Start 2,360 feet, end 4,840 feet (high point 4,840 feet)
Trailheads: Rock Creek Recreation Area (start) and Pleasant Garden Overlook (end)
Type: Hiking

Details: Starting at the Rock Creek Recreation Area entrance, walk or drive east on the paved road through the picnic and camping areas. The paved road passes through a very pleasant grove of sweet gum, hemlock, tulip poplar, rhododendron, and other vegetation. The pavement turns into gravel and continues about 75 yards, where it ends at a USFS gated road. A footbridge crosses Rock Creek on the left side of the gravel road just before you get to the gate. A trail sign at the bridge indicates

"Rattlesnake Ridge Trail No. 26." Cross the bridge and, on the other side, watch for a trail to the left, which is the Rattlesnake Ridge Trail; a trail sign may be posted to indicate the left turn. The trail then runs in a northerly direction through laurel slicks and will cross over a small, nearly dry stream several times. Continue on the trail as it climbs around the side of a wooded hill. You will note pines overhead, along with trailing arbutus, galax, and other species found in warm dry exposures. At 0.8 mile the trail will briefly connect with Dick Creek ORV road (FS 307). Turn sharply east-southeast away from the ORV road to begin a steep ascent up Rattlesnake Ridge.

The Rattlesnake Ridge Trail climbs a dry exposed ridge covered with table mountain pines, along with bracken, clubmosses, teaberry, lichen, and reindeer moss. Bear sign can often be spotted. The view from the trail reveals the ridge to be climbed ahead and more distant ridges to the west. Near the top of the ridge the trail passes through open woods with grassy areas. Eastern hemlock, Fraser magnolia, and red spruce are predominant species at this elevation. Blackberries and blueberries will reward the climber in season, as will good views of Unaka and other mountains in the area. The trail comes out of the forest at the Pleasant Garden Overlook at 3.0 miles near the Unaka Mountain gravel road. The Ravens Lore Interpretative Trail is at the Pleasant Garden Overlook; it is a loop trail of 0.38 mile.

Rock Creek Falls (Trail No. 148)
Length: 2.3 miles
Elevation Change: Start 2,360 feet, end 3,400 feet (high point 3,400 feet)
Trailhead: Rock Creek Recreation Area (start and dead-end)
Type: Hiking

Comments: The trail begins as a USFS road but converts to a trail. Rock Creek Falls is a small but beautiful series of cascades at the base of Unaka Mountain.

Details: Start at the entrance of the Rock Creek Recreation Area and follow the paved road through the area to the USFS gated gravel road. Walk around the gate and continue up the USFS road, with the creek on your left as you walk upstream. Do not cross the footbridge a short distance before the gate on your left (this bridge leads to the Rattlesnake Ridge Trail). The road will soon ford the creek, and you can wade, rock-hop, or cross on a one-log bridge with hand cable. Continue on up the road, with the creek now on your right. The road begins a gentle eastward climb. The creek flows over moderate-sized rocks and is shaded by laurel. A second creek crossing is required, with a cable for support (all that remains of a former bridge). The road has by this point become a trail passing between ridges on the north and south side of the creek. Two more creek crossings are required before the top of

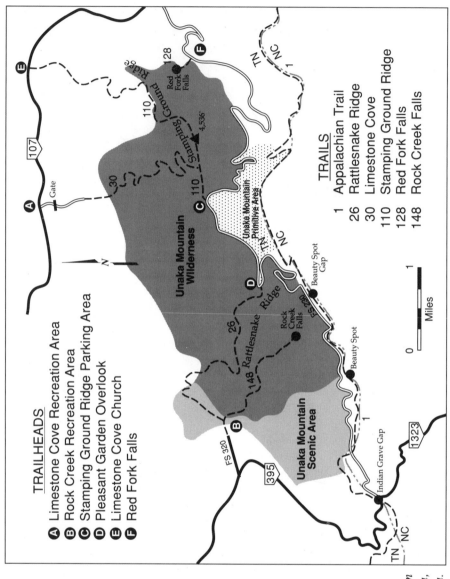

TRAILHEADS

Ⓐ Limestone Cove Recreation Area
Ⓑ Rock Creek Recreation Area
Ⓒ Stamping Ground Ridge Parking Area
Ⓓ Pleasant Garden Overlook
Ⓔ Limestone Cove Church
Ⓕ Red Fork Falls

TRAILS

1 Appalachian Trail
26 Rattlesnake Ridge
30 Limestone Cove
110 Stamping Ground Ridge
128 Red Fork Falls
148 Rock Creek Falls

*Unaka Mountain
Wilderness, Scenic Area,
and Primitive Area.*

Rock Creek Falls can be seen. The trail climbs moderately, passing several smaller falls and laurel-covered rock outcroppings. Rock Creek Falls is reached at 2.3 miles. Rock Creek Falls is really more of a cascade, falling over sculptured rocks in a dark, shaded area of the forest. The rocks are quite slippery; be careful.

Stamping Ground Ridge (Stamping Ground) (Trail No. 110)

Length: 2.5 miles
Elevation Change: Start 2,360 feet, end 4,709 feet (high point 4,709 feet)
Trailheads: Limestone Cove Church (start) and Stamping Ground Ridge Parking Area (end)
Trail Connections: Limestone Cove Trail
Type: Hiking

Comments: Walk south up the drive across the road from the Methodist Church (a private drive serving several houses). The trail enters the woods, going west of the houses. This trail was part of the AT prior to its rerouting around 1954. This is also known as Stamping Ground Trail.

Details: The trail begins by entering a grove of handsome eastern hemlock and rhododendron. A creek comes in from the left, and the trail soon crosses it. The path proceeds through a tunnel of rhododendron and enters the creekbed and mingles with the creek for about 0.2 mile. The trail breaks into the open following a dry creekbed continuing to the west. Watch carefully for a sharp turn south up the mountain at 0.7 mile from the church; note that there is a spur just before you reach the turn.

The trail climbs steadily and straight toward the Stamping Ground with a gap visible in the ridge ahead. Vegetation in the area includes galax, trailing arbutus, pipsissewa, and scrubby trees. The trail passes a dry creek drainage, then swings up and toward the west, beginning to climb around the ridge.

As you stop to look back to the north, the view is of Stone Mountain across the valley of Limestone Cove. There is a spring on the left side of the trail at 2.3 miles, close to the top of the ridge. The vegetation includes red spruce, and club moss carpets the ground. The trail becomes open, with beautiful views of the surrounding mountains dominated by Unaka Mountain. The Stamping Ground Ridge Parking Area Trailhead is reached at 2.5 miles.

Red Fork Falls (Trail No. 128)
Length: Less than 0.25 mile
Elevation Change: Negligible
Trailhead: Red Fork Falls (start and dead-end)
Type: Hiking

Comments: Red Fork Falls is a major falls of about 100 feet, including a picturesque series of cascades above and below the falls. The falls gets its name from the rainbow of colors present when the setting sun hits the water. This is no longer an official trail.

Details: The trail begins on the north side of Unaka Mountain Road and descends to the creek. Cross the creek, passing through an area used for camping and picnicking. Again cross the creek about 50 yards from the first crossing. Pick up the trail, following the creek to the top of the falls. Caution should be used in approaching the falls. The trail is exposed, and roots and slick rocks make accidents very possible.

Limestone Cove (Trail No. 30)
Length: 2.8 miles
Elevation Change: Start 2,280 feet, end 4,520 feet (high point 4,520 feet)
Trailheads: Limestone Cove Recreation Area (start) and Stamping Ground Ridge Trail (end)
Trail Connections: Stamping Ground Ridge Trail
Type: Hiking

Comments: Locate the USFS road that goes to the left (east) of the camping area at the Limestone Cove Recreation Area. Follow this road south about 0.5 mile to the Limestone Cove Trail junction on your right. There is a foot-trail marker there; the trail has fresh yellow blazes and is cleared to the top of Stamping-Ground Ridge. USFS Trail signs may not have been installed.

Details: The trail begins as a gentle climb on a wide grassy trail. Old roads crossing or connecting can cause confusion in spots, and one should look for the yellow blazes. A USFS sign "Unaka Mountain Wilderness" is at about 0.3 mile from the campground road. A box for registration is a short way beyond.

After the USFS sign is passed, there follows a gentle but persistent climb for about 0.5 mile to Rocky Branch. The trail then crosses Rocky Branch, beginning a steady, moderate, sometimes steep, winding climb up to Stamping Ground Ridge.

The trail is shaded for much of the route up the mountain. Water can be found at several locations. The trail uses the remains of old logging roads and is in good shape and easy to follow.

At 2.8 miles the trail joins the Stamping Ground Ridge Trail, which is about 0.4 mile from the Stamping Ground Ridge Parking Area Trailhead.

Future Trails

The USFS is in the process of clearing a horse trail which, when completed, will be about a 3-mile loop and known as the Little Dark Hollow Trail (No. 28). This trail will be in the Little Dark Hollow and Dark Hollow section of the Unakas, not within the Wilderness. The trail will be accessed via Rock Creek Recreation Area on the foot trail leading to Dick Creek jeep road. It will climb out of Dick Creek Gap in a westerly direction (on the opposite side from the Rattlesnake Ridge Trail). A steep 0.2-mile climb will be required to reach the top of the ridge out of Dick Creek Gap. However, you will be rewarded by great views across Dick Creek, Rattlesnake Ridge, and the Unaka Mountains. This trail is to be completed sometime in the early 1990s.

10. NOLICHUCKY PRIMITIVE AREA

This 1,970-acre Primitive Area is a completely forested triangle formed by the TN-NC state line, the Nolichucky River corridor, and the AT corridor. It is in Unicoi County and the Unaka Ranger District just southeast of, and up the Nolichucky River from, Erwin, TN. The Area itself has no trails, but the contiguous AT and off-trail hiking allow one to enjoy an isolated and otherwise inaccessible portion of the Unaka Mountains. Open forests of large hemlocks and protected watersheds of numerous clear streams flowing into the Nolichucky River and Jones Branch are among its attractions. Five species of rare fauna have their habitat in the Nolichucky River just outside the Area: three species of river snail and two species of pearly mussel.

HISTORY

Much of the Area was logged 40 years or so ago but has since recovered almost completely. Since then the geographical isolation of the Area provided by the TN-NC state line, the Nolichucky River, and Johnson Rock Ridge has mainly protected the Area, with only some ORV abuse being present. The designation of the Area in 1988 as a Primitive Area under the CNF's Management Plan has eliminated most ORV abuse.

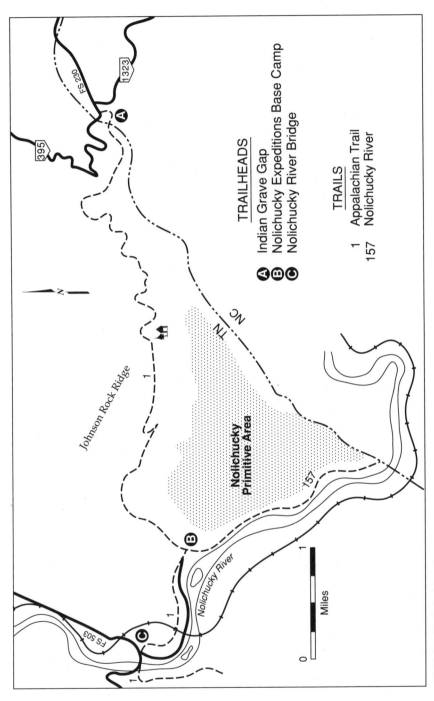

Nolichucky Primitive Area.

TRAILHEADS AND MAPS

Nolichucky River Bridge and
Nolichucky Expeditions Base Camp Trailheads

Approach via either TN 107 or US 19. From the intersection of TN 107/81 with US 23/19 (just outside Erwin, TN), drive south on the four-lane US 23/19 for 2.8 miles, at which point the four lanes are reduced to two. Six tenths of a mile beyond this point, turn left off the highway onto a side road marked with a small brown sign (also on the left side of the highway): "Cherokee N.F.-Chestoa .75 Mile." After 0.4 mile, cross a two-lane bridge (with a protected walkway for AT hikers) over the Nolichucky River, and immediately turn right onto a paved road. The Jones Branch section of the AT terminates at this Nolichucky River Bridge. Chestoa Recreation Area, 0.25 mile ahead on the right, has parking for several cars.

Continue on the paved road to its end, 1.4 miles from the bridge, at Nolichucky Expeditions Base Camp, a commercial whitewater rafting operation. The AT passes by here, and the Nolichucky River Trail begins here. For those who need help in arranging a car shuttle, it is useful to note that during the whitewater rafting season members of Nolichucky Expeditions staff (telephone 615/743-7111) are frequently available for a fee to help with car shuttles. One or more cars may be left at the Base Camp; tenting and cabin facilities are available at the Base Camp or adjoining Nolichucky Campground.

Indian Grave Gap Trailhead

Indian Grave Gap is located where TN 395 (paved) intersects the AT. A paved pull-off here will hold several parked cars. A gravel road runs steeply northeast from Indian Grave Gap about 3.0 miles to Beauty Spot on the AT. To reach Indian Grave Gap, drive northeast through Erwin, TN, on Mohawk Drive, then turn right onto Tenth Street, which soon becomes Rock Creek Road and TN 395. A highway sign for Mitchell County marks the end of TN 395, the TN-NC state line, and Indian Grave Gap. Driving distance to the gap is 12.0 miles from Erwin. The road continues into NC as NC 1323 for 4.0 miles to Poplar. To find the AT, walk directly across the highway from the paved parking strip at the end of TN 395 and look for a white AT blaze on a series of stone steps leading up the bank.

Topographic Maps: Huntdale, NC-TN; Chestoa, TN-NC.

TRAIL DESCRIPTIONS

AT (Jones Branch Section, Trail No. 1)
Length: 8.4 Miles
Elevation Change: Start 3,360 feet, end 1,720 feet (high point 3,480 feet)
Trailheads: Indian Grave Gap (start) and Nolichucky Expeditions
Base Camp or Nolichucky River Bridge (end)
Type: Hiking

Comments: This section of the AT is maintained by the Tennessee Eastman Hiking Club and includes a trail shelter at Curley Maple Gap. AT through-hikers will usually travel this section from south to north; however, the majority of day-hikers will prefer to hike it from north to south since a car shuttle can be arranged to permit a downhill trip. The description below is of the downhill route.

Details: Climb the stone steps up the steep bank at Indian Grave Gap and note the small metal sign reading: "Appalachian Trail: Curley Maple Gap Shelter 4.1 Mi.; Nolichucky River 8.4 Mi." After an initially steep climb, the trail climbs gently for nearly a mile before leveling off. At 0.4 mile a side trail on the left runs uphill 100 yards to a grassy meadow with a few trees. It has been used as a campsite but has no water. The trail passes over a rounded crest at 1.0 mile to begin a steady descent all the way to the Nolichucky River. Mixed hardwoods and patches of rhododendron characterize this portion of Jones Branch, with an abundance of diverse wildflowers in season—tradescantia, coreopsis, whorled loosestrife, and blue-bead lily, to name a few. Further on, where the trail is drier, the heath family is abundantly represented, with arbutus, laurel, wintergreen, and azalea.

At 1.5 miles, the trail crosses the ridge and continues to descend, but with the valley on the left instead of the right. A switchback is encountered at 1.6 miles. The trail passes beneath frequent long rhododendron tunnels; the abundance of vegetation precludes good views from this altitude, but at about 2.0 miles the hiker is offered one of the few glimpses into the valley below. The trail crosses small streams at 2.8 (spring), 3.0, and 3.6 miles.

The trail crosses an abandoned dirt road at 4.0 miles with the foundation of an old Civilian Conservation Corps shelter nearby. A bit further on, the concrete-block Curley Maple Gap AT shelter with a corrugated metal roof nestles beside the trail. It accommodates six people, and a spring is 100 feet south on the AT. The spring may be disappointingly stagnant at first, but you will find running water by following the stream downhill where it becomes Jones Branch after several confluences. The fall of the stream is rapid away from the trail, and soon it becomes audible only in the distance. The trail plays catch-up by means of switchbacks at 5.0 and 5.3 miles, enabling the hiker to rock-hop across Jones Branch at mile 5.5. Leucothoe, nettles, and sedges become plentiful here in the narrow, flat valley. The nature of this narrow flood plain is responsible for occasional trail destruction by heavy rains. Five additional stream crossings are encountered at miles 5.7, 6.3, 6.6, 6.7, and 7.0—most of them aided by means of improved log bridges.

At 7.1 miles, the AT emerges from a rhododendron and hemlock forest onto a gravel road that borders the Nolichucky Expeditions Base Camp and turns right away from Jones Branch. Here is a junction with Nolichucky River Trail, well marked with a USFS sign that also carries the admonition "Dead End, 2 Miles." At 7.2 miles the AT abruptly turns right to cross a gully with the aid of a well-constructed footbridge, although there is no water in dry weather. At the end of this bridge, only a few yards from the boundary of the Nolichucky Expeditions property, a sign invites you to visit their camp store.

From the bridge the AT gradually climbs a steep ridge while running parallel to Nolichucky River and to the paved road leading to Nolichucky Expeditions Base Camp. The river is continuously visible due to the steepness of the terrain. The AT eventually levels out and traverses a couple of small swampy areas where old railroad ties provide stepping stones. After crossing the Clinchfield Railroad tracks at 8.3 miles, the AT descends easily to the paved road and Nolichucky River at 8.4 miles. Here a new (1991) two-lane bridge with protected walkway facilitates the AT crossing of Nolichucky River. Although the Jones Branch section of the AT terminates here, the AT continues toward No Business Knob and an AT shelter.

Nolichucky River (Trail No. 157)
Length: 2.0 miles
Elevation Change: Start 1,720 feet, end 1,800 feet (high point 1,800 feet)
Trailhead: Nolichucky Expeditions Base Camp (start and dead-end)
Type: Hiking

Comments: This trail is an official USFS trail but for the most part should be considered only a crude manway as of the early 1990s. It is marked with yellow paint blazes and occasional yellow diamond-shaped sheet metal markers. The trail begins as a woods trail, leads to a riverside path, and gradually deteriorates to a rough scramble over scree and boulders. Since the trail generally follows the river's edge and frequently crosses sand bars, flood conditions of the Nolichucky River can be expected to inundate the footpath. Flooding can especially be expected during the months of March, April, May, and possibly August. The Nolichucky River is quite scenic along the trail, with no roads and only a railroad on the other side. The trail begins at a sign on the AT located less than 0.1 mile from the Nolichucky Expeditions Base Camp.

Details: From its junction with the AT, the trail leads through a short wooded area and passes along the rear boundary of Nolichucky Campground before descending to Nolichucky River at 0.2 mile. The trail then follows a well-used riverside path that leads to several vantage points for watching canoes and rafts as they negotiate river rapids. Alder thickets are frequent along the trail, interspersed with rhododendron, willow, dog hobble, and an occasional hemlock. Poison ivy is common in some places. Flowering spurge, crested dwarf iris, joe-pye-weed, and cardinal flower will be observed in season.

The trail traverses a number of sand bars. Where these are large enough to accommodate boating parties, piles of beverage cans may have accumulated. Variety is provided by the occasional scramble up the steep hillside because of impenetrable thickets, and sometimes the trail calls for a scramble over large boulders near the river's edge. The trail gradually degenerates into a rough manway, which in turn becomes less and less distinct, especially beyond 1.3 miles. The trail's route may thereafter be followed on up the river to the TN-NC state line at 2.0 miles. This last portion of the trail should, however, be considered off-trail hiking. Simply proceed upriver, always keeping the river within sight and sound.

11. SAMPSON MOUNTAIN WILDERNESS AND PRIMITIVE AREA

The 8,319-acre Sampson Mountain Wilderness and the adjacent 6,324-acre Primitive Area are rugged and beautiful. They are dominated by very steep slopes and drained by swift-flowing, rock-bottomed streams. A number of impressive, precipitous, and very high falls and cascades occur in the Areas. The most outstanding of these are the 475-foot-high Buckeye Falls and the 200-foot-high Painter Creek Falls. Although a portion of these falls would probably more accurately be classified as cascades, they are nonetheless very impressive, especially when water flow is plentiful. Some accounts claim Buckeye Falls to be the highest waterfall in the eastern United States. The Areas are located in Washington, Unicoi, and Greene counties and the Unaka and Nolichucky ranger districts.

Wildlife is varied and abundant in the Areas. The Sampson Mountain Wilderness, along with the Bald Mountain Ridge Scenic Area and adjacent USFS areas, is probably the best bear habitat north of the GSMNP in TN. Black bear or their sign is frequently seen, despite heavy hunting pressure. Trout fishing is excellent in several of the swift-flowing, rock-bottomed streams.

The Sampson Mountain Wilderness and Primitive Area is a portion of an outstanding outdoor recreation area, adjacent to the 8,653-acre Bald Mountain Ridge Scenic Area and the AT Corridor. A large protected USFS area also lies across the AT in NC. Balds, high cliffs, and rock outcrops afford magnificent views of the TN Valley to the west and the mountains of NC to the east.

The Areas are covered in second-growth forest, having been logged in the early part of the century and extensively burned. However, a number of large trees can be found in the Areas. A wide diversity of shrubs is also found, including laurel, rhododendron, flame azalea, and blueberry. There is also an excellent variety of wildflowers, such as violets, bloodroot, anemone, trillium, lady's-slipper, showy orchis, and foamflowers. There have been few botanical surveys in the Areas, but rare species found outside the Areas probably also occur in the Areas. These species include turkeybeard, long-flowered alumroot, and Buckleya.

The trail system in the Areas is in great need of maintenance and expansion. Many of the trails lead up creek valleys and gradually fade out, going nowhere. Confusing old roadbeds that go nowhere lead off the main trails. Few circuit hikes are possible at this time because of the lack of trail connections. Despite these limitations, the Areas have high potential for future trail development and improvement. There are several opportunities to connect trails that would take relatively little construction. If these connecting trails were built, some present trails extended and maintained, and the confusing maze of old roadbeds allowed to fade under the vegetation, the Areas could have an excellent trail system tying into the AT and the adjoining Bald Mountain Ridge Scenic Area.

HISTORY

Much of the Areas was logged in the 1930s. Signs of logging roads can still be seen, especially on the lower slopes of the Clark Creek watershed. In 1952 a large section was burned to the mineral soil. Some timber-salvage operations took place after the fire. Another fire in 1981, the Painter Creek fire, burned 1,600 acres. These past abuses are still somewhat in evidence, but the Areas have greatly recovered and the streams run clear and sparkling.

The Sampson Mountain Wilderness was designated by the US Congress in 1986. The Sampson Mountain Primitive Area was designated in 1988 in the CNF Management Plan. Unlike most primitive areas, motor vehicles are allowed on one dirt road into the Sampson Mountain Primitive Area; timber harvesting will not be allowed.

TRAILHEADS AND MAPS

Access to the trails in Sampson Mountain Wilderness is from TN 107. Take it east from the junction with the US 11E bypass in Greeneville. Go through Tusculum and cross the Elbert Kinser Bridge at 4.0 miles.

Horse Creek Recreation Area Trailhead

At 6.7 miles along TN 107, turn right onto FS 94 at a National Forest Recreation Site sign immediately before several dumpsters. A sign for Horse Creek Recreation Area appears 0.3 mile along the road. There is another Horse Creek Recreation sign at 0.8 mile, when the road takes a sharp right. At 2.8 miles enter USFS land and pass the turnoff to Old Forge Campground at 2.9 miles. Horse Creek Campground is on the left. After you pass the campground, the pavement ends in a parking and picnic area that provides access to Squibb Creek Trail, Turkey Pen Cove Trail, and Middle Spring Ridge Trail as well as much of Bald Mountain Ridge Scenic Area.

Cassi Creek Trailhead

At mile 11.4 on TN 107, turn right on Maple Swamp Road. Go 1.1 miles until Maple Swamp Road intersects Cassi Creek Road (County 5404) and Liberty Creek Drive. Go straight through the intersection onto Cassi Creek Road. Stay on Cassi Creek Road until the pavement ends at 3.2 miles. A wide place in the road provides limited parking on the right before the dirt road crosses a small creek. To hike the Cassi Creek Trail continue up the road, which gradually narrows into a trail.

Painter Creek Road Trailhead

At mile 12.2 on TN 107, turn right on Painter Creek Road. Continue on it for 2.0 miles. At 2.0 miles a parking area on the right can accommodate several cars. The pavement ends, and a gate blocks the road at 2.1 miles. To hike the Painter Creek Trail, walk around the gate and continue up the road.

Sallys Hole, Hell Hollow Trail, Sill Branch Road, and Clark Creek Road Trailheads

At mile 15.4 on TN 107, turn right on Clark Creek Road just before TN 107 crosses Clark Creek. The pavement ends at the boundary to CNF, but continue along the gravel road (FS 25). Near the boundary, about 1.6 miles from TN 107, the road crosses Clark Creek on a bridge. The trailhead to the Sallys Hole Trail (No. 109) is just across the bridge to the left of the road; look for a trail marker. At 2.8 miles, the Hell Hollow Trail (No. 124) begins on the right side of the road just after a side stream comes in from the right. It begins as a dirt road that angles up to the right.

After approximately 3.4 miles an old dirt road leads off to the left, but access is blocked by large rocks. This road was formerly the Sill Branch Road, FS 25A. It follows Sill Branch for approximately 0.5 miles to the confluence of the North Fork and the South Fork of Sill Branch. Sill Branch Trail and Sill Branch Spur Trail begin at the confluence.

Continuing up Clark Creek Road, at 4.2 miles the road ends at rock barricades just before a crossing of Clark Creek. This is the Clark Creek Road Trailhead. An ORV road formerly continued up Clark Creek but is now the initial portion of Clark Creek Trail.

Topographic Maps: Greystone, TN-NC; Flag Pond, TN-NC; Telford, TN.

TRAIL DESCRIPTIONS

Squibb Creek (Trail No. 23)
Length: 2.2 miles
Elevation Change: Start 1,920 feet, end 2,800 feet (high point 2,800 feet)
Trailhead: Horse Creek Road (start and dead-end)
Trail Connections: Turkey Pen Cove Trail and Middle Spring Ridge Trail
Type: Hiking

Comments: The Squibb Creek Trail follows Squibb Creek to a lovely waterfall. The trail dead-ends at this point, but Turkey Pen Cove Trail and Middle Spring Ridge Trail lead off of Squibb Creek Trail. In fact, USGS topographic maps label Middle Spring Ridge Trail as part of Squibb Creek Trail. However, these topographic maps do not show a trail extending up Squibb Creek, nor do they show Turkey Pen Cove Trail. This guide will adopt the new names used by the USFS on signs in the Areas.

Details: Take the Horse Creek Road that begins at the parking area near Horse Creek Campground and follows Horse Creek upstream. After 0.12 mile, look for a wooden bridge across Horse Creek and a sign for Squibb Creek Trail. The Squibb Creek Trail begins at the bridge.

Cross Horse Creek on the bridge and parallel Squibb Creek along the left bank. At 0.2 mile on the Squibb Creek Trail another wooden bridge takes the trail to the right bank of the creek. At 0.3 mile the trail crosses another wooden bridge to the left side of the creek. At 0.4 mile the trail emerges into a clearing that contains an A-frame cabin. The cabin is on a parcel of private land within the National Forest. Note the double yellow blazes on the tree to the left of the cabin. Cross in front of the cabin and note another set of double blazes. Angle to the right down to the creek, cross the creek, and continue upstream on the right side of the creek. At 0.49 mile

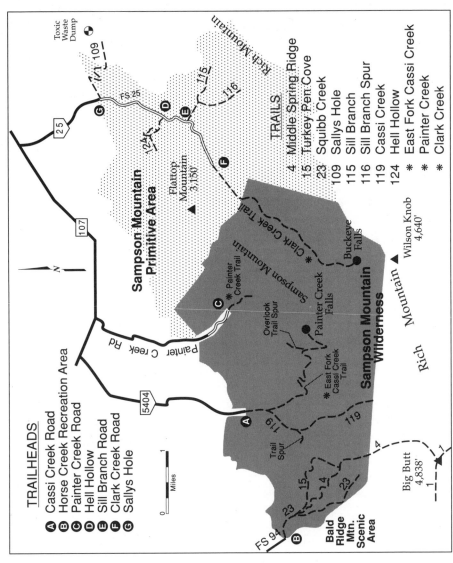

Sampson Mountain
Wilderness and
Primitive Area.

cross back to the left side of the creek. At 0.54 mile cross a side stream that comes in from the left. At 0.56 mile cross another stream that comes in from the left. The trail then skirts through the edge of the stream. Across the stream is a sign designating the Turkey Pen Cove Trail: "Turkey Pen Cove, 1.75 Miles." It also has arrows pointing up the trail for "Middle Spring Ridge Trail, .1 Mile," and "Squibb Creek Trail." Squibb Creek Trail climbs out of the streambed and cuts back toward Squibb Creek. At 0.6 mile note double blazes. A few steps past the blazes, look closely for the Middle Spring Ridge Trail as it turns left up over a mound.

To continue on Squibb Creek Trail follow the yellow blazes up Squibb Creek. At 0.9 mile the trail crosses Squibb Creek to the right bank, and at 1.2 miles the trail crosses back to the left side. Look for double blazes at 1.3 miles; the trail turns sharply left up the bank. After this point the trail may be difficult to follow unless it has had recent maintenance. Continue following the creek as the trail crosses it several times. Watch for yellow blazes. At 2.2 miles the trail ends at a small waterfall.

Turkey Pen Cove (Trail No. 15)
Length: 1.8 miles
Elevation Change: Start 2,000 feet, end 3,440 feet (high point 3,440 feet)
Trailheads: Squibb Creek Trail (start) and Middle Spring Ridge Trail (end)
Type: Hiking

Comments: The Turkey Pen Cove Trail leaves the Squibb Creek Trail and travels up Turkey Pen Cove Branch. It then ascends a side ridge of Middle Spring Ridge and intersects the Middle Spring Ridge Trail 0.57 mile from the Wilderness boundary. It appears to follow an old road for part of its length, but the section going up the ridge appears to be new. The trail is yellow blazed. You will need to watch carefully for the blazes because the trail itself is difficult to follow in places.

Details: Take the Squibb Creek Trail for 0.56 miles. After crossing a tributary that comes in from the left, skirt through the edge of the stream, looking for a sign across the stream that says: "Turkey Pen Cove Trail, 1.75 Miles; Middle Spring Ridge Trail, .1 Mile; Squibb Creek Trail." To take the Turkey Pen Cove Trail, cross the stream and follow the yellow blazes.

The trail starts on the left bank of the stream and passes through rhododendron, hemlock, and hardwoods. At 0.2 mile cross to the right side of the stream. In places the trail is overgrown with rhododendron. After 0.34 mile, the trail heads uphill into a narrow cove on an old roadbed. At 0.42 mile the trail leaves the roadbed, angles to the right across the slope above the stream, and crosses a small side stream at 0.48 mile. The trail then descends to cross the main stream at 0.51 mile. At

0.56 mile cross the stream back to the right side and continue upstream on an old roadbed. In this section blazes are few and the trail confusing, so follow directions carefully and watch closely for blazes.

At 0.6 mile the trail appears to fork. Take the right-hand fork; the left fork fades out and disappears quickly. The trail crosses a side branch that comes in from the right at 0.63 mile. Bear right along the left bank of this tributary. The other tributary is off to the left through thick rhododendron, running roughly parallel to the one you are following. At 0.75 mile the trail crosses the stream to the right side and heads up the slope away from the stream into more open forest. Look for blazes at 0.9 mile and 0.92 mile. Cross back to the left of the small stream near its source at 1.05 miles and traverse the slope. Between 1.13 and 1.33 miles the trail goes through a series of switchbacks as it goes up the side of the ridge through pines. At 1.39 miles the trail passes over the point of the ridge and heads up the left side of the ridge and then along the ridgeline. There are spectacular views along this section. At 1.57 miles the trail goes up steeply over rock outcrops with great views to the northeast. The trail continues to travel along the ridgecrest as it levels out. The trail intersects the Middle Spring Ridge Trail at 1.8 miles. To the right 1.45 miles is the intersection with the Squibb Creek Trail; to the left about 2.2 miles is Big Butt.

Middle Spring Ridge (Trail No. 4)
Length: 3.6 miles
Elevation Change: Start 2,000 feet, end 4,838 feet (high point 4,838 feet)
Trailheads: Squibb Creek Trail (start) and AT (end)
Type: Hiking

Comments: This trail ascends Middle Spring Ridge between Squibb Creek and Turkey Pen Cove. The trail quickly ascends to the ridgecrest, which it follows as it climbs to Rich Mountain. The trail exits Sampson Mountain Wilderness at 2.0 miles, but the trail itself can be followed to Big Butt. Much of the land outside the Wilderness is presently in private ownership. The trail is not blazed. It is not difficult to follow in the Wilderness, but the privately owned land is laced with old roads and trails that make finding the way difficult. Actually getting to Big Butt and connecting to the AT require cutting through a blueberry heath that separates the end of the trail from the AT.

Details: Take the Squibb Creek Trail for 0.6 mile. After crossing a tributary that comes in from the left, skirt through the edge of the stream, looking for a sign across the stream that says: "Turkey Pen Cove Trail, 1.75 Miles; Middle Spring Ridge Trail, 0.1 Mile; Squibb Creek Trail." To take the Middle Spring Ridge Trail, continue past the sign away from the creek as the trail climbs slightly. Seventy yards past the sign, look for double yellow blazes beside the trail. Shortly after seeing the double blazes, look for a trail that leaves Squibb Creek Trail and goes over a small mound to the left. This is the Middle Spring Ridge Trail. One tenth of a mile up the trail is a game clearing. The trail ascends steeply through rhododendron. Turkey Pen Cove Branch can be heard to the left. The trail continues to climb through tulip trees, maples, and hemlock. A group of particularly large hemlocks can be found at 0.3 mile. The trail levels off somewhat through pine forest. Views into the Squibb Creek Gorge can be seen at 0.8 mile. The trail goes through a series of switchbacks from 1.0 mile to 1.2 miles and then steeply ascends the ridgecrest. The grade gradually lessens, and the Turkey Pen Cove Trail intersects as a side ridge joins the main ridge at 1.45 miles. The trail continues to follow the ridge as it gradually climbs. At 2.06 miles a sign designates the Wilderness boundary. At 2.34 miles the trail comes out of thick mountain laurel into a small clearing. A roadbed leads to the left and the right. To the left, the old roadbed leads down into the Cassi Creek drainage before fading out.

Continue to the right along the roadbed, which intersects another road at 2.37 miles. To the left the road dead-ends after 0.3 mile. Turn right on the road and continue uphill. The road reaches a large clearing of exposed ground on the rounded point of the ridge. At the beginning of the clearing, to the right, is a trail that leads 1.1 miles across the headwaters of Squibb Creek before ending on a knob near the boundary between Sampson Mountain Wilderness and Bald Mountain Ridge Scenic Area. Water is available 0.2 mile down this trail. To reach Big Butt, continue through the bare area and pick up the jeep trail on the far side. The trail goes through switchbacks at 2.6 and 2.7 miles. At the second switchback continue on the middle jeep trail. The other jeep trail leads toward Wilson Knob. Switchbacks at 3.0 miles and 3.1 miles bring the trail to the ridgeline. Continue along the ridgeline to a clear area at 3.3 miles. Pass through a rock pile at 3.5 miles. A bald covered with blueberries is reached at 3.6 miles. There is no sign of the trail here. To reach Big Butt, a 4,838-foot knoll, and the AT, you will have to make your way through the thick growth of blueberries to the southwest. A few hundred yards of this will bring you to the clearings of Big Butt, which connect to the AT. To the right (southwest) along the AT are the Coldspring Mountain Parking Area, Horse Creek Road (FS 94), and Sarvis Cove Trail, all within the Bald Ridge Mountain Scenic Area.

Cassi Creek (Trail No. 119)

Length: 2.5 miles
Elevation Change: Start 1,800 feet, end 2,600 feet (high point 2,600 feet)
Trailhead: Cassi Creek Road (start and dead-end)
Trail Connections: East Fork Cassi Creek Trail
Type: Hiking

Comments: The Cassi Creek Trail follows Cassi Creek to the confluence of the stream's West and East forks. It then follows the West Fork of Cassi Creek until the Middle Fork of Cassi Creek branches off. A section of the Cassi Creek Trail continues a short distance up the West Fork before fading out. This section could be made to connect to the Turkey Pen Cove Trail. Another section of the Cassi Creek Trail continues up the Middle Fork before fading out. It could connect to the Middle Spring Ridge Trail. The trail has been blazed recently.

Details: At the point where the Cassi Creek Road ends at a wide place in the road (which has been used as a dump), continue on the old roadbed. Cross a small tributary stream. Follow yellow blazes past dirt barriers. At 0.3 mile the trail goes up a streambed. At 0.35 mile cross Cassi Creek to a gravel bar, go upstream on the gravel bar a few yards, and then cross back to the right side of Cassi Creek. At 0.43 mile cross West Fork Cassi Creek. The East Fork Cassi Creek Trail bears left and follows the East Fork Cassi Creek. The Cassi Creek Trail turns right along the West Fork. A hiker's sign can be seen a few feet down the trail. Follow yellow blazes up the creek and cross the creek at 0.5 mile. At 1.0 mile the trail crosses the creek to the left side. Shortly afterwards a hiker's sign is seen where the trail branches.

One of the trail sections turns right across the creek and follows the West Fork Cassi Creek, with yellow blazes, for about 0.25 mile before fading out. Another 0.5 mile in the direction the trail is heading would connect it with the Turkey Pen Cove Trail.

The other section of the trail continues up the Middle Fork of Cassi Creek for another 1.4 miles. Continuing on this section of the trail, which is also marked with yellow blazes, the creek is crossed several times. At 1.5 miles an old roadbed comes in from the right. Continue to follow the yellow blazes as the trail crosses the creek several times, heading upstream. The trail passes through a lovely valley, which then narrows. The last blaze is seen at 2.45 miles, and the trail soon ends at 2.5 miles. Old roadbeds can be seen, but these quickly fade out. There is potential to link this trail with the Middle Spring Ridge Trail, but the trail at this point lies out of the Sampson Mountain Wilderness Area on land that is presently under private ownership.

East Fork Cassi Creek (No USFS Number)
Length: 3.4 miles
Elevation Change: Start 1,880 feet, end 2,720 feet (high point 2,920 feet)
Trailhead: Cassi Creek Trail (start and dead-end)
Type: Hiking

Comments: The East Fork Cassi Creek Trail connects the Cassi Creek drainage with the Painter Creek drainage. This trail, as is the case with most of the trails in the Areas, needs development and integration into a trail system that makes overall sense. At present it is not included in the CNF trail system. The trail itself, as far as it goes, is in fairly good condition and is not hard to follow. However, it does not connect with Painter Creek Trail and is not marked or blazed. A car shuttle can be made between Cassi Creek and Painter Creek but requires crossing a section of difficult terrain. The East Cassi Creek Trail ends 0.25 mile above Painter Creek Falls; Painter Creek Trail does not begin until about 1.25 miles below the falls.

Painter Creek Falls is a lovely falls of about 200 feet. As with Buckeye Falls, some of this distance might be classified a cascade. Waterflow is considerably greater than Buckeye Falls. The falls itself should be approached with extreme caution. According to a local resident, at least two people have lost their lives in accidents on Painter Creek Falls.

Details: East Fork Cassi Creek Trail begins at the confluence of the West and East Forks of Cassi Creek. After crossing West Fork Cassi Creek on the Cassi Creek Trail, bear left up the right bank of East Cassi Creek on an old roadbed. After about 150 feet, cross the creek to the left side. The trail crosses the creek again at 300 feet and thereafter five times between 0.1 and 0.7 mile as it gradually gains elevation. The trail is on the left of the creek at 0.8 mile when it turns sharply to the left (north) away from the creek and begins to climb the slope. The old roadbed that the trail follows parallels a branch of East Cassi Creek that is below to the left. At 1.0 mile an old roadbed comes in from the left; it goes down toward the branch before fading out. The trail itself bears to the east. At 1.14 miles the trail turns to the southeast and begins to circle the point of a ridge. By 1.5 miles the trail has come back around to the east and is going downhill with the branch getting closer on the left. At 1.7 miles the trail crosses the branch and turns to the northeast going uphill. The trail climbs the slope through pine, laurel, and rhododendron.

At 1.9 miles the trail, which had been heading north and northwest, switches back to the east and parallels the section of the trail below. The trail turns southeast and then south before switching back to the northeast through young pines at 2.3 miles. The trail enters a gap at 2.4 miles. Two other trails leave the gap. One leads uphill to the north and goes 0.38 mile to the top of a knob. The other trail goes downhill to the south toward Painter Creek. The trail to the south descends quickly and reaches Painter Creek at 2.8 miles. Cross Painter Creek and follow it downstream. A side stream comes in from the right at 2.9 miles. Cross the creek to the left bank just before they join. Cross the creek to the right side at 3.05 miles and back to the left side at 3.2 miles. The trail, which had been following an old roadbed, narrows and by 3.4

miles has faded out completely. To reach Painter Creek Falls, continue downstream along the creek for 0.25 mile. Approach cautiously, as the terrain falls off precipitously. The safest descent past the falls appears to be off to the left of the falls. Painter Creek Trail can be picked up 1.25 miles downstream from the falls (or 1.5 miles downstream from the end of East Cassi Creek Trail). There are stretches along the creek that appear to be trail; other sections require struggling through rhododendron.

Painter Creek (No USFS Number)
Length: 1.1 mile
Elevation Change: Start 1,760 feet, end 1,960 feet (high point 1,960 feet)
Trailhead: Painter Creek Road (start and dead-end)
Type: Hiking

Comments: The Painter Creek Trail, in its present form, leads only a portion of the distance up Painter Creek toward Painter Creek Falls. To reach the falls you will need to continue up the stream for another 1.25 miles. There are stretches along the creek that appear to be remnants of a trail or to be trail worn by people traveling to the falls. Other stretches are difficult to negotiate because of thick rhododendron. After the trail ends, the terrain also climbs appreciably. The creek climbs to approximately 2,400 feet at the foot of the 200-foot falls. Extreme caution should be taken at the falls; at least two people have died here. At present this trail is not included in the CNF trail system.

Relatively little trail construction would be required to make a loop between Cassi Creek and Painter Creek. An extension of the Painter Creek Trail by 1.25 miles up Painter Creek would reach the falls; a section only 0.25 mile from the end of East Cassi Creek Trail would also reach the falls, so that the two trails could tie in together. In its present state, cross-country hiking is required to reach the falls or make the loop from the East Cassi Creek Trail.

Details: Parking for several cars can be found to the right of Painter Creek Road shortly before it ends at a gate. To take the trail, continue past a house on the right and through the gate. The pavement ends at the gate. Continue up the road. At 0.2 mile turn left off the main road and skirt the left side of a large meadow. The road leads to a house on the other side of the meadow. At 0.3 mile you pass a barn as you enter the forest. At 0.34 miles cross Painter Creek to the right side. Cross the creek four times between 0.41 and 0.54 mile. Continue up the right side of the creek. At 0.9 mile cross the creek to the left side and then cross a side stream that comes in from the left and continue up the creek. At 1.06 miles the roadbed narrows and the trail gradually fades out. To continue, cross another tributary stream that comes in from the left at 1.2 miles. Continue up the creek, crossing when necessary to find better terrain. Sections of the creek are easy to negotiate, with the trail being worn by hikers coming up the creek; other sections are choked with rhododendron and are difficult. At 2.25 miles the foot of Painter Creek Falls is reached. East Cassi Creek Trail can be found 0.25 mile up the creek. The safest route seems to be to skirt the falls far to the right. Extreme caution should be exercised, as the terrain slopes steeply in this area.

Clark Creek (No USFS Number)

Length: 3.6 miles
Elevation Change: Start 1,840 feet, end 3,000 feet (high point 3,000 feet)
Trailhead: Clark Creek Road (start and dead-end)
Type: Hiking

Comments: The Clark Creek Trail leads up Clark Creek, which is a swift-flowing, rock-bottomed stream with numerous cascades and clear pools. Numerous creek crossings are required, but the stream's low volume often allows rock hopping. The trail is a good one for seeing wildflowers, especially large-flowered trillium. On the headwaters of one of the branches of Clark Creek lies Buckeye Falls. Buckeye Falls is at least 475 feet high and by some accounts is the highest falls in the eastern United States. Strictly speaking, much of this height is a cascade and not a true waterfall. Water volume is never great, and it is difficult to see the whole falls at one time because of the great height involved. Nevertheless, Buckeye Falls is spectacular, especially when the stream is running full. Great caution should be taken around this falls, as is true with all waterfalls. This trail is not currently a part of the CNF trail system.

Details: Park at the end of Clark Creek Road near some rock barriers to ORVs. Immediately cross the first stream ford. Continue up the old road as it parallels Clark Creek and crosses the creek four more times. At 0.8 mile a side trail comes in from the right. Continue left, in the direction of a red arrow painted on a tree, as the right-hand road is a dead-end. Continue along the creek, which is crossed two more times. After the first crossing, climb over a series of earth berms and enter the Wilderness. It is marked by a wooden sign and, on up the trail after the second crossing, a trail register. At 1.3 miles the trail climbs steeply above the creek to the right. At 1.5 miles the jeep trail ends at dirt barriers and a foot trail continues above the creek.

Descend steeply to the creek and cross to the left side at 2.0 miles. An alternate is to continue 100 feet on the right, and then cross. Continue up the creek, which at this point forms numerous clear pools with a solid rock bottom. The trail becomes rough and rocky. Cross the creek numerous times, as the trail continues up the creek. Look for a small and deep triangular pool that is perfect for a summer swim. An old engine block is located at 3.0 miles but may be hard to spot. Shortly afterwards, the trail follows a ridge in the middle of the creek before crossing a few more times and then going up the middle of the creek. Look for a branch coming in from the left at about 3.2 miles; note a red arrow painted on a tree. At 3.4 miles another branch comes in from the left. Look for red painted arrows on two trees; a faint trail continues up Clark Creek. Turn left and hike up the branch. You will begin to see a cascade ahead after about 0.1 mile, and then Buckeye Falls. The trail becomes indistinct as it follows the creek and is very steep. At 3.6 miles you will reach the base of the falls. Although the water volume is not great, the falls are quite impressive. A huge exposed amphitheater-like rock wall spreads across the mountain. On the right side the cascades tumble down from far above. The view of the upper portion of the falls is blocked by vegetation. A view of the upper reaches of the falls can be had from the ridge to the right of the falls. However, this is not recommended because the slope leading up to the ridge is very steep and unstable. At least one person has been injured coming down this slope. Wilson Knob lies at the top of this ridge above Buckeye Falls.

Sallys Hole (Trail No. 109)
Length: 2.0 miles
Elevation Change: Start 1,580 feet, end 2,400 feet (high point 2,400 feet)
Trailhead: Sallys Hole (start and dead-end)
Type: Hiking

Comments: The Sallys Hole Trail climbs up Furnace Stack Hollow to a gap in Embreeville Mountain. It then descends into Bumpus Cove, which is a closed toxic-waste landfill on the Superfund List. It is recommended that you hike only as far as the gap on Embreeville Mountain. In 1991 the CNF deleted this trail from their official trails system.

Details: Park on the left of the road shortly after driving over the bridge near the USFS boundary; look for the trail marker. The trail goes up the creekbed to the left of the road. The creek is crossed many times as the trail continues up the stream. After 0.5 mile the trail turns sharply to the right at a yellow diamond trail marker on a beech tree. The trail leaves the creek and goes uphill past several large hemlocks and pines. At 0.8 mile the trail reaches the crest of a pine-covered ridge. There are nice views back into the Clark Creek Valley. At 1.2 miles continue straight past an old logging road. A few yards past this road is an intersection. Two logging roads turn off to the right; one logging road turns off to the left. The trail to Bumpus Cove continues straight ahead. The trail reaches the back of Bumpus Cove at 2.0 miles, but this route is not recommended because of aesthetic and health concerns.

Hell Hollow (Trail No. 124)
Length: 0.9 mile
Elevation Change: Start 1,720 feet, end 2,400 feet (high point 2,400 feet)
Trailhead: Hell Hollow (start and dead-end)
Type: Hiking

Comments: The Hell Hollow Trail follows the stream of Hell Hollow up the east flank of Sampson Mountain. As one would expect from the name, the trail travels through dense rhododendron and laurel stands. There is potential for extending this trail to Flattop (elevation 3,150) on Sampson Mountain and for connecting it to trails in the Sampson Mountain Wilderness.

Details: At 2.8 miles on the Clark Creek Road, look for a creek coming in from the right (west). Park on the right of the road. Head due west on the left side of the creek up a dirt road. At 0.2 mile cross the creek to the right and head rather steeply uphill through laurel thickets. At 0.7 mile head downhill through pines. Cross the creek to the left side at 0.8 mile and turn to the right up the creek. The trail continues up the creek through hemlock and laurel but fades out at about 0.9 mile.

Sill Branch (Trail No. 115)
Length: 0.6 mile
Elevation Change: Start 1,960 feet, end 2,400 feet (high point 2,400 feet)
Trailhead: Sill Branch Road (start and dead-end)
Type: Hiking

Comments: USFS has closed the Sill Branch Road, and its 0.5-mile distance should be added to the trail mileage. Hike up the former road to a trail junction. Follow the trail leading up the left-hand fork (North Fork) of Sill Branch. The Sill Branch Trail follows the North Fork of Sill Branch uphill for about 0.6 mile. Some old maps show a road leading further up Rich Mountain, and it may be possible to follow the old roadbed further up the mountain.

Sill Branch Spur (Trail No. 116)
Length: 0.8 mile
Elevation Change: Start 1,960 feet, end 2,400 feet (high point 2,400 feet)
Trailhead: Sill Branch Road (start and dead-end)
Type: Hiking

Comments: USFS has closed the Sill Branch Road, and its 0.5-mile distance should be added to the trail mileage. Hike up the former road to a trail junction. Follow the trail leading up the right-hand fork (South Fork) of Sill Branch. The Sill Branch Spur Trail follows the South Fork of Sill Branch uphill for about 0.8 mile. The USFS may close the Sill Branch Road, in which case its 0.5-mile distance should be added to the trail mileage.

12. BALD MOUNTAIN RIDGE SCENIC AREA

The Bald Mountain Ridge Scenic Area covers 8,653 acres of the CNF (Nolichucky Ranger District) in Greene County, TN, including the steep western side of the Bald Mountains as they rise some 3,000 feet above the valley floor. The Area is rather rugged for the most part, with many rocky exposures and cliffs fringing the upper slopes of Bald Mountain Ridge. Some of these cliffs offer outstanding views of the TN Valley, such as those near the end of the Horse Creek Road, and the magnificent Blackstack Cliffs on the AT.

Most of the trails into the Area follow one of the four major drainages that dissect the main ridge. The streams are not very large, but the trails cross them repeatedly (without the benefit of footbridges) because the steepness of the narrow valley walls leaves little space for both stream and trail. As the streams near the main ridge, they rapidly steepen and numerous small waterfalls and cascades are found along most of the trails. Care must be followed when hiking several of these trails up to the AT, for although they are marked with yellow or blue blazes, they are rarely used, very steep, and have not received maintenance in several years. In summertime the upper reaches of the Sarvis Cove, Artie Hollow, and Phillips Hollow trails should not be attempted without a topographical map and compass.

The Area is covered with a young to middle-aged, second-growth forest, with some large cove hardwoods found in the sheltered hollows. The Area has many fine examples of open oak forests on the high ridges, especially above Round Knob and along the AT. Closed oak forests, rich in mountain laurel, rhododendron, blueberry, and flame azalea are especially common on the dry, rocky, south-facing slopes of the lower foothills of Green Ridge, Greystone Mountain, and Reynolds Ridge. Some of this dry forest was ravaged by fires in the drought years of the late 1980s.

The ruggedness of the terrain in the Area makes it prime habitat for reclusive animals, such as wild turkey, ruffed grouse, fox, and black bear. The region around Sarvis Cove and Horse Creek is designated by the TWRA as a bear preserve. Scheduled bear hunts with dogs are conducted in early winter. Check with the USFS before attempting a hike in November and December to avoid these hunts.

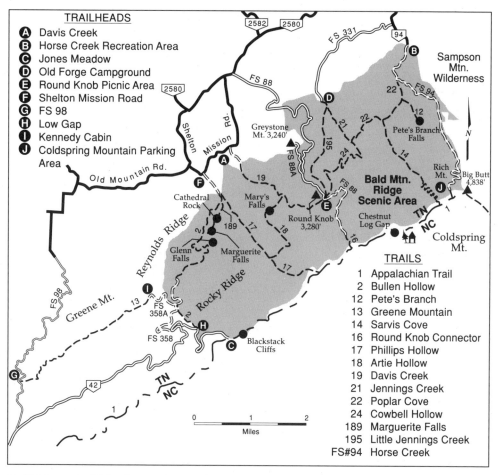

Bald Mountain Ridge Scenic Area.

HISTORY

The Area was extensively clear-cut until it was acquired by the USFS about 1930.
Evidence of logging remains on some trails, in the form of old rails, rotted rail ties, and
various metal debris. The ruggedness of the terrain generally spared the Area from
further harvesting until the present time. The Area has served as a favorite recreational area for local residents through the years, especially the swimming holes at
the campgrounds at Horse Creek and Old Forge, and the grassy balds on Coldspring

Mountain. The back-country trails, however, receive little use, affording a true wilderness experience. The Viking Mountain Resort, a failed resort venture at the southwestern corner of the area between Jones Meadow and Blackstack Cliffs, was auctioned in 1989 and purchased by the USFS; several homes and cottages there have been dismantled.

The Area is in the center of the former Jennings Creek RARE II area. The CNF Wilderness Coalition supported wilderness designation for this Area during the late 1970s and the RARE II process. However, in the early 1980s the USFS issued plans for major road construction and clear-cutting in the Area. This action was appealed by the Sierra Club, leading to amendments to the USFS's ambitious plan in 1983. The Sierra Club, in conjunction with the USFS, the Tennessee Conservation League, hunters' groups, and ORV organizations subsequently negotiated a settlement as to the fate of the Area. This led to designation of the Sampson Mountain Wilderness and the creation of the Bald Mountain Ridge Scenic Area from most of the old RARE II area's acreage. The compromise allowed some of the existing roads to remain open but stopped any future road construction and clear-cutting. The Scenic Area was designated in 1988 in the CNF Management Plan.

TRAILHEADS AND MAPS

Horse Creek Recreation Area
and Old Forge Campground Trailheads

Take TN 107 east out of Greeneville off US 11E. Follow TN 107 through Tusculum and across the Nolichucky River about 4.0 miles from Greeneville. Continue on TN 107 about 3.0 miles from the river and turn right onto County 94 (Horse Creek Road) at a USFS sign for the Horse Creek Recreation Area on the right, about 0.3 mile past the second intersection with TN 351. After about 0.8 mile the road takes a sharp right at an intersection. Look for the USFS sign. Just past the intersection Greystone Road enters from the right (west), leading to the trailheads at Round Knob and Shelton Mission Road (see below). The road bears right again at a rocky knoll and travels about 0.3 mile further to the Horse Creek Recreation Area at 2.7 miles from TN 107. The gravel road (FS 331) to Old Forge Campground enters from the right about 100 yards ahead. To the left is a parking lot for the swimming area. Straight ahead it is about 0.2 mile to the Horse Creek Campground and 0.5 mile to the trailhead for the Horse Creek and Squibb Mountain trails. To reach Old Forge Campground turn right (west) on FS 331 and follow it about 2.4 miles to its end at the Old Forge USFS Campground and the Little Jennings Creek and Jennings Creek trails.

Jennings Creek in Bald Mountain Ridge Scenic Area.
Photo by E. Kenneth McDonald.

Coldspring Mountain Parking Area Trailhead

The Coldspring Mountain Parking Area can be reached only by four-wheel-drive vehicle and is at the south end of FS 94, the Horse Creek Road, on Coldspring Mountain; FS 94 is often used as a trail and is described in the Trail Descriptions. It begins at the Horse Creek Recreation Area Trailhead described above and climbs up toward Coldspring Mountain along Horse Creek.

Round Knob Picnic Area and Shelton Mission and Trailheads

To get to both Round Knob Picnic Area and Shelton Mission Road trailheads, turn right (west) on Greystone Road as mentioned above (Greystone Road is on the Horse Creek Road, County 94, about 1.0 mile from the County 94-TN 107 junction). Bear left at the first intersection, passing a church on the right. The road curves around a knoll and passes Greystone F.W.B. Church about 3.3 miles from the road to Horse Creek. Follow the road over Jennings Creek at 3.4 miles (you are now on County 2580), then look for a gravel road on the left at 3.7 miles, just before crossing another creek (Water Fork). A USFS sign marks the location of the road (FS 88). Turn left on FS 88, which climbs 4.5 miles to the Round Knob Picnic Area and several trailheads. To reach Shelton Mission Road access, continue past the road to Round

Knob, passing a large piped spring on the left. Take the first paved road to the left, 0.25 mile from the road to Round Knob. This is Shelton Mission Road. Follow the road 1.25 miles to a stone foundation on the right. Directly across the road is the Davis Creek Trail Trailhead. There is a trail sign but very little room for parking. Continue along Shelton Mission Road, past Shelton Mission Church, reaching the Bullen Hollow Trail Trailhead 1.0 mile from the Davis Creek Trailhead, or 2.2 miles from the last intersection.

An alternate route to the Round Knob area is on TN 351. When proceeding east on TN 107, take the first right (south) onto TN 351 after crossing the Nolichucky River (Elbert Kinser Bridge). Take TN 351 for about 4.5 miles, taking the fourth left turn in the Bird Island Community. Follow the road 2.0 miles until it descends into another road and turn left. Follow this road about 3.2 miles to Shelton Mission Road or 3.5 miles to the gravel road to Round Knob. To the right, it is about 6.0 miles back to Greeneville along TN 350. After turning left, follow the road past a sand and gravel quarry at 2.0 miles from TN 351. Turn right at the next intersection, following signs to Greystone F.W.B. Church. At 3.2 miles from TN 351 you will pass the Greystone School. At 4.7 miles the Shelton Mission Road turns right. At 5.0 miles FS 88 turns right and proceeds up to the Round Knob Picnic Area.

FS 98 Trailhead

Take TN 70 east from Greeneville about 15 miles to unmarked Bald Mountain Road (County 42), which enters on the left just before the state line. There is a sign at the road for a summer camp, and a stone structure and the ruins of a chalet that once served as the entrance to a defunct development. If approaching from NC, take TN 208 to the TN-NC state line and look for County 42 about 0.5 mile from the state line on the right. Follow the paved County 42 1.6 miles; then turn left onto an unmarked, gravel road sometimes referred to as Greene Mountain Road (FS 98). Follow the gravel road 1.0 mile and look for a horse-trail sign on the right immediately before a hairpin turn to the right. There is parking space for a couple of cars along the roadside on the left shoulder of the road.

Kennedy Cabin, Low Gap, and Jones Meadow Trailheads

Three trailheads are located off the Bald Mountain Road (County 58), a poorly maintained county road, though usually passable by automobile, that provided access to the now defunct Viking Mountain development at Jones Meadow. Use the directions for the FS 98 Trailhead above to locate Bald Mountain Road. Continue on Bald Mountain Road for 2.7 miles past the FS 98 turnoff, at which point the road changes to a rough dirt road. Follow the dirt road 1.7 miles. To reach the Kennedy Cabin Trailhead turn left at this point on a gated USFS road (FS 358). Follow the dirt road 0.8 mile to an intersection, and bear left. The right fork leads approximately 50 yards to the upper section of the Bullen Hollow Trail. That trail leaves a saddle to the right, leading approximately 0.5 mile to Low Gap, while to the left of the saddle it follows the road about 0.75 mile before continuing as an ORV trail. To reach the Kennedy Cabin Trailhead, proceed on the left fork 0.7 mile, reaching a turnaround in a grassy clearing. The trailhead is to the left, marked by trail signs. There is ample space for parking.

To reach the other two trailheads, continue on the Bald Mountain Road for approximately 0.6 mile from FS 358 to an obvious gap. This is the Low Gap Trailhead, and the Bullen Hollow Trail begins on the left (west) side of the gap. The Jones Meadow Trailhead is reached by continuing on the Bald Mountain Road until it ends at Jones Meadow, where parking is available. Most of the failed development's land at Jones Meadow has been acquired by the USFS. To reach the AT, walk approximately 100 yards downhill from the parking area or walk up the gated road, past the ruins of cabins and a lodge, and along a dirt road that leads to the right of the clearly visible Blackstack Cliffs. That road meets the AT at a side trail leading about 100 yards to the cliffs.

Topographic Maps: Greystone, TN-NC; Davy Crockett Lake, TN-NC.

TRAIL DESCRIPTIONS

Horse Creek (Cold Spring Mountain) (FS 94)
Length: 4.7 miles
Elevation Change: Start 1,800 feet, end 4,550 feet (high point 4,550 feet)
Trailheads: Horse Creek Recreation Area (start) and Coldspring Mountain Parking Area (end)
Trail Connections: Poplar Cove Trail and Squibb Creek Trail
Type: Road

Comments: The Horse Creek Road (also known as Cold Spring Mountain Road) is, for the most part, an ORV road that provides access to the Horse Creek watershed, the AT near Big Butt, and fine views near its terminus on Coldspring Mountain. The road is wide, graded, and receives regular use by ORVs, especially during the summer, and you may want to avoid it during that period. It is otherwise a pleasant walk and may be used to create loop hikes. The road is gated near the AT, where there is a small parking area. No vehicles are allowed on the AT nor within an adjacent corridor. The road is not suitable for two-wheel-drive vehicles.

Details: The road begins near the entrance of the Horse Creek Campground, where there are ample parking, toilets, and drinking water. There is no trail sign, but the gravel jeep road is quite evident as it follows Horse Creek south away from the campground.

The road passes a foot-bridge leading to the Squibb Creek Trail before crossing Horse Creek at 0.1 mile. The Squibb Creek Trail and Middle Spring Ridge Trail can be used to reach the AT (see Sampson Mountain Wilderness, above). The road then follows Horse Creek through mature second-growth forest and among occasional sandstone outcrops. At 0.5 mile the road forks in a grove of white pine and hemlock. Take the left fork, which crosses the creek, then recrosses. At 0.8 mile the road forks again. Here the right fork is the Poplar Cove Trail, which leads to Jennings Creek on the AT via the Sarvis Cove Trail. The Horse Creek Road veers left along a rutted jeep road, climbing gently. At 1.6 miles the road enters a clearing among the sycamore, pine, and rhododendron. Note the large boulders of white quartzite. At 1.7 miles the road again crosses Horse Creek and continues climbing, leaving the stream. At 2.3 miles the road begins its ascent out of the valley at a wide switchback. The road climbs through a very young forest of pine, mountain laurel, and galax.

At about 3.0 miles an abandoned road enters from the right. The Horse Creek Road continues climbing, passing several small branches. The road skirts a boulder field at a switchback at 3.5 miles as the forest becomes rich in beech, birch, and hickory. The road climbs steadily through several switchbacks, passing boulders and outcrops of white quartzite. To the north, there are fine views of cliffs, and heath balds near the ridgecrest. The road flattens at 4.4 miles and arrives at a turnaround where a side trail to the right leads to a clifftop affording excellent views of the valley and ridge in the vicinity of Greeneville, as well as the entire Bald Mountain Ridge Scenic Area. The road continues past the turnaround, reaching a gate at 4.6 miles, where the road goes right to the Coldspring Mountain Parking Area. A trail continues uphill, reaching the junction with the AT at 4.7 miles. To the right (southwest) it is about 0.2 mile to the Sarvis Cove Trail and the grassy bald summit of Coldspring Mountain. To the left (northeast) it is 0.4 mile to the Middle Spring Ridge Trail near Big Butt (4,838 feet).

Sarvis Cove (Trail No. 14)
Length: 2.9 miles
Elevation Change: Start 2,320 feet, end 4,560 feet (high point 4,560 feet)
Trailheads: Poplar Cove Trail (start) and AT (end)
Type: Hiking

Comments: This trail provides a nice alternate route to the Horse Creek Road, which is heavily used by ORVs. The trail begins as a wide trail but is overgrown, steep, and hard to follow in its last mile. The trail generally follows an old logging road along Sarvis Creek, in a mature second-growth forest through Sarvis Cove. The upper reaches of the cove house a mature grove of fairly large oaks and hemlocks.

Details: The trail leaves the Poplar Creek Trail about 1.0 mile from the Horse Creek Road. There is no trail sign, but the Sarvis Cove Trail heads left (south) along the creek while the Poplar Creek Trail goes right (west), uphill.

Past the trail intersection, the trail ascends gently along the creek, tunneling through rhododendron in a young forest. Here the trail is wide and walking is pleasant. The trail begins to climb more steeply and crosses Sarvis Creek at 0.4 mile. The forest is largely mature hardwoods, rhododendron, and hemlock. Spring wildflowers grow in profusion in this rich wood. At 1.3 miles the trail crosses the stream again at the confluence of two branches. Note the rotting railroad bridge near a nice cascade in the main stream. The trail continues to ascend along the creek, passing a small waterfall at 1.4 miles and several smaller rapids and cascades. At about 1.8 miles you will reach another beautiful cascade down a moss-strewn cleft in the bedrock. At 2.0 miles the trail narrows and leaves the creek, beginning a steep ascent through a hemlock-dominated forest. The trail climbs through about 12 switchbacks and is poorly graded. The trail may be difficult to follow in summer, so look carefully for yellow blazes. The trail reaches the ridgecrest at 2.8 miles at a rocky crag of white quartzite on the left of the trail. Just past the rocks, a side trail leads to the parking lot at the end of the Horse Creek Road. The Sarvis Cove Trail continues 0.1 mile to meet the old AT at 2.9 miles. To the left the Horse Creek Road is about 0.2 mile. To the right is a nice bald area across which runs the recently relocated AT, marked by white blazes.

Bullen Hollow (Trail No. 2)
Length: 3.9 miles
Elevation Change: Start 1,860 feet, end 3,970 feet (high point 4,080 feet)
Trailheads: Shelton Mission Road (start) and Low Gap (end)
Trail Connections: Greene Mountain Trail and Marguerite Falls Trail
Type: Motorcycle

Comments: This wide, graded trail passes through a diverse assemblage of forest types, from a superb example of closed oak forest to a mature cove hardwood forest in lovely Bullen Hollow. The trail serves as the access to the Marguerite Falls Trail, a fascinating walk through a rugged, steep valley. This trail is unique among the trails in the Bald Mountain Ridge Scenic Area, for it climbs along the ridgetop instead of up the stream valley. Water is available at several locations, and potential campsites are located near the trailhead and in Bullen Hollow. The Bullen Hollow

Trail is presently designated by the USFS as an ORV trail. There have been efforts to reclassify it as a hiking trail by the Sierra Club and other conservation groups. Until and if it is reclassified, you may encounter ORVs on this trail.

Details: The trail begins on Shelton Mission Road about 2.6 miles from the intersection with Greystone Road. There is a trail sign marking the trailhead on the left of Shelton Mission Road. Parking is available at an old spring on the right. High-clearance vehicles can continue along the trail for the first 0.4 mile, where there are several campsites and more parking.

The trail follows a wide jeep trail for the first 0.4 mile, which receives occasional motor traffic. At 0.4 mile, the Phillips Hollow Trail begins on the left. There is a trail sign saying that Marguerite Falls is 0.6 mile straight ahead and that the AT is 2.7 miles to the left (across the creek) on the Phillips Hollow Trail. The Bullen Hollow Trail follows the route to Marguerite Falls, bearing right, following the creek. At 0.5 mile the trail bears right again, ascending the ridge. The Marguerite Falls Trail continues straight ahead (see trail description below). Both trails are marked by yellow blazes. The trail ascends steadily and is wide and rutted, passing an access trail back to the Marguerite Falls Trail at 0.7 mile. At 0.8 mile the trail forks twice on a very steep grade, but the various side trails all rejoin as the trail levels, upon climbing out of the steep-sided valley carved by West Fork at 1.0 mile. The trail enters a dry, open forest of pine, several different oaks, laurel, sourwood, sassafras, and huckleberry. The trail climbs moderately around the south side of Reynolds Ridge, passing good views to the left of Cathedral Rocks on neighboring Rocky Ridge, and the nearly denuded slopes of surrounding ridges exposed by recent forest fires. These burned slopes allow observation of the tilted layers of 570-million-year-old sandstone that comprise the front of the Bald Mountains.

At 1.3 miles the trail passes a slow spring in a rhododendron thicket. The oaks and pine give way to hemlock, maple, and poplar as the trail enters Bullen Hollow, reaching Bullen Branch at 1.6 miles. The area is fairly overgrown, but suitable camping space is available. The trail then climbs out of the hollow, passing an old road grade on the left at 2.5 miles. The trail begins climbing more steeply up Henry Ridge through a forest of mature oaks and maple. At 3.0 miles the trail descends gently to a gap and reaches a very wide jeep road. From here, follow the road to the right, skirting the top of Henry Ridge, passing fine views of Blackstack Cliffs to the southeast and the TN Valley to the north. The trail rejoins Reynolds Ridge at 3.4 miles at a wooded gap. Look closely for the Bullen Hollow Trail, which leaves the road to the left, uphill. The jeep road descends from the gap about 0.8 mile and joins Bald Mountain Road. The trail climbs a knob, then descends, reaching Low Gap at 3.9 miles.

Marguerite Falls (Trail No. 189)
Length: 0.6 mile
Elevation Change: Start 2,000 feet, end 2,500 feet (high point 2,600 feet)
Trailhead: Bullen Hollow Trail (start and dead-end)
Type: Hiking

Comments: The Marguerite Falls Trail provides an excellent side trip off the Bullen Hollow and Phillips Hollow trails for a short day hike. The trail follows West Fork through an impressive gorge cut through tilted beds of Cambrian-period sandstone and among large cove hardwoods.

Details: The trail begins at 0.5 mile on the Bullen Hollow Trail. At 0.1 mile a cutoff back to the Bullen Hollow Trail enters from the right, heading uphill about 0.1 mile. The trail then crosses West Fork several times, passing through the middle of the stream at 0.3 mile. By now the trail has entered into the gorge; notice the vertical sandstone cliffs on the southeast side of the creek. The trail then climbs by large hardwoods to the right of the creek and follows the base of the cliffs along a small talus slope. The trail then rejoins the creek, passing several small waterfalls among sandstone boulders. At 0.5 mile there are good views of Cathedral Rock, an impressive promontory that juts out of the bluffs. At 0.6 mile, a double blaze marks the trail to Marguerite Falls to the left. An obscure trail continues straight ahead and dead-ends at a small cliff. Marguerite Falls is a very pretty cascade fanning out over thin layers of bedrock. A nice campsite is reached by climbing through the talus to the right of the falls and up the small cliff to the top of the falls. Another small waterfall, Glen Falls, is reached by scrambling up the creek about 0.1 mile further. Glen Falls, about 8 feet high, enters from a branch (Bullen Branch) on the right and drops into a small, rock-walled glen.

Phillips Hollow (Trail No. 17)
Length: 2.7 miles
Elevation Change: Start 1,960 feet, end 4,240 feet (high point 4,240 feet)
Trailheads: Bullen Hollow Trail (start) and AT (end)
Trail Connections: Artie Hollow Trail
Type: Hiking

Comments: The Phillips Hollow Trail provides a pleasant walk, followed by a steep, arduous ascent to the AT along Dry Creek and its tributaries. The upper portion of the trail is very steep and overgrown but is quite scenic, featuring some fine trees, impressive bluffs, and boulder fields. Route-finding ability is necessary, especially in summer, so be sure to carry a map and compass. Water is plentiful, but camping space is quite limited due to the steepness of the terrain.

Details: The trail begins at 0.4 mile on the Bullen Hollow Trail, where a trail sign indicates the intersection in an open, forested area. There is ample parking at the Bullen Hollow trailhead.

The Phillips Hollow Trail goes left, crossing Dry Creek. The trail is marked by yellow blazes as it passes along the valley cut through Cambrian sandstone, which is visible on both sides of the valley. Notice how much more mature the forest is along the creek valley (cove) as compared to several yards up the rugged, boulder-strewn slopes. The trail soon becomes much rougher and reaches the stream confluence of Dry Creek, which goes right, and the east fork, which the trail follows. The USGS topographical map shows the trailhead of a Spruce Thicket Trail at this point, generally following Dry Creek to the vicinity of the Blackstack Cliffs. No trail is evident here, so follow the blue blazes that mark the Phillips Hollow Trail. At about 0.6 mile the trail becomes rougher, passing several blow-downs. Look for cross-bedding in the sandstone outcrop on the left.

The trail crosses the East Fork at 0.7 mile, then passes several consecutive cascades as it ascends through a slightly younger forest. The trail then negotiates many stream crossings, passing at 1.4 miles a small clearing on the right, which appears to be an old homesite or logging camp. The trail ascends steadily through rhododendron and tall second-growth timber, reaching the terminus of the Artie Hollow Trail at 1.6 miles. An obscure trail sign nailed to a tree on the right marks the direction to the AT and Phillips Hollow but does not mention the Artie Hollow Trail, which enters at a sharp angle on the left.

The trail continues ahead along an obvious footpath into a more mature forest and crosses the creek again at a tree with blazes on both sides. The trail leaves the branch and ascends the right side of the valley, skirting a talus slope. The trail here is well constructed into the large rocks, but watch for stinging nettles in the summer. At 1.9 miles the trail rejoins the stream, which now is quite small, and begins ascending steeply, generally following the creekbed. Here the trail is virtually non-existent in places and is overgrown by rhododendron, making walking difficult. At 2.2 miles the trail reaches a moss-covered rock ledge with a small cascade on the right. This is a good spot to rest and look back down at the mature hardwood forest that covers this steep slope. Look for the trail to the left of the rock ledge as it continues to climb steeply through rhododendron along a ravine. At 2.5 miles the trail reaches a wooded glade where the trail is again evident. Continue ascending along a gentle grade, reaching the AT at 2.7 miles. The trail is rather overgrown in the last

0.1 mile, so look for the blue blazes. The old Fox Cabin site is near the end of the trail and is now marked only by a dense briar patch. A trail sign here reads, "USFS Trail, 3.4 miles-Shelton Mission Road." To the left (east) on the AT it is 0.6 mile to the Round Knob Connector and 1.6 miles to Jerry's Cabin Shelter. To the right (west) it is 1.8 miles to Blackstack Cliffs, offering outstanding views of the TN Valley, and approximately 2.0 miles to the Bald Mountain Road.

Davis Creek (Trail No. 19)

Length: 3.3 miles
Elevation Change: Start 1,850 feet, end 3,100 feet (high point 3,100 feet)
Trailheads: Shelton Mission Road (start) and Round Knob Picnic Area (end)
Trail Connections: Artie Hollow Trail and Cowbell Hollow Trail
Type: Hiking

Comments: The Davis Creek Trail is a wide path that generally follows an old road up Davis Creek to a former homesite, then climbs steeply up to Round Knob Picnic Area on a footpath. The trail crosses Davis Creek many times, so bring an extra pair of socks. There are numerous camping spots along the creek. The upper mile or so passes an extensive burned-over area on Round Knob.

Details: The trailhead is on Shelton Mission Road, 0.4 mile northeast of Shelton Mission Church and 1.0 mile from the Bullen Hollow Trailhead. When coming from the north, look for an old stone foundation near several homes on the right, 1.25 miles off Greystone Road. There is a trail sign off the road that says (incorrectly as to mileage), "Round Knob 4 miles—Constructed by YCC (Youth Conservation Corps) 1978." There is room for maybe one car at the trailhead, so it might be better to drive the extra mile to the Bullen Hollow Trailhead and walk back along the road.

Past the trail sign, the trail ascends along a wide road through a hardwood and pine forest. At 0.1 mile the trail turns right, off the wider road, at a double blaze. The trail then climbs over several low rocky ridges, through a young second-growth forest that is burned over in places. At 0.7 mile a double blaze marks a wide trail that enters from the right, leading to some private homes. The Davis Creek Trail heads left, joining Davis Creek. The trail then makes many wet stream crossings, passing a small dam on the left at 1.2 miles. The walking here is very pleasant, along the old road with a gentle grade. The trail passes through a mature, second-growth cove hardwood forest, crossing Davis Creek several more times. At 2.2 miles the rather faint Artie Hollow Trail begins on the right (look for a double blaze on a tree). The Davis Creek Trail continues ahead, crossing Davis Creek a final time. A rather conspicuous road enters from the left at 2.3 miles, heading uphill beside a branch.

The trail continues to the left of Davis Creek and crosses the branch. To the left, the trail skirts an extensive burned-over area that covers much of Greystone Mountain and Round Knob. This area was decimated by wildfires during the drought of the late 1980s. The trail passes a series of sandstone bluffs at 2.5 miles and crosses another branch. The trail then turns left (east) and follows the branch, past an old homesite, and through a wonderful grove of large trees. Here the trail begins its ascent of Round Knob, crossing the branch a final time at 3.0 miles. At 3.1 miles, the trail again skirts the burned-over area. Avoid the many side trails leading left to the burned forest. These were apparently constructed during the fire-fighting effort. The Davis Creek Trail continues climbing the ridge on a steep grade. Within site of the covered picnic area at Round Knob, the trail bears left and crosses a knoll and ends at a trail sign at the north end of the picnic area. Across the road is the trailhead for the Cowbell Hollow Trail, which leads to Jennings Creek. To the right the Round Knob Connector begins at the gate and heads about 1.8 miles to the AT.

Artie Hollow (Trail No. 18)
Length: 1.9 miles
Elevation Change: Start 2,280 feet, end 3,200 feet (high point 3,400 feet)
Trailheads: Davis Creek Trail (start) and Phillips Hollow Trail (end)
Type: Hiking

Comments: This trail follows an old logging railroad grade up secluded Artie Hollow, past a nice waterfall, and through a fairly mature forest of cove hardwoods. The trail crosses the stream repeatedly, so expect to get your feet wet. Through connections with the upper Davis Creek Trail and Phillips Hollow Trail, and with the AT, one can make a nice day-long loop hike from Round Knob of about 5.5 miles. Water is abundant, and some campsites are available, especially near the trailhead.

Details: The trail begins at about 1.7 miles on the Davis Creek Trail or about 1.1 miles from Round Knob. There is no trail sign, so look carefully to the right of the trail just before the last crossing of Davis Creek. If you are descending from Round Knob, this would be your first major stream crossing.

The trail passes beside Davis Creek briefly, then crosses the branch that leads up Artie Hollow. There is a nice campsite at the crossing. The trail ascends gently through an open forest of poplar and hemlock to the left of the branch for about 0.3 mile, then begins crossing the stream regularly. At 0.5 mile the trail climbs left slightly away from the branch and passes pretty Mary's Falls, which drops some 30 feet off a sandstone bluff. Past this point the trail becomes rougher, following an old logging road, where evidence of rotted ties, spikes, and rails can be seen. The trail now crosses, and sometimes runs through, the branch. The trail is quite overgrown in some places but generally follows the stream. At 1.3 miles the trail reaches the confluence of two branches in a clearing caused by several blow-downs. The Artie Hollow Trail follows the right fork, ascending to the right of the creek along a ravine. The trail begins ascending away from the stream at 1.4 miles and climbs through a couple of switchbacks, tunneling through dense rhododendron. At 1.6 miles the trail reaches a dry gap in an unnamed ridge. The forest here changes abruptly to pine, laurel, and galax in an old burned-over area. The trail then descends very steeply through rhododendron and young hardwoods and reaches a small branch at 1.7 miles and then turns west, following to the right of the branch and becoming rough (look for blazes). The trail then crosses the branch and leaves it, skirting the side of a ridge. At 1.9 miles the Artie Hollow Trail terminates at an intersection with the Phillips Hollow Trail. There is an obscure trail sign nailed to a tree. To the left, it is 1.1 rough miles to the AT. To the right it is about 2.0 miles to Shelton Mission Road at the Bullen Hollow Trailhead.

Jennings Creek (Trail No. 21)

Length: 1.5 miles
Elevation Change: Start 1,920 feet, end 2,280 feet (high point 2,280 feet)
Trailheads: Old Forge Campground (start) and Cowbell Hollow Trail (end)
Trail Connections: Poplar Cove Trail
Type: Horse

Comments: The Jennings Creek Trail follows beautiful Jennings Creek, crossing it repeatedly. The trail is wide and easy to follow to the intersection with the Cowbell Hollow Trail. From that point a manway follows the creek another 1.5 miles, which is not covered in this description. Old maps show the trail extending up to Chestnutlog Gap on the AT, but this trail is no longer evident and must be considered off-trail hiking. There are plans to improve the old trail to the AT in the future, so check with the USFS. This trail can be used to make a 5.0-mile-loop day hike from Old Forge via the Cowbell Hollow and Little Jennings Creek trails with a stop at Round Knob for lunch. This trail has a marvelous show of spring wildflowers, notably wild iris, trillium, trailing arbutus, and several varieties of violets.

Details: The trail begins at the trail sign at the entrance to the Old Forge Campground. Here, in addition to campsites, there are ample parking, toilets, drinking water, and a swimming hole. The sign indicates it is 3.0 miles to Round Knob via the "Big Jennings Creek Trail." The road to Old Forge is closed after the first snow and/or bad weather in winter. If you choose to walk the road to the trailhead, add an additional 2.7 miles from the gate.

The trail leaves the south end of the campground and immediately crosses Jennings Creek. A side trail to the right before the crossing heads 100 yards to a swimming hole at a small waterfall. At 0.1 mile the trail crosses a large branch and reaches the Little Jennings Creek Trail Trailhead (No. 195). An interesting carved stone sign on the right of the trail indicates it is 2.0 miles to Round Knob via the Little Jennings Creek Trail. The topographic map calls this stream "Round Knob Branch." The Jennings Creek Trail continues along Jennings Creek and crosses it at 0.3 mile. Note here the recent scars left by forest fires on the neighboring ridges. The mature cove hardwoods along the creek escaped destruction. At 0.7 mile, after several stream crossings, the trail enters an area of open forest where wildflowers grow in profusion in late April and early May. Note particularly the large white trillium, foam flower, and abundant wild iris. At 1.0 mile the Poplar Cove Trail terminates on the left, having come 0.7 mile from the beginning of the Sarvis Cove Trail and 1.7 miles from the Horse Creek Road. The Jennings Creek Trail continues along the creek through cove hardwoods (buckeye, poplar, hemlock, oak, hickory) and rhododendron. The trail reaches the trailhead of the Cowbell Hollow Trail on the right at 1.5 miles. It leads 1.1 miles to the Round Knob Picnic Area. An obscure Jennings Creek Trail continues another 1.5 miles or so along the creek. Look for signs of the trail in the dry slough at the trail intersection.

Cowbell Hollow (Trail No. 24)
Length: 1.4 miles
Elevation Change: Start 2,280 feet, end 3,100 feet (high point 3,100 feet)
Trailheads: Jennings Creek Trail (start) and Round Knob Picnic Area (end)
Trail Connections: Davis Creek Trail
Type: Horse

Comments: The Cowbell Hollow Trail climbs out of the Jennings Creek watershed to reach Round Knob with trail connections to Davis Creek and the AT via the Round Knob Connector. The trail begins in a rich cove forest and climbs through an interesting open oak and pine forest, then enters a more mature closed oak forest near Round Knob.

Details: The trail begins at about 1.4 miles along the Jennings Creek Trail. There is no trail sign, but the trail is quite evident as it follows a branch entering from the right (west) of the Jennings Creek Trail. Look for the familiar yellow blazes.

The trail follows the branch into Cowbell Hollow along a moderate grade through a forest of cove hardwoods (yellow buckeye, yellow poplar, eastern hemlock, sugar maple, flowering dogwood). The grade steepens at 0.4 mile and the trail leaves the branch, climbing sharply. The trail negotiates several switchbacks while climbing an unnamed ridge. Here the forest is composed of red maple, oak, pine, rhododendron, and mountain laurel, with an understory of wintergreen, galax, and trailing arbutus. The trail descends gently, and at 1.3 miles on the right, the terminus of the Little Jennings Creek trail is marked by a trail sign. Straight ahead is the Round Knob Picnic Area. The trail is badly littered along the last 100 yards approaching the terminus at 1.4 miles. At Round Knob there are picnic tables, toilets, and an excellent piped spring to the left of a shelter with a large stone fireplace. To the left of the trail, the Round Knob Connector Trail (here a narrow jeep road) leads 1.7 miles to the AT. To the right, the Davis Creek Trail terminates at the north end of the parking area, having come 2.8 miles from Shelton Mission Road.

Little Jennings Creek (Round Knob Branch) (Trail No. 195)
Length: 2.1 Miles
Elevation Change: Start 1,920 feet, end 3,100 feet (high point 3,100 feet)
Trailheads: Old Forge Campground (start) and Round Knob Picnic Area (end)
Type: Horse

Comments: This trail provides a nice alternate route to Round Knob from Old Forge. It passes through a mature cove forest along the creek, with abundant wildflowers in April and May. This is also known as The Round Knob Branch Trail.

Details: The trail begins on the Jennings Creek Trail 0.1 mile from Old Forge Campground. Look for the sign carved in a large stone, "Round Knob 2 miles," along the Little Jennings Creek Trail. The trail follows Little Jennings Creek (Round Knob Branch) off to the right.

After the intersection, the trail passes through a narrow valley of yellow poplar, red maple, sycamore, and rhododendron. Spring wildflowers grow in profusion. Look for wild iris, violets, Solomon's seal, false Solomon's seal, jack-in-the-pulpit, trillium, and wild ginger (little brown jugs). The trail climbs gently, crossing the creek repeatedly. At 1.1 miles the grade steepens as the valley narrows, and the trail enters a grove of young eastern hemlocks, red maple, and ash (look for a patch of showy orchids). At 1.4 miles an unmarked trail enters from the right, descending along the ridge. A double blaze marks the trail intersection.

The Little Jennings Creek Trail continues to follow the creek, but about 100 feet above the valley floor. The trail continues to climb and rejoins the creek, which is now quite small. At 1.8 miles the trail enters a ravine in a rhododendron and laurel slick and begins climbing, passing an old tire and some household waste. The creek disappears and the trail enters an open oak forest at 2.0 miles. At 2.1 miles the trail terminates at the Cowbell Hollow Trail, which enters from the left, having climbed 1.4 miles from Jennings Creek. To the right it is 0.1 mile to the Round Knob Picnic Area.

AT (Jones Meadow to Big Butt Section) (Trail No. 1)

Length: 6.1 miles
Elevation Change: Start 4,420 feet, end 4,800 feet (high point 4,800 feet)
Trailheads: Jones Meadow (start) and Coldspring Mountain Parking Area (end)
Trail Connections: Phillips Hollow Trail and Sarvis Cove Trail
Type: Hiking

Comments: The AT skirts the TN-NC state line, which forms the southeastern boundary of the Area. This section is quite scenic at either end. The Blackstack Cliffs at the southwestern end offer an outstanding view of the entire Area and the TN Valley. The balds on Coldspring Mountain at the northeastern end are an excellent example of southeastern grassy balds and have views of the Appalachians to the southwest. The AT generally follows the ridgecrest of the Bald Mountains, making for very gentle grades. Camping is available at Chestnutlog Gap (Jerry's Cabin), where there is a fine spring, and on the balds on Coldspring Mountain. Car access is from Jones Meadow; four-wheel-drive vehicles can also access the trail on Horse Creek Road to the Coldspring Mountain Parking Area. Horse Creek Road can also be walked (see description, above). Vehicles are not allowed on the AT nor within an adjacent corridor.

Details: The trail passes below the developed land that formerly belonged to the Viking Mountain Resort, passing numerous springs. This failed development was closed in 1985 after years of financial difficulties. The CNF acquired most of the land and buildings in 1989. The buildings have now been largely dismantled, including a stone lodge and several houses built below the cliffs. At 0.8 mile a trail to the right leads about 15 yards to Whiterock Cliff, with fine views to the southeast of the Black Mountains in North Carolina. At 1.0 mile the trail to the left leads 75 yards to the top of Blackstack Cliffs and excellent views. The Blackstack Cliffs, incidentally, are actually composed of gleaming white quartzite that only appear black when viewed from a distance. This white quartzite forms the impressive cliffs that rim the rugged face of the Bald Mountains. The trail continues through dense rhododendron to Bearwallow Gap at 1.2 miles, where the trail bears left and skirts the rocky summit of Big Firescald Knob. The trail follows the level ridgecrest and passes the terminus of the Phillips Hollow Trail at 2.8 miles, where a trail sign indicates that Shelton Hollow Road is 3.4 miles distant. The trail descends gently, passing the terminus of the Round Knob Connector at 3.4 miles near the summit of Bald Mountain (4,360 feet). The trail sign here states that it is 2.0 miles to Round Knob; the actual distance is about 1.8 miles.

The trail continues through an open forest, passing the Fork Ridge Trail on the right at 4.2 miles. This trail has climbed 2.0 miles from Big Creek Road in NC. The AT descends to Chestnutlog Gap (4,150 feet) at 4.5 miles, which is the site of Jerry's Cabin, an AT shelter that sleeps six on wooden bunks. To the left, follow blue blazes to an excellent piped spring at the headwaters of Jennings Creek. Chestnutlog Gap is relatively flat and has a pleasant forest of hemlock and white pine, making it an excellent spot to camp. The trail then leaves the gap along a rerouted section that climbs moderately via switchbacks to reach a grassy bald on Coldspring Mountain at 5.0 miles. The AT skirts to the right of the bald, but side trails lead through it, including the old AT. The Sarvis Creek Trail terminates at 5.3 miles on the left on the old AT. Look for the "Hiker Trail" sign and blue blazes at the end of the bald for the Sarvis Creek Trail. At this point the old AT is marked by green blazes and leads 0.2 mile further to the terminus of the Horse Creek Road. From the Sarvis Creek Trail junction the AT continues along the ridgecrest on a rocky trail, reaching Big Butt at 6.1 miles. From there the AT turns south, while the Middle Spring Ridge Trail continues along the ridgecrest, before descending 4.5 miles along Middle Spring Ridge to the Squibb Creek Trail and the Horse Creek Campground. The boulder-strewn summit of Big Butt (4,838 feet) is reached by proceeding another 100 yards or so and taking the surveyor's cut to the right.

Poplar Cove (Trail No. 22)
Length: 1.7 miles
Elevation Change: Start 2,030, end 2,110 feet (high point 2,750 feet)
Trailheads: Horse Creek Road (start) and Jennings Creek Trail (end)
Trail Connections: Sarvis Cove Trail and Pete's Branch Trail
Type: Horse

Comments: This trail provides access from the Horse Creek watershed to Sarvis Cove and Jennings Creek. The trail follows a jeep road to a camping area on Sarvis Creek; afterward it becomes a well-graded trail leading through an unnamed gap, then descending to Jennings Creek. The trail passes mostly through an oak, pine, and laurel forest, typical of south-facing slopes of the southern Appalachians.

Details: The trail follows the jeep road through the clearing, passing a camping area on the right at 0.1 mile. The trail continues past the boulders placed to prohibit ORV use beyond this point. The trail crosses Sarvis Creek and reaches the trailhead for the Pete's Branch Trail at 0.2 mile, where there is a signpost but no trail sign. That trail leads 0.6 mile to a small cascade (Pete's Branch or Sierra Falls). The Poplar Cove Trail ascends above the creek, which is obscured by pine, rhododendron, and mountain laurel. At 1.0 mile the Sarvis Cove Trail begins on the left, following the creek. The Poplar Cove Trail turns right, ascending beside a dry ravine. The trail climbs steadily along a rocky trail and enters an oak forest. At 1.3 miles the trail reaches a dry gap on Middle Ridge, which is quite littered.

A manway leads to the right, following the ridgetop towards Green Ridge. The Poplar Creek Trail descends from the gap, passing a burned-over area on the right. The trail descends steeply through an open forest of small pines, oaks, huckleberry, and laurel. The trail tunnels through dense rhododendron and descends into a ravine (Poplar Cove) via a couple of steep switchbacks. The Poplar Cove Trail terminates at 1.7 miles at the Jennings Creek Trail. To the left it is 0.5 mile to the Cowbell Hollow Trail and 2.0 miles to Round Knob Picnic Area. To the right it is 1.0 mile to Old Forge Campground.

Pete's Branch (Trail No. 12)
Length: 0.6 mile
Elevation Change: Start 2,160 feet, end 2,600 feet (high point 2,600 feet)
Trailhead: Poplar Cove Trail (start and dead-end)
Type: Hiking

Details: This trail leaves the intersection with the Poplar Cove Trail as an overgrown road, tunneling through a rhododendron thicket. The trail climbs to a clearing at 0.3 mile, where the road ends. The trail, now a footpath, continues uphill, climbing gently through second-growth timber. Passing alongside the eroded streambed the trail climbs, joining an obscure old road that enters from the left (note double blaze). The trail climbs gently along Pete's Branch, which stairsteps through angular blocks of quartzite. At 0.5 mile the trail becomes rather rough as it approaches a steep ravine with a tangle of blow-downs, which take careful negotiating. Several hundred yards beyond, the Pete's Branch Trail reaches Pete's Branch Falls (Sierra Falls) at an impressive rocky bluff. The small waterfall splashes through a cleft in the quartzite face. The large fold on the left wall and the numerous fractures in the bedrock attest to the powerful mountain-building stresses that accompanied the original uplift of this region some 250 million years ago. A rich grove of yellow poplar, buckeye, and hemlock has matured in this steep-sided valley, forming an amphitheater-like setting.

Round Knob Connector (FS 88 and Trail No. 16)
Length: 1.8 miles
Elevation Change: Start 3,100 feet, end 4,290 feet (high point 4,290 feet)
Trailheads: Round Knob Picnic Area (start) and AT (end)
Type: ORV road and trail

Comments: The Round Knob Connector is mainly an ORV road (FS 88) that climbs a broad ridge to the base of Bald Mountain and the AT corridor. Vehicles are thereafter prohibited; a badly rutted trail (Trail No. 16) leads on up to the AT. The jeep road receives regular use in the summer months, so use care if you travel this section on foot. There is a campsite at the end of the jeep road.

Details: The road begins at the end of the parking lot for the Round Knob Picnic Area. The Cowbell Hollow Trail ends on the left. The Round Knob Connector follows the jeep road through the gate.

The trail ascends on a rutted, wide trail through a second-growth forest of oak, sugar maple, and rhododendron. The road climbs through two switchbacks as it ascends a side ridge, reaching the ridgetop at 0.9 mile. The forest is mostly pine and oak with an understory of mountain laurel, greenbriar, galax, and wintergreen. The road follows the ridgecrest, then descends. Note the angular pieces of white quartzite in the road. At 1.1 miles the road forks in a gap; the right fork leads about 200 yards to a small stream. The Round Knob Connector continues on the left fork and resumes climbing. At 1.5 miles the road ends at a grassy turnaround after cresting a small knob. Boulders block the road where "Hiker Trail" signs mark the trail, which continues uphill. There is ample camping or parking space here. The trail climbs fairly steeply out of the gap. Beware of numerous side trails, apparently remnants of past ORV use. The trail bears right near the ridgecrest of the Bald Mountains. Bald Mountain is now wooded; however, grassy balds can be found on Coldspring Mountain, past Jerry's Cabin, about 1.8 miles east. To the right (west) it is 0.6 mile along the AT to the Phillips Hollow Trail.

Greene Mountain (Trail No. 13)
Length: 3.6 miles
Elevation Change: Start 2,480 feet, end 3,930 feet (high point 3,930 feet)
Trailheads: FS 98 (start) and Kennedy Cabin (end)
Type: Horse

Comments: The trail climbs, then follows, the rocky crest of Greene Mountain. The trail is rather steep for the first mile and is relatively flat thereafter as it travels along the ridgetop. The Greene Mountain Trail is just outside the boundaries of the Area but is quite scenic, has outstanding blackberries in season, and often contains evidence of black bear. The Sierra Club has supported adding Greene Mountain to the Scenic Area. Greene Mountain forms a prominent front to the higher range behind it, the Bald Mountains. Although mostly forested, the trail does afford some fine wintertime views. Since it is largely a ridgetop trail, there are no sources of water. The trail is easy to follow for the most part and is marked with diamond-shaped, yellow metal tags.

Details: The trail begins as a wide, graded path climbing somewhat steeply away from the road. The trail continues climbing steeply through several switchbacks in a second-growth forest, then across a rocky, burned-over clear-cut. This clearing affords some views to the south and east. Climb through very young pines and sassafras, reentering the woods at 0.7 mile. The trail continues climbing up a side ridge of Greene Mountain, passing through several small saddles. Look for pink ladies' slippers on the dry, rocky stretches during late spring, as well as trailing arbutus, galax, and Indian pipe. The trail reaches the crest of Greene Mountain at 1.5 miles in second-growth of oak and hickory. Giant Solomon's seal, false Solomon's seal, turk's cap lilies, and touch-me-not (jewelweed) grow in profusion, often obscuring the trail. The trail then follows the ridgecrest and descends into an unnamed gap at 2.1 miles. Climbing out of the gap, pass several very large rhododendron and mature hardwoods. The top of Greene Mountain is a rather flat, wide ridge; hereafter the walking is level and pleasant. Descend gently, passing some views to the southeast of Camp Creek Bald and Jones Meadow, and into a gap at 3.1 miles where a grassy woods road enters from the right. The Greene Mountain Trail continues straight ahead (look for metal markers) as an old road. Follow the road along a gentle grade, reaching another intersection at 3.3 miles, and bear left on a larger road. These roads are gated, so they receive very little use. Follow the road for about 1.0 mile, then turn left and cross an earthen barrier. Follow the road past numerous blackberry and blueberry bushes, crossing another road at a large clearing at 3.55 miles. Reach the trail end and trail signs at 3.6 miles. One sign indicates a horse trail; the other says "Foot Trail Only." The area at the trail's end is named Kennedy Cabin on the USGS map, although no structures are now present. From here it is 0.7 mile along the road to access the Bullen Hollow Trail and another 0.5 mile to the Bullen Hollow Trail's starting point at Low Gap.

13. DEVIL'S BACKBONE PRIMITIVE AREA

This 6,986-acre Area near Newport, TN, in the Nolichucky Ranger District is named after the crest of Stone Mountain, which is marked on the topographical maps as "Devil's Backbone." The east side of the crest is quite steep, with some sections rising as much as 600 to 800 feet within a 300-yard distance. The profile of the crest can be seen from several vantage points and truly does suggest a spine. The high point on the Devil's Backbone is at Hall Top, where TN maintains an active fire tower. The vistas from the tower (which is accessible by a dirt road) are impressive. They include many of the northeastern peaks of the GSMNP and, when conditions permit, a view all the way across the French Broad River Valley to the Cumberland escarpment.

The Primitive Area's crest extends about 6.0 miles in a generally north-south direction on the east and west sides of I-40 near the Hartford, TN, exit. The Area lies on both sides of the crest extending about 2.0 or 3.0 miles out from the center, and the GSMNP is just to the south. I-40 traffic and the Pigeon River between Hartford and the Foothills Parkway interchange both pass around the southern end of Stone Mountain between the two sections of the Devil's Backbone Area.

HISTORY

The area was logged in the early 1900s, and many old logging roads may be found throughout. Some farms existed prior to federal acquisition of the land, but those old homesteads are now deep in the forest and not easily located. A dirt road extending 4.0 miles from near Hartford to the top of Stone Mountain was constructed for a timber sale in the mid-1980s. At least one clear-cut exists on the east side of Stone Mountain, as evidence of fairly recent logging activities.

The Area was designated as a Primitive Area by the CNF Management Plan in 1988.

TRAILHEADS AND MAPS

Hall Top Fire Tower Trailhead

To reach the Hall Top Fire Tower by car, take the Wilton Springs exit from I-40 (interchange 440) and head northeast on a two-lane blacktop (TN 73). Go 2.2 miles on TN 73 to an intersection at Sweetwater Creek and turn right on Sweetwater Road (County 207). There is a Shady Grove Baptist Church sign pointing to the right at the intersection. Go 1.1 miles on County 207 and take the right fork onto FS 207 where the blacktop ends. In another 2.1 miles take the right fork; after 0.9 mile more take another right turn and go through the USFS gate at Low Gap. Another 3.3 miles brings you to the

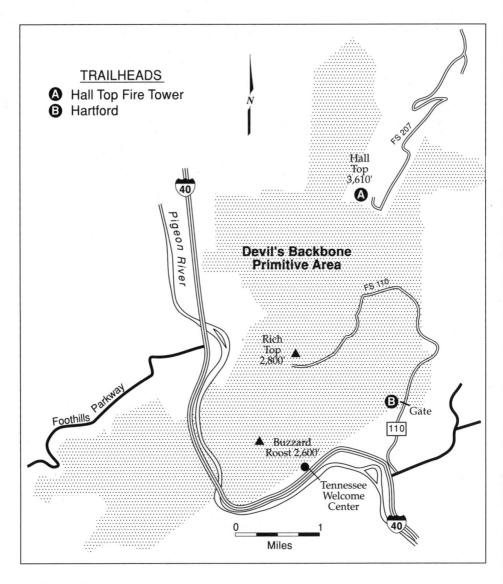

Devil's Backbone Primitive Area.

tower. Total distance from the end of the blacktop to the fire tower is 6.3 miles, but the road is very rocky and twisted, and it takes about 40 minutes. It is best traversed in a pickup truck or ORV.

Hartford Trailhead

Another Devil's Backbone entry point exists near the Hartford I-40 exit (Interchange 447), but this access provides only an 8.0-mile round-trip hike on the gated logging road (FS 110) from Mill Creek to Rich Top at the southern end of the "Backbone." To get there, exit at Hartford and, on the east side of the interstate, go north beside some dumpsters next to the exit. In 0.25 mile turn right at Mill Creek Church on County 110 and go 1.0 mile to a locked gate where there is a small parking area.

Topographic Maps: Hartford, TN-NC; Newport, TN; Waterville, TN-NC; Neddy Mountain, TN. (The first two maps cover most of the Area.)

TRAIL DESCRIPTIONS

Unfortunately, there are currently no hiking trails in the Devil's Backbone Area. There were trails in the past, and there are plans for some in the future, but any hikes in the Area at present are either a walk on dirt roads or an off-trail bushwhacking adventure. In the process of preparing this guide we explored the dotted lines (indicating old trails) on the topographical maps and found no usable trails. The gated FS 110 road can be walked through the Area.

We did, however, find some illicit back-country marijuana farms in those hills, far from any road or trail. Consequently we do not recommend off-trail hiking in the Area from late spring to early fall. If you do hike in the Area during that period, be aware that off-trail hiking could elicit hostile reactions from a nervous marijuana grower.

The State of Tennessee Department of Tourism operates a visitor center along I-40 just north of Hartford. The center is on federal land administrated by the USFS. The District Ranger has mapped out several hiking trails starting from the center, but as of the early 1990s only preliminary planning has been accomplished. The schedule for construction of these trails is dependent on future funding. When they have been constructed and mapped, the resulting increased usage will undoubtedly discourage the hemp-growing activities.

The small portion of the Area south of I-40, which borders the Foothills Parkway, is quite inaccessible and undeveloped and will probably remain so.

14. APPALACHIAN NATIONAL SCENIC TRAIL

Of the over 2,100 miles covered by the AT, about 215 are found in the CNF between Damascus, VA, and the GSMNP. The northern reaches of this section are located wholly within the CNF. However, after climbing the Highlands of Roan, the trail straddles the boundary between the CNF in TN and the Pisgah National Forest in NC.

This section of the AT contains highly varied and rewarding walking throughout its entire length. The trail follows long wooded ridges, such as on Iron Mountain and the Bald Mountains, passing through northern evergreen forests, high grassy balds, and rhododendron gardens in the Highlands of Roan, or through deep gorges at Laurel Fork and the Nolichucky River. However, some of the most pleasant walking occurs among the numerous old fields, pastures, and small communities of upper east TN.

This part of the AT is maintained by three hiking clubs that are members of the Appalachian Trail Conference: the Tennessee Eastman Hiking Club, the Carolina Mountain Club, and the Smoky Mountains Hiking Club. The AT was built and is maintained to established standards; its route is marked with the characteristic white blazes. The overall route is fairly stable, although small relocations to improve it are continually being made.

There are 25 shelters and 36 campsites on this length of the AT. The shelters are three-sided structures sleeping six to eight people and usually spaced 5 to 10 miles apart. Water is available from springs near the shelters and campsites and at other places along the AT. There are 40 road access points, with the distance between them ranging from 0.6 to 15.6 miles and averaging 5.4 miles. These access points, plus a few side trails, allow hikes of any length to be selected.

Limits of space in this publication and the length of this trail allow only a brief summary of the AT route through the CNF. For simplicity, this section of the trail has been divided into 16 sections. For each section, the route is briefly described in the north-to-south direction, giving the amount of climbing, the number of shelters, and a few outstanding features. Each section has road access at each end, and some have intermediate road crossings, as noted.

These 16 sections, routes, and mileage correspond to the sections, routes, and mileage in the *Appalachian Trail Guide to Tennessee-North Carolina*, published by the Appalachian Trail Conference (see Bibliography). The guidebook gives detailed trail descriptions in both directions, plus general historic and descriptive material, with excellent maps. Use of this guidebook is highly recommended for planning hikes on the AT. Note that the Appalachian Trail Conference guidebook mileage may vary slightly from the measured mileage for this guidebook.

1. *Damascus, VA, to US 421 (Low Gap, TN), 14.6 miles.* Beginning at Damascus Town Hall, the AT ascends 1,400 feet southwest in 3.3 miles to the crest of Holston Mountain. The remainder of this section is on the crest of Holston Mountain, with no major changes in elevation. The section has one shelter and one road crossing.

2. *US 421 (Low Gap) to TN 91, 6.9 miles.* From Low Gap, the AT follows the crest of Holston Mountain southwestward for 3.4 miles. It then follows Cross Mountain southeastward for the remaining 3.5 miles. The climb is about 1,800 feet in either direction. This section has one shelter.

3. *TN 91 to Watauga Dam Road, 15.6 miles.* From TN 91 the first mile of the AT goes to the southeast on Cross Mountain. It then turns southwest and follows the crest of Iron Mountain. The trail gains 700 feet in elevation in the first 5.6 miles, has only minor elevation changes in the next 7.0 miles, and descends 1,300 feet in the last 3.0 miles. The section has two shelters and one road crossing.

4. *Watauga Dam Road to Dennis Cove Road, 14.3 miles.* The AT crosses the top of Watauga Dam, skirts Watauga Lake for 2.3 miles, and then parallels US 321 for 1.3 miles. It next ascends 1,700 feet to the crest of Pond Mountain and drops steeply into Laurel Fork Gorge, up which it then proceeds 2.8 miles, passing Laurel Falls. The section has about 3,800 feet of climbing in either direction. The section has two shelters. Note that an AT relocation will change this route and mileage; see Pond Mountain Trail, above.

5. *Dennis Cove to US 19E, 18.9 miles.* The AT climbs 1,000 feet to the crest of White Rocks Mountain, follows its crest for 3.7 miles, and then passes over numerous small side ridges for 5.9 miles to Walnut Mountain Road. It drops into Sugar Hollow, then ascends into woods and old farms, finally descending through Bishop Hollow and above Bear Branch. The section has much climbing, about 6,500 feet in either direction. The section has one shelter and three intermediate road crossings.

6. *US 19E to Carvers Gap, 12.9 miles.* The AT first climbs 1,900 feet in 2.6 miles to Doll Flats on the TN-NC line, and then another 1,000 feet in 2.4 miles to the summit of Hump Mountain. For the remaining 7.9 miles it continues along the state line on beautifully spacious grassy summits, including Yellow Mountain and Grassy Ridge. Total climbing is 5,700 feet southward and 2,400 feet northward. The section has three shelters.

7. *Carvers Gap to Hughes Gap, 4.6 miles.* The first 1.8 miles of the AT are on an old road in dense evergreen woods to Roan High Knob (6,267 feet); the famous rhododendron gardens are found nearby. The remainder, also in woods, descends steeply to Hughes Gap. Total climbing is 2,400 feet southward and 4,800 feet northward. The section has one shelter and one road access near midpoint.

8. *Hughes Gap to Iron Mountain Gap, 8.1 miles.* This section is entirely in woods on the crest of Iron Mountain. The climb is about 2,400 feet in either direction. The section has one shelter.

9. *Iron Mountain Gap to Nolichucky River, 19.2 miles.* For the first 7.0 miles, the AT follows the wooded crest of Iron Mountain and Unaka Mountain to Deep Gap. For the next 3.8 miles to Indian Grave Gap, the trail passes through woods and balds, including Beauty Spot. From there it continues along the ridge and then descends to the Nolichucky River near Erwin, TN. This section has 6,300 feet of climbing going northward and 4,300 feet southward. There are two shelters and two intermediate road crossings.

10. *Nolichucky River to Spivey Gap, 10.2 miles.* The AT first climbs 1,500 feet up Cliff Ridge in 1.9 miles. Beyond, it follows Temple Ridge and skirts No Business Knob with little change in elevation. Traveling southward there are 3,300 feet of climbing and 1,500 feet traveling northward. The section has one shelter.

11. *Spivey Gap to Sams Gap, 12.2 miles.* The AT first climbs 1,100 feet to High Rocks in 1.1 miles. It then descends to Whistling Gap and ascends Little Bald in the next 2.6 miles. It continues for 2.5 miles on the crest of the Bald Mountains to Big Bald. Beyond, it descends to Street Gap and the remainder of the section, through hardwoods and old fields. The section has one shelter.

12. *Sams Gap to Devil Fork Gap, 7.7 miles.* The AT first follows the crest of the Bald Mountains through forests and fields for 3.2 miles westward to Rice Gap. Beyond, it goes northward over Frozen Knob, Big Flat, and Sugarloaf Knob to the end of the section. There are two road crossings and one shelter on this section.

13. *Devil Fork Gap to Allen Gap, 20.1 miles.* The AT first follows the crest of the Bald Mountains northwestward for 5.5 miles to Big Butt. It then heads southwestward on the ridgeline through forest and open areas, passing over Cold Spring Mountain, Big Firescald Knob, the rocky face of Blackstack Cliffs, and Camp Creek Bald. The section has three shelters and one road crossing.

14. *Allen Gap to Hot Springs, 14.4 miles.* The AT first ascends the Bald Mountain Range ridgeline, climbing 1,400 feet in 6.1 miles to reach Rich Mountain. It then descends 1,400 feet in 2.5 miles to Tanyard Gap. Beyond, it passes through woods and open areas to Pump Gap and then Lovers Leap Ridge, descending to the end of the section at Hot Springs, NC. From north to south, there are 2,600 feet of climbing, with 3,500 feet from south to north. The section has one shelter and two intermediate road crossings.

15. *Hot Springs to Max Patch Road, 20.0 miles.* In the first 10.1 miles, the AT ascends 3,400 feet to the top of Bluff Mountain. In another 3.7 miles it reaches Lemon Gap. For the next 5.4 miles it generally ascends across side ridges to reach the open summit of Max Patch with a panoramic view of the surrounding CNF and Pisgah

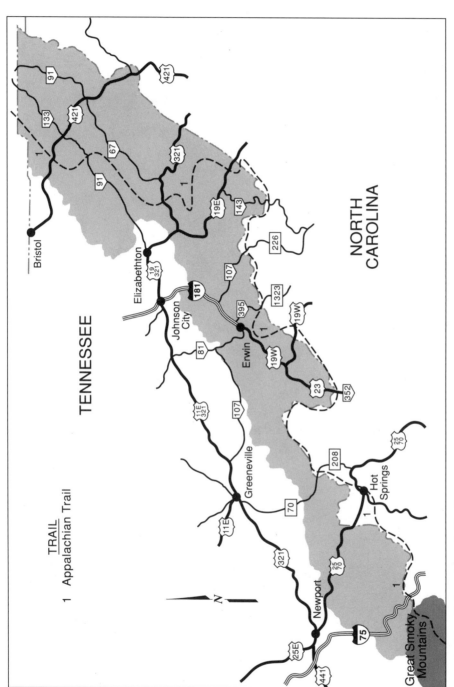

Appalachian National Scenic Trail.

National Forests and south to the GSMNP. From north to south, the section has 5,800 feet of climbing, with 1,800 feet from south to north. There are two shelters and two intermediate road crossings in this section.

16. *Max Patch Road to Davenport Gap, 15.3 miles.* The first 10.1 miles of this section of the AT generally follow the crest of Snowbird Mountain along the state line. The trail passes Brown Gap, Groundhog Creek Gap, and Wildcat Top. Thereafter it descends along Painter Branch, reaching I-40 at the Pigeon River in another 3.3 miles. In another 1.9 miles it reaches Davenport Gap. From north to south, there is a net descent of 2,300 feet. This section has one shelter and three intermediate road crossings.

Section C

The Cherokee National Forest's Wilderness Trails—South

15. CITICO CREEK WILDERNESS, JOYCE KILMER-SLICKROCK WILDERNESS (TN PORTION), AND HAW KNOB PRIMITIVE AREA

Citico Creek Wilderness, at 16,226 acres the largest wilderness in CNF, is in Monroe County and the Tellico Ranger District. Its 13 trails, covering 57.4 miles, provide immense opportunity for exploration of the Area. The Wilderness is dominated by the long, high ridge of the Unicoi Mountains on the east, with three steeply sloped ridges leading west from the main ridge. These ridges—Brush Mountain, Pine Ridge, and Sassafras Ridge—are cut by swift-flowing stream valleys, which drain to the west. The terrain is very rugged, with 90 percent of the slope area exceeding 30 degrees. Elevation ranges from a low of 1,400 feet to a high of 4,600 feet.

Citico Creek Wilderness is not an isolated Wilderness. It adjoins the 17,013-acre Joyce Kilmer-Slickrock Wilderness Area, most of which is in NC but 3,881 acres of which are in TN and the CNF. The combined wildernesses, consisting of 33,239 acres, together with the contiguous 1,060-acre Haw Knob Primitive Area, constitute a unique treasure of the Wilderness Preservation System, with many outstanding features, scenic areas, and points of interest. There are numerous ecological, geographic, and trail connections between the two Wilderness Areas. While this guidebook will concentrate on the Citico Creek Wilderness, there are a number of opportunities to join these Areas into longer excursions. It should also be noted that the GSMNP, a de facto wilderness area, lies only 4.0 miles to the north.

The Citico Creek Wilderness contains the entire upper drainage of Citico Creek, which consists of two major tributaries, the North Fork Citico Creek and the South Fork Citico Creek. In addition there are at least eight tributary streams to Citico Creek in the Area. The streams in the Area are characterized by unusually large channels, resulting from the narrow, steep-walled valleys, the steep gradients of the valleys (averaging 13 percent), and the high amount of precipitation (averaging about 70 inches per year). All of these factors contribute to swift, clear-flowing streams, even though they were heavily damaged by logging abuses of the early

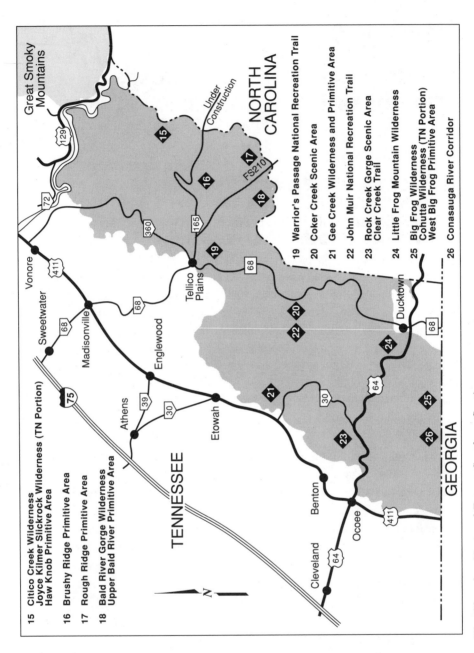

The Cherokee National Forest, Southern Section.

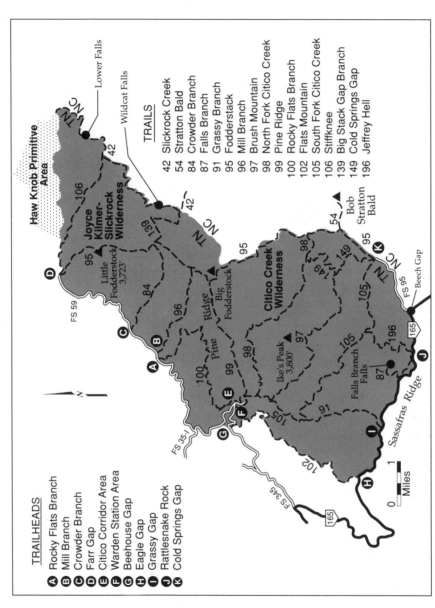

TRAILHEADS

Ⓐ Rocky Flats Branch
Ⓑ Mill Branch
Ⓒ Crowder Branch
Ⓓ Farr Gap
Ⓔ Citico Corridor Area
Ⓕ Warden Station Area
Ⓖ Beehouse Gap
Ⓗ Eagle Gap
Ⓘ Grassy Gap
Ⓙ Rattlesnake Rock
Ⓚ Cold Springs Gap

TRAILS

42 Slickrock Creek
54 Stratton Bald
84 Crowder Branch
87 Falls Branch
91 Grassy Branch
95 Fodderstack
96 Mill Branch
97 Brush Mountain
98 North Fork Citico Creek
99 Pine Ridge
100 Rocky Flats Branch
102 Flats Mountain
105 South Fork Citico Creek
106 Stiffknee
139 Big Stack Gap Branch
149 Cold Springs Gap
196 Jeffrey Hell

Citico Creek Wilderness, Joyce Kilmer-Slickrock Wilderness (TN Portion), and Haw Knob Primitive Area.

Hikers plan route on Bob's Bald, which adjoins Citico Wilderness.
Photo by Lance McCold.

20th century. Beginning in 1960 the watershed itself was extensively studied for eleven years in a joint project of the USFS, TVA, and TWRA (at that time the Game and Fish Commission). Relics of the study can be seen in the gauging station weir on the North Fork Citico Creek near its confluence with the South Fork Citico Creek. Surface water quality is in general excellent, the water being soft, imperceptible in color, and with an average pH of 6.8. Eagle Branch and some of the upper reaches of streams along the Tellico-Robbinsville Road were affected by exposure of iron pyrite rock formations in the construction of the road in the late 1970s. This resulted in unnatural acid concentrations in these streams. Grassy Branch and Eagle Branch were especially affected.

HISTORY

The Areas have maintained and regained their wilderness character through a long history of human use. The first humans to use the Areas were the American Indians. It is not known when this use first began, but there were extensive Cherokee Indian settlements near Citico Creek along the Little Tennessee River during precolonial times. The primeval forest and rugged terrain of the Citico Creek Area were extensively used for hunting and other purposes by the Indians. The name Citico derives from the Cherokee word *sitiku*, meaning place of clean fishing wa-

Looking toward Bob's Bald and the eastern boundary of Citico Wilderness from Hangover Mountain. Photo by Roger Jenkins.

ters. It may still be possible to find artifacts and remnants of camp sites left by these early people.

English Army Lieutenant Henry Timberlake explored nearby in the 1750s. The Cherokee Nation, under much coercion, ceded the Areas, along with all their holdings east of the Mississippi River, to the US in 1835 in the Treaty of New Echota. There may have been scattered pioneer families that settled the Citico Creek area in the mid-1800s. The area was owned by wealthy plantation families as a mineral investment and was frequently hunted during this period. Following the Civil War, the land went to northern investors. The Citico Creek area was owned during the late 19th century by George Peabody Wetmore, a wealthy US Senator from Rhode Island.

The Citico Creek area was acquired by Smoky Mountain Timber and Improvement Company in the early 1900s. The land was surveyed and a railroad line constructed from the junction of the North and South Forks of Citico Creek to Maryville, TN, where it connected with the Little River Railroad, which came out of the GSMNP. This railroad line was completed about 1910. Logs were removed on smaller tramways built up the stream valleys and on the mountain slopes. Remnants of these tramways and other relics of logging can still be seen in the Areas. Names and ownership of the land had changed by the 1920s. Babcock Land and Timber Company

*Falls Branch Falls in
Citico Wilderness.
Photo by Roger Jenkins.*

and Tellico River Lumber Company continued the timber operations in the early 1920s. In 1925 a disastrous wildfire, fueled by logging slash and debris and exacerbated by very dry weather, burned about half of the Citico Creek Wilderness, especially in the lower elevations. Two people were killed, and many of the structures necessary for timber harvesting were destroyed. The cost of replacement was prohibitive; the timber companies were forced to abandon operations in the higher elevations. Logging operations continued only along Doublecamp Creek until 1929. This halt to the logging resulted in stands of old-growth forest being left in the inaccessible places that had not yet been cut. In the higher elevations large trees and relatively untouched stands of the primeval forest can still be found. Probably the largest of these are a 187-acre cove hardwood forest near Falls Branch Falls and a 200-acre hemlock-hardwood stand between Glen Gap and the headwaters of Indian Valley Branch.

After the logging period, a number of families settled along the creeks. They farmed some of the areas left cleared by the logging operations and used the balds for summer pasture. The USFS bought the Citico Creek area in 1935 from Babcock

North Fork of Citico Creek.
Photo by Lance McCold.

and Tellico River Lumber Companies. Only 11 percent of the Citico Creek Wilderness has been harvested since 1935.

In the 1930s, what is now the Citico Creek Wilderness was considered for wilderness designation by the USFS in a broader proposal for a Citico-Cheoah Primitive Area. This never came to pass but, as it recovered, the Citico Creek area became known for its natural character. In the 1970s support grew for designating the Citico Creek area as wilderness. The Eastern Wilderness Act, enacted on January 3, 1975, created the Citico Creek Wilderness Study Area and the Joyce Kilmer-Slickrock Wilderness. Subsequently, the Citico Creek Wilderness Area was designated by Congress in 1984. The Haw Knob Primitive Area was established in 1988 in the CNF Management Plan.

Since the 1920s, natural processes have healed much of the damage caused by logging abuses and fire. The remnants of the old-growth forest have been surrounded by second-growth forest. Wildlife has rebounded, and the Areas are once again renowned for bear, turkey, deer, and other animal life. The much-abused streams once again flow clear and pure, and trout and other water inhabitants abound. The headwaters of Citico Creek are an important habitat for brook trout, since its numerous waterfalls provide barriers to exclude the introduced rainbow trout, with which the brook trout has a hard time coexisting. Several rare animals occur in the Areas, including the star-nosed mole, woodland jumping mouse, masked shrew, and northern water shrew. Two rare salamanders, the seepage salamander and *Desmognathus sp.* are found in the Areas. The black bear and eastern brook trout found in the Areas are considered sensitive species by the USFS. Rare plants found in the Areas include lesser prickly sedge, Fraser's sedge, a huckleberry known as *Gaylussacia ursina*, Blue Ridge St. John's Wort, Coville's Rush, ginseng, and hedge nettle. As the decades and centuries pass, it is hoped that the Areas, in their protected status, will again approach their primeval condition.

TRAILHEADS AND MAPS

There are two main routes to the Citico Creek Wilderness and adjacent Areas. A third route uses sections of the other two routes. All routes turn off US 411.

One route to the Areas turns off US 411 onto TN 68 in Madisonville, TN. Take TN 68 to Tellico Plains (approximately 14 miles). When TN 68 intersects TN 165 in the middle of Tellico Plains, take a left on TN 165. Go 0.65 mile east to where TN 165 makes a junction with TN 360. Take a right at the junction to stay on TN 165. The following mileages are given for this route measured from this point. TN 165 continues past a group of stores and cabins and passes a CNF sign. The road runs along the south bank and then the north bank of Tellico River. Shortly after passing the Ooesterneck Creek parking area at 4.2 miles, the road forks. The right fork continues along the river past the Tellico Ranger Station and to Bald River Falls. Take the left fork and continue on TN 165 over rolling hills. At 13.7 miles TN 165 intersects with FS 345 on the left. This road leads to Indian Boundary Lake and Recreation Area and, by way of the Citico Creek Road, to the Warden Station Area and the Doublecamp Road area. To reach trailheads along the Tellico-Robbinsville Road, continue along TN 165.

The other main route is by the Citico Creek Road, which turns off US 411 onto TN 360 at Vonore, TN. After 7.4 miles from Vonore, TN 360 turns right across a bridge. Do not turn right across the bridge, but continue straight on the Citico Creek Road. The pavement ends 16.6 miles from Vonore. At this point do not turn left across Citico Creek on the concrete bridge, but continue on the right side of Citico Creek on the gravel road. Continue on Citico Creek Road (FS 35-1) as it goes deeper into the CNF. Pass through Jakes Best Campground at 24.2 miles from Vonore. Doublecamp Road (FS 59) turns left off Citico Creek Road (28.0 miles) at Doublecamp Campground. Citico Creek Road continues up Citico Creek and makes a hairpin turn away from the creek at 29.5 miles. The road (FS 29) that continues straight ahead and crosses the creek goes to the Citico Corridor Area. Continuing on the Citico Creek Road for about 0.1 mile takes you past the turnoff to the Warden Station Area on the left. At 31.9 miles from Vonore, FS 35-1 intersects FS 345 at the entrance to Indian Boundary Recreation Area. Bear left on FS 345 to reach the Tellico-Robbinsville Road (TN 165) after 1.3 miles (33.2 miles from Vonore).

The third route avoids stretches of gravel along the Citico Creek Road and makes use of parts of both of the previous routes. As in the second route, take TN 360 south off US 411 in Vonore. After 7.4 miles stay on TN 360 by turning right across the bridge (this is where you would go straight to go along the Citico Creek Road). 12.1 miles from Vonore, TN 360 turns left at a stop sign shortly after passing a small sawmill. Continue on TN 360 until it intersects TN 165 (at 22.8 miles from Vonore) shortly after crossing the Tellico River on the outskirts of Tellico Plains. Take a sharp left onto TN 165. Directions and mileages from the first route can be followed from this point.

The best route to take to Citico Wilderness depends on your point of origin, what trailhead you plan to use, and personal preferences. Some factors should be considered. The gravel section of the Citico Creek Road is narrow in places; it is crowded during some weekends of the year; and, depending on the season and the weather, it can be very dusty or rutted. The third route mentioned above, following TN 360, stays entirely in the country and is very scenic. But you may need to keep up with mileages carefully and watch for turnoffs to stay on this route.

Doublecamp Road (FS 59) Trailheads:
Rocky Flats Branch, Mill Branch,
Crowder Branch, and Farr Gap

Four trailheads lie along Doublecamp Road (FS 59), which turns off the Citico Creek Road at Doublecamp Campground. Mileages are given from this turnoff. Trailheads are located on the right (southeast) side of this 6.7-mile road, which ends at Farr Gap, as follows: Rocky Flats Branch Trail (No. 100) at 2.5 miles, Mill Branch Trail (No. 96) at 2.7 miles, Crowder Branch Trail (No. 84) at 3.5 miles, and Fodderstack Trail (No. 95) in Farr Gap at 6.7 miles. The road is gravel but is in good condition. Most of the trailheads have limited and informal parking areas but there are wide places in the road nearby, and the road is wide enough to park along without impeding the rather sparse traffic. Farr Gap, which is the trailhead for Fodderstack Trail, has several designated parking places.

Citico Corridor Area Trailhead

There are a number of trailheads in this area and the nearby Warden Station Area. The Citico Corridor Road (FS 29) turns off the Citico Creek Road 2.4 miles northeast from the entrance to the Indian Boundary Recreation Area and 1.6 miles southeast from Doublecamp Road. At the hairpin curve, leave Citico Creek Road and cross the low-water bridge to the corridor. There are a number of meadows that are extensively used for car and truck camping. Parking can be found along the Corridor Road and along the margins of the meadow. Trailheads for Pine Ridge Trail (No. 99) and Rocky Flats Trail (No. 100) are nearby, although Rocky Flats Trail will be described from the trailhead along Doublecamp Road. The South Fork Trail can also be accessed by following the corridor road for 0.25 mile until it dead-ends into Citico Creek. A rather difficult ford of the creek leads to the old road on the other side of the creek which soon becomes the South Fork Trail. However, this trail will be described from the nearby Warden Station Area, which does not require the creek crossing.

Warden Station Area Trailhead

To reach the Warden Station Area take the Citico Creek Road toward Indian Boundary for 0.1 mile past the Citico Corridor Area. A turnoff to the left is marked by trail sign No. 105. Parking is very limited. There is space for one or two cars to park where the South Fork Trail turns off the road. More parking can be found in the Citico Corridor Area nearby. Ruins of the Warden Station can be found along the early sections of the trail. The trail stays high on the western side of Citico Creek and crosses two small streams. After about 0.5 mile the trail opens up into a large park-like game clearing, with some large fruit trees. At the other side of the clearing is an old road that runs along Citico Creek. The South Fork Trail leads off to the right; to the left a short distance the old road crosses Citico Creek to the corridor area. Trailhead connections to the North Fork Citico Creek Trail (No. 98), Ike Camp Branch Trail (No. 97—also known as Brush Mountain Trail), Grassy Branch Trail (No. 91) and Jeffrey Hell Trail (No. 196) lie along the South Fork Citico Creek Trail. The South Fork, the North Fork, and Ike Camp Branch trails will be described from their trailheads in the Warden Station Area. Grassy Branch and Jeffrey Hell trails will be described from their trailheads along the Tellico-Robbinsville Road.

Beehouse Gap Trailhead

This low gap at 2,580 feet is on the Citico Creek Road 0.9 mile southwest from the Citico Corridor Area and 1.5 miles northeast from the entrance to the Indian Boundary Recreation Area. A trailhead for the Flats Mountain Trail, with space for three or four cars, is in the gap. This trail will be described from its trailhead along the Tellico-Robbinsville Road, and ending at Beehouse Gap.

Tellico-Robbinsville Road (TN 165) Trailheads:
Eagle Gap, Grassy Gap, and Rattlesnake Rock

Access to several trailheads lies along the Tellico-Robbinsville Road (TN 165). This road, which originally would have passed through the present Joyce Kilmer-Slickrock Wilderness, was rerouted to its present path in order to spare that Wilderness. Construction of the road disturbed pyrite mineral deposits, which caused acid pollution in some nearby streams. The impact was heavy upon several streams on the other side of the road from Citico Creek Wilderness. Grassy Branch and Eagle Branch on the Citico side of the road sustained damage from this pollution.

From the intersection of TN 165 and FS 345, take TN 165 as it skirts the southern edge of the Citico Wilderness. Numerous turnoffs along the road give spectacular views of the Citico watershed and of other parts of the Tellico Ranger District. Mileages to trailheads are given from the junction of TN 165 and FS 345. The Flats Mountain Trail (No. 102) Trailhead is at 4.8 miles in Eagle Gap. The Grassy Branch Trail (No. 91) Trailhead is at 6.3 miles and a large parking area in Grassy Gap. The trailhead for both Falls Branch Trail (No. 87) and Jeffrey Hell Trail (No. 196) is at 8.4 miles near an area known as Rattlesnake Rock Parking Area (note this trailhead is before the Rattlesnake Rock Scenic Overlook).

Cold Spring Gap Trailhead

At the TN-NC state line near Beech Gap (9.85 miles beyond the Indian Boundary turnoff from Tellico-Robbinsville Road), FS 217H turns off to the left. This dirt road travels 1.9 miles through thick forest to a trailhead complex and parking area for several cars at Cold Spring Gap near Strawberry Knob. The road is barely passable by two-wheel-drive car. Portions of the road have deep ruts, large rocks, and large mud holes. The South Fork Citico (No. 105), Cold Spring Gap (No. 149), Fodderstack (No. 95), Brush Mountain (No. 97), and North Fork Citico (No. 98) trails all have trailheads that can be accessed from Cold Spring Gap (the latter two via Cold Spring Gap Trail). Most of these trails will be described from the other ends of the trails. Only Cold Spring Gap Trail, which was formerly a section of FS 217H, will be described from Cold Spring Gap. If you do hike from this area and do not have a truck or four-wheel drive, you may want to consider treating the 1.9 miles of FS 217H as a trail and park near the Tellico-Robbinsville Road.

Topographic Maps: Whiteoak Flats, TN-NC; Big Junction, TN-NC; Tapoca, TN-NC; Santeetlah Creek, NC. (The first two maps cover all of the Citico Creek Wilderness.)

TRAIL DESCRIPTIONS

General Comments: Most of the trails are on old tramways or roads in the lower elevations and tend to be fairly easy to follow and have reasonable inclines. In the higher elevations the trails tend to be much fainter and are sometimes very steep. In fact some of these sections are in need of rerouting in order to decrease erosion as well as make the trails more accessible to hikers. Expect to get wet if you cross the lower portions of either North Fork Citico Creek or South Fork Citico Creek. You may want to take extra tennis shoes or "water shoes" if your feet are tender. Otherwise just take off your boots, roll up your pants, and wade. Some of the upper portions of the trails tend to follow streambeds. Not only can these trails be a muddy mess, but they also adversely affect the water quality downstream. The upper portions of many of the trails have developed as "paths of least resistance" and are in great need of rerouting.

All of the trails have been blazed at one time or another. Traditionally, this has been performed on trees with swatches of white paint. On some of the trails these blazes are quite noticeable and easy to follow. On other trails the painted blazes are old and faded, and many of the blazed trees have died and fallen over. Given that some of these trails have had little travel, they can be quite difficult to follow. The USFS has cleared and reblazed some of the trails since they were hiked for this guidebook, which should make them easier to follow. The new blazes are rectangles cut out of the bark of the trees. As the cuts heal, scar tissue will form that presumably can be followed. So look for these new blazes, as well as the old painted blazes.

The only topographic map that shows all of the present trail system is the Joyce Kilmer-Slickrock Wilderness and Citico Creek Wilderness map issued by the USFS. This map can be obtained from the CNF. While it shows present trail layout, it does not show abandoned trails or old roadbeds. Ideally, the USFS map, in conjunction with the USGS topographic maps, gives the best picture of the Areas. If you must choose between them, the USFS map will be a better guide to the present trail system.

Fodderstack (Trail No. 95), including Stratton Bald (Nantahala National Forest Trail No. 54) and Big Stack Gap Branch (Trail No. 139)
Length (Trail No. 95): 10.6 miles
Elevation Change (Trail No. 95): Start 2,800 feet, end 4,400 feet (high point 5,160 feet)

Trailheads: Farr Gap (start) and Cold Spring Gap (end)
Trail Connections: Crowder Branch Trail, Big Stack Gap Branch Trail, Mill Branch Trail, Pine Ridge Trail, North Fork Citico Creek Trail, and Stratton Bald Trail
Type: Horse

Comments: This trail runs along the Unicoi Mountain Range dividing Citico Wilderness and Joyce Kilmer-Slickrock Wilderness. It passes near the crests of Little Fodderstack, Big Fodderstack, and Rockstack. Bob Bald, which is a short distance along Stratton Bald Trail in North Carolina's Nantahala National Forest, offers excellent campsites and spring water. It is one of the finest grassy balds in the southern CNF and offers excellent views. Flame azaleas and phlox bloom profusely in the early summer.

The Fodderstack Trail provides access to several trails in the Citico Wilderness, as well as the Joyce Kilmer-Slickrock Wilderness, and provides the potential for utilizing these for a multiple-day backpack trip. Several small campsites can be found along the trail, and larger sites can be found short distances down the Crowder Branch, Mill Branch, and Stratton Bald trails. Water is usually not found on the trail, but springs are found at Crowder Place and Bob Stratton Bald. In addition water can be found down the creek drainages off the ridgecrest.

The trail begins at Farr Gap, 6.7 miles along the Doublecamp Road. While it is possible to hike Fodderstack Trail from the trailhead at the Cold Spring Gap area near Beech Gap, the Doublecamp Road is in much better condition than FS 217H from Beech Gap to the trailhead at Cold Spring Gap. The Doublecamp Road is graveled and in fair condition. A parking area near the Fodderstack Trailhead has space for several cars.

Details: The Fodderstack Trail begins at the high point of Farr Gap a short distance up the Doublecamp Road from the parking area. From the gap you can look into the Joyce Kilmer-Slickrock Wilderness. A short distance after the Fodderstack Trail turns right off the road, the Stiffknee Trail (No. 106) turns left (southeast) and descends into the Slickrock Creek watershed. The Fodderstack Trail leads straight ahead through a mixed forest of oak, hickory, tulip trees, sourwood, pine, and maple. The trail reaches a ridge after about 0.39 mile and turns east along it. The trail remains on the ridge as it turns southeast and goes through forest alternating with old clearings grown up in white pine and blackberries. Good views are possible from some of these clearings, especially in winter.

After 1.0 mile the trail turns south and ascends rather steeply to skirt Little Fodderstack to the west of its summit after 1.5 miles. Look for chestnut sprouts. At 1.7 miles the trail turns sharply from southwest to southeast. An old overgrown trail continues west along the ridge at the switchback. As the main trail continues around Little Fodderstack, a faint trail can be seen to the left following the ridgeline for 0.25 mile to the summit of Little Fodderstack. The main trail ascends to a sister knob of Little Fodderstack at 2.1 miles. From the knob, look back for good views of Little Fodderstack. Near the top of the knob is a small clearing to the left of the trail that could accommodate a tent. As one continues beyond the knob along the ridgeline, it may be possible to see Hangover, a prominent rock outcrop in the Joyce Kilmer-Slickrock Wilderness, to the southeast. The trail reaches a gap at 2.5 miles, with a possible campsite to the left of the trail. A side trail splits off from the main trail at 2.6 miles and goes to the top of a partially cleared knob to the right. The trail reaches the top of another knob at 2.9 miles before descending rather steeply to the gap above Crowder Place at 3.04 miles. The Crowder Branch Trail leaves the gap to the right and passes through Crowder Place, which has numerous campsites and a dependable spring 0.2 mile down the trail from the gap.

The trail climbs out of the gap and at 3.2 miles reaches a trailhead with a clearing that can accommodate several tents. The Big Stack Gap Branch Trail turns left and descends 1.8 miles into Joyce Kilmer-Slickrock Wilderness.

The Big Stack Gap Branch Trail is a hiking trail that provides access to Slickrock Creek and the Joyce Kilmer-Slickrock Wilderness trail system. It is blazed with bear-preserve signs and initially follows a ridge down into Slickrock Valley. At 0.6 mile it drops off the ridge to the south and descends across a series of coves to Big Stack Gap Branch. The trail then follows an old logging skidroad along the branch to its end at 1.8 miles at Slickrock Creek. The Slickrock Creek Trail (No. 42) goes left (north) 2.7 miles downstream to the Stiffknee Trail (No. 106; see description below), which turns left and leads back up out of the valley to Farr Gap. Trail No. 42 continues along Slickrock Creek for 1.8 miles to Lake Cheoah and on to a trailhead at US 129. The Slickrock Creek Trail goes right (south) up Slickrock Creek to its headwaters and up a steep climb to Naked Ground and a junction with the Stratton Bald Trail (No. 54), a distance of approximately 6.0 miles.

The Fodderstack Trail continues to climb gently past the Big Stack Gap Branch Trail junction along the ridgecrest until it tops out at about 3.7 miles. The trail then steeply descends to Big Stack Gap at 4.2 miles. Mill Branch Trail descends to the right (west) out of the gap. Several very large oaks are in the gap. A large branch of one of these oaks has fallen and has partially obscured the unsigned beginning of Mill Branch Trail.

The trail climbs out of the gap and up the northwest slopes of Big Fodderstack Mountain. At 4.7 miles the trail makes a sharp turn to the left; at this point a trail appears to continue straight ahead, but this "trail" soon disappears. The main trail makes a sharp right within a few yards. The trail heads south but gradually bears to the southwest as it continues to climb around Big Fodderstack. The trail reaches a rocky clearing on the point of a spur ridge at 5.0 miles. The Pine Ridge Trail traverses down the south side of the ridge to the southwest at this point.

Fodderstack Trail makes a sharp turn to the southeast at the intersection with Pine Ridge Trail and continues up the ridgeline for a short distance before turning east and skirting below the summit of Big Fodderstack. A short bushwhack will take you to the summit (4,200 feet) for good views to the east of the Slickrock Creek Valley. The trail turns back to the southeast and descends along a ridge coming down from Big Fodderstack. Nearby the TN-NC border leads up from the Slickrock Valley and now shares the ridgeline with the trail. The trail reaches Harrison Gap at 6.19 miles. The gap is long and shallow, with numerous large oaks. The trail steeply ascends out of the gap at 6.6 miles, heading south, and then turns east along a ridgeline where there is evidence of a recent burn. At about 7.0 miles, the trail levels out as it skirts the west side of Rockstack before descending into Glen Gap at 7.3 miles. There is space for one or two tents, and water can be found down the stream drainages on each side of the gap.

The trail climbs out of Glen Gap and ascends along the ridgeline. The trail runs near the state line for the next 2.0 miles. At 7.9 miles notice a large boulder with double horizontal slashes and "NC" painted in orange. The trail reaches Chestnut Knob at 8.1 miles. Descend gradually through a hemlock grove to Cherry Log Gap at 8.3 miles. Several large, straight black cherry trees are in the gap. The North Fork Trail turns right at the gap (to the southwest) and heads into the Citico drainage.

Fodderstack Trail climbs out of Cherry Log Gap moving south along the ridgeline. At 8.6 miles the trail reaches a clearing that could accommodate two or three tents. Turn left after passing the clearing; be careful not to bear right down an old trail with faint white blazes. This trail descends through overgrown sections and numerous blow-downs to the Cold Spring Gap Trail. Look for newer blazes as the Fodderstack Trail turns left on the far side of the clearing and steeply ascends. There are switchbacks at 9.0 miles, 9.1 miles, and 9.3 miles before the trail intersects the Stratton Bald Trail at 9.4 miles. Bob Stratton Bald is in the Nantahala National Forest at 0.4 mile along the Stratton Bald Trail (No. 54), which turns left (east) at the intersection.

The Stratton Bald Trail, a hiking trail, and the Bob Stratton Bald it leads to are in NC but make a good side-hike or camping area. The bald is often referred to as "Bob's Bald," and maps label it as both "Bob Bald" and "Stratton Bald." The correct name is probably "Bob Stratton Bald" since it was named after Robert B. Stratton, a mountain man who lived nearby in the late 1800s. He reportedly bought 100 acres of Swan Meadows for $9.40 in 1872. The portion of the original bald that remains clear is 5,261 feet high and provides one of the best views in the entire area. The GSMNP is in the distance to the north with the Slickrock Creek valley below. The USFS clears the bald periodically so there are numerous grassy campsites, with reliable water on the southeast of the grassy area.

The Fodderstack Trail turns right (southwest) from the Stratton Bald Trail junction and passes through blackberries and rhododendron as it descends down the backbone of the ridge. A short section that followed an eroded gully at 9.7 miles was replaced and revegetated in 1990; avoid the replaced section. There are a number of large, gnarled trees on this section of the trail; a particularly large tree is reached at about 9.8 miles. The forest opens up considerably before descending steeply at 10.1 miles. The trail continues to descend steeply along the ridge for 0.5 mile to end at Cold Spring Gap at 10.6 miles.

Crowder Branch (Trail No. 84)
Length: 2.6 miles
Elevation Change: Start 1,920 feet, end 3,360 feet (high point 3,360 feet)
Trailheads: Crowder Branch (start) and Fodderstack Trail (end)
Type: Hiking

Comments: The Crowder Branch Trail follows Crowder Branch from Doublecamp Road to Crowder Place, an old homesite. There is a large meadow at Crowder Place, as well as an excellent spring, an old orchard, and impressive displays of pink ladyslippers and dwarf crested iris. The trail itself is short but relatively difficult. It is steep in places and stays in the stream for long stretches, especially near the end. Nevertheless, the trail is well worth the effort it takes to travel it. The stream is beautiful, the valley contains good examples of cove hardwood forest, and Crowder Place is one of the best campsites in the Citico Wilderness. A very scenic and enjoyable day-hike can be negotiated using Crowder Branch Trail, Mill Branch Trail, and the section of the Fodderstack Trail between these two trails.

The trail starts at 3.5 miles on the Doublecamp Road just past a large meadow, known as Crowder Field, to the right of the road. There is a parking area/campsite across the road from the trail sign with "No. 84" on it. There is additional parking for one or two cars immediately across a small bridge over Crowder Branch. Additional parking can be found back at the meadow.

Details: The trail crosses Crowder Branch at 0.1 mile and parallels the stream. At 0.2 mile the trail crosses the branch again and follows an old wet roadbed that acts as a diversion stream in wet weather. Look for white blazes. The trail crosses the branch again and then joins an old roadbed (at 0.4 mile) that follows the branch closely through cove hardwood forest. The trail crosses the branch several times until the trail ascends steeply to the slope above the branch at 0.8 mile. Notice a cascade and pool on the branch to the right below. There are more excellent views of the branch as the trail moves up the slope above it. Cross a small side stream at 1.0 mile. Here are excellent views of the branch through towering trees. At 1.2 miles the trail descends to a flat area near the creek that could serve as a small campsite.

The trail ascends steeply out of the flat area, crosses a side stream, and rejoins the old roadbed. Below is a towering cove hardwood forest with large, exceptionally straight trees. The trail continues along the left (north) side of Crowder Branch. At 1.7 miles cross a small side stream and then ascend the slope steeply. At 1.8 miles a crossing of Crowder Branch is reached. To follow the established trail, cross here and ascend steeply along its right (south) side. It is possible to continue along the north side on an old roadbed a few yards above the branch. This route is heavily overgrown with rhododendron and is essentially cross-country in many places. However, it avoids some of the sloshing through the streambed that the established trail requires. This alternate route rejoins the main trail near Crowder Place and may offer promise for rerouting the trail in the future.

To continue on the main trail, ascend beside the stream on the south side of the branch. Cross the branch to the left (north) side at 1.9 miles through a tangle of fallen logs and rock steps. The trail enters the streambed at 2.0 miles and is in and out of the stream for much of the remaining distance to Crowder Place. At 2.3 miles exit the stream to the left and follow it as it enters a clearing at 2.4 miles. Ruins of an old building are to the right. The branch (now a trickle) comes from the covered spring to the left. The spring is very dependable, and there are campsites nearby. Many more additional sites are available as the trail bears right around the ruins and enters a large meadow, known as Crowder Field. Several old apple trees still stand in the meadow. The Crowder Branch Trail intersects with the Fodderstack Trail at 2.6 miles. There are also potential campsites at this intersection. This trail junction is at 3.04 miles on the Fodderstack Trail from the Farr Gap Trailhead.

Mill Branch (Trail No. 96)
Length: 2.5 miles
Elevation Change: Start 1,860 feet, end 3,380 feet (high point 3,380 feet)
Trailheads: Mill Branch (start) and Fodderstack Trail (end)
Type: Hiking

Comments: This trail parallels Mill Branch up the northwest flank of Pine Ridge. However, for most of its length the stream is out of sight, and the main stream is crossed only once, although some small side branches are also crossed. The trail is in good condition for most of its length except for some areas near Big Stack Gap. Stretches of the trail are quite steep. An excellent day-hike can be put together using Mill

Branch Trail, Crowder Branch Trail, and the portion of the Fodderstack Trail between them. Mill Branch roughly parallels Crowder Branch, but the two trails give very different perspectives of their respective streams. There is no marker for Mill Branch Trail on Fodderstack Trail, and a blow-down of large oak branches obscures Mill Branch Trail here. However, Big Stack Gap is easily recognized as the deepest gap on this stretch of the Fodderstack Trail. A beautiful campsite in a grove of large trees dominated by a huge red oak is 0.1 mile down the trail from Big Stack Gap.

The trail begins at 2.7 miles on the Doublecamp Road immediately after crossing Mill Branch on the road. The trail is on the right (east) side of the road and is designated by a trail sign with No. 96. There is limited space for parking at the trailhead.

Details: The trail starts out on an old railbed through tall hemlock and pines along Mill Branch. There is a clearing on the left that has been used for camping. For the first 0.5 mile the trail is wide, relatively flat, and lined with ferns. The evergreens gradually give way to deciduous trees. The trail runs close to Mill Branch until at 0.5 mile it climbs the slope and leaves the stream far below to the right. A couple of small side streams are crossed at 0.7 and 0.8 mile, and then a pine forest is entered as the trail continues to traverse the slope. At 1.0 mile the trail passes through rhododendron to reach the only major stream crossing. This is one of the two major forks of Mill Branch; it curves around the nose of the ridge just across the stream and flows to the right to intersect the other fork that has descended on the other side of the ridge. Cross the first fork and ascend very steeply the slope of the ridge. The second fork of Mill Branch flows in the valley below to the right.

The trail continues to ascend along the slope of the ridge from 1.05 miles to 1.75 miles, heading southeast and then east. The trail is very steep and without switchbacks but is in good condition. There is evidence that the trail is on the bed of an old narrow-gauge rail spur like those that went up many of the valleys to carry out timber early in this century. At 1.6 miles look for railroad ties exposed in the trail. These particular ties are made of chestnut and are very resistant to decay. At 1.75 miles the trail crosses the brow of the ridge and levels off. The fork of Mill Branch that was crossed at the bottom of the ridge lies to the left, and the trail remains relatively level as it passes through this "hanging valley" of this fork of Mill Branch. At 1.9 miles look for bits of coal left from the old rail spur; at 2.0 miles look for a large coil of cable from logging days.

Shortly after passing the cable, the trail passes through a small tributary stream and seep area. At 2.3 miles another muddy seep area is entered. At 2.4 miles a grove of large trees lies to the right of the trail. This grove, which contains a large buckeye and several maples and tulip trees, is dominated by a huge northern red oak. There is space for one or more tents in the area surrounded by these trees; water can be obtained in the stream nearby. The trail ascends rather steeply past the grove and enters Big Stack Gap at 2.5 miles. There are several large northern red oaks in the gap. A huge branch (larger than most trees) from one of these trees has fallen, partially obscuring the junction of Fodderstack Trail with Mill Branch Trail. There is room to camp in the gap. The Crowder Branch Trail is 1.2 miles to the left (northeast) along Fodderstack Trail.

Rocky Flats Branch (Rocky Flats) (Trail No. 100)
Length: 4.5 miles
Elevation Change: Start 1,880 feet, end 1,680 feet (high point 2,960 feet)
Trailheads: Rocky Flats Branch (start) and Citico Creek Corridor (end)
Type: Hiking

Comments: This trail is very challenging. It has received little use and is difficult to follow, especially in the middle. However, the trail goes through a variety of different environments and passes impressive ruins of an old homestead. It is well worth the effort if you do not mind the sometimes difficult task of searching for traces of the trail. The trail is probably somewhat easier to follow starting from Doublecamp Road rather than in the opposite direction. The blazes are old and sporadic, but recent maintenance may improve them. Look for grouse and signs of bear along this trail.

The trail begins at mile 2.5 on the Doublecamp Road, before crossing Mill Branch. The trail begins on the right (southeast) side of the road at the FS trail sign No. 100. There is parking for two or three cars on the opposite side of the road. This is also known as Rocky Flats Trail.

Details: The trail climbs uphill heading southeast; no blazes are visible. After turning briefly east, the trail continues southeast through second-growth mixed hardwoods and pine. After 0.5 mile the trail turns south along an old roadbed. At 0.7 mile the trail is almost blocked by young saplings; bear to the right through the trees and then downhill toward the south. At 0.9 mile the trail leaves the roadbed and heads southwest to the right of a small stream. Look for sporadic blazes.

The trail passes several rock structures in ruins and through the remains of an old house. An almost intact chimney is to the right of the trail; ruins of another chimney are to the left of the trail. The trail enters the stream at 1.1 miles, heading downstream. Go through the stream for about 60 feet and look for a white blaze and an old roadbed on the left side of the stream. A huge old chestnut log lies across the trail at 1.2 miles. It has footholds cut in its side to climb over. The trail comes out into an open forest of hardwoods and hemlock. Follow blazes to the south and then to the southeast. Ascend a gentle slope through hickories. At 1.25 miles the last blaze for some time is passed. Go through a patch of ferns and start up a broad valley.

Turn sharply right just past the ferns at 1.3 miles (there is no blaze, but the turn is 150 feet past the last blaze).

The trail proceeds steeply upslope. Look for a blaze about 200 feet upslope; turn sharply right (northwest) just past the blaze. The trail follows the contour of the slope and passes over a ridge at 1.4 miles. It then descends into and crosses a dry drainage with hemlocks and poplars towering above. The trail is now heading northwest. At 1.6 miles pass through a dense stand of young pine and hemlock. The trail heads downhill into another dry drainage and turns right (southwest) along the slope of the opposite side of the drainage; watch for blazes. Go over a small ridge at 1.7 miles and head southwest and then south. At 1.8 miles the trail goes through an extensive blow-down that has been somewhat cut and cleared. The trail encounters and parallels a small stream for a short distance before entering the stream at 1.9 miles. It emerges about 30 feet downstream on the opposite bank.

Head uphill through rhododendron. At 1.95 miles cross a small drainage and head sharply uphill (southwest). The trail tops out on a ridge and takes a sharp left to the south back along the slope of the ridge. Notice white quartz boulders at 2.1 miles. Continue around the contour of Pine Ridge heading generally west, topping spur ridges and descending into dry drainage channels. Look closely for the sporadic blazes.

At 2.9 miles the trail descends into a valley with a small stream after making two switchbacks. Cross the stream and turn right (west). Follow the stream as it bears to the southwest. The trail crosses the stream three more times and at 3.4 miles goes down the middle of the stream for about 40 feet and emerges on the left of the stream. Cross the stream two more times. As the trail tops the ridge at 3.55 miles, turn sharply left to the northeast and climb the rocks along the ridgecrest. You will need to look closely for this turnoff as the trail appears to continue straight along the ridge. If you continue straight along the ridge on the alternate trail, there is a view of Citico Creek to the left. The alternate trail then continues around the ridge and reaches Citico Creek after 0.2 mile. If you cross Citico Creek on the alternate trail, you will reach the Citico Road approximately half way between Doublecamp and the Citico Corridor area. This is where the designated trail formerly ended.

Continuing along the designated trail, climb steeply over rocks on the ridgecrest to the northeast. Spectacular views of Citico Creek are below to the right. The trail runs along the dry south slope above Citico Creek. At 3.8 miles the trail flattens out and runs through open hardwoods. At 4.3 miles the trail again comes out on the dry south slope above Citico Creek. At 4.4 miles the trail crosses a small stream and descends along the stream through rhododendron. At 4.5 miles the trail comes out in a meadow in the Citico Corridor area. A trail sign by a large forked tulip tree indicates Trail No. 100.

Pine Ridge (Trail No. 99)

Length: 3.55 miles
Elevation Change: Start 1,720 feet, end 4,000 feet (high point 4,000 feet)
Trailheads: Citico Corridor Area (start) and Fodderstack Trail (end)
Type: Horse

Comments: The Pine Ridge Trail follows Pine Ridge to its junction with the Fodderstack Trail near the top of Big Fodderstack Mountain. For most of its length the trail follows the southern flank of Pine Ridge just below its backbone as it climbs to the east-northeast. The middle portion of the trail goes through a series of small coves along the ridge side alternating with exposed south slope. There are some excellent views of the North Fork drainage along this trail. Iris and phlox bloom on the lower portion of the trail in the spring, and flame azaleas can be seen in late June on the middle portion of the trail. The trail is relatively dry, although a small stream is crossed on the lower portion, and a spring occurs in the last mile. The spring may dry up when rain is not plentiful. There are three small areas that could be used for tent sites, but they are not near water sources.

The trail starts in the Citico Corridor Area about 0.1 mile up the dirt road from the concrete low-water bridge. Look for a horse-trail sign on the left. A hiker's trail sign is a few feet past the first sign. The two trails that turn off to the left join after a few feet.

Details: The trail will appear to fork after a very short distance. Take the right fork; the left fork dead-ends. At 0.1 mile the trail comes to an overlook over Citico Creek. At 0.2 mile the trail crosses a beautiful small stream and then begins to climb up the slope and away from Citico Creek. At 0.4 mile the trail enters a small cove. At 0.5 mile the trail turns sharply north. Huckleberries are along the trail here. The trail turns sharply to the east again at 0.56 mile as it goes through a mixed pine and hardwood forest. At 0.8 mile the trail bears back to the north. At 1.4 miles there is a potential campsite for one tent. At 1.8 miles there is a larger potential campsite downslope to the right; there are signs this site has been used as a hunter's camp in the past. At 1.9 miles there is another small flat area to the right of the trail that could be used for tents.

The trail crosses a dry drainage at 2.31 miles; there are several large trees in this area. Bear have been sighted in this area, and there may be signs of boar. Enter a small cove area at 2.4 miles and then cross a dry drainage area. At 2.6 miles the trail slants across the steep side of the ridge with rock outcrops above the trail and then goes around a ridge point where there is a potential campsite on the point of the ridge to the right. At 2.7 miles there are views through the trees of the North Fork of

Citico drainage. Water flows out of rocks beside the trail at 2.75 miles. A spring emerges below the trail at 2.8 miles; the spring has good flow in wet weather but may dry up in dry weather. At 3.3 miles the trail angles north; there is a view of Big Fodderstack Mountain to the east through the pines. The trail passes through a section overgrown with mountain laurel and has great views before intersecting with the Fodderstack Trail at 3.55 miles. From here the Fodderstack Trail goes northeast toward Crowder Place and southeast toward Glen Gap.

South Fork Citico Creek (Trail No. 105)
Length: 8.5 miles
Elevation Change: Start 1,720 feet, end 4,400 feet (high point 4,400 feet)
Trailheads: Warden Station Area (start) and Cold Spring Gap (end)
Trail Connections: North Fork Citico Creek Trail, Brush Mountain Trail, Grassy Branch Trail, and Jeffrey Hell Trail
Type: Hiking

Comments: The South Fork Citico Creek Trail follows the South Fork Citico Creek from the Warden Station Area to its headwaters below Cold Spring Gap. There is at least one stream crossing in the lower section of the trail that will require care, especially if the creek is high. Sections of the trail may be overgrown with blackberries, and portions of the trail may be difficult to find unless the trail has received recent maintenance. There are spectacular views of the Citico Creek Gorge in the middle section and a spacious meadow near its end that will accommodate several tents. Spring wildflowers abound along this trail. The trail provides access and connections to several other trails; it is a key trail for exploring the Citico Wilderness, as well as being a very scenic and enjoyable hike.

The trailhead for the South Fork Citico Creek Trail begins at the turnoff to the Warden Station Area from the Citico Creek Road 2.3 miles from the Indian Boundary Recreation Area entrance and 1.7 miles from Doublecamp (see the trailhead access for the Warden Station Area, above). Note that this trailhead is not across the low-water bridge at the Citico Corridor Area. It is 0.1 mile up the ridge along the Citico Creek Road toward Indian Boundary past the turnoff to the Corridor Area. A USFS trail sign with "No. 105" designates the beginning of the trail. There is parking for only two or three cars at the trailhead. It is much better to park across the low-water bridge at the Corridor area and walk the 0.1 mile up Citico Creek Road to the trailhead.

Details: Follow the old road until it reaches an end at a dirt barrier. Continue past the barrier as the trail narrows and passes ruins of the Warden Station and a small stream at 0.16 mile. Cross another small stream at 0.25 mile. The trail then traverses the steep slope above Citico Creek through rhododendron. Another small stream is crossed at 0.4 mile before reaching a clearing and the remnants of an old orchard at 0.5 mile. Continue through the clearing to reach an old roadbed at 0.6 mile and a wooden trail register. The South Fork Citico Creek Trail turns right along the roadbed. Back to the left the roadbed crosses Citico Creek and reaches the Citico Corridor area; the concrete low-water bridge at the turnoff from the Citico Creek Road is 0.32 mile away but requires a rather difficult crossing of Citico Creek.

The trail follows the roadbed along Citico Creek and passes a concrete blockhouse at 0.9 mile. The North Fork Citico Creek Trail turns left across a footbridge at 0.97 mile. The South Fork Citico Creek Trail continues along the right side of the creek. At 1.2 miles a stream enters the creek on the opposite bank; this is Ike Camp Branch. The Brush Mountain Trail begins at an unmarked creek crossing 250 feet further upstream. A flat area at 2.0 miles would accommodate one or two tents. At 2.13 miles, as you approach an obvious stream crossing, the trail leaves the old roadbed and angles back to the right, up, and across the slope to avoid two stream crossings. If desired, the roadbed can be followed across the two crossings. A tributary stream is crossed at 2.2 miles. The old roadbed is rejoined at 2.39 miles. A small area with a fire ring and room for a tent is passed at 2.54 miles. At 2.6 miles the Grassy Branch Trail leaves the South Fork Trail and continues along the right bank of the creek. The South Fork Trail crosses the creek at this point to the left (north) side and requires wading. At 2.7 miles a stream (Eagle Branch) flows into South Fork Citico Creek on the opposite bank. A short distance later, a side trail to the right leads to a cable strung across the creek; this is an alternative trailhead for Grassy Branch Trail.

At 3.1 miles is a small campsite. The trail leaves the roadbed at 3.5 miles and angles steeply up the slope to the left. At 3.6 miles the trail ascends to the left of a small stream ravine for 0.1 mile. The trail then crosses the stream and proceeds up the stream. About 50 feet beyond the crossing, despite the presence of a path up the creekbed, do not continue up the streambed. Instead, cut sharply back to the right, go up the slope very steeply, and traverse the ridge steeply until it rejoins the roadbed (or railbed) at 3.9 miles. At 4.0 miles the trail comes to a fork of the railbeds. The South Fork Trail takes the left fork (note the blazes) and angles upslope of the other roadbed, which appears to go back down to the creek; do not go downward at this point. At 4.2 miles coal can be seen in the trail. A stream ravine crosses at 4.4 miles. At 4.7 miles the slope to the north of the trail is a blackberry slick, presumably due to fires that swept through the area after logging. The trail itself is heavily overgrown with blackberry briars, grape vines, and greenbriar, and may be difficult to negotiate unless it has had recent maintenance. This section of the trail affords spectacular views of the South Fork Citico Creek Gorge below. The view is more noticeable when hiking the trail in the opposite direction, so be sure to look back to the west if hiking up the trail. At 4.8 miles look for a tree growing up through a pile of large cables. A stream crosses the trail at 5.3 miles. Shortly past the stream turn back for another view over the creek gorge. A jumble of boulders is crossed at 5.4 miles.

The trail rejoins the South Fork Citico Creek, and there is a series of falls and cascades at 5.5 miles. At 5.8 miles is an opening to the left (north) of the trail that has a fire ring and scraps of old iron; space for a tent could be found. Small creeks cross the trail at 5.9 and 6.2 miles. There is a small campsite 100 feet up the second stream. At 6.25 miles the Jeffrey Hell Trail comes in from the right, having come from the Tellico-Robbinsville Road. The South Fork Citico Creek Trail continues straight ahead, remaining on the north side of the creek. At 6.5 miles a cleared area containing iron pieces, fire rings, and space for a tent is passed. Cross Citico Creek (wading may be required) to the right (south) side at 7.0 miles. Much of the trail may be wet in this area during rain. The old railbed is very prominent here, and pieces of slag and old iron pieces can be seen at 7.3 miles. A large grassy meadow beside the trail at 7.4 miles makes a lovely campsite for several tents. Spring beauties abound here in April.

The trail continues through a forest of young, straight tulip trees and through several small streams. The trail continues to cross and be in small streams as it passes through rhododendrons along the old railbed. Around 8.0 miles leave the railbed, ascending moderately. The trail follows the streambed for a short distance and then steeply climbs the adjacent slope. Spring wildflowers, including trout lily and spring beauty, abound in this area in April. The trail continues uphill to the east through rich forest, crosses the stream, and continues steeply through open woods. After a final stream crossing, the trail again ascends steeply up to Cold Spring Gap at 8.6 miles. There is a small parking area in the gap.

North Fork Citico Creek (Trail No. 98)

Length: 5.45 miles
Elevation Change: Start 1,800 feet, end 4,400 feet (high point 4,400 feet)
Trailheads: South Fork Citico Creek Trail (start) and Fodderstack Trail (end)
Trail Connections: Cold Springs Gap Trail
Type: Hiking

Comments: The North Fork Trail follows the North Fork of Citico Creek from its confluence with the South Fork Citico Creek to near its source below Cherry Log Gap. The gap is a short distance up the hollow above the creek. There are several beautiful waterfalls along the upper portion of the creek, and the trail passes through some of the wildest and most scenic portions of the Citico Creek Wilderness. The trail crosses Citico Creek many times. Several of these crossings are in the lower portion of the creek and can be difficult, especially after a heavy rain. The trail was newly blazed in the summer of 1989.

This trail begins at 0.8 mile of the South Fork Trail at a hiker's sign, just past the ruins of an old concrete building. The trail leaves the South Fork Trail to the left, crossing the South Fork Citico Creek on a wooden bridge.

Details: From the footbridge the South Fork Citico Creek can be seen flowing into the North Fork Creek to the left. At 0.1 mile there is an old weir (notched dam) on the North Fork Creek. The trail fords the creek to the left side at 0.5 mile and then back to the right side after about 0.1 mile. There is a campsite to the right of the trail in between these crossings. It is possible to avoid both crossings by climbing the slope on the right side of the creek. However, this route is quite difficult as it passes through a thick growth of rhododendron. Continuing on the right side of the creek, a potential campsite overlooking the creek is passed at 0.62 mile. The trail, which remains fairly level, continues along the right bank of the creek. A pair of crossings occur at 1.4 miles and again 0.1 mile later, bringing the trail back to the right side of the creek. At 1.6 miles the trail crosses a tributary stream that flows into the North Fork Creek from the right. There is a large camping area to the right of the trail at 2.1 miles.

The trail continues to parallel the creek closely, for the most part on an old rail-road bed. The trail crosses part of the creek at 2.2 miles to an island, which it follows for 0.1 mile before recrossing back to the right side of the creek. At 2.5 miles the trail crosses the creek to the left side. A tributary is crossed at 2.7 miles; potential camp-sites are to the left of the trail soon afterwards. The trail crosses back to the right side of the creek at 3.0 miles. A flat, raised area at 3.1 miles would make a good camp site. The creek is crossed to the left side at 3.2 miles and enters a flat area suit-able for camping. The trail turns sharply left and climbs a very steep slope. Watch for blazes. The trail intersects the old railbed and turns right. It reaches a large tribu-tary at 3.5 miles. This is a lovely area, and there are flat spots nearby that might be suitable for camping. Debris from logging days may be found.

After crossing the tributary, the trail continues through a relatively flat area be-fore beginning to climb rather steeply beside the creek. At 3.95 miles the trail passes between two enormous boulders. As the trail climbs steeply, there is a view of a beautiful waterfall (30 to 40 feet high) and cascade to the right. The trail goes up and over a gigantic moss-covered boulder beside the creek and crosses the creek to the right side at 4.1 miles. The trail goes through thick rhododendron and crosses the creek to the left side above a large cascade at 4.2 miles. The creek divides just above the crossing; follow the left branch. Notice the large cable as the trail crosses back to the right side of the creek. The trail crosses the creek a number of times in the next 0.5 mile. Look for a view of a waterfall ahead through the vegetation. The trail crosses the creek on the lip of this waterfall at 4.7 miles. Another waterfall is reached at 4.8 miles. There is space for a tent near the base of this waterfall. The trail climbs a steep slope and switchback beside the fall. At 4.84 miles the Cold Spring Gap Trail comes in from the right to join the North Fork Trail.

The North Fork Trail continues east southeast on the right of the creek but soon crosses to the left. At 5.0 miles the trail bears to the left; an old route can be seen bearing to the right back toward the stream. The trail follows an old railbed, which will have water flowing over it in wet weather. At 5.2 miles the trail is dry and the forest opens up as rhododendron disappears from the understory. The trail climbs steeply between two ridges. Beech, cherry, silverbell, and sugar maple trees are passed as the trail climbs up the hollow and comes out at Cherry Log Gap to intersect the Fodderstack Trail at 5.45 miles. Note the large cherry trees in this broad gap. The Fodderstack Trail leads south out of the gap toward Bob Bald and north out of the gap toward Chestnut Knob and Glen Gap.

Brush Mountain (Ike Camp Branch) (Trail No. 97)
Length: 4.4 miles
Elevation Change: Start 1,880 feet, end 4,360 feet (high point 4,360 feet)
Trailheads: South Fork Citico Creek Trail (start) and Cold Spring Gap Trail (end)
Type: Hiking

Comments: The Brush Mountain Trail ascends Brush Mountain from a generally western direction. The trail follows Ike Camp Branch for about 2.0 miles before leaving the stream, passing below Ikes Peak, and then continuing through beautiful forest stands and some large trees on the slopes and coves of Brush Mountain. The trail is frequently referred to as the Ike Camp Branch Trail, but we will use the USFS designation of Brush Mountain Trail to avoid confusion with the Ike Branch Trail in the adjacent Joyce Kilmer-Slickrock Wilderness. The trail is sometimes difficult to follow and passes through areas of windblown trees and overgrowth, but it has outstanding scenery and conveys a sense of wild remoteness and isolation. There are signs of logging and a small gauge rail line in the area up Ike Camp Branch. Signs of wildlife, including bear, bobcat, and boar are often seen, especially in the middle portion of the trail. Because of elevation gain, this trail is quite challenging when hiking up it (which is how the trail details below describe it).

The trailhead is one of the more difficult parts of the trail to locate; at the time this trail was scouted there was no trail sign. At 1.2 miles on the South Fork Citico Creek Trail look for a stream flowing into the opposite side of the South Fork Citico

Creek. This stream (Ike Branch) will be the first tributary of any size past the North Fork Citico Creek. Walk another 250 feet, looking for a rock cairn on the side of the trail. Also look for large boulders on each side of Citico Creek that look as though they once supported a bridge. Look for a blaze on a tree on the opposite bank and cable and wire on the tree. Cross the South Fork Citico Creek at this point.

Details: Cross the South Fork Citico Creek to the blazed tree on the opposite bank. Depending on the water level, this crossing may be difficult. There are remnants of cable and wire attached to this tree. Look for rectangular cut-out blazes on the trees, as well as old white blazes and sporadic large painted reddish orange circles. The trail follows Citico Creek downstream for about 140 feet and then turns right (east), going up the hillside. Ike Camp Branch can soon be seen downslope to the left.

The trail goes up the narrow valley of Ike Camp Branch. Note the old rail ties at 0.2 mile. In the spring, spring beauties, Canadian yellow violets, and trillium occur frequently on this trail near the stream. At 0.4 mile the trail crosses Ike Camp Branch to the left; it crosses back to the right side a short time later. The stream and the trail are both heading to the southeast. The trail remains for some time on a shelf to the right and above the stream. You may see an old engine block beside the trail. At 1.0 mile the trail moves briefly away from Ike Camp Branch and is wet from a side stream flowing down the trail. At 1.1 miles the trail approaches Ike Camp Branch again and crosses to the left bank. Pieces of coal from the old narrow-gauge train line may be spotted around 1.3 miles in an area overgrown with many grape vines. At 1.5 miles the trail goes up to the left around, and then over, a large boulder and then crosses the branch to the right bank. The trail heads upstream to the east. The trail soon enters the stream and travels in and out of the stream for the next 0.4 mile. You should watch closely for the trail during this stretch. At 1.6 miles the branch divides; look for a tree with a white blaze and a gray swatch painted around it. Follow the left branch. At 1.85 miles railroad ties in the streambed give a stairstep appearance. By 1.9 miles the stream has virtually disappeared; the trail heads upslope to a saddle below Ikes Peak at 2.1 miles.

In the saddle the trail turns sharply right to the southeast and follows the ridge. The trail descends steeply at 2.3 miles to cross a small hollow and ascends the other side to a small cleared area (at 2.4 miles) that could accommodate one tent. The trail descends through a hardwood forest with a rhododendron understory to a boggy area at 2.5 miles. The trail heads east through open forest with a fern understory and then passes through a grove of hemlocks to a grove of large cherry trees. The trail continues through a forest of mixed northern hardwoods until it tops out on a peak at 2.8 miles. The elevation here is 4,013 feet. The trail turns east and descends past a grove of large cherry trees. The trail ascends through a dense stand of hemlock and then descends steeply through a dense stand of hemlock and rhododendron. At 3.1 miles the trail reaches a grove of large tulip trees. There is a pile of buckets, other rubbish, and a pile of coal at 3.2 miles. There are signs that a road once came in at this point.

The trail turns southeast and ascends through hemlock and hardwood to reach rock outcrops along the ridgeline at 3.6 miles. There are good views into Jeffrey Hell from this vantage point. The trail turns east along the ridgeline but soon drops off the ridgecrest to the left (north) and descends sharply downslope. At 3.76 miles look for a large silverbell tree with a blaze, showing where to angle across the slope. There is a large cherry tree with a blaze at 3.8 miles. Other large trees can be seen, including buckeye, hemlock, and beech. There follows an extensive blow-down that makes traversing this section of the trail difficult. Rock outcrops are to the right at 4.1 miles. Bear right at 4.3 miles after the trail goes up through rhododendron and passes between two large hemlock trees. At 4.4 miles the trail passes through an overgrowth of blackberry bushes. Push through these bushes or skirt around them to intersect the Cold Spring Gap Trail at 4.4 miles. To reach Cold Spring Gap, turn right and walk 1.5 miles.

Flats Mountain (Trail No. 102)

Length: 6.2 miles
Elevation Change: Start 3,600 feet, end 1,960 feet (high point 3,853 feet)
Trailheads: Eagle Gap (start) and Beehouse Gap (end)
Type: Hiking

Comments: The Flats Mountain Trail follows the ridge of Flats Mountain from its high point near Eagle Gap down along the edge of the Citico Creek Wilderness to Beehouse Gap outside the Wilderness. There are spectacular views of Indian Boundary Lake and much of the Tellico Ranger District, as well as views into the Citico Creek Wilderness, especially when leaves are off the trees.

The Flats Mountain Trail is well maintained and easy to follow. When hiked from Eagle Gap to Beehouse Gap, as described, the trail is practically all downhill and particularly enjoyable, with many outstanding vistas. Hawks can often be sighted in the higher elevations. Wildflowers of many kinds may also be found in the spring and summer.

Water is generally not available on the Flats Mountain Trail, and few campsites are available except on the meadows on Flats Mountain, so this trail is better suited for a day hike than for backpacking. If a backpack trip is undertaken, water can be obtained in wet weather at a spring at 1.4 miles or off-trail on the lower portion of the trail.

The trail begins at Eagle Gap on the Tellico-Robbinsville Road, 4.8 miles east of TN 165 and FS 345 junction. A USFS hiker's sign "No. 102" can be seen on the left side of the road. A gravel road that turns off the main road at this point leads to adequate parking.

Details: Follow the gravel road from Eagle Gap uphill. Bear left at the first turn. This jeep road is a remnant of the old road that ran along Sassafras Ridge before the Tellico-Robbinsville Road was built. The road is gated at 0.1 mile. There are outstanding views of the Citico Creek Wilderness, Bob Stratton Bald, and the Unicoi Mountain Range as the trail climbs the ridge. The trail reaches a grassy meadow (a former wildlife management clearing) on top of Flats Mountain at 0.5 mile. There are great views of the Tellico Ranger District. The trail exits on the right side of the meadow and heads northeast into a second grassy meadow (also a former food plot) at 0.7 mile. Cross this meadow in the long direction and leave the meadow at the far end, heading northeast. Continue down the ridge through a dry oak forest. At 0.9 mile a side trail to the left leads down to rock outcroppings from which there are tremendous views to the northwest of Indian Boundary Lake, Tellico Lake, and in the distance the TN Valley. There will be a number of other views of this panorama as the trail winds down the mountain, but the view from these rocks is by far the best.

Continuing northeast along the main trail, two sharp switchbacks occur at 1.0 mile around the high point of Flats Mountain. The trail traverses across the mountain to the east. A flat area at 1.2 miles has been used as a camping area. At 1.3 miles the trail continues down the mountain with a switchback to the northwest. At 1.4 miles a small stream crosses the trail from a spring that emerges a few yards above the trail; this spring probably does not run in dry weather. While going around a switchback to the east at 1.6 miles you may catch a glimpse of Indian Boundary Lake. Another switchback to the southwest occurs at 1.8 miles. Do not take the dim trail that heads straight down the ridge; it rejoins the main trail but is so steep without the switchbacks that it poses an erosion problem. The trail switches back to the northeast at 1.9 miles and heads down the ridgeline. The trail passes through a stand of table mountain pine at 2.0 miles. A gap in the trees allows a view into the Citico watershed to the east. Another view up the Citico drainage at 2.5 miles gives good views of the Unicoi Mountains. A small gap at 2.8 miles has a fire ring and could serve as a dry campsite. Red blazes at 2.9 miles mark the Wilderness boundary, which the trail generally follows. The trail turns to the southwest a couple of times but quickly resumes its descent along the ridge to the northeast. The trail goes through a gap at 3.3 miles and then tops out on a knob covered with table mountain pine at 3.5 miles.

The trail goes down a steep, straight descent at 3.6 miles. Big Fodderstack can be seen straight ahead. At 3.7 miles is a good view up the South Fork Citico drainage to the southeast; to the northwest is the last of the views of Indian Boundary Lake. There is the site of a recent fire (1989) at 3.9 miles, with a jumble of blowdowns and small pines and other seedlings emerging. The trail makes another steep, straight descent to the northeast and then turns sharply to the south at 4.1 miles. There is another good view into the South Fork Citico drainage through the dead pines; listen for the sound of water. The trail turns sharply back to the northeast at 4.3 miles and then gradually turns to the north. Red blazes at 4.9 miles mark the boundary of the Wilderness; the remainder of the trail lies outside the Wilderness. The trail gradually turns to the northwest. There is a large area of blow-down at 5.1 miles. A dim trail that comes in from the right at 5.7 miles at a white blaze and flag lead into the Citico drainage. The trail continues northwest through mixed pine and hardwoods. The trail comes out on the Citico Creek Road at Beehouse Gap at 6.2 miles. A parking area for several cars is directly across the road from the trailhead. A USFS sign gives the elevation at Beehouse Gap as 2,580 feet, but this should be 1,960 feet.

Grassy Branch (Trail No. 91)
Length: 2.3 miles
Elevation Change: Start 3,400 feet, end 2,160 feet (high point 3,400 feet)
Trailheads: Grassy Gap (start) and South Fork Citico Creek Trail (end)
Type: Hiking

Comments: The Grassy Branch Trail follows Grassy Branch and then Eagle Branch as they descend to South Fork Citico Creek. The trail follows Grassy Branch as it passes through a lovely hanging valley, with plentiful spring wildflowers, then flows dramatically out of the valley in a series of falls and cascades to join Eagle Branch. There are a number of inviting pools along Eagle Branch. Two alternate leads near the end of the trail give a choice of routes for reaching the South Fork Citico Creek Trail. The trail seems to have more than its share of snakes.

Construction of the Tellico-Robbinsville Road exposed iron pyrites that resulted in acid contamination in the upper portion of Grassy Branch in the 1970s. Mitigation measures were undertaken with some success. Additionally, the small amount of water originating in the polluted area is vastly diluted by the time Grassy Branch reaches Eagle Branch and South Fork Citico Creek. Still, one should not rely on Grassy Branch for drinking water (there are old signs along the branch, which have mostly fallen over, warning that the water is contaminated).

The trail begins at a parking area to the left and below the Tellico-Robbinsville

Road at Grassy Gap, 6.3 miles past the TN 165 and FS 345 junction. There is a parking area to the left just before the Grassy Gap sign. Follow the hiker's sign (No. 91) out of the parking area into a beautiful grassy meadow.

Details: The trail passes through the meadow, which is bordered by oaks and hickories to the east and a hemlock grove on the western edge. Cross the small stream at the far side of the meadow and enter a boggy area. At 0.1 mile the trail passes through dense rhododendron and hemlock. The trail crosses the stream again and is in and out of the water for the next 0.2 mile. At one point the branch runs briefly underground. At 0.3 mile the trail is on the slope above the left side of the stream. The trail passes through young, second-growth cove hardwoods. During the next mile the trail and branch gradually enter a hanging valley that has an open understory with herbaceous cover and wildflowers abounding. Two small side streams come in from the left at 0.6 mile and 0.8 mile. There is a fallen sign at the second stream that warns that the water is contaminated. Shortly past the second stream, two large hemlocks beside the trail probably predate the logging in the Area. The trail crosses and is in Grassy Branch several times during the next 0.5 mile. At 1.1 miles, while the trail is to the right of Grassy Branch, a side stream enters from the east. Since this stream does not have its source near the Tellico-Robbinsville Road, it should be uncontaminated by acid runoff.

At 1.3 miles the branch begins its descent out of the hanging valley as a series of cascades and falls. The trail descends rather steeply along the slope to the right of the branch. Note the high bluff on the other side of the branch. As the trail moves away from the branch, look back up the valley for spectacular views of the water falling and cascading out of the hanging valley. At 1.5 miles the trail crosses over the nose of a spur ridge coming down from the right and descends into a small stream channel. As the trail resumes its descent along the slope of the main ridge, Grassy Branch can be seen joining Eagle Branch in the valley below. The trail reaches Eagle Branch at 1.6 miles and crosses it to the left side; it crosses to the right side at 1.7 miles. At 1.8 miles is a nice pool in the stream below a small waterfall just after the branch is crossed back to the left side. At 1.9 miles a small stream comes in from the left. Cross Eagle Branch to the right at 2.0 miles.

Continue along the right side of Eagle Branch until it reaches South Fork Citico Creek at 2.3 miles. There is a cable stretched across the creek that can be used with caution to cross. The South Fork Citico Creek Trail is on the other side of the creek at 2.4 miles. The trail junction is at 2.6 miles on the South Fork Citico Creek Trail from the Warden Station Area Trailhead.

Alternately, cross Eagle Branch to the left side at 2.2 miles and follow that trail through rhododendron. Cross Clemmer Cove Branch at 2.3 miles and intersect the

South Fork Citico Creek Trail at 2.4 miles before it crosses the creek. Which trail you take in the last section will depend on whether you plan on going up or down the South Fork Citico Creek Trail.

Falls Branch (Trail No. 87)
Length: 1.3 miles
Elevation Change: Start 3,960 feet, end 3,520 feet (high point 3,960 feet)
Trailhead: Rattlesnake Rock Parking Area (start and dead-end)
Type: Hiking

Comments: The Falls Branch Trail is a short but very beautiful trail to the 80-foot Falls Branch Waterfall. The Falls Branch Area was a scenic area before the Citico Creek Wilderness was designated. During this period the trail left directly from the old Sassafras Ridge Road and traveled a fraction of a mile to the falls. After the Tellico-Robbinsville Road was constructed, the trail was rerouted along part of the old Sassafras Ridge Road and the trailhead was placed at the Rattlesnake Parking Area. Be careful along the last section of the trail near the falls as the rocks will be wet, moss-covered, and very slippery.

The trail begins at a parking area on the left of the Tellico-Robbinsville Road near Rattlesnake Rock, 8.4 miles east of the TN 165 and FS 345 junction. USFS hiker's signs with "No. 87" and "No. 196" can be seen leading from the western end of the overlook parking lot.

Alternatively, for a shorter hike, park at the scenic overlook at 7.15 miles past the turnoff to Indian Boundary Recreation Area. This scenic overlook is immediately before the "million dollar bridge" (so named because it is rumored to have cost in excess of that amount) that spans a cove on the side of the mountain. A section of the old Sassafras Ridge Road can be found to the west of the bridge. This road joins the other trail to the falls. The old road is heavily overgrown; the other route is recommended for beauty and a more aesthetic approach.

Details: Follow the trail that leaves the western side of the parking lot. It is marked with hiker signs for Trail Nos. 196 and 87. The trail goes downhill for 250 feet, at which point the trails divide. Jeffrey Hell Trail (No. 196) turns right; Falls Branch Trail (No. 87) turns left. Falls Branch Trail goes through rich northern hardwood forest over the broad, flat, old Sassafras Ridge roadbed. At 0.3 mile there is a switchback. At 0.45 mile note a large gnarled maple. Shortly afterwards an old roadbed enters from the left. At 0.8 mile is a switchback. At 0.9 mile look for the trail to turn off to the right at a curve in the roadbed. Watch for blazes. An arrow painted on a large hemlock points toward the falls. The trail passes through rhododendron and then descends along a stream through a cove hardwood forest of large trees. This is part of one of the larger areas of old-growth forest that was never logged. In the spring many wildflowers grow in this area. At 1.1 miles the trail crosses a streambed that may be dry; continue to follow the blazes through a switchback at 1.2 miles.

As the trail levels off there is a view of the falls ahead; the sound of the falls should be loud by this point. Cross a small stream and then go down a steep, slippery slope. The view of the falls continues to get better at points along this approach. Another small stream is crossed, and then the main stream is reached at 1.25 miles. The view of the falls is excellent from this vantage point, but if you want to get closer, cross the stream and pass through a cleft in a large boulder. Note the birch tree with its roots clasped to the side of the boulder. Follow the trail up the left side of the stream. At 1.3 miles the foot of the falls is reached. Nearby is a birch tree with large arched roots with space to crawl under. Someone has fashioned a rock seat here. There is an excellent view from the rocks below the falls. Do not attempt to climb on the falls, as they are very slick and dangerous.

Jeffrey Hell (Trail No. 196)
Length: 2.2 miles
Elevation Change: Start 3,960 feet, end 3,320 feet (high point 3,960 feet)
Trailheads: Rattlesnake Rock Parking Area (start) and South Fork Citico Creek Trail (end)
Type: Hiking

Comments: The Jeffrey Hell Trail follows an old roadbed as it gradually descends through Jeffrey Hell toward the South Fork Citico Creek. Jeffrey Hell gets its name because of the dense growth of rhododendron and mountain laurel that makes off-trail hiking difficult. There is also the legend that a man named Jeffrey went looking for his hunting dogs in the area. Before he left, he made the statement, "I'll find them if I have to go to hell to get them." He was never seen again. The first part of the trail descends very gradually and is fairly easy hiking. However, the last 0.5 mile of the trail leaves the roadbed and heads very steeply downhill to intersect the South Fork Citico Creek Trail. The trail passes through some interesting old-growth cove hardwood and hemlock forest during its descent along the old roadbed. There are few places to camp along the Jeffrey Hell Trail, but it is a good route to obtain access to the middle portion of the South Fork Citico Creek Trail quickly or when the lower portion of the trail is inaccessible because the creek is high.

The trail begins at a parking area on the left of the Tellico-Robbinsville Road near Rattlesnake Rock, 8.4 miles east of the TN 165 and FS 345 junction. USFS hiker's signs with "No. 87" and "No. 196" can be seen at a trail leading from the west side of the overlook parking lot. There is abundant parking at the overlook.

Details: The two trails head downhill together for a very short distance until they intersect an old roadbed. The Falls Branch Trail turns left. The Jeffrey Hell Trail turns right and descends gradually along the roadbed past some rather large buckeye and silverbell trees. The trail passes a large maple at 0.2 mile and passes a seep area. A stream passes under the trail at 0.5 mile through a culvert left from the old road. There is a rock wall bordering the trail across the stream. The stream, Falls Branch, flows down the small valley to Falls Branch Falls, which is accessed from the Falls Branch Trail. The Jeffrey Hell Trail continues around the contours of the mountain, heading in a generally northerly direction. Two small clearings are passed at 1.0 mile. A grove of large hemlocks is passed to the left of the trail at 1.2 miles. A large hollow buckeye also can be seen to the left of the trail. These are probably remnants of the forest that grew here before logging in the 1920s. An old road or trail can be seen to the left at 1.5 miles. A small clearing is reached at 1.7 miles. The old roadbed turns left to the southwest; the trail bears right, leaves the roadbed, and heads very steeply downhill to the northeast. As the trail descends the slope, turn east at a double-blazed tree. An old oil drum can be seen beside the trail. A small stream is reached at 1.8 miles. The trail is in and out of the water for the next 0.4 mile, as the trail continues to descend the slope more gradually. Logging cables and cinders from the old tramway that came up the South Fork Citico Creek during logging days can be seen in this stretch of trail. An eroded streambed that contains considerable amounts of cinders is reached right before South Fork Citico Creek is crossed. The South Fork Citico Creek Trail is reached at 2.2 miles after the creek is crossed. There is a small campsite at this point, which is 6.25 miles on the South Fork Citico Creek Trail from the Warden Station Area Trailhead.

Cold Spring Gap (Trail No. 149)

Length: 3.2 miles
Elevation Change: Start 4,400 feet, end 3,840 feet (high point 4,400 feet)
Trailheads: Cold Spring Gap (start) and North Fork Citico Creek Trail (end)
Trail Connections: Brush Mountain Trail
Type: Hiking

Comments: The Cold Spring Gap Trail follows the roadbed of the former road (FS 217H) that now ends at Cold Spring Gap. The trail follows the contours of Brush Mountain and connects the Fodderstack Trail, the South Fork Citico Creek Trail, and the North Fork Citico Creek Trail; the Brush Mountain Trail intersects the Cold Spring Gap Trail about halfway between the other trails. The trail is broad and in excellent condition. It makes a good connector in putting together longer hikes in the Areas. There are usually numerous signs of bear along this trail, indicating that they also use the trail as a connector.

The trailhead for the Cold Spring Gap Trail is at Cold Spring Gap, which is 1.9 miles from Beech Gap at the turnaround to FS 217H past Strawberry Knob. This road at present is barely passable to cars, with sections having deep ruts, large exposed rocks, and large mud holes. If you do not want to risk getting your car stuck, you may want to leave it parked near Beech Gap and hike the road. The USFS may do some maintenance work on this road, so it may be more passable in the future. If you do drive in, there is space for several cars at the gap.

The trail begins at vehicle barriers on the north side of the gap, opposite from where the road enters the gap. The Fodderstack Trail enters the gap from the northeast; the South Fork Citico Creek Trail enters the gap from the northwest. Two other old roadbeds also enter the gap from the southwest and the southeast. A horse-rider sign incorrectly designates the Cold Spring Gap Trail as USFS No. 158.

Details: Follow the trail over the mounds of dirt that act as vehicle barriers. The flat, wide, gravel trail passes through mixed hardwoods and hemlock forest. At 0.75 mile one of the sources of the South Fork Citico Creek flows under the trail. The trail climbs after crossing the creek but soon levels off again. Wild strawberries grow along the trail. At 1.3 miles there is a large clearing growing up in blackberries. To the right through the briars is a connector to an old abandoned trail leading up to the Fodderstack Trail. At 1.4 miles note a large hemlock growing to the left of the trail. At 1.5 miles another clearing growing up in blackberries is reached; the Brush Mountain Trail enters this clearing from the left. Follow the trail as it continues to curve around the mountain.

At 1.7 miles an old roadbed comes in from the left to join the trail at a clearing. At 1.9 miles is a very large birch tree where a small stream crosses the trail. Shortly after the tree is another clearing. Through thick blackberries on the right of the trail is a roadbed that joins the abandoned connector trail that leads up the mountain to Fodderstack Trail. Another clearing occurs at 2.4 miles and shortly afterwards one of the headwater streams for the North Fork Citico Creek crosses under the trail. The trail goes through a grove of very large hemlocks at 2.6 miles. At 2.98 miles there is a small clearing with a fire ring. At 3.0 miles the trail narrows, passes over dirt vehicle barriers, and descends steeply to reach one of the main branches of the North Fork Citico Creek at 3.2 miles. The North Fork Citico Creek Trail has come up the stream from the left and proceeds upward to the right. This junction is at 4.84

miles on the North Fork Citico Creek Trail from the South Fork Citico Creek Trail Trailhead. Cherry Log Gap is 0.6 mile to the right along the North Fork Citico Creek Trail.

Stiffknee (Trail No. 106),
including Slickrock
(Nantahala National Forest Trail No. 42)
Length: 3.4 miles
Elevation Change: Start 2,840 feet, end 1,400 feet (high point 2,840 feet)
Trailhead: Farr Gap (start) and Slickrock Creek Trail (end)
Type: Hiking

Comments: Stiffknee Trail is one of three trails connecting the trail systems of the contiguous Citico Creek Wilderness and Joyce Kilmer-Slickrock Wilderness (the others are Big Stack Gap Branch and Stratton Bald; see Fodderstack Trail for details on these). It is also the only trail in the Haw Knob Primitive Area, and only slightly touches the Primitive Area.

Details: The trail starts on the east side of the Farr Gap parking area and is marked. It is outside the Wilderness boundary for 0.8 mile as it traverses down the side of a ridge, in and out of small coves. At 0.8 mile it reaches Stiffknee Gap just below Stiffknee Top. At this point it is skirting the edge of the Primitive Area to the northeast. The trail then enters the Joyce Kilmer-Slickrock Wilderness and descends into the headwaters of Little Slickrock Creek. After reaching the creek, the trail follows it for slightly over 2.0 miles to Slickrock Creek. The trail is initially a rocky footpath beside the creek, but after 2.4 miles the trail appears to follow an old railroad bed. The creek is crossed five times.

At the junction of the trail with Slickrock Creek is the Slickrock Creek Trail (No. 42), which goes both up and downstream. This is the longest (13.3 miles) and one of the most beautiful of the Joyce Kilmer-Slickrock Wilderness trails as it winds its way along Slickrock Creek from Lake Cheoah to the high mountains above the valley. The elevation gain along the way is substantial—3,700 feet; however, most of this gain is in the last 5.0 miles. The trail is entirely in the Nantahala National Forest. To the left (downstream) the trail leads to Lower Falls at about 1.2 miles from the junction of Stiffknee and Slickrock trails. Continue on downstream to Calderwood Lake, then to the east along the lake. The trailhead at US 129 is reached at 4.75 miles. To the right (upstream) from the Stiffknee-Slickrock trails junction, you will pass the spectacular Wildcat Falls at 8.55 miles. On upstream at 5.9 miles on the right (west) is the Big Stack Gap Branch Trail, which leads up to the Fodderstack Trail and the Citico Creek Wilderness. Shortly thereafter the climbing will begin, and at 13.3 miles the trail reaches Naked Ground and the Haoe Lead Trail (No. 53). To the right (west) 0.6 miles on the Haoe Lead Trail will lead you to the Stratton Bald Trail (No. 54). Another 1.3 miles on the Stratton Bald Trail will lead you across the scenic Bob Stratton Bald to the Fodderstack Trail and the Citico Creek Wilderness.

16. BRUSHY RIDGE PRIMITIVE AREA

The 4,220-acre Brushy Ridge Primitive Area lies in Monroe County, TN, in the Tellico Ranger District. It is bordered on the north by Sassafras Ridge and the Tellico-Robbinsville Road (TN 165). On the south, it is bordered by North River and the North River Road (FS 217). Between the Tellico-Robbinsville Road and North River Road is a beautiful area of forest, streams, and ridges. Three trails begin along the North River Road and ascend along stream valleys through the Area to the Tellico-Robbinsville Road along Sassafras Ridge. These stream valleys are separated by ridges that intersect Sassafras Ridge at right angles; the ridges, except McIntyre Lead on the east, are also in the Primitive Area.

The Primitive Area is across the Tellico-Robbinsville Road from the Citico Creek Wilderness and shares many of the same plants and animals. Cove hardwood forest spreads up the stream valleys; oak complexes dominate the slopes; pines are mixed with oaks on the ridges; and pines dominate the dry south slopes.

HISTORY

The Brushy Ridge Primitive Area is covered in second-growth forest, having been logged extensively in the early 20th century. Old narrow-gauge tramways from this period were used to harvest the timber. The railbeds from these tramways form the trails along the streams in the lower elevations of Brushy Ridge today. Construction on the Tellico-Robbinsville Road during the 1970s exposed iron pyrites that drained into Hemlock Creek and McNabb Creek, resulting in severe water quality degradation in these streams. Neutralization structures have been built at the headwaters of these streams to help correct the problem.

The Area was designated as a Primitive Area (Managed) in 1988 in the CNF's Management Plan. Unlike most primitive areas, limited timber harvesting may be allowed (see Section A).

TRAILHEADS AND MAPS

It is possible to access all three trails in the Area from either the North River Road or the Tellico-Robbinsville Road. For detailed alternate directions to the Tellico-Robbinsville Road, see the Citico Wilderness section, above.

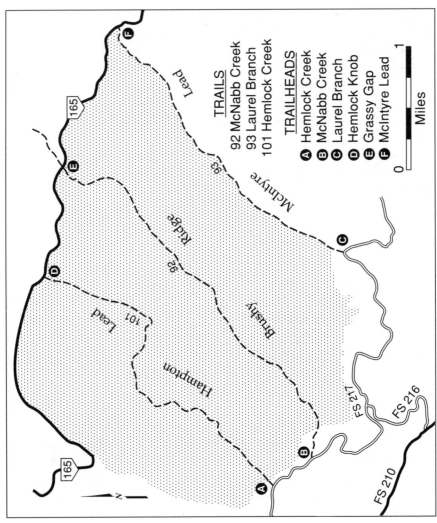

Brushy Ridge Primitive Area.

North River Road Trailheads:
Hemlock Creek, McNabb Creek, and Laurel Branch

Turn off US 411 onto TN 68 in Madisonville, TN. Take TN 68 to Tellico Plains (approximately 14.0 miles). When TN 68 intersects TN 165 in the middle of Tellico Plains, take a left (east) on TN 165. Go 0.65 mile to where TN 165 makes a junction with TN 360. Take a right at the junction to stay on TN 165. This road, the Tellico-Robbinsville Road, continues past a group of stores and cabins and passes a CNF sign. The road runs along the south bank and then the north bank of the Tellico River. Shortly after passing the Ooesterneck Creek Parking Area at 4.2 miles, the road forks. Take the right fork, which is the paved Tellico River Road (FS 210). Continue along the Tellico River Road past the Tellico Ranger Station and past Bald River Falls on the right. At 5.5 miles past Bald River Falls, turn left off the Tellico River Road onto the North River Road (FS 217). Hemlock Creek Trail is 1.4 miles on the North River Road; McNabb Creek Trail is 1.8 miles on the North River Road; and Laurel Branch Trail is 4.9 miles on the North River Road. FS 217 can also be reached from the east by turning right (north) off the Tellico River Road onto FS 216.

Tellico-Robbinsville Road Trailheads:
Hemlock Knob, Grassy Gap, and McIntyre Lead

To access the trailheads along the Tellico-Robbinsville Road, take the left fork when the Tellico River Road turns right just after the Oosterneck Creek Parking Area and continue on TN 165 over rolling hills. At 13.7 miles TN 165 intersects with FS 345. This road leads to Indian Boundary Recreation Area. To reach trailheads along the Tellico-Robbinsville Road, continue along TN 165. From the intersection of TN 165E and FS 345, continue on TN 165E as it skirts the southern edge of the Citico Creek Wilderness. Numerous turnoffs along the road give spectacular views of the Citico watershed and of the Tellico Ranger District of the CNF. Hemlock Creek and the Hemlock Creek Trailhead are 4.5 miles from the turnoff to Indian Boundary on TN 165; Grassy Gap and the McNabb Creek Trailhead are 6.3 miles from the turnoff to Indian Boundary on TN 165; and McIntyre Lead and the Laurel Branch Trailhead are 7.1 miles from the turnoff to Indian Boundary on TN 165.

Topographic Maps: Big Junction, TN-NC; Bald River Falls, TN-NC.

TRAIL DESCRIPTIONS

Hemlock Creek (Hemock) (Trail No. 101)
Length: 3.48 miles
Elevation Change: Start 1,760 feet, end 3,800 feet (high point 3,800 feet)
Trailheads: Hemlock Creek (start) and Hemlock Knob (end)
Type: Hiking

Comments: This is a beautiful, easy trail in its lower sections as it follows Hemlock Creek. The trail at this point follows an old roadbed or narrow-gauge railbed. The trail crosses the creek a number of times before it veers away from the stream at about the halfway point. The last half of the trail is very steep and largely unmaintained. There is no water on the last half of the trail. This is also known as Hemlock Trail.

Details: The trail begins on the north side of the road at a small parking area and a sign for Trail No. 101. Follow the nearly level trail as it passes through second-growth forest. At 0.37 mile, rock hop across Hemlock Creek; there is a wire cable that can be used for support. Continue along the trail, making several easy crossings of Hemlock Creek and small side branches. The trail comes to a large flat area suitable for camping at 0.83 mile as it continues its almost level progress along the creek. The trail begins a gentle ascent and passes several more possible campsites.

At 1.2 miles the railbed fades into a well-marked, easy trail. At 1.85 miles, with the creek to the left, the trail angles sharply to the right. It ascends moderately up a ravine but quickly becomes much steeper. This section is quite strenuous and the trail is obscure. Stick to the ravine and look for white blazes on trees.

The trail reaches a small saddle at 2.27 miles. Continue a more moderate ascent along a spur, coming to several small saddles. The trail along this section is better marked and not as obscure as the previous section. At 3.4 miles the trail ends its ascent. The trail traverses left and leads to Hemlock Knob and the Tellico-Robbinsville Road at 3.48 miles. The trail is marked by USFS trail sign as No. 101. Parking is available along the shoulder of the road.

McNabb Creek (Trail No. 92)
Length: 3.82 miles
Elevation Change: Start 1,800 feet, end 3,400 feet (high point 3,400 feet)
Trailheads: McNabb Creek (start) and Grassy Gap (end)
Type: Hiking

Comments: McNabb Creek Trail is a scenic trail that follows McNabb Creek for most of its distance. There are many creek crossings. The trail ascends gently for the first two-thirds of its length; it then becomes moderately steep for the last third. The upper reaches of McNabb Creek, while appearing to be clear, are contaminated by acid drainage from iron pyrite exposed by the construction of the Tellico-Robbinsville Road.

Details: The trail begins on the north side of the North River Road at a camping area with a pit toilet and a turnaround loop, and is marked by USFS trail sign No. 92. Follow the gently ascending trail as it follows an old railroad grade through second-growth forest of rhododendron and conifers. Frequent crossings of McNabb

Creek, a beautiful mountain stream, require rock hopping or shallow wading. Although water along these lower stretches may be drinkable, hikers should note the Comments section above on acid drainage.

At 0.64 mile is a level campsite to the left of the trail next to the creek; there is another campsite at 1.88 miles, below the trail near the creek. At 1.93 miles an old orange game-and-fish-commission sign is attached to a tree. The sign, marked No. 54, is partly engulfed by the bark of the tree, with the bark growing over the top and bottom edges. At 2.51 miles the trail steeply ascends the hillside for 0.1 mile; the creek is to the right of the trail. The trail then ascends more gradually along the old railroad grade. The McNabb Creek Valley becomes much narrower; this section is easy hiking.

At 2.93 miles a metal sign warns against the contaminated water. The trail is now passing through a mixed forest of hardwoods, conifers, and rhododendrons. At 3.25 miles, after crossing a small branch, the trail begins a steep ascent. Another warning sign is encountered, after which you come to a small dam across McNabb Creek, which is much smaller at this point.

Continue to ascend via moderate switchbacks heading toward the highway visible above. The trail traverses the hillside on the east side of the creek, paralleling the highway for a short distance through open forest. The trail switches back to the left, ascends the hillside, and emerges on the Tellico-Robbinsville Road at 3.82 miles next to a USFS sign for Trail No. 92. There is a small area on the road shoulder for parking. About 100 yards west of the trailhead is a sign: "Grassy Gap—Elevation 3,400 feet." Grassy Gap provides beautiful views to the south. A road at the gap heads down the north side of the ridge to a large parking area with a trailhead for the Grassy Branch Trail into Citico Creek Wilderness.

Laurel Branch (Trail No. 93)
Length: 3.06 miles
Elevation Change: Start 2,000 feet, end 3,800 feet (high point 3,800 feet)
Trailheads: Laurel Branch (start) and McIntyre Lead (end)
Type: Hiking

Comments: Laurel Branch Trail is a pleasant trail for the first two-thirds of its length, with several stream crossings. The trail then becomes fairly steep during the last third of its length. Good displays of spring wildflowers can be found along this trail.

Details: The trail begins on the north side of the road at a bridge over Laurel Branch, with a USFS sign designating Trail No. 93. Follow the trail, which follows an old railbed, through second-growth forest consisting mostly of rhododendron and pine. There are small wooden footbridges over Laurel Branch at 0.18 mile and 0.66 mile. The trail crosses the creek several times in the first 2.0 miles. These crossings are usually easily negotiated over rocks. At 1.44 miles, there is a storage tank and pipe-line on the right. The trail leaves the old railbed at 1.63 miles. The railbed turns to the left while the trail veers to the right and becomes less distinct.

The trail crosses the branch at 2.5 miles, and the grade becomes considerably steeper. In the spring, this is a good section to see Dutchman's breeches, trillium, and wild geraniums.

The trail becomes more obscure at 2.65 miles; look carefully for trail blazes. The trail becomes steeper and is not graded or maintained. During wet weather, it would be difficult to negotiate. When leaves are off the trees during the winter, a good view down the valley can be glimpsed at 2.86 miles. The trail ends on McIntyre Lead at the Tellico-Robbinsville Road at 3.06 miles. A USFS sign designates Trail No. 93. To the east, parking spaces are available at a scenic overlook.

17. ROUGH RIDGE PRIMITIVE AREA

The Rough Ridge Primitive Area is about 2,970 acres in size, located in Monroe County, TN, and the Tellico Ranger District in the upper reaches of the Tellico River, generally east of Tellico Plains. It is bounded on the northeast by the TN-NC state line; Rough Ridge Creek and Sycamore Creek also form its boundaries, and the crest of Rough Ridge runs through the center of the Area. The steep mountain slopes are covered with typical southern Appalachian hardwoods, pine, rhododendron, dog hobble, mountain laurel, and a wide variety of other flora. The fall colors are gorgeous; the Primitive Area supports a wide variety of wildlife typical of the southern mountains of Appalachia, including the larger species such as black bear, deer, wild hogs, and possibly turkey. Hunting is a favorite activity in the Area.

There are no maintained trails in the Primitive Area, so any hiking will necessarily be off-trail, with a topographical map being essential. A dirt road along Sycamore Creek provides easy access to its western and northern sides from the Tellico River Road. Another dirt road along Rough Ridge Branch, starting from the end of the Tellico River Road, provides access from the southeast. The Davis Creek, Big Oak Cove, and Stateline USFS campgrounds are near the Area.

HISTORY

Like much of the Tellico River basin, the Area was heavily logged in the early part of the 20th century. However, it has recovered quite well from abusive logging practices of that time and provides a unique recreational opportunity without roads or trails. Nearby and just to the east of the Area in NC's Nantahala National Forest is the Snowbird Creek Area, which has been proposed for wilderness designation.

The Area was designated as a Primitive Area in 1988 by the CNF Management Plan.

*Rough Ridge
Primitive Area.*

TRAILHEADS

Ⓐ Pheasant Field Fish Hatchery
Ⓑ Stateline Campground

Grassy Top
4,979'

N

Rough Ridge Primitive Area

Ridge

Rough

Looking Glass Mtn.

Tellico River

FS 210

FS 61

FS 2105

FS 24

TN.
NC.

0   Miles   1

TRAILHEADS AND MAPS

Pheasant Field Fish Hatchery
and Stateline Campground Trailheads

Directions to the old roads on Sycamore Creek and Rough Ridge Branch are given
from the intersection of TN 165 and TN 68 on the west side of Tellico Plains, TN.
From the intersection of these highways follow TN 165 up the Tellico River to a junction at 5.3 miles. Turn right up the Tellico River on paved FS 210. Continue 14.8
miles upriver on FS 210 from this junction, passing Bald River Falls and the Tellico
Lodge area, to a bridge that crosses to the north side of the Tellico River, where the
Pheasant Field Fish Hatchery is located. There is ample parking here. The old dirt
logging road (FS 61), which is now closed to all vehicles, goes up Sycamore Creek to
the northeast from the north end of the bridge and provides access to the Area from
the west and north. To get into the Primitive Area from the south, continue up the
Tellico River road about 3.0 miles from the fish hatchery bridge to near the TN-NC
state line and the USFS Stateline Campground, where there is adequate parking. The
Tellico River Road is on the north side of the river at this point. The dirt logging
road (FS 210G) up Rough Ridge Creek, which is closed to public vehicles, goes
northeast from the Tellico River Road, starting just west of Rough Ridge Branch,
and provides access to the Area from the southeast.

Topographic Map: Big Junction, TN-NC.

18. BALD RIVER GORGE WILDERNESS
AND UPPER BALD RIVER PRIMITIVE AREAS

The Bald River Gorge Wilderness and Upper Bald River Primitive Areas together
consist of 14,181 acres, the entire Bald River watershed except for a few acres around
Bald River Falls and 198 privately owned acres near Sandy Gap. This watershed is
in the upper region of the Tellico River basin generally east of Tellico Plains in Monroe County, TN, and in the Tellico Ranger District. The large size and outstanding
beauty of the Areas make the watershed a significant recreation, wildlife, and scien-
tific resource. Little Bald, Beaverdam Bald, Sled Runner Gap, Rocky Top, Round
Top, Hazelnut Knob, and Sandy Gap are landmarks located on the TN-NC state
line ridge, which forms the southern boundary. Waucheesi Bald, which dominates
the high ridgeline to the southwest, is accessible by car from Basin Gap.

Bald River, originating on the north side of Little Bald at the southeast corner of
the Area, is relatively small but is clean, cold, fast-moving, and very attractive. Several
tributaries such as Henderson Branch, Brookshire Creek, Kirkland Creek, Waucheesi

Creek, and Big Cove Branch contribute their share of clean, cold water. Cascades are numerous, contributing significantly to the beauty of the Areas. Trout thrive here, as do trout fishermen who prefer a challenge in a wilderness setting. During late fall and early winter hunting is a major activity in the Area.

The mountain slopes are covered with typical southern Appalachian hardwoods, pine, rhododendron, dog hobble, mountain laurel, and a wide variety of other flora. Wildflowers are plentiful and the fall colors are gorgeous. The Areas support a wide variety of wildlife typically found in the southern Appalachians, including the larger species such as black bear, deer, wild hogs, and turkey.

Only 3,721 acres, the Bald River Gorge Wilderness, are permanently protected from logging and other developments. This Wilderness is the steep-sided gorge north of FS 126, extending north to, but not including, a few acres around Bald River Falls. The balance of the Areas (10,460 acres) consists of four Primitive Areas, which are roughly split evenly between unmanaged (5,190 acres) and managed (5,270 acres) categories. The unmanaged portion is generally west of Brookshire Creek, and the managed portion is generally east of Brookshire Creek.

Bald River Falls, at the north end of Bald River (outside of the Wilderness) where it flows under the Tellico River Road, is one of the most impressive waterfalls in TN. The Bald River Trailhead is here, and this trail is the most heavily used in the Areas. A gravel road passable by cars, FS 126, traverses the Areas from Green Cove Gap on the east to Basin Gap on the west. Holly Flats Campground is on this road. The road provides good access to the Upper Bald River Primitive Areas.

HISTORY

Much of these Areas was logged during the early part of the 20th century, utilizing a railroad extending up the Tellico River. The track that went into the Bald River watershed left the main track on the Tellico River a short distance below Bald River Falls, gaining elevation to get above the falls and the cliff on the west side of the falls. It entered the Bald River watershed and made its first crossing of the river a short distance above the falls. It then continued to the headwaters of the river and several of its tributaries. The trail that now follows the river and the two major trails in the Primitive Areas utilize much of this old logging grade.

Farming in this remote area was impractical even for the hardy mountaineers that inhabited this region of TN and NC in bygone days. There is no obvious evidence of farming in the gorge area along the Bald River Trail, but the lay of the land along FS 126 and in the small valleys south of this road is such that it could have supported subsistence mountain farms, as did most of the Appalachian Mountains. There is evidence today that such a farm did exist in the headwaters of Brookshire Creek near Beaverdam Bald, and two other remote cabin sites are found on Brookshire

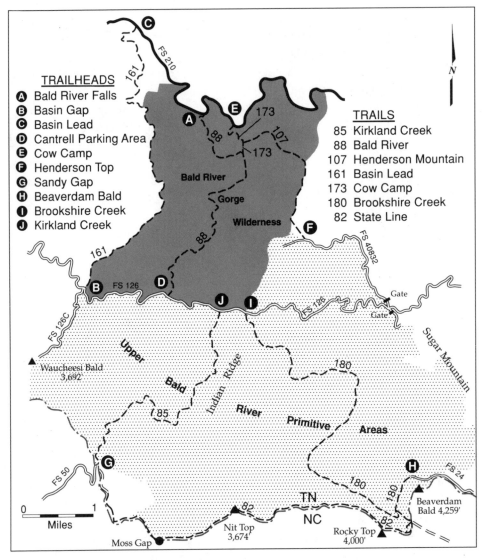

Bald River Gorge Wilderness and Upper Bald River Primitive Areas.

Creek. An area-wide archaeological survey would probably disclose further evidence of other mountain farms, logging camps, and possibly sites used by the Cherokee Indians. One Cherokee cemetery is reported to be located on Indian Ridge, which is between Kirkland and Brookshire creeks.

With the depletion of the timber resources and withdrawal of the logging railroads, the Areas recovered their wilderness character. Some timber harvesting has occurred since the 1960s: several clear-cuts south of Henderson Top and in the 1980s a clear-cut in the head of Bald River. Efforts to protect the entire watershed under the provisions of the Wilderness Act of 1964 began in the early 1970s but were unsuccessful. After a lengthy struggle by conservationists, the 3,721-acre Bald River Gorge Wilderness Area was added to the wilderness system in 1984 and the Primitive Areas were designated as a Primitive Area in the CNF's 1988 Management Plan. Portions of the Primitive Area are managed, and limited timber harvesting may be allowed in such portions (see Section A).

The Areas are popular for hunting, fishing, camping, hiking, horseback riding, and pleasure driving on FS 126. The trails in the Areas utilize the old logging roads, except for the Cow Camp and Henderson Mountain trails. NC's Nantahala National Forest Trail No. 82 borders the Primitive Area on the state line ridge from Sled Runner Bald to Sandy Gap, and makes loop trips possible. This trail, although poorly maintained, is easy to follow by experienced hikers from Sled Runner Gap, just south of Beaverdam Bald, to Sandy Gap. The trail is generally described in the descriptions of the Brookshire Creek and Kirkland Creek trails.

TRAILHEADS AND MAPS

The trails are described from their low-elevation ends, the most practical starting point. The trailheads are located on the paved Tellico River Road (FS 210) and gravel FS 126, and driving directions to them start from the intersection of TN 165 and TN 68 on the west side of Tellico Plains, TN. Trailheads for one trail, the State Line Trail (Trail No. 82; a NC Nantahala National Forest Trail) are included in the description of the Brookshire Creek and Kirkland Creek trails. Its trailheads are Sandy Gap and Beaverdam Bald.

Tellico River Road (FS 210) Trailheads

Basin Lead Trailhead

From the intersection of TN 165 and TN 68 on the west side of Tellico Plains follow TN 165 up the Tellico River to a junction at mile 5.3. Keep right up the Tellico River. This is FS 210. Continue 4.4 miles on FS 210 to a footbridge across the river, where a small sign identifies the Basin Lead Trail, No. 161. Parking space is very limited. One space exists on the narrow shoulder near the end of the bridge, and two or three spots can be found about 200 feet upriver at a small highway bridge across a branch of the Tellico River. If you want to make a loop trip on this trail and the Bald River Trail (No. 88), it is suggested that you park here and walk 1.9 miles upriver to begin hiking on the Bald River Trail (see the trailhead description below). The south ends of these trails are also 1.9 miles apart on FS 126, with the south end of the Basin Lead Trail being at Basin Gap. There is adequate parking space at the south ends of both trails.

Fisherman risks slippery footing at base of Bald River Falls.
Photo by E. Kenneth McDonald.

Bald River Falls Trailhead

Continue on FS 210 for 1.9 miles (a total of 6.3 miles on FS 210) to a small parking
area on the east side (upriver) of Bald River Falls. You cannot miss the falls. A large
sign identifies this as the location of the Bald River Falls Picnic Area parking site. A
small sign with the number 88 on it marks the north end of the Bald River Trail (No.
88). Primitive toilet facilities are available here. In late spring, summer, and early
fall, finding a parking space here may be difficult. Roadside parking where the
shoulder permits is usually acceptable. The south end of this trail is on FS 126 where
the Bald River flows under this FS 126, 1.9 miles east of Basin Gap.

Cow Camp Trailhead

Continue on FS 210 for 0.9 mile past Bald River Falls (a total of 7.2 miles on FS 210)
to a bridge and cross the bridge to the east (upstream) end. Park on the wide shoulder between the pavement and the river. There is adequate parking space here but
no facilities. The north end of the trail is behind the guard rail at the west (downstream) end of the bridge. A small trail marker here identifies this as Trail No. 173,
and a small wooden stairway behind the guard rail helps you over a steep embankment onto the trail proper.

This trailhead also serves as the trailhead for the Henderson Mountain Trail (No. 107). The north end of the Henderson Mountain Trail is at an unmarked junction with the Cow Camp Trail on the ridgecrest about 0.6 mile from the Tellico River Road.

Upper Bald River Road (FS 126) Trailheads

Henderson Top Trailhead

From the intersection of TN 165 and TN 68 on the west side of Tellico Plains follow TN 165 up the Tellico River to a junction at 5.3 miles. Keep right up the Tellico River. This is FS 210. Continue 13.9 miles upriver from this junction on FS 210, passing Bald River Falls and the Tellico Lodge area, to a graveled road on the right (south) side of FS 210. This is the east end of FS 126, the road to Green Cove and the upper Bald River area. Follow FS 126 uphill to the top of the ridge at Green Cove Gap and park in the gap. Although it is not identified on topographical maps, you should have no problem recognizing the gap. Walk north on a logging road, FS 40832, 2.5 miles to a gap about 0.25 mile southeast of Henderson Top's highest point, where the logging road goes through the gap. The Henderson Mountain Trail is on the right side of the road (north), but the trailhead is unmarked and difficult to find. Hiking up the trail from the Tellico River Road is the suggested route if you have any doubts about finding the trailhead.

Brookshire Creek Trailhead

Continue on FS 126 through Green Cove Gap and down Henderson Branch to its confluence with Bald River on the left (south) side of the road, 5.1 miles from the Tellico River Road. Here is the first significant forest opening after you begin your descent from Green Cove Gap down Henderson Branch. There is no defined parking area at this opening, but there is ample parking space. Nor is there a trail marker, but the former logging road going south across Henderson Branch and up Bald River is very obvious. There is evidence of camping activities on both sides of the road. There are no facilities here, but Holly Flats Campground is only 0.8 mile further west on this road. The south end of this trail is also unmarked and is at a wild-life-management clearing on the north side of Beaverdam Bald. It is accessible by an unimproved logging road (FS 24) from the Tellico River Road, using a high-clearance vehicle. Locating it is for those who enjoy searching for obscure trailheads using maps and local information.

Kirkland Creek Trailhead

Continue on FS 126 for 0.4 mile past the Brookshire Creek Trailhead (a total of 5.5 miles on FS 126) to a small graveled parking area on the south side of FS 126. This is at the confluence of Bald River and Kirkland Creek. There is parking space for four or five vehicles, but others could be parked on the shoulder of FS 126. A small sign identifies this point as one end (the north end) of Trail No. 85. There are no facilities here, but Holly Flats Campground is only 0.4 mile further west on this road.

The south end of the trail is at the head of Kirkland Creek on the TN-NC state line at Sandy Gap. There is no identifying marker at this end, but it is possible to reach this end by an unimproved dirt logging road (FS 50) that comes up from the NC side of the ridge. Use maps and inquire locally if you approach from NC.

Cantrell Parking Area Trailhead

Continue on FS 126 for 0.9 mile past the Kirkland Creek Trailhead (a total of 6.4 miles on FS 126) to the Bald River and Cantrell Parking Area. The Bald River Trail is on the right (north) just before crossing the river to the Cantrell Parking Area. You will pass the USFS Holly Flats Campground on the left 0.4 mile from Kirkland Creek.

Basin Gap Trailhead

Continue on FS 126 for 1.9 miles past the Bald River Trail (a total of 8.3 miles on FS 126) to Basin Gap. The Waucheesi Mountain Road (FS 126C) turns left (south) in the gap while the Basin Lead Trail is on the right (north) side. Note that FS 126C may be closed to vehicles.

Beaverdam Bald Trailhead

Beaverdam Bald is reached by FS 24, a dirt road that requires a four-wheel-drive vehicle. FS 24 turns off FS 210 (Tellico River Road) at the Big Oak Cove Campground. It then proceeds south to the TN-NC state line, then generally west along the state line, past Little Bald and Grassy Gap, to Beaverdam Bald. A USFS map may be necessary to follow this road. Near the east side of Beaverdam Bald the road forks. The left (south) fork goes to the top of Beaverdam Bald at 4,259 feet. On top is a wildlife clearing. On the other side (west) of the clearing is an old ORV track that originally descended 0.5 mile along the state line down to Sled Runner Gap. However, to discourage ORV use from NC, the USFS has cut numerous trees along the old track, and it is now difficult to navigate. Instead of taking the left fork mentioned above where FS 24 splits, take the right (north) fork to reach the Beaverdam Bald Trailhead. The right fork of FS 24 goes a short distance and ends at a second wildlife clearing at 3,920 feet in a saddle on the northwest side of Beaverdam Bald and northwest of the first wildlife clearing at the mountaintop mentioned above.

This second clearing is the Beaverdam Bald Trailhead. On the west side of the clearing the Brookshire Creek Trail begins traversing around Beaverdam Bald toward, but not to, Sled Runner Gap. Just above a former homesite, at about 0.4 mile from the trailhead, the Brookshire Creek Trail turns sharply to the right (northwest) and proceeds down Brookshire Creek. About 100 to 200 feet before reaching the sharp right turn, you can turn left (southeast) and proceed on an obvious track about 0.25 mile up a slight incline to Sled Runner Gap. ORVs sometimes come up from NC to Sled Runner Gap and, prevented by the cut trees from following the state line directly up to Beaverdam Bald, they cross over to the Brookshire Creek Trail and then up to the Bald. At Sled Runner Gap the unmarked State Line Trail begins to the right (south) and swings to the west, climbing up toward Rocky Top on an easy grade.

Sandy Gap Trailhead

The access road to Sandy Gap turns off TN 68 on the north side of the Hiwassee River bridge, 1.5 miles north of the Farner, TN, post office and 1.1 miles southeast of the Womble Branch Trailhead for the John Muir Trail. FS 311 turns off TN 68 at the bridge and proceeds up the Hiwassee River; the mileage numbers hereafter specified begin at the bridge. The first several FS road junctions are unsigned. The FS 311 pavement ends in 200 feet, and a good-quality gravel road continues. FS 311 turns left away from the river at 0.35 miles. Continue on up the river on FS 37. At 2.15 mile you enter NC and the road number changes to FS 1322 (there is a NC sign but no number sign). At 3.8 miles is a fork; take the left fork (FS 338) instead of the right fork (FS 1323), which crosses a creek. Pass a Circle Valley Home sign at 5.7 miles and reach an intersection at 7.3 miles. FS 1326 will come in from the left; continue straight ahead on FS 1325, past a turnoff on the right for FS 1326. This and future intersections have small road number signs. Continue past FS 82 on the left at 9.55 miles. At 9.8 miles turn left on FS 1327 off FS 1325. Finally, at 10.35 miles reach a fork with a mailbox in the middle; take the left fork (FS 50) and not the right fork (FS 1328). Pass FS 50A and a parking area on the left at 11.25 miles and climb up to Sandy Gap and the road's end at 14.0 miles. As you drive into the gap, there will be four possible trails: (i) on your right (southeast) will be an ORV road that is also the State Line Trail (No. 82); (ii) straight ahead is the old, abandoned Kirkland Creek Trail, which drops directly down into the valley; on your left (northwest) will be two trails, (iii) a trail leading up the ridge and another trail (iv), below the one leading up the ridge, traversing around the northeast side of the ridge. The latter trail on the northeast side of the ridge is Kirkland Creek Trail (No. 85).

Topographic Maps: Bald River Falls, TN-NC; Unaka, TN-NC; Big Junction, TN-NC.

TRAIL DESCRIPTIONS

Basin Lead (Basin Gap) (Trail No. 161)
Length: 6.0 miles
Elevation Change: Start 1,180 feet, end 2,740 feet (high point 3,000 feet)
Trailheads: Basin Lead (start) and Basin Gap (end)
Type: Hiking

Comments: This trail is best suited for hiking from the Tellico River Road. If you want to make a long loop, you can hike to Basin Gap, go east on FS 126 to Bald River, turn north on the Bald River Trail (No. 88), go downstream on this trail to the Tellico River Road, and then west 1.9 miles on the road to the starting point. This is also known as Basin Gap Trail.

Except for the first 1.1 miles and a few hundred feet of trail at a point high up the ridge, this trail is old logging grades along or near the ridgetop. The trail is forested along its entire length with Appalachian hardwoods and some pine. It is a pleasant walk after a short steep section leaving the Tellico River Gorge. One high point along the way offers reasonably good views of distant mountains when the leaves are down, and Waucheesi Bald looms above Basin Gap on the final approach to this gap. There is one site that could be used by a small party for camping, although water may not be available in very dry weather.

Details: The trail crosses the footbridge over the Tellico River and ascends on a steep grade with switchbacks, along a poor treadway and over blow-downs to 0.4 mile, where the grade eases along Basin Lead. White paint blazes mark the route up the steep grade. Once you are out of the gorge, it is easy hiking along the ridgecrest to the top of a small knob at 1.1 miles. The forest here is hardwood mixed with some pine, and this will be the type of forest along the full length of this trail, although the pine component varies in density along the way. Just across the high point of the knob, an old logging grade becomes the trail. From time to time you will see other old logging grades intersecting the trail grade, but the brush has been cut from the one used for the trail and blazes have been painted on trees, so following the correct one is not a problem.

The trail descends slowly from the knob, contouring with the variations of the ridgetop, and reaches a small watercourse at 1.5 miles, where water may be available. At 1.6 miles there is an area where a small party could find usable tent sites and water should be available most of the time.

At this point the trail levels out, then begins an easy ascent to intersect another logging road at 1.75 miles. This road is still being used by the USFS. Make a sharp left-turn upgrade on this road. At 2.4 miles a wet-weather spring is encountered at a junction with another old logging road. Keep left. An earthen vehicle barrier is soon encountered, and this appears to be the point beyond which the USFS vehicles are no longer used.

The trail soon levels out and descends slowly to a shallow gap at 3.1 miles, where old logging roads go in several directions. Veer left on a level grade (look for blazes). It is easy hiking on a moderate grade to 3.7 miles, where the logging road ends temporarily. On top of the ridge there is a small rock outcropping. On a clear day when the leaves are down, reasonably good views of some of the distant mountains can be seen. At 4.2 miles the trail rejoins the old logging road and continues easily to Basin Gap. The final approach to Basin Gap is on a slight downhill grade where Waucheesi Bald may be seen looming high above the gap. FS 126 is reached at 6.0 miles. The gap is on the ridgecrest where FS 126 going west leaves the Bald River watershed. A road (FS 126C) going uphill to the south on the west side of the ridge goes to Waucheesi Bald; the road may be closed to public vehicular use.

Bald River (Trail No. 88)

Length: 4.8 miles
Elevation Change: Start 1,380 feet, end 1,860 feet (high point 1,860 feet)
Trailheads: Bald River Falls (start) and Cantrell Parking Area (end)
Trail Connections: Cow Camp Trail
Type: Hiking

Comments: It is suggested that this trail be hiked by starting at the Bald River Trailhead. This trail follows Bald River from the Tellico River Road (FS 210) at Bald River Falls and ends on FS 126. It passes through a largely deciduous forest with some white pine and hemlock mixed in. Rhododendron, mountain laurel, and dog hobble, along with the conifers, provide an adequate amount of green color in winter. The trail utilizes an old logging grade on some stretches, but other parts of it are a narrow outsloping tread in need of widening. The rhododendron encroaches on the trail in some locations but is not a serious problem. Wildflowers and fall colors adorn the landscape in season.

Easy access to the river is provided for those who trout fish. The river is small but relatively clean since there is only one small campground and some logging activity upstream. It tumbles over numerous cascades and rock ledges on its way to the Tellico River. Several small sites suitable for backpacking campsites exist along the river. This trail receives heavy use, except in winter.

A loop hike can be made by turning west on FS 126 at the south end of the trail and proceeding 1.9 miles to Basin Gap on FS 126, where the south end of the Basin

Lead Trail can be found. Here you would turn north and follow the Basin Lead Trail to the Tellico River Road, then upriver 1.9 miles on the road to Bald River Falls.

A shorter loop can be made by retracing the route from FS 126 to an unmarked trail junction on the Bald River, 1.4 miles from the Bald River Trailhead. This is the north end of the Cow Camp Trail (No. 173). Here you would turn east and proceed to the top of a low ridge where another unmarked trail junction exists, the north end of the Henderson Mountain Trail (No. 107). It is then downhill to the Tellico River Road and 0.9 mile downriver to the Bald River Trailhead.

Details: Starting at the trailhead where a small sign identifies Trail No. 88, the trail bears left uphill, then switches back to reach a small picnic area on the river above the falls at 0.15 mile. It continues upriver on an old logging grade to 0.5 mile, where it switches back to the left to gain elevation to the top of a high rock outcropping lying a short distance ahead. At 0.6 mile the trail reaches the top of the rocks where an unmaintained manway leads out onto them. The river makes a U-bend around the base of the rocks, cascading over several rock ledges. A good view of a large cascade can be seen a short distance upstream. The trail gains a little more elevation over a rocky tread, then descends slowly to the large cascade at 0.7 mile.

At 1.4 miles there is an unmarked trail junction where the Cow Camp Trail (No. 173) joins this trail. Trail No. 88 continues upriver. A small campsite is reached about 350 feet beyond this junction. Except in wet weather the river would be the source of water for campers. Pawpaw Cove Creek is crossed at 1.8 miles, and at 2.3 miles there is a good campsite. The trail continues on an easy grade, crossing small stream courses which may or may not have water in them, depending on recent weather. Small campsites exist at 2.7 miles and at 4.2 miles. At this last site, Big Cove Branch can be seen entering Bald River on the west side.

The end of a low ridge in a river bend is crossed at 4.5 miles, where the trail then descends to a large cascade. At 4.8 miles the trail reaches FS 126, which traverses the Bald River watershed. The river flows under this road about 50 feet to the west, where there is adequate parking space at the Cantrell Parking Area. Holly Flats Campground is on this road 0.5 mile to the east.

Cow Camp (Trail No. 173)
Length: 0.8 mile
Elevation Change: Start 1,500 feet, end 1,650 feet (high point 1,940 feet)
Trailheads: Cow Camp (start) and Bald River Trail (end)
Trail Connections: Henderson Mountain Trail
Type: Hiking

Comments: This is a short trail crossing a low ridge to Bald River through a hardwood and mixed pine forest. It ends at an unmarked trail junction on the Bald River Trail (No. 88). One small water course is crossed shortly after leaving the road. This trail provides access to the Henderson Mountain Trail (No. 107), the north end of which is at an unmarked junction on the ridgecrest. It can also be used in combination with the Bald River Trail to make a short loop hike, starting at either trailhead (see description of the Bald River Trail, above).

Details: After parking at the upstream end of the bridge across the Tellico River, walk back across the bridge, step over the guardrail onto a wooden stairway (six or seven steps), and you are on the trail. The trail follows an easy grade southwest along a small stream course, which may be dry in summer, for about 0.25 mile. Then it switches back to the left, contouring around a small ridge and gaining elevation until it reaches the ridgecrest at 0.6 mile, with an elevation gain of about 440 feet. There you will find an unmarked trail junction. The trail to the east is the Henderson Mountain Trail (No. 107). The Cow Camp Trail continues south, downhill through a hardwood forest with pine mixed in. At 0.8 mile the trail joins the Bald River Trail at another unmarked junction.

Henderson Mountain (Trail No. 107)
Length: 2.7 miles
Elevation Change: Start 1,940 feet, end 2,660 feet (high point 2,800 feet)
Trailheads: Cow Camp Trail (start) and Henderson Top (end)
Type: Hiking

Comments: The Henderson Mountain Trail is an opening (no tread construction) along the ridgecrest of Cow Camp Lead and an unnamed lead extending northwest off Cow Camp Lead. It is marked by white blazes (most of them reasonably visible), occasional evidence of someone having cut some blow-downs or underbrush many years ago, and some evidence of people having walked it. It makes virtually no compromise in its grade as it follows the ridgecrest. There are no campsites or water on this trail though there may be some water on the Cow Camp Trail (except in dry weather), a short distance from the Tellico River Road.

The trail is forested along its full length with hardwoods, but occasionally some pine is mixed in. One short section has numerous dead pine across the trail, presumably killed by southern pine beetles several years ago. On a clear day when the leaves are down, there are good views of the distant mountains. Wild turkey have been seen along this trail.

Details: From the parking area at the upstream end of the bridge across the Tellico River, walk back across the bridge, step across the guard rail at the west (downriver) end of the bridge, and you are on the Cow Camp Trail (No. 173). Ascend the six or seven wooden steps and follow the trail as it contours to the left around the hillside to a small watercourse. Follow this branch 0.25 mile, where it switches back to the left and continues on a moderate grade through a hardwood forest to the ridgecrest at 0.6 mile. On the ridgecrest you arrive at an unmarked trail junction, the beginning point for Trail No. 107, the Henderson Mountain Trail. Turn east along the ridgecrest, going over low knobs following an obvious path about 0.25 mile. Here it descends to the left and contours around to the right into a hollow at 0.35 mile from the unmarked junction. A human-made rockpile can be seen here. Look for blazes going southwest up a steep grade and follow these. The grade soon eases, as the trail veers to the right to reach a shoulder on the ridge. It then switches back to the left up a steep grade, eases again, and soon reaches the top of a knob at 0.8 mile. The trail descends to a shallow gap at 1.0 mile and continues on with alternately steep and easy grades to 1.6 miles, where it reaches Cow Camp Lead.

Turning south on Cow Camp Lead, it is easy going to 2.3 miles, where a steep grade is reached on the north side of Henderson Top. A short distance up the grade the trail veers to the left, reaches a shoulder, and contours around to the southeast side of Henderson Top, where at 2.4 miles there is a clear-cut and burned area to the southwest. This was probably a controlled burn. The trail descends southeast along a firebreak, where a logging road becomes visible 50 feet to the south of the trail at 2.6 miles. A few hundred feet more and the trail ends on FS 40832 at 2.7 miles. There is no trail marker here, blazes are difficult to see even with the leaves down, and the path is obscure. This logging road can be followed 0.6 mile southeast to the south end of the Panther Branch Trail (No. 162), which comes up from the Tellico River Road or 2.5 miles to FS 126 at Green Cove Gap.

Brookshire Creek (Trail No. 180)
Length: 6.3 miles
Elevation Change: Start 1,900 feet, end 3,940 feet (high point 3,940 feet)
Trailhead: Brookshire Creek (start) and Beaverdam Bald (end)
Trail Connections: State Line Trail
Type: Horse

Comments: This trail is best suited for a hike to Beaverdam Bald and return by the same route or a loop backpack using this trail, Nantahala National Forest State Line Trail (No. 82), and the Kirkland Creek Trail. Trails in this area are in general poorly maintained, so you should be prepared to make your way through, over, or around blow-downs on the trail. There are several stream crossings, of which at least one and possibly others, depending on the weather, will require wading.

The trail uses old logging grades for most of its length, passing through a hardwood forest with some pine and a generous amount of rhododendron. Wildflowers are plentiful in the spring, and the fall colors are beautiful. Brookshire Creek generally forms the boundary between the managed and unmanaged portions of the Primitive Areas. Accordingly, limited timber harvesting may occur to the east of Brookshire Creek (see Section A).

Details: Starting at FS 126 you must immediately cross Henderson Branch, then continue up Bald River generally going southeast on a former logging road. A variety of deciduous trees and undergrowth with some pine line the trail. A good campsite is found at 0.75 mile, and the first Bald River crossing occurs at 1.1 miles. The trail remains close to Bald River and is very easy hiking. At 1.7 miles is another good campsite and, as the grade steepens a little, a small but attractive waterfall about 15 feet high is found at 2.4 miles. A very short distance beyond this, the old Bald River logging road crosses Brookshire Creek at some very pretty cascades. Turn right (south) before crossing Brookshire Creek up a steep embankment, staying on the west side of Brookshire Creek, where the old logging grade is not present.

At 2.7 miles the trail again reaches the old logging grade on Brookshire Creek. There is a good campsite here on the west side of the trail. From here to the south end, the trail is on and off the old logging road. At 2.9 miles the trail crosses Brookshire Creek and goes a very short distance up a steep grade, but at no time is the trail difficult. At 4.2 miles there is evidence of an old cabin site on the east side of the trail, and at 4.7 miles small cascades greet you. In spring, wildflowers are everywhere and, since the trail is always in a hardwood forest, fall colors will be beautiful along these streams.

Another old cabin site can be seen at 5.0 miles on the southwest side of the trail, and a third one is found at 5.7 miles. Here a small party can find suitable camping space along Brookshire Creek. This area appears to have been a mountain farm site in the distant past. Sled Runner Gap is a short distance to the south, but the trail does not go to this gap as shown on the current CNF trail map. A short distance up the trail from the cabin site the trail switches back to the east, contouring upward and around Beaverdam Bald to reach a wildlife management clearing at 6.3 miles in a gap on the northwest side of 4,259-foot Beaverdam Bald. At 6.2 miles, just before reaching the clearing, there is a spring (at least in wet weather) about 20 feet below the trail, making the wildlife-management clearing a suitable campsite. A logging road, FS 24, can be found on the east side of the clearing. This road provides access, with high-clearance vehicles, to this end of the trail from the Tellico River Road. Water may also be found just below this road on the east side. A short distance east of the wildlife clearing, along the logging road, FS 24, a junction is reached where you can switchback to the west and go to the wildlife clearing at the top of Beaverdam Bald.

A very short distance above the switchback and cabin site mentioned above, you can find an easy route to Sled Runner Gap by walking southeast for about 0.25 mile. ORVs have in the past and may still be illegally using this access to get from NC through Sled Runner Gap to the logging road (FS 24) on the east side of the wildlife management clearing. At Sled Runner Gap you can find State Line Trail (No. 82, unmarked), a Nantahala National Forest trail. It seldom sees any maintenance work but can be easily followed along the ridgecrest 6.0 miles west to Sandy Gap at the south end of the Kirkland Creek Trail. These three trails (Brookshire Creek, State Line, and Kirkland Creek) make a good loop trip for backpackers. A suggestion for backpacking this loop: start on the Brookshire Creek Trail, camp at the wildlife management clearing on the north side of Beaverdam Bald, follow State Line Trail from Sled Runner Gap to Sandy Gap, then go down the Kirkland Creek Trail. There is no water on State Line Trail, and neither water nor a suitable campsite is available at Sandy Gap. The current Kirkland Creek Trail goes northwest from Sandy Gap on an old logging grade, not downhill to the northeast as shown on some maps still in use.

Kirkland Creek (Trail No. 85)
Length: 4.6 miles
Elevation Change: Start 1,885 feet, end 2,580 feet (high point 2,580 feet)
Trailheads: Kirkland Creek (start) and Sandy Gap (end)
Trail Connections: State Line Trail No. 82
Type: Hiking

Comments: This trail is best suited for a roundtrip hike, starting and ending at the Kirkland Creek Trailhead, a hike of about 9.2 miles. The trail is poorly maintained, so you should be prepared for blow-downs across it. There are also several stream crossings, some of which will require wading, including Bald River about 50 feet from the parking area. Old logging grades are used for most of the trail, and only one short steep grade is encountered on the whole length of the trail. A predominantly hardwood forest with some pine and a generous quantity of rhododendron provides a delightful environment year round. Spring wildflowers and fall colors add significantly to its beauty.

Details: Park your vehicle, walk 50 feet, and wade Bald River to start this easy hike up parts of two small, clean, attractive streams. The trail follows old logging grades most of the way to Sandy Gap. Look carefully and you will see some evidence of an effort made many years ago to improve the trout habitat on the first 0.5 mile or so of Kirkland Creek. It is quite level along this part of the stream and could have supported subsistence farming. No cabin sites are obvious from the trail, but a little exploring in some of the wide, flat areas may reveal evidence of past habitation.

At 0.9 mile from the parking area is a good campsite on the creek about 150 feet off the trail on the west side. There are several creek crossings, and the next one is at 1.0 mile; this crossing requires wading, as will several others. At 1.2 miles there is another good campsite for a small party. Water is never a problem until you leave Waucheesi Creek. Wildflowers are plentiful in the spring, and in the fall this hardwood forest will show a typical display of very colorful Appalachian hardwood foliage. Rhododendron and some pine provide green in the view year round. Another good campsite is found at 1.8 miles.

At 1.9 miles cross Waucheesi Creek and make a turn to the west up this creek. Its confluence with Kirkland Creek is out of sight in the rhododendron to the east. The trail up Kirkland Creek shown on old topographical maps can be found here, but it has not been maintained in years, which will be immediately obvious if you choose to follow it south through the rhododendron. Continue up Waucheesi Creek, making several crossings, most of which can be crossed on small rocks, except in wet weather. The grade will increase slightly before reaching 2.7 miles, where there is a rocky crossing with large slippery rocks.

At 2.9 miles the valley floor is level, with a good campsite. The creek is flowing eastward at this point. Make a turn to the south toward the ridge, looking carefully for painted blazes. The trail goes straight up the side of the ridge, reaching the crest at 3.1 miles. You will find another old logging road here going westward along the ridge. The logging grade on the creeks was the original logging access into this area. The one on the ridge was constructed much later. Except in wet weather, there will be no water between Waucheesi Creek and Sandy Gap. The trail continues on old logging roads as it makes its way along the ridge, or contours around the mountain, swinging to the south with easy grades up and down. Painted blazes mark the way, but these are not repainted often, so look carefully. At 4.6 miles you reach the dirt logging road, FS 50, at Sandy Gap on the ridgecrest. The south end of the old trail that followed Kirkland Creek, which may still be shown on your topographical map, can be found here. There are no trail markers, no water is nearby, and there are no suitable campsites at this gap. Note also that 198 acres are privately owned southeast of Sandy Gap.

If you decide to take a shortcut from this gap to the Kirkland Creek Trail at the confluence of Waucheesi Creek and Kirkland Creek, be prepared to bushwhack through extensive rhododendron, other assorted brush and briars, and soggy bottomland.

A part of NC's Nantahala National Forest State Line Trail (No. 82) runs generally along the ridgecrest between Sandy Gap and Sled Runner Gap, several miles to the east near the south end of the Brookshire Creek Trail. Although there is no trail marker at Sandy Gap for Trail No. 82, it goes uphill to the southeast on the very rough logging road leaving the gap. The logging road ends and becomes a trail about 0.4 mile southeast of Sandy Gap. The trail then continues on to Sled Runner Gap (no trail markers here either) and Beaverdam Bald.

State Line (Nantahala National Forest Trail No. 82)
Length: 6.0 miles
Elevation Change: Start 2,600 feet, end 3,920 feet (high point 3,920 feet)
Trailheads: Sandy Gap (start) and Beaverdam Bald (end)
Type: Hiking

Comments: This is a Nantahala National Forest Trail that essentially runs along the TN-NC state line between Sandy Gap and Sled Runner Gap near Beaverdam Bald. It is not marked or well maintained but is excellent for loop backpacking, using the Kirkland Creek and Brookshire Creek trails. Wonderful views of mountain ranges in all directions are available in winter. Wear long pants in the summer because of profuse briars. Although not marked, there are sporadic NC "wildlife game lands" signs along the state line.

Details: Begin hiking up the ORV road that leads up and to the southeast out of Sandy Gap. Do not be tempted to drive a two-wheel-drive car up the road. The road climbs up to the ridgecrest and at 0.1 mile reaches a road fork. Take the right fork, which continues up a steep ridge, instead of the good road, which traverses around the side of the hill to the left. Continue along the ridge with good views to the right of the TN-NC state line. At approximately 0.4 mile the road contours to the left side of a 2,861-foot knoll. Do not take the road; instead, proceed on the trail that leads straight up the ridge to the right. State Line Trail becomes a true trail at this point as it climbs over the knoll. Hipps Gap is on the other side of the knoll at 0.75 mile, after a steep descent.

On the other side of Hipps Gap the trail ascends steeply, continuing along the ridge. It somewhat levels off at 0.95 mile as the ridge and trail turn northeast. The trail moves off to the right side of the ridge and turns southeast with the ridge at 1.2 miles. Shortly thereafter it passes through a rhododendron tunnel. At 1.45 miles the trail makes a distinct swing to the right, away from the ridge and around the side of the Hazelnut Knob ridge, which is straight ahead. As it traverses the ridge, note many rock outcrops; the trail passes just below one that has two trees literally growing out of it. A small spring also flows out of a blow-down.

As the trail rounds the ridge and heads down toward an obvious gap (Moss Gap), be alert for a trail junction. Most people go on down to the gap, where there is a possible campsite; beyond the gap the trail ultimately disappears. Instead of going down to Moss Gap, look for another trail at 1.75 miles, coming down from the ridge above and running into the trail you are on, creating a V about 0.1 mile from the gap. Do an almost complete turn and start back up the other trail, directly up the ridge line. If you miss it, turn around in the gap and follow the ridgeline. The trail immediately passes through a mass of wild grape vines and climbs steeply upward. It then levels off and gradually loops to the right and east to reach Hazelnut Knob at 2.2 miles. On the way up to the knob, watch for a stone with "1812/1816" carved on it.

After Hazelnut Knob, the trail turns northeast and continues along the ridgecrest at 3,674-foot Nit Top at 3.1 miles. The trail drops somewhat and then ascends again to Round Top at 3.65 miles. An old trail drops off to the south just before Round Top. Just beyond Round Top at 3.95 miles is a 3,698-foot unnamed peak. Beyond that peak the trail begins a long gradual ridgetop ascent, staying at or near the state line, to the east and then southeast, reaching 4,000-foot Rocky Top at 5.65 miles. Beyond Rocky Top the trail curves almost 90 degrees, starting out southeast and finishing north, as it drops down to Sled Runner Gap. Sled Runner Gap at 6.0 miles is the official end of the trail. The trail formerly continued across the gap and along the state line up to Beaverdam Bald. However, ORVs from the NC side sometimes came up to Sled Runner Gap and used the trail for access to Beaverdam Bald. The USFS cut numerous trees across the trail, thus making the old route difficult for ORVs. Hikers can follow the old route through briars and fallen trees for 0.5 mile to Beaverdam Bald. However, a better option is to turn left (northwest) at Sled Runner Gap and walk slightly downhill for about 0.25 mile to the Brookshire Creek Trail. ORVs sometimes illegally take the same route. Turn right (north) on the Brookshire Creek Trail and follow it about 0.4 mile up to the Beaverdam Bald Trailhead located in a wildlife clearing at 3,920 feet. FS 24 enters this clearing on its east side. Water can usually be found below the trail on both sides of the wildlife clearing, making it a good place to camp.

19. WARRIOR'S PASSAGE NATIONAL RECREATION TRAIL

The Warrior's Passage Trail is a remaining portion of a trail that served Cherokee Indians traveling between villages, British soldiers who built Fort Loudon, and South Carolina traders eager to reach the "Overhill" towns. Some adventurers, interested in the gold once found in nearby Coker Creek, used the trail to cross the

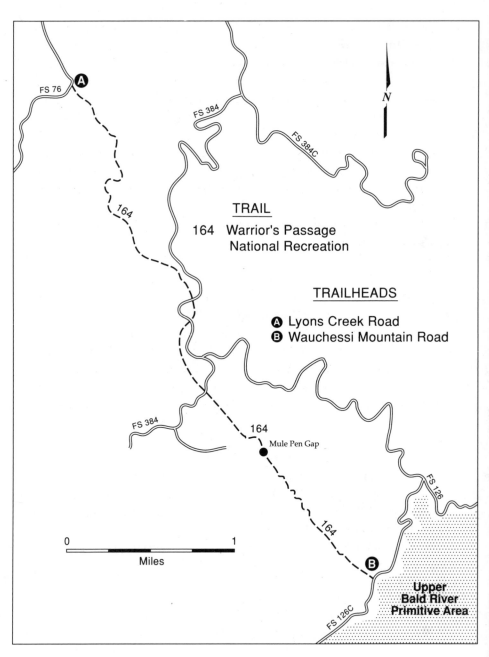

Warrior's Passage National Recreation Trail.

southern Appalachian Mountains. Under the 1988 CNF Management Plan, the trail is protected by a 200-foot corridor.

The trail begins with moderate ups and downs but is very steep the last couple of miles and makes several stream crossings (two of which must be waded at times of high water levels). It has many forks and branches, so following the blazes is necessary to stay on the trail. At some places, especially road crossings, the blazes are difficult to locate, so you must be observant.

The USFS includes the 2.9 miles along FS 76 to the signpost marking the beginning of the trail as part of the trail itself, assigning it a total length of 8.1 miles. The length of the actual hiking trail from the signpost on FS 76 to Waucheesi Mountain Road is 5.2 miles.

The trail is not well maintained; there are numerous blow-downs, particularly on the upper portion of the trail, and it is heavily overgrown in some places.

TRAILHEADS AND MAPS

Lyons Creek Road Trailhead

Follow TN 165 southeast out of Tellico Plains, TN. Take the right fork (a continuation of TN 165) at a sign for Bald River Falls just outside Tellico Plains. Drive 1.2 miles on TN 165 from the sign and turn right on an unmarked paved road, which is Lyons Creek Road, FS 76. (The Tellico Beach Drive-In is opposite the turnoff for this road.) Continue up FS 76, which turns to gravel, for 2.9 miles until you see the Boy Scouts signpost ("BSA-WP") on the left. There is no USFS trail sign marking this trail.

Waucheesi Mountain Road Trailhead

FS 126C, known as the Waucheesi Mountain Road, turns south off the Bald River Road, FS 126. To reach FS 126 follow TN 165 5.3 miles from the intersection of TN 165 and TN 68 on the west side of Tellico Plains. At that point, turn right on FS 210 and follow it for 13.9 miles to FS 210 on the right. Turn right on FS 210, a gravel road, and follow it past Holly Flats Campground to a sign for Waucheesi Mountain and FS 126C. Turn left on FS 126C and proceed up the mountain if the road is open; it may be closed by the USFS, which would require walking up the road. The trailhead is about halfway up Waucheesi Mountain on the west side of the road.

Topographic Map: Bald River Falls, TN-NC.

TRAIL DESCRIPTION

Warrior's Passage National Recreation Trail (No. 164)

Length: 5.2 miles
Elevation Change: Start 1,600 feet, end 3,200 feet (high point 3,200 feet)
Trailheads: Lyons Creek Road (start) and Waucheesi Mountain Road (end)
Type: Hiking

Comments: The trail is blazed with a vertical rectangle with a dot or line above and below the rectangle. The trail is described from FS 76, Lyons Creek Road, to FS 126C, the Waucheesi Mountain Road.

Details: The trail begins at the signpost on the left side of FS 76. At about 0.1 mile it branches to the right. It forks right again at 0.28 mile and crosses a stream, which may be dry at times. The trail then climbs through a rhododendron grove at 0.36 mile and makes a sharp left turn at 0.47 mile.

At 0.66 mile the trail turns right and at 0.75 veers left. At 1.0 mile, you will be at Wildcat Creek. Here the trail turns sharply left, follows the creek for a few yards, and then crosses. The stream must be waded at this crossing. The trail begins to climb after the crossing and is steep at times. At 1.2 miles it branches to the right, descends, and crosses a small unnamed branch twice at approximately 1.3 miles. At 1.7 miles the trail leaves the branch and climbs steeply up the hillside. The trail crosses an abandoned road at 1.9 miles, bears left, and at 2.0 miles comes upon a USFS road. Do not cross the road. Instead, turn right and continue parallel to the road. The trail does cross the road at 2.3 miles and again at 2.8 miles. It then goes downhill, approaches a stream, and turns left.

You should be observant at this point because the route can be a bit confusing for the next hundred yards or so. After making the above-mentioned left turn, the trail turns right at about 2.9 miles, where a stream must be crossed. This right turn can be difficult to spot because the blaze is not conspicuous. Additionally, it appears that the trail goes straight ahead instead of turning right. In fact, if you do go straight, you will find a couple of blazes and a marker post further on. This is apparently a route that the Warrior's Passage Trail followed in the past, but it is now abandoned. This route eventually disappears in thick undergrowth, so do not waste your time.

When you make the right turn at 2.9 miles, the trail will be quite evident on the other side of the stream, although there are no blazes until the trail branches left at 3.1 miles. You should be alert for this left turn because it is also not conspicuous and is not marked with a blaze. After making this left, the trail begins to climb sharply and the blazes will be observed once again. At 3.7 miles, the trail branches right and thereafter, at 3.8 miles, crosses FS 126, the last road crossing.

At 4.0 miles the trail forks left and begins a steep ascent which does not abate until the Waucheesi Mountain Road is reached. After veering left again at 4.5 miles it branches right at 4.9 miles, where a marker post will be found. The trail continues its steep climb, reaching its upper termination on the Waucheesi Mountain Road at 5.2 miles.

You may now choose to turn right up the road and hike the 0.8 mile to the Waucheesi fire tower, which has an elevation of 3,692 feet. Those who do so will be rewarded with a spectacular 360-degree view of the surrounding mountains and the Bald River watershed.

20. GEE CREEK WILDERNESS AND PRIMITIVE AREA

Gee Creek, a rugged, hanging valley cut out of the extreme western "Chilhowee" face of the southern Appalachians, was the first officially designated Wilderness wholly in the CNF, receiving that status in 1975. The creek's watershed is easily visible from US 411 just north of the Hiwassee River bridge. What you see is a V-shaped cut in the steep, otherwise continuous face of Starr and Chestnut Mountains. The creek and its major tributary, Poplar Springs Branch, begin as northeast-to-southwest streams, parallel to and behind Starr Mountain. Only in the last 0.5 mile of Gee Creek does the watershed abruptly turn some 60 degrees to cut east-west through the ridge face. Were it not for Gee Creek, Chestnut Mountain would simply be the end of Starr Mountain and deserve no separate name.

The 2,493-acre Wilderness includes virtually all of the watershed of Gee Creek. In the 1960s and 1970s the USFS toyed with the idea of limiting Wilderness designation to areas of 5,000 or more contiguous acres. No better argument against that idea exists than Gee Creek. It is compact, varied, and self-sustaining. Its three trails represent three entirely different experiences. The Gee Creek Trail itself is the nearest thing to instant exposure to wilderness a hiker will find in the CNF. Adjacent to the Wilderness's eastern boundary is a 1,400-acre Primitive Area which is a motorized and managed area (see Section A).

From an elevation of 2,100 feet at the headwaters of Gee Creek and Poplar Springs Branch, the system loses 1,100 feet of elevation within the Wilderness, down to 1,000 feet elevation at the Gee Creek Trailhead. Most of this elevation drop is fairly evenly distributed over 4.0 to 5.0 miles of watershed, but the last 350 feet is suddenly, lavishly lost in the final 0.5 mile, creating many waterfalls, some 20 to 25

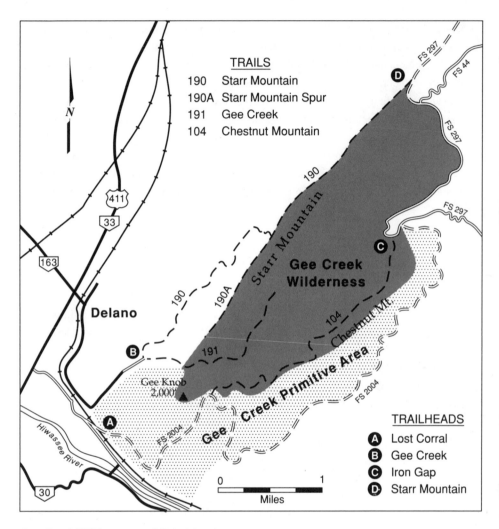

Gee Creek Wilderness and Primitive Area.

feet high, along the Gee Creek Trail. Hemlock, tulip trees, and rhododendron fill the lowest elevations of the gorge while the higher elevations are dominated by Virginia pine, white oak, and red oak, with some hickory. The highest point is the 2,560-foot crest of Chestnut Mountain. Rainbow trout, first introduced in 1905, might be hiding in any of the deeper pools of the main watershed.

The Gee Creek Areas also contain a cave, some impressive bluffs, and are near the Hiwassee River. From the Gee Creek Campground (which is outside the Areas) it is possible, for those with the proper equipment and experience, to go white-water canoeing, caving, rock climbing, and hiking all in one weekend. Note that, because of its small size, overnight camping is not allowed in the Wilderness itself.

None of the three trails in the Wilderness intersects with one another, and the USFS has no plans to connect them. Accordingly, loop hikes will require some off-trail or road hiking. The areas are in Polk and Monroe Counties and the Hiwassee Ranger District.

HISTORY

The oldest signs of man in the Areas are the remains of a concrete flume and rock crusher on the lowest section of Gee Creek, vestiges of an iron-mining venture during the years 1825-60. The mine was operated by Tennessee Copper Company, whose employees sought a certain type of iron ore used as an additive in copper smelting. They lived in the nearby—now deserted—community of Austral. The USFS says the entire drainage was logged as recently as 45 years ago, but some large trees, mostly hemlock, were left in the gorge. Starr Mountain, the first buffer to the prevailing westerly winds over the TN Valley, was the scene of many forest fires in the 1920s. In the early 1970s (prewilderness) three wildlife-management clearings were made on Chestnut Mountain, but they have blended into the forest and are not noticeable from the trail.

Starr Mountain, which forms the western boundary of the Wilderness, is named for Caleb Starr, a young Pennsylvanian Quaker who moved into the area from NC after the Revolutionary War. Caleb and his descendants were historical figures in TN and, subsequently, Oklahoma. Caleb married Nancy Harlan, granddaughter of Nancy Ward, known as the "Wild Rose of the Cherokees." He owned Starr Mountain and amassed a fortune in land, livestock, and slaves. The area was then under Cherokee jurisdiction, but Caleb's son, James Starr, persuaded President Jackson to sign a treaty that gave 640 acres to white settlers. The following unrest culminated in the Trail of Tears; since the Starrs were part Indian, the entire family, including Caleb and Nancy, moved to Oklahoma. James was later murdered for his role in selling out the Cherokees. Tom Starr, Caleb's son, and Sam Starr, Caleb's grandson, became notorious outlaws in the Southwest; Tom started killing at age 19 to avenge the death of his father, and Sam rode with the well-known Younger gang. Another

Double cascade on Gee Creek Trail. Photo by Roger Jenkins.

relative, Henry Starr, was also an infamous southwestern outlaws, as was Sam's wife, Belle Starr.

The Wilderness was designated as such by Congress in 1975. The area adjacent to the eastern boundary of the Wilderness was designated as a Primitive Area (Managed) in 1988 by the CNF Management Plan. Vehicles will be allowed on one road (FS 2004) in the Primitive Area, and limited timber harvesting may be allowed—unlike most primitive areas (see Section A).

TRAILHEADS AND MAPS

Gee Creek Trailhead

Turn east off US 411 on a paved road south of Etowah (5.0 miles south of the old Etowah train depot and 1.3 miles north of the Hiwassee River bridge) opposite a Gulf station and the Delano Branch of the Benton Banking Company. There should be a Gee Creek Wilderness directional sign on US 411. Follow the main paved road until it crosses some railroad tracks, then turn right. The road follows along the left side of the railroad tracks through a small community and then turns away from the tracks to the left (1.4 miles from US 411), just before the tracks cross Gee Creek. Follow the road until the pavement runs out next to the last house. Continue on the rough but passable dirt road until you come to the trailhead (2.2 miles from US 411).

There is a bulletin board with a map of the Area and a small parking lot. To the left, you will find the trailhead for Starr Mountain Trail only about 30 yards up the road on the right-hand side (you may even be able to see the first of the white trail blazes from the parking area). To the right is the Gee Creek Trailhead; walk up the jeep road (which has been closed to vehicles) and cross Gee Creek on a footbridge to enter the Wilderness.

Lost Corral Trailhead

Turn east off US 411 at the Gee Creek Campground sign 0.4 mile north of the Hiwassee River. Follow the large dirt-and-gravel road 0.7 mile, cross Gee Creek, and pass the ranger's residence on the left. Then take the second dirt road to the left, at 0.8 mile, which will immediately cross the railroad tracks (elevation at the tracks is exactly 750 feet). Just beyond the railroad tracks is a large dirt parking area. On the left back corner of the parking area is the access to Gee Cave. (*Do not* enter the cave without using the proper equipment and checking in with the USFS in advance.) On the right back corner of the lot is a gate that is the trailhead for the Chestnut Mountain Trail; the trail begins as an ORV road.

Iron Gap Trailhead and Starr Mountain Trailhead

It is a long, roundabout car ride to the upper ends of both Starr Mountain and Chestnut Mountain trails, both of which end at FS 297. The better decision may be to return by the route you came or—if you can hike nearly 15 miles in a day, counting the walk between the lower trailheads, or camp along the route—make a roundtrip of it using FS 297 as a connector. To reach FS 297, take TN 30 from US 411 to Reliance. At Reliance, turn left on TN 315 and cross the river on a new bridge. Take TN 315 north to the little community of Springtown. Just above Springtown (5.3 miles on TN 315), FS 297 (unpaved) turns off to the left at Merrell's Cemetery; there is no sign identifying FS 297. It is a long, winding 4.3-mile dirt road—preferably traversed in a four-wheel-drive or pickup—to Iron Gap, the trailhead for the Chestnut Mountain Trail. There is a bulletin board in the gap. From there it is about 2.4 miles on FS 297 to the junction with Yellow Creek Road. Vehicles may not be allowed beyond the Yellow Creek Road junction on FS 297, but it is only about a 15-minute walk on the road to the Starr Mountain Trailhead.

In addition to the USFS, you have two sources of information: the TN State Park Ranger's office building just south of the Hiwassee River (on the hill on the west side of US 411) and, possibly, at the Gee Creek Campground and Picnic Area, either the overnight campground just west of the ranger's residence or the new picnic ground and visitor's center (just beyond the turnoff to the Chestnut Mountain Trailhead/parking lot, on the right). Both Campground and Picnic Area are administered by the TN Department of State Parks. There should be registration boxes at all the trailheads.

Topographic Maps: Oswald Dome, TN; Etowah, TN; Mecca, TN.

TRAIL DESCRIPTIONS

Starr Mountain (Trail No. 190)
and Starr Mountain Spur (Trail No. 190A)
Length: 5.0 miles (Trail No. 190)
Elevation Change: (Trail No. 190) Start 920 feet, end 2,300 feet (high point 2,380 feet)
Trailheads: Gee Creek (start) and Starr Mountain (end)
Type: Hiking

Comments: The Starr Mountain Trail was recently constructed (mid-1980s) by linking together a series of preexisting jeep tracks and trails at various levels of the mountain. It is *not* the trail shown on the 1967-vintage Etowah topographical map.

The lower stretches of the Starr Mountain Trail are pretty, very secluded, and trash-free. The upper stretches top out on one of the very few level ridgetop trails in TN, a different experience altogether from plateau trails, even those following the escarpments. The middle stretch of this trail passes through some brief but fierce tangles of blackberry and other thorned bushes; long pants and long-sleeved shirts are advised. In the summer there is virtually no water on Starr Mountain.

Details: From the trailhead just above and to the left of the parking area, climb the short switchback, following the first of the "dotted i" white blazes. After about 100 yards, the trail turns right along a logging road. At 0.2 mile the trail leaves the logging road with a sharp left turn up a bank. The trail has been rerouted at this point to go around a clear-cut made in 1991. The trail follows the edge of the clear-cut and a burned area. It is well marked with white blazes; the blazes should be watched carefully because several old logging roads cross the trail. At 0.6 mile the trail leaves the burned area and veers left into a mixed pine hardwood grove. At 1.1 miles the Huber Chemical Plant is visible to the left.

At 1.2 miles and for the next 0.4 mile, watch carefully for the trail to switchback to the right (uphill), leaving the more obvious old graded beds. It does this several times. This is the area in which the USFS has cut new sections of ungraded trail to connect old, preexisting graded trails at different contour levels. It is also an area entangled with blackberry bushes.

At 1.2 miles, you will encounter the first of the sudden switchbacks to the right.

It will immediately put you on another old track headed left. There are intermittent blazes here. At 1.3 miles the trail cuts through a rockslide. At 1.6 miles the old trailbed goes straight ahead, but the newly marked trail switches back suddenly to the right again and hooks up with another old trailbed directly above. This turn may not be marked. Turn left along the old trailbed. At 1.7 miles the trail enters a large, open rockslide area, with many blown-down trees. There is a full view of the valley and the chemical plant. At slightly over 2.0 miles, the Starr Mountain ridgecrest, ruggedly fitted with house-sized boulders, comes into view though the trees on the right. At 2.8 miles the trail begins switching back to the right to approach the ridgecrest. At almost due north the town of Etowah can be seen through the trees. In another 70 yards, the trail switches back to the left just beneath the rocks of the ridgecrest, near a lone hemlock tree. Just beyond the hemlock tree the trail switches back and forth as it ascends steeply to the crest. At 2.9 miles, the trail tops out on the ridgecrest of Starr Mountain, at 2,300 feet elevation, and turns left (north). From here on, the trail simply follows the nearly level ridgecrest to the northeast.

At the point the trail reaches the ridgecrest, you can turn right (south) and hike along the mountain crest for about 1.8 miles to the point of Starr Mountain, which provides spectacular views of the entire area. This short dead-end trial is the Starr Mountain Spur (Trail No. 190A).

Within a few hundred yards after reaching the crest and turning left, the Starr Mountain Trail passes what may be the highest point of the ridge at 2,380 feet, just to the left of the trail. Beyond this point, the USFS and/or neighboring landowners have marked every 50 yards or so of the boundary with multiple splashes of red or orange paint—frequently both colors—on the larger trees. The land on the bluff side of the paint markers is not wilderness.

The trail passes a property corner marker—a steel post and rock also painted bright red—at 3.25 miles and 2,330 feet elevation. At roughly 3.6 miles the trail enters a beautiful, heavily shaded section of ridgecrest with many large rocks, offering panoramic views of the countryside.

At 4.8 miles the mountain becomes a true knife-edge ridge, and the trail, entering a pretty grove of pines, slopes down to the right of the ridgecrest. At this point, you should begin watching the trail-blazes carefully. Within a few yards the trail will suddenly cut up the ridge to the left, through some knee-high rocks, to follow the ridgecrest once again. There is a blazed pine tree on the left at the point of the turn, but it is easy to miss and follow what looks like the main track straight ahead into a maze of blow-downs and frustration.

At 5.0 miles the Starr Mountain Trail ends at FS 297 in spectacular fashion, with a full view of the town of Etowah and the TN Valley to the left (northwest) and panoramic views of the mountains to the east, from the upper limits of Tellico all the way south—75 miles or so—to Little Frog Mountain and the southern tip of Chilhowee Mountain. There is an old campsite (no water) at the junction of the trail and FS 297.

If you turn right at this point and follow the jeep track down the mountain, it is 2.6 miles, mostly level or downhill, along FS 297 to the Chestnut Mountain Trailhead at Iron Gap. Within a few minutes you will encounter the only major junction, a road to the left following Yellow Creek down the mountain to the Bullet Creek area. To reach Iron Gap, stay to the right—straight ahead—and follow the main road along the top of the ridge. The large ridge to the south, visible from much of the road, is Chestnut Mountain.

Gee Creek (Trail No. 191)
Length: Approximately 1.9 miles
Elevation Change: Start 920 feet, end 1,400 feet (high point 1,400 feet)
Trailhead: Gee Creek (start and dead-end)
Type: Hiking

Comments: The Gee Creek Trail is not a planned, graded trail but an old fisherman's path that finds the easiest route up the gorge. At present, the trail must be considered a dead-end for all but experienced off-trail hikers. You must descend the same way you hiked up. In high water, after continuous rains or one- to two-inch storms, the creek may be impassable. Even in moderate flow, some crossings are difficult, with sharp differences in depth, jagged rocks, and big waterfalls just downstream, waiting for the clumsy hiker. Some hikers may be tempted to try cutting up the canyon on the pathless sides in order to avoid a particular crossing. Do not try it. The lower gorge contains unusually hard rock formations and deceptive leaf-litter ground cover which looks anchored but in fact rides atop moisture on the rock base and gives way at the slightest pressure. Experienced off-trail hikers—not to mention the uninitiated—could find themselves in extremely dangerous situations. If you cannot make a creek crossing in the lower gorge, stop.

Details: From the parking lot at the bulletin board, walk the trail to the right, which is a jeep road, for 0.5 mile. One hundred yards beyond a small turnaround, downhill on a short spur road to the creek, you will see a new wooden footbridge. At 0.7 mile the trail passes alongside the old concrete flume built by the Tennessee Copper Company before the Civil War. The entire creek flows through the flume. Some very large boulders have fallen on top of the upper end of the flume, a rare occasion to date a geologic event at a glance. Were it not for the flume, the viewer would have no idea whether these rocks had fallen within the past two centuries or over two thousand years ago.

At 0.8 mile, the trail reaches the first of two back-to-back beautiful waterfalls, each about 20 to 25 feet high. The second waterfall flows through a sharp rectangular cut in the rock bed of the creek. Below this second waterfall, the trail crosses Gee Creek to the north side. In less than 0.1 mile it crosses back to the south side. This is what tempts the foolhardy to try bushwhacking to avoid high water crossings. At approximately 0.9 mile the trail reaches an impressive campsite. The creek is cascading to the left; to the right, towering over the campsite, is a 150-foot bluff. The whole scene is shaded with hemlocks. Just above this campsite, on the opposite side of Gee Creek, but in plain view of the trail, is a very unusual side-stream waterfall that slants on a 45-degree angle from the upper left to lower right down a perfectly cut channel in the rock.

At approximately 1.0 mile, the trail crosses Gee Creek two more times in rapid succession and ends up at a level semi-clearing on the south (right) side of the stream. A large hemlock, one of the biggest trees left in the Gee Creek Areas, sits near the center of this level area. By this point the gorge is leveling out in elevation and has turned sharply to the northeast. From here on, creek crossings—on average—become much safer. The trail, however, begins to fade. It continues to be recognizable for about 1.9 miles, with several creek crossings, but the benefit of hiking that far (there are no more spectacular waterfalls) is probably outweighed by the fact that every creek crossing must be redone on the return trip.

Chestnut Mountain (Trail No. 104)
Length: 5.6 miles
Elevation Change: Start 760 feet, end 1,880 feet (high point 2,560 feet)
Trailheads: Lost Corral (start) and Iron Gap (FS 297) (end)
Type: Horse

Comments: This trail is an old ORV road. Most of the route—3.8 miles—is off-limits to vehicles and is already overgrown. All the elevation gain is in the first 3.0 miles; the stretch on top of Chestnut Mountain is mostly level or a gentle downhill slope. Beyond the gap at Gee Knob (where the trail leaves the ORV road) there is a real sense of solitude all the way to Iron Gap.

Details: Begin at the gatepost at the back right corner of the Lost Corral parking lot. Follow the jeep trail to the right (FS 2004), ignoring a path to the left and an old, lesser jeep trail in the center that climbs the slope directly ahead. You want the more used road to the right. After starting up FS 2004 also ignore any smaller trails that take off up the hillside; stay on the main ORV road. At 0.8 mile, after some rather steep sections, the ORV road enters the watershed of Coffee Creek, which drains from the gap between Gee Knob and Chestnut Mountain. The trail comes within sight of Coffee Creek at 1.6 miles and bends hard to the left to begin the climb to the gap.

At 1.8 miles the jeep trail forks. Take the left (higher) fork, labeled by the USFS "dotted-i" blaze. There should be a hiking trail marker here designating Trail No. 104. Several deep pits just beyond the sign are meant to stop vehicle entry. The gap between Gee Knob and Chestnut Mountain is reached at 2.1 miles. In the winter this site offers the first views into Gee Creek gorge. The trail goes to the right and should be marked with another Trail No. 104 sign, plus a blaze. The trail immediately becomes rockier, wilder, and steeper as it begins the climb up Chestnut Mountain. At 2.3 miles—in winter—the first full views of the entire gorge may be seen. At 2.5 miles the TN Valley to the west comes into full view. Shortly thereafter, at about 2.8 miles, the trail begins some fairly steep switchbacks which will abruptly end at the top of Chestnut Mountain.

The highest elevation, the top of Chestnut Mountain, is reached at 3.3 miles. From this point, it will take less than half the time to get to Iron Gap that it took to reach the top of the mountain; it is all downhill, or level, and gently graded.

At 3.7 miles the old trail crosses the first of two springs spaced only a few dozen yards apart. They probably run in all but the driest seasons. From here the trail is a relatively uneventful, but very pleasant, walk down the top of Chestnut Mountain, gradually easing off to the left (north) of the crest. At 5.1 miles the trail begins a sharper descent. A sizable stream crosses the trail at 5.4 miles. Just beyond the stream the trail is strewn with several table-sized boulders that look oddly out of place. From here the trail begins a short, much steeper descent to Iron Gap. Just before the gap is a USFS sign-in box, another series of ORV prevention pits, and a row of posts for good measure. The gap and FS 297 are reached at 5.6 miles. The elevation here is about 1,900 feet. To the left on FS 297 it is 2.6 miles to Starr Mountain Trailhead.

You may be tempted to try following an old jeep road that begins at Iron Gap and heads down into the Gee Creek watershed to the left of the last few feet of Chestnut Mountain Trail. The road fades out at about 0.5 mile, however, and the hiker is left facing masses of rhododendron that continue off and on for more than a mile, followed by a pathless stretch of gorge in which repeated creek crossings must be made. Only experienced off-trail hikers should attempt bushwhacking down Gee Creek.

21. COKER CREEK SCENIC AREA AND UNICOI MOUNTAIN TRAIL

Coker Creek is a small, 375-acre Scenic Area in Polk County, TN, and the Hiwassee Ranger District near the Hiwassee River. It protects an especially scenic portion of Coker Creek before it flows into the Hiwassee River. The most outstanding sight in the Scenic Area is Coker Creek Falls, a series of ledge falls, up to 40 feet in height, that rival any other falls in the CNF. The falls are located in a narrow, densely forested gorge, with evergreens along Coker Creek and deciduous trees on the slopes. The Scenic Area itself is a small part of a large valley through which Coker Creek flows to the Hiwassee River. The larger, and unprotected, valley is bounded on the west by Duckett Ridge Road (FS 22), on the east by TN 68 and Unicoi Mountain, and on the south by the Hiwassee River. The Unicoi Mountain Trail (FS 83) runs along Unicoi Mountain, providing outstanding views of the gorge and the Hiwassee River Valley.

The forest is second-growth, and hardwood species typical of the southern Appalachians dominate the Area along with some large old-growth hemlock and white pine. Vegetation also includes sassafras, ginseng, flame azalea, mountain mint, mountain laurel, rhododendron, the uncommon Carolina hemlock, Fraser's sedge, and Allegheny cliff fern. Many wildflowers bloom from early spring through fall. Sandberry, blackberry, and blueberry can also be found. Most wildlife species of the southern Appalachians are present, including a large number of wild turkeys.

HISTORY

Just north of the Scenic Area, near Ironsburg and beside Coker Creek, a few foundation stones remain from the Tellico (formerly Carroll) Ironworks. Carroll Ironworks purchased the ironworks from the Cherokee Indians who originally built "the works" prior to the War of 1812. During the winter of 1863, General Sherman's army destroyed the ironworks. Panning for gold occurred in the Coker Creek area before the 1847 California Gold Rush, with Coker Creek being one of the few TN gold-producing areas. An operation partially owned by T. F. Peck proved quite profitable. Just before 1900, a railroad was built to the area and was a major factor in attracting large timber operations during the first quarter of the 20th century. W. C. Heyser, then C. A. Scott, and finally Babcock Logging Company cut over much of the area during that period. In 1933, 85,000 or more acres were sold to the USFS by the timber companies, forming the core of the current Tellico Wildlife Management Area. The Coker Creek Community commemorates that past and sponsors an annual Autumn Gold Festival featuring gold panning and other festival-type activities.

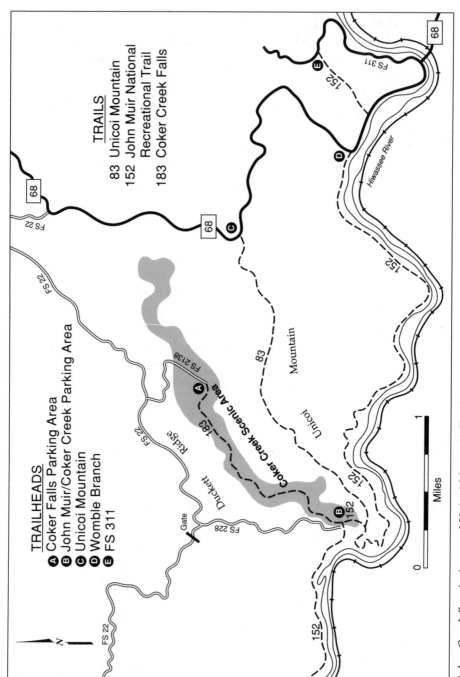

Coker Creek Scenic Area and Unicoi Mountain Trail.

The Scenic Area was designated in 1988 in the CNF Management Plan. The Unicoi Mountain Trail is not within a protected area at present but has a required 200-foot protected corridor under the Management Plan.

TRAILHEADS AND MAPS

Unicoi Mountain Trailhead

Follow TN 68 south from Tellico Plains, TN, through the Coker Creek Community. South of the Community, about 12.5 miles from Tellico Plains, note the Ironsburg Methodist Church on the right. Start keeping mileage there. At 0.1 mile further, note on the left signs for "Coker Creek Falls 4" and the Calvary Baptist Church. At 3.5 miles from the Methodist Church, the highway takes a sharp left turn downhill. At the turn, on the right, is a small parking area with a gated logging road going downhill. On the uphill side of the logging road is a series of dirt mounds (barriers to ORVs). A trail is visible in the center of the mounds heading up the ridge; this is the Unicoi Mountain Trail (No. 83).

Note that another 0.3 mile down TN 68 brings you to the Unicoi Mountain motorcycle trail on the left side of the road, heading up the mountain to Buck Bald. Although a motorcycle trail, it is not used very much by ORVs and is a scenic hike. Another 2.2 miles on TN 68 brings you to the John Muir Trail (No. 152). Womble Branch runs into the Hiwassee River near this point; the trailhead is on the right where TN 68 first comes down to the Hiwassee River.

Duckett Ridge Road Trailheads: Coker Creek Falls Parking Area and John Muir/Coker Creek Parking Area

Follow TN 68 south from Tellico Plains, TN, for about 12.5 miles through the Coker Creek Community. South of the Community, note the Ironsburg Methodist Church on the right. Just beyond the Church, opposite the Calvary Baptist Church, turn right at a sign (on the left) for "Coker Creek Falls 4." You are now on FS 22, Duckett Ridge Road. At 0.9 mile take a left fork at a sign reading "Coker Creek Falls." Continue straight past a fork to the left where the pavement ends. At 3.8 miles on the left you will see a sign for "Coker Creek Falls." At this point you can go to the Coker Creek Falls Parking Area or the John Muir/Coker Creek Parking Area.

A dirt road turns left at the Coker Creek Falls sign (FS 2138) and proceeds 1.0 mile steeply down into the Coker Creek Gorge and the parking area for the Coker Creek Falls Trail (FS 183) and Coker Creek Falls. The road is very rough; you might want to walk. A short distance down the road, proceed left where a spur logging road goes right. The road ends at a small parking lot beside Coker Creek. The trail proceeds downstream from the lot. There is space for a few tents at the parking lot.

Coker Creek Falls. Photo by Roger Jenkins.

If you continue on Duckett Ridge Road, past the "Coker Creek Falls" sign, for 1.6 miles, you will reach FS 228, which turns left and leads to the John Muir Trail, Unicoi Mountain Trail, and Coker Creek Falls Trail. Duckett Ridge Road makes a sharp U-bend back to the right, and FS 228 proceeds straight ahead from that point. FS 228 is another bad road, but not as bad as the road down to the falls parking area. It gradually goes downhill to Coker Creek. At 1.6 miles on FS 228 is a parking area above the creek. The John Muir Trail (No. 152) goes west, toward the Hiwassee River, from the right side (west) of this parking area. A very bad road continues a short distance down to the creek, where there is an area used for ORV camping. At the end of the road, about 0.2 mile from the parking area above the creek, are two trailheads. Coker Creek Trail (No. 183) proceeds straight ahead up the left side of Coker Creek. The eastern portion of the John Muir Trail crosses Coker Creek on a wooden bridge built during the summer of 1990. It proceeds up Coker Creek a very short distance on an old logging road, then turns back to the south and up to a gap. At about 0.45 mile from the bridge there is a trail up the ridge to the left; this is the Unicoi Mountain Trail (No. 83). A sign marks the trailhead as "Unicoi Mountain Trail No. 83, State Highway 68 4." The John Muir Trail continues straight ahead through the gap.

Topographic Maps: McFarland, TN; Farner, TN-NC.

TRAIL DESCRIPTIONS

Unicoi Mountain (Trail No. 83)
Length: 4.25 miles
Elevation Change: Start 1,240 feet, end 1,800 feet (high point 2,080 feet)
Trailheads: John Muir/Coker Creek Parking Area (start) and Unicoi Mountain (end)
Type: Hiking

Comments: The trail is described from the John Muir/Coker Creek Parking Area, off the Duckett Ridge Road, to TN 68 but can easily be hiked in either direction; if you arrange a shuttle, you will not have to backtrack. Trail mileage is given from the parking area, not the John Muir Trail Trailhead where the official trail begins.

Details: The trail (initially on the John Muir Trail) begins at the upper end of the creekside camping area at a trail sign marked with a hiker logo and the number "152." The trail immediately crosses Coker Creek on a very well-built wooden bridge. Immediately on the other side of Coker Creek, the trail proceeds left up the ridge on an old logging road. Note that the old road comes in from the right after having crossed the creek; this road formerly provided ORV access to this side of Coker Creek. At 0.06 mile there is another hiker logo and John Muir Trail sign, together with another sign for Trail 152. Just beyond those signs, the trail swings sharply around to the right and heads gradually upward across a series of ridges. Where the trail turns sharply right, there are signs of an old road proceeding up Coker Creek, to the left. The trail is marked with white blazes, a short blaze over a long blaze. Gradually the trail leaves the Coker Creek gorge bottom and its hemlock forest and climbs into a mixed deciduous forest.

At 0.45 mile there is a junction of four trails, which is where the Unicoi Mountain Trail officially begins. The John Muir Trail, Trail No. 152, proceeds straight ahead and is well marked. The Unicoi Mountain Trail makes a sharp left turn at a huge beech tree and heads up the ridge. It is also marked, with a hiker logo and number "83." There is also a mileage sign pointing out the two trails: "Unicoi Mountain Trail No. 83, State Highway 68 4; John Muir Trail No. 152, State Highway 68 5." In addition to the John Muir Trail and Unicoi Mountain Trail, an old road proceeds across the gap behind the mileage sign. After leaving the John Muir Trail, the Unicoi Mountain Trail is a true trail which does not follow old logging roads. As you proceed up the ridge on Trail No. 83, a huge clear-cut is visible directly to your left in the distance. At 0.6 mile the top of the ridge is reached, and the trail simply crosses and traverses around to the right of a knoll toward a gap. At 0.7 mile the trail passes above and to the left of the gap previously mentioned and continues to traverse along the side of the ridge. Above the gap is a profusion of small white pines which are particularly scenic on winter hikes when hardwood leaves are gone. At 0.8 mile is a sharp gully on the left which leads a short distance up to the ridgetop. The abundant white pines continue and get larger under a canopy of large deciduous trees. Wildflowers are plentiful on this trail in the spring and include wild iris, several varieties of trillium, lady slippers, and maidenhair ferns. Poison ivy is also present, especially at the TN 68 end of the trail.

At 1.0 mile the trail reaches the top of the ridge and crosses a gap, proceeding now to the left side of the ridge and a knoll on the ridge. After going around the knoll, the trail reaches a beautiful gap between two knolls on the ridge, flat and wide, at 1.15 miles. This is an especially nice place with the sound of the Hiwassee River wafting up from below and a portion of the river visible on the right side of the trail. Straight ahead is another knoll with large white rock outcrops visible in the winter. It would be a great campsite if water were carried from below. This is the closest the trail comes to the Hiwassee River. The trail proceeds past the gap around the left side of the knoll, from which a view is available in winter directly to the left of the clear-cut previously seen. The clear-cut appears to be the only distraction from the scenic beauty of the lower Coker Creek gorge.

At 1.35 miles the trail returns to the ridgetop, which is fairly level at this point. The Hiwassee River is still off to the right. The trail soon leaves the ridgetop and traverses along the left side of the ridge, looking steeply down into the Coker Creek gorge. The trail proceeds slightly downward to another gap at 1.6 miles. At this point the valley on the right is narrow with the opposite ridge quite close. The trail then heads up the ridge on the other side of the gap, traversing to the left. After going around a small knoll, the trail ascends very gradually, and in almost a straight line, toward a side ridge running down into the Coker Creek gorge. Just before you reach the ridge, notice a small rock up to the right in a gully. This is a very crude spring that might provide water in wet weather.

At 2.0 miles the ridgetop is reached. At this point you can easily get lost. A strip of grass runs directly to the right, between the forest and an oldclear-cut, up to the top of the ridge, and is tempting. Do not take it. Further, a strip of green grass runs to the left out to the edge of the ridge overlooking Coker Creek gorge. There are great views from that point, looking west, with Chestnut Mountain and Oswald Dome Mountain looming prominent on the horizon. However, instead of going left or right, you should go straight ahead into the briars, brush, and remnants of what was a large clear-cut that may have been followed by fire. After a short distance (300 feet or less) there is an obvious trail that leads directly along the side of the ridge, overlooking Coker Creek gorge, but it can be quite overgrown, particularly in summer and at the start. Although the views are outstanding in the distance, the immediate surroundings are less than scenic. Long pants are advisable through this section. There are no trail markings, but the obvious trail and evidence of some maintenance will keep you headed in the right direction. Finally, at 2.2 miles, the clear-cut ends and the woods resume. The trail again becomes obvious, with blazes, and traversing generally up the side of the ridge.

At 2.6 miles you will reach the top of the ridge at a point between the two highest knolls on the ridge, one to the left at 2,160 feet, and the other to the right at 2,120 feet. At this point, the trail simply crosses over the ridge and traverses down on the other side below the knoll to the left. In the winter the views are outstanding from this point looking south over the Hiwassee River gorge to the mountains on the horizon. The ridgeline will continue on your left and, at around 2.8 miles, the absence of trees on the other side of the ridge indicates an old clear-cut. At 2.9 miles, you will reach a gap and will see an old logging road coming up from the right. To the left is the previously mentioned clear-cut and in the distance a more recent clear-cut at the bottom of the ridge. The trail, however, avoids most of the clear-cut and proceeds down the old logging road straight ahead, to the left side of the ridge. The trail follows this old road to TN 58.

As you walk out the ridge, you will get a good view of the whole clear-cut to the left and the destruction resulting from the clear-cut. Particularly noticeable are the logging roads which continue to be, years later, raw sores on the side of the ridge. Soon, however, the road leaves sight of the clear-cuts and, at 3.0 miles, the trail reaches the top of the ridge and proceeds along the ridge. The trail at this point is wide and almost level, making for very easy walking. The trail gradually follows the ridge, traversing around knolls, and leading slightly upward. At 3.35 miles, the trail begins descending, continuing along the ridgetop. White oaks blanket the right side of the trail at this point. The trail is consistently almost on top of the ridge, with great wintertime views both to the left and right. At 3.67 miles, the trail leaves the ridgetop and heads down the right side of the ridge. At 3.8 miles, the trail makes a sharp cut away from the ridge toward the right. At 3.9 miles another old logging road comes in from the right and the trail proceeds straight ahead, level, and on top of the ridge. At 4.06 miles the trail cuts to the right, again away from the ridgetop and to the right of the ridge. After a short distance the trail begins to descend more steeply, down toward TN 58. At 4.2 miles you reach the first of a series of earthen bumps designed to keep out ORVs. Just beyond the third of these bumps is the trailhead sign "Unicoi Mountain Trail No. 83; Coker Creek 5." Finally, at 4.25 miles you will reach the last of the earthen mounds, and you will see TN 58 directly ahead with a gravel logging road proceeding down to the right.

Coker Creek Falls (Trail No. 183)
Length: 2.7 miles
Elevation Change: Start 1,360 feet, end 940 feet (high point 1,360 feet)
Trailheads: Coker Creek Falls Parking Area (start) and John Muir/
Coker Creek Parking Area (end)
Type: Hiking

Comments: The trail is well marked with two white blazes, a square blaze above a rectangular blaze. It is also fairly open, with the usual blow-downs, and is very easy to hike. The roaring of Coker Creek is almost always present. It can be hiked easily in either direction but is described from the Coker Creek Falls Parking Area to the John Muir/Coker Creek Parking Area.

Details: The trail proceeds down Coker Creek from the parking lot. A sign at the beginning indicates "Coker Creek Falls Trail No. 183, John Muir Trail No. 152 3." Coker Creek Falls are located just downstream at 0.1 mile from the parking area and the initial trail sign. You will hear their roar before you reach them and will be impressed by the series of spectacular waterfalls as you walk down the trail. The falls are formed by rock ledges that extend completely across the creek, 75 feet or so. There are four major ledge falls that vary in height from 5 feet to 40 feet, with shoals between the falls. Dense evergreen trees cover both banks and accentuate the white water and roaring noise. A short loop side trail goes down to the lower, and largest, fall.

Below the falls at 0.2 mile the trail heads up to the top of a ridge and away from the creek. You will see occasional views of additional, smaller falls and will constantly hear the roar of the creek as you proceed along this trail. An old logging road comes in from the right at 0.4 mile. The trail then dips down to the creek and back up on the side of the gorge, then back down and back up again. Thereafter, a series of steep switchbacks lead toward Coker Creek and at 1.1 miles is the first small tributary stream you will encounter, coming in from the right. On the other side of the small creek there is one long switchback up the hill to the side of the gorge. The trail at this point follows the steep gorge side, in some cases looking almost directly down at Coker Creek below.

The trail then descends to another small tributary creek coming in from the right at 1.7 miles, and then continues just above Coker Creek. It thereafter descends even lower down toward Coker Creek, where the creek has somewhat flattened. The trail at this point (1.8 miles) runs level and straight along an old logging road. However, at 2.2 miles, the trail leaves the old road, which is washed out in a bend of Coker Creek ahead, and goes up the side of the ridge to the right. It then descends again down to the old road and more level walking. However, the old road and trail almost immediately angle up the hill to the right and then turn sharply to the right. Do not go straight ahead on the old road, which continues to a creek ravine and stops. Instead, head up the ridge on the old road for about 50 feet, where the trail leaves the old road and cuts sharply back to the left. Be careful here and do not continue up the old road. After what is essentially a Z-series of turns, you should be following the white blazes down Coker Creek. The trail then goes down into and around the creek ravine, then down the Coker Creek gorge above Coker Creek.

After a short distance the trail returns again down to the creek and ends at 2.7 miles at the John Muir/Coker Creek Parking Area. There is a large bare area beside Coker Creek at this point where ORVs come down to the creek for car camping. There are also trail signs for the Coker Creek Falls Trail and the John Muir Trail, which crosses Coker Creek to the left on a wooden bridge. The John Muir Trail also proceeds the other way through the camping area to the right, up the access road a short distance to the bench above, and then to the left down Coker Creek toward the Hiwassee River.

Although the Coker Creek Trail officially ends at the FS 228 parking area, the creek continues a short distance to the Hiwassee River. A walk down to the river is rewarded by scenic views up and down the river, huge clear pools in Coker Creek, giant shale bluffs and boulders, and roaring rapids. To take this walk, continue through the parking area on the John Muir Trail and turn left off the road at the west end of the parking area. After leaving the road you will see three trail signs, the first stating "John Muir Trail No. 152, Appalachian Power House 4." After two more signs, look for a trail descending sharply to the left. Follow it down to the river, but be careful, as the trail and rocks are dangerous.

22. JOHN MUIR NATIONAL RECREATION TRAIL

The John Muir National Recreation Trail was built in 1972 through the efforts of the Youth Conservation Corps and the Senior Community Service Employment Program. The trail follows the scenic Hiwassee River, named after the Cherokee Indian word *ayuwasi* (meadow). The first 3.0-mile section is designed for senior citizens and is quite easy to walk. This section of the river is known for trout fishing and canoeing. As many as 50,000 white-water rafters use the river every year, and it is one of the nation's outstanding scenic streams.

The trail was named because it is believed Sierra Club founder John Muir traveled this section of the Hiwassee River during a walk from Kentucky to Florida as documented in his book *A Thousand Mile Walk to the Gulf*. On September 19, 1867, John Muir wrote, "My path today led me along the leafy banks of the Hiwassee, a most impressive mountain river. . . . The finest of forests are usually found along

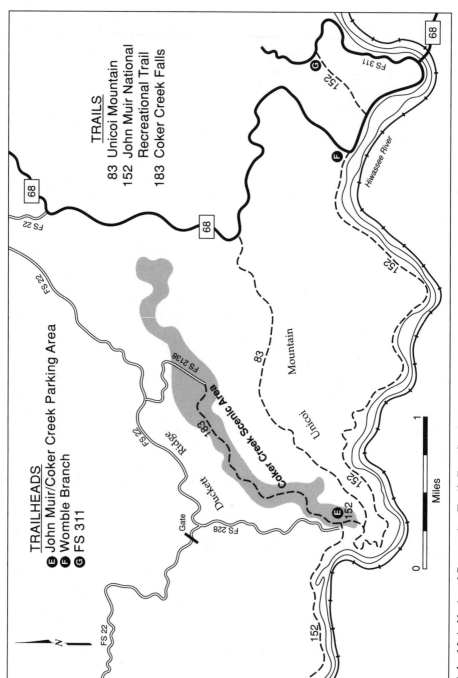

John Muir National Recreation Trail, East Section.

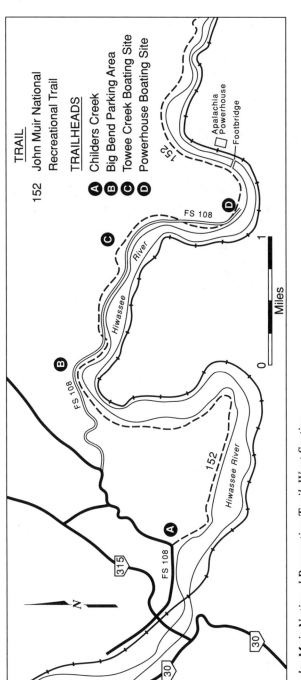

John Muir National Recreation Trail, West Section.

Footbridge across Hiwassee River near Apalachia Power Plant. John Muir Trail goes underneath far end of bridge. Photo by Roger Jenkins.

[the] banks, and in multitude of falls and rapids the wilderness finds a voice. Such a river is the Hiwassee, with its surface broken to a thousand sparkling gems, and its forest walls vinedraped and flowery as Eden."

There is a great variety of wildlife present along the trail, including songbirds, as well as grouse and wild turkey. The larger animals are beaver, raccoon, fox, deer, and wild boar. Water-related wildlife is especially prevalent along this trail. A wide variety of wildflowers may be found along the trail, including squaw root, blood-root, toothwort, fire pink, columbine, stargrass, trillium, white and yellow trout lilies, rattlesnake plantain, wild sorrel, dog hobble, bishop's cap, fairy wand, little brown jug, yuccas, and wild ginger. The trail is protected by a minimum 200-foot corridor pursuant to the 1988 CNF Management Plan.

TRAILHEADS AND MAPS

FS 108 Trailheads: Childers Creek, Big Bend Parking Area, Towee Creek Boating Site, and Powerhouse Boating Site

From the north, take US 411S through Etowah, TN, cross the Hiwassee River, go 0.5 mile, and turn left on TN 30. From the south follow US 411N and turn right on TN 30 just before crossing the Hiwassee River. Go 5.7 miles on TN 30 and turn left onto

Fishermen in the Hiwassee River. View from the John Muir Trail. Photo by Roger Jenkins.

TN 315 at the new bridge that crosses the river (Reliance Bridge). At the end of bridge, take the first road to the right, which is FS 108, a paved road which later becomes gravel. Go about 0.5 mile on paved FS 108 and turn right into the parking area for the John Muir Trail at Childers Creek. If you keep going down FS 108 for 0.7 mile you will come to a small gas station/store that rents rafts to go down the river. Turn right at the store and follow FS 108, keeping right where it forks and continuing as it becomes unpaved. This gravel road leads to the Apalachia Power-house and the starting point for float trips down the Hiwassee River. FS 108 also provides additional trailheads for the John Muir Trail at the Big Bend Parking Area, Towee Creek Boating Site, and finally, near the road's end, the Apalachia Power-house Boating Site.

Womble Branch and FS 311 Trailheads
TN 68 runs south from Coker Creek, TN, and north from Ducktown, TN, crossing the Hiwassee River just below Apalachia Lake. From Coker Creek proceed south on TN 68 into Polk County. After mile marker 3, where the road comes down to Hi-wassee River and takes a distinct bend to the southeast along the river, look for a pull-off on the left. Womble Branch runs into the Hiwassee River at this point. Park in the pull-off, walk across TN 68, and proceed down the trail along the Hiwassee

Upper Hiwassee River from footbridge near Apalachia Power House. John Muir Trail runs along the left bank. Photo by Roger Jenkins.

River. The trail mileage to Childers Creek Trailhead is 17.7 miles from this point. Or you can stay on the north side of TN 68 and hike the John Muir Trail to its actual starting point to the north on FS 311 (see below). The trailhead for hiking north climbs a steep bank on stairs on the north side of TN 68. If you approach this trailhead on TN 68 from the east, drive north from Ducktown on TN 68, past the Farner Post Office, cross the Hiwassee River, and at 2.6 miles from the post office the trailheads will be on your left and right just as the road turns north away from the river.

The Womble Branch Trailhead is the preferred starting point from the eastern end of the trail. However, the actual eastern starting point is off FS 311, which is further south on TN 68. FS 311 is a dirt road that turns back to the left (north) just before the TN 68 bridge that crosses the Hiwassee River. At 0.3 mile the road forks; stay on the right fork and proceed 1.7 miles to a large kudzu patch on the left. There is just enough room to pull a car off the road at the concrete bridge that crosses Watertank Branch at the end of the kudzu. The trailhead can be found on the left about 100 yards down the jeep road that cuts through the kudzu. The road is extremely muddy in wet weather. The trail climbs over the ridge down to TN 68 and the trailhead described above.

Other Trailheads: See Coker Creek Scenic Area section.

Topographic Maps: McFarland, TN; Farner, TN-NC.

TRAIL DESCRIPTION

John Muir National Recreation Trail (No. 152)
Length: 18.85 miles
Elevation Change: Start 600 feet, end 1,100 feet (high point 1,200 feet)
Trailheads: Childers Creek (start) and FS 311 (end)
Trail Connections: Coker Creek Trail, Unicoi Mountain Trail
Type: Hiking

Comments: The trail is identified with either the number "152" (although some USFS maps show it as No. 108) or "JM" for John Muir. The entire trail essentially follows the north bank of the Hiwassee River.

Details: The trail begins at Childers Creek Trailhead. There is a footbridge across Childers Creek, and the trail starts off in a southeasterly direction through a meadow, with the river in the distance. After a short way, you begin walking beside the first of many towering bluffs on your left, with the Hiwassee River directly on your right. The rock formations consist of micaceous quartzite, quartz schist, mica slate, and mica schist. If the water level is low enough you will see the rock formations, which create exciting but only moderately difficult rapids for canoeists and rafters.

At 1.5 miles the trail begins to head north and you begin walking away from the river through large stands of hemlocks, with rhododendrons covering the bluffs. Before long you lose sight of the river completely, as you begin going through a marshy area. The trail eventually widens as it goes along an old logging trail. At 3.0 miles you come to the Big Bend parking lot. There are roadside facilities available.

For the next 3.0 miles the trail proceeds along the river and the USFS road that goes up to the Apalachia Power Plant. The trail can be very muddy at times, depending on the weather conditions.

Once you arrive at the Power Plant at 6.0 miles, there is a suspension bridge that goes over the Hiwassee River. Do not cross the bridge; instead, the trail continues down under the bridge along the north side of the river (the side opposite the Power Plant). At 6.75 miles a large outcropping rock looms about 50 feet overhead. The trail goes around to the left and, depending on the water level, it may be under water. At this point you begin climbing away from the main river and are going around Big Rock Island. At 7.2 miles the trail begins a series of nine switchbacks to the left, then to the right. The trail returns to the river for a brief stretch, then heads back into the forest of hemlocks, popular, redbuds, dogwoods, yellow buckeyes, ash, ironwoods, sycamores, and cucumber magnolias.

At 8.8 miles, switchback to the left at a "No. 152" trail marker. A trail continues straight ahead that goes down to the river. There are some very interesting rock formations caused by water erosion; these are definitely worth exploring. This section of the river is called the Narrows. Once you begin the series of switchbacks at marker No. 152, you are climbing up the side of the mountain and following the contour of the bluffs. You occasionally get a glimpse of the river several hundred feet below. This last section of the trail is not used as much as the first 6.0 miles and consequently may be in need of trail maintenance; you may find downed trees across the trail as well as washed-out switchbacks.

At 11.2 miles you top out on the bluffs with a magnificent view of the river. You begin heading back down the bluffs with another series of switchbacks for another 0.5 mile. Near the bottom, at 11.7 miles, the John Muir Trail merges with a trail from the right that goes down along Coker Creek to its junction with the Hiwassee River. This short but difficult side trail provides a scenic close-up view of the river, bluffs, and Coker Creek. Proceed straight ahead on the John Muir Trail and you will quickly reach the Duckett Ridge Road; follow it down to Coker Creek and to the left up Coker Creek past some primitive vehicle campsites. At the end of the camping area the Coker Creek Trail goes straight ahead while the John Muir Trail forks off to the right across Coker Creek. A bridge constructed in 1989 allows a dry crossing.

Once again you head into the forest, and in late spring you see a wide profusion of mountain laurel, flame azalea, and rhododendrons in bud; in early summer the rhododendrons will be in full bloom. About 0.45 mile from Coker Creek there is a junction. The Unicoi Mountain Trail (No. 83) begins here and proceeds left up the ridge. An old road continues across the gap behind the mileage sign that reads "Unicoi Mtn Trail No. 83, State Hwy 68 4; John Muir Trail No. 152, State Hwy 68 5." Continue following the John Muir Trail marker back around to the right, down a long-forgotten roadbed. Cross the small streambed and begin going up the side of the mountain, following its contours.

At 13.6 miles you begin a series of switchbacks down the mountainside. At 14.5 miles you will cross a footbridge made of two logs. At 15.4 miles is a beautiful waterfall cascading from the left with rhododendron abounding.

The final leg of the trail goes through the forest and along an old roadbed. At times the ferns and poison ivy almost cover the trail. It can be very soggy and sometimes downright muddy after abundant rainfall. The trail finally comes out at TN

68 just south of TN 68 mile marker 3. The trail to this point has covered 17.7 miles. It continues up the ridge on the other side of TN 68 for approximately 1.15 miles to FS 311 and the trail's end at 18.85 miles. Because of difficult access this last section is not hiked as frequently as west of TN 68. There are plans to extend the John Muir Trail even further.

23. ROCK CREEK GORGE SCENIC AREA AND CLEAR CREEK TRAIL

This 220-acre Scenic Area is in Polk County, TN, and the Ocoee Ranger District near Ocoee Lake, and is one of the CNF's oldest scenic areas. Rock Creek, a clear mountain stream with 11 waterfalls along its rugged gorge path, is the focal point of this Area. One of the falls drops 60 feet over a sheer rock bluff while another cascades 180 feet. The Area is close to the many recreational opportunities and developments on Chilhowee Mountain and is within hiking distance of Ocoee Lake developments. Adjacent to the Scenic Area is the 5.4-mile Clear Creek Trail and the 1.6-mile Benton Falls Trail.

HISTORY

Once many of the Cherokee Indians were driven out of this area in 1838, settlers moved in to develop the area for pasture land and agriculture. The two best-known settlers, McCamy and Cronin, built Benton Springs Road up Chilhowee Mountain. During the Civil War, there was a Confederate camp nearby, and the area had its share of Civil War homicides. In early 1865, it is reported that Civil War troops were ambushed on Benton Springs Road. One of these legendary soldiers managed to crawl down the mountain to the Greasy Creek community to get help. Years later, a resort area was developed on Chilhowee Mountain where tourists came from surrounding states to enjoy the cooler summer temperatures and the fresh spring water provided by Benton Springs. The Area was first designated for protection as a Scenic Area in 1965 because of its popularity with local tourists for recreation, and such designation was continued in the CNF's 1988 Management Plan. The Clear Creek Trail and Benton Falls Trail are not within the protected Scenic Area but, under the CNF Management Plan, a forest corridor should be maintained along each trail (some past clear-cuts remain evident on the Clear Creek Trail).

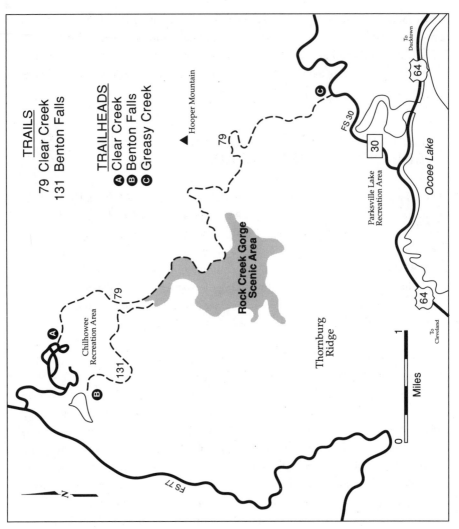

Rock Creek Gorge Scenic Area and Clear Creek Trail.

TRAILHEADS AND MAPS

Chilhowee Recreation Area Trailheads

The usual approach to Chilhowee Recreation Area is from the west. Starting from the intersection of US 411 and US 64, drive east on US 64. Look for FS 77 on the left after passing the Ocoee District Ranger Station and driving along Ocoee Lake for a short distance. If approaching from the east, drive west on US 64 and look for FS 77 on the right after driving some distance along Ocoee Lake. Turn onto paved FS 77, which is signed by number and is known as Oswald Road (although the name is not signed). Benton Falls Trail and Clear Creek Trail Trailheads are located off FS 77.

Benton Falls Trailhead

Drive 3.8 miles on FS 77 to an overlook. Proceed and at 4.1 miles turn right into the Chilhowee Recreation Area, indicated by a sign that says "Cherokee Campground." Go 0.5 mile to a parking area for Lake McCamy (although there is no sign to indicate a lake). Park there if you can. The lake is popular for swimming in the hot summer months so you may have to park away from the area. The trailhead is immediately to the left of the swimming area. Two signs clearly indicate the beginning of the trail.

Clear Creek Trailhead

Continue by taking a left turn at the Lake McCamy parking lot described above and proceed down the hill, past all the camping loops, to the dump station at a dead-end circle. The Clear Creek Trailhead is at the dump station.

Greasy Creek Trailhead

When approaching the Area from the west, start at the intersection of US 411 and US 64 and drive east on US 64. Pass the Ranger Station on the left at the entrance to the CNF and continue 2.1 miles to TN 30. Turn left. Approaching from the east, drive west on US 64; look for TN 30 shortly after crossing a bay of Ocoee Lake; turn right. Go 1.0 mile on paved TN 30 to the trailhead on the left. Landmarks for the trailhead include a picnic table on the right just before the trailhead and a bridge that crosses Greasy Creek immediately beyond the trailhead.

Topographic Map: Oswald Dome, TN.

Trail Information: Unfortunately, trails in the Rock Creek Gorge Scenic Area itself exist only as dotted lines on a topographical map. As of the early 1990s, funding for construction awaits submission of a design narrative by the USFS. Contact the Ocoee

District Ranger for the status of these trails. Two trails are proposed for the gorge: the Rimrock Trail (3.0 miles, Trail No. 77), encircling the gorge, and the Scenic Spur Trail (0.8 miles, Trail No. 78), into the gorge. Access to both trails will be from the Clear Creek Trail running from the Chilhowee Recreation Area to Greasy Creek.

TRAIL DESCRIPTIONS

Clear Creek (Trail No. 79)
Length: 5.4 miles
Elevation Change: Start 1,800 feet, end 880 feet (high point 2,000 feet)
Trailheads: Clear Creek (start) and Greasy Creek (end)
Type: Hiking

Comments: The Clear Creek Trail provides an easy hike from the Chilhowee Recreational Area. For a moderately more demanding hike, consider beginning at Greasy Creek and walking the opposite direction to the Recreation Area. The trail largely follows old roads through a second-growth forest of deciduous and evergreen trees, skirting the north side of the Rock Creek Gorge on Chilhowee Mountain. The trail is marked with white blazes.

The first section of the trail from Chilhowee Recreation Area passes through, and is marred by, an area near the trail which was, apparently by mistake, clear-cut a number of years ago; the trail may be relocated in the future to avoid the clear-cut. A scenic view of the Hooper Mountain Range enhances one section of the trail. Wooden bridges are provided for two creek crossings, but at other times wading or crossing on rocks is necessary. Beware of extremely slippery rocks. An initial elevation gain of 190 feet is misleading because there is an overall loss of 820 feet from trailhead to end. The trail ends at Greasy Creek Trailhead on TN 30 where a bridge and a picnic area on the far side of the road make good landmarks if hikers choose to use a car shuttle.

Details: The Clear Creek Trail passes through mixed evergreen and deciduous second-growth forest. Both the short Chilhowee Recreation Area Azalea Trail and Arbutus Trail join the Clear Creek Trail briefly during the first 0.5 mile. Cross the creek on a small wooden bridge at 0.4 mile. Just past the bridge, to the left of the trail, several acres were completely cleared and plowed under in 1990. Log debris from past clear-cuts sometimes litter both sides of the trail for the first 2.7 miles, providing graphic evidence of the need for protected trail corridors. Franklin Spring Branch parallels the trail in this area. Cross a second small wooden bridge and take a right (southwest) onto an old road at 0.7 mile. Turn right away from the clear-cut at 1.7

miles and then left onto an old road at 2.1 miles. Step across a small creek at 2.3 miles and follow the trail as it snakes uphill to the 2.7-miles mark, which is the highest point of the trail (elevation 2,000 feet).

The trail begins a descent at 2.9 miles and then becomes steeper and more narrow at 3.1 miles. As the steep descent begins, enjoy a view of the Hooper Mountain Range on the left. The trail again winds uphill from 3.7 miles to 3.8 miles, descends with a switchback at 3.9 miles, and then levels out for a while beginning at 4.4 miles as it follows an old road cut into a hillside. Another descent leads to the trail's lowest elevation (990 feet) at 4.8 miles. Cross a 15-foot-wide creek at 5.0 miles and then again at 5.1 miles. Wading is recommended because the rocks are slippery. Finally, the trail joins an old road to end at Greasy Creek Trailhead on TN 30.

Benton Falls (Trail No. 131)

Length: 1.6 miles
Elevation Change: Start 1,880 feet, end 1,600 feet (high point 1,880 feet)
Trailhead: Benton Falls (start and dead-end)
Type: Hiking

Comments: The Benton Falls Trail is an easy trail, sometimes level and sometimes downhill, which proceeds 1.6 miles through a mixed deciduous forest. The trail dead-ends at Benton Falls, a 65-foot waterfall, which makes the walk well worthwhile. This well-worn trail varies from 4 to 6 feet wide. The only difficulties are presented by areas where the trail is rocky, and by the somewhat steep descent on rock stairs at the end of the trail to the falls. The trail is marked with blue blazes.

Details: The trail begins at Lake McCamy with a sharp right turn and a short descent and then levels off to continue along the forest floor beside a small creek that appears to flow out of the swimming lake. Thereafter turn left at the visitor registration stand and continue on level trail through mostly deciduous forest of secondary growth. At 0.2 mile cross through a power-line right-of-way with high wires overhead. Undergrowth on the forest floor is relatively sparse on the first part of the trail, but medium and large gray boulders litter the area, on trail and off trail. A thick carpet of ferns can be found to the left of the trail at 0.4 mile. Sand has been put down in some locations along the trail, probably to cover muddy spots.

At 1.0 mile, the trail begins a gradual descent, and at 1.05 miles an unidentified trail dead-ends at Benton Falls Trail from the left. Within sight on the left is a large blackberry bush; look for ripe berries in June and July. The trail curves to the right and becomes quite wide. At 1.35 miles large rhododendron bushes are located to the left below you. Soon afterward a sign warns of slippery footing around the falls and points out that three people have been hospitalized as a result of falling while climbing the rocks at the falls.

A sharp left turn begins the sudden and final descent to the bottom of the falls on a trail now much narrower and rockier. Just after a switchback at 1.45 miles a side trail to the left leads to the top of the falls. Thereafter, a log fence railing prevents hikers from stepping off the left edge of the trail. Rocks taken from the immediate area have been embedded to serve as steps. At 1.55 miles, the trail levels out; at 1.6 miles, look up to enjoy beautiful Benton Falls. The falls drop from a high rock ledge down a rock face onto another rock ledge and then into a small pool littered with medium and large gray boulders.

24. LITTLE FROG MOUNTAIN WILDERNESS

The Little Frog Mountain Wilderness covers some 4,684 acres, located east of Cleveland, TN, in Polk County and the Ocoee Ranger District. From its highest point at Sassafras Knob, at 3,322 feet, to approximately 1,200 feet at the Ocoee River near Power House No. 3, the Area is one of beauty and variety. It offers a taste of wilderness to the novice or the experienced backpacker. The trails will lead you along ridges, through gaps, across streams, and down into a beautiful valley while traveling through a second-growth forest. Dry Pond Lead and Little Frog Mountain form a horseshoe-shaped valley that isolates Pressley Cove, giving it a wild character. Many species of flowering plants, trees, and shrubs are present, including the flame azalea, mountain laurel, rhododendron, trailing arbutus, crested dwarf iris, mayapple, bloodroot, toothwort, magnolia, dogwood, and redbud. A panoramic view of this Area could formerly be seen from the Sassafras Knob fire tower, which was dismantled in 1989. The solitude and splendor of the Area is in sharp contrast with the devastation in the Copperhill/Ducktown area just to the east.

HISTORY

Little Frog Mountain Wilderness is in the Ocoee Ranger District of the CNF. The word *Ocoee* is a Cherokee Indian term meaning "apricot vine place" (translation: maypop or passion flower plant). The passion flower plant produces a seed capsule, with a pulpy inside, which was eaten by the Indians. The Area was designated as a Wilderness by the US Congress in 1986, after having been designated a wilderness study area in 1984.

Most of the Wilderness was timbered in the past, but only a few obvious signs remain, and even they are now rapidly disappearing into forest growth. Jenkins Grave Gap is named for Thomas Jenkins, a mail carrier who froze to death in 1854.

Little Frog Mountain Wilderness.

CAMPBELL COVE LAKE

N

FS 68

FS 68A

Sassafras Knob

Jenkins Graves Gap

Little Frog Mountain Wilderness

Little Frog Mountain

Pressley Cove

Dry Pond Lead

76

125

76

C

B

Boyd Gap

64

OCOEE NO. 3 LAKE

138

D

64

A

Ocoee No. 3 Powerhouse

Ocoee No. 2 Dam

TRAILHEADS
A Dry Pond Lead
B Rock Creek
C Kimsey Highway
D Rogers Branch

TRAILS
76 Dry Pond Lead
125 Rock Creek
138 Rogers Branch

0   1
Miles

Rhododendrons alongside a small cascade in Little Frog Wilderness.
Photo by Roger Jenkins.

His grave is about 100 yards off FS 68 between Sassafras Knob and Dry Pond Lead Trailhead. The grave of Viola Morgan is also there; her tombstone reads "Nov. 17, 1897." Henry Smith and his family lived in a house that stood on the north side of US 64 just east of Boyd Gap and the Wilderness boundary until the early or mid-1950s. He was a mountain man who worked for TWRA and its predecessor as a game warden.

Perhaps the most interesting historical aspect of the Little Frog Wilderness is its location near the infamous Ducktown/Copperhill copper-processing plants. Emissions from those industries reduced their immediate location, and several miles around, to a desert-like appearance or worse, with little vegetation. Reforestation efforts have been partially successful; only a core area around the plants remains barren. The damage to the Wilderness has been slight, perhaps because it was protected by the ridge of Little Frog Mountain and an upwind location.

The Kimsey Highway (FS 68), located to the north of the Area, was started in 1914, but the contractor soon bankrupted. Dr. Lucius Kimsey of Ducktown pushed for finishing the road until Polk County completed the construction in 1920. For some time the Kimsey Road was the only road between the Copper Basin and the Tennessee Valley. A road built along the Ocoee River to haul copper was abandoned sometime after a railroad was constructed in 1890, leaving only the Kimsey Road. The road along the Ocoee River was reconstructed in the late 1920s or early 1930s, and the Kimsey Road fell into disuse. There are some current efforts to relocate US 64 away from the Ocoee River because of overcrowding and the winding nature of the road.

TRAILHEADS AND MAPS

Dry Pond Lead Trailhead

This trailhead, on US 64, is approximately 18.6 miles east of the US 64-US 411 intersection; the intersection is east of Cleveland, TN. Simply drive up the Ocoee River on US 64 to Power House No. 3, which is about 0.5 mile above Ocoee Dam No. 2 and a launch ramp; you will probably see rafters and kayakers on the river. The trailhead marker, "Dry Pond Lead, No. 76," is on the north side of US 64 directly across from Power House No. 3 and Thunder Rock Campground. Parking for the trail is along US 64 or the small parking area beside Power House No. 3. The ranger station is 2.9 miles inside the USNF boundary heading east on US 64 from Cleveland. The trailhead can also be approached from Ducktown, TN, by following US 64 westward to Power House No. 3 for 7.6 miles from the TN 68-US 64 junction.

Rock Creek Trailhead

This trailhead, on US 64, is approximately 21.3 miles east of the US 64-US 411 intersection. It is also 2.7 miles east from Power House No. 3 and Thunder Rock Campground. Parking for the trail is at the trailhead on an old paved road to the left of US 64. The trailhead is approximately 20 yards beyond and to the right of a mound of dirt placed across the old road. The trail descends sharply to the left of the "Rock Creek No. 125" trail sign. If you approach from the east, the trailhead is on the right side of US 64 at 4.9 miles west of the US 64-TN 68 junction in Ducktown, TN.

Rogers Branch Trailhead

This trailhead is about 0.5 miles west (downstream) on US 64 from the Dry Pond Lead Trailhead (see above). The Ocoee Dam No. 2, a boat launch ramp, and a parking area are on the south side of US 64; the trailhead is on the north side and is well marked.

Kimsey Highway Trailhead

The Kimsey Highway, a gravel USFS road, stretches from east to west across the CNF, north of the Area, and provides access to the Dry Pond Lead Trail and the old Sassafras Lookout Tower site. From the intersection of US 64 and TN 68 in Ducktown,

*Pressley Cove in
Little Frog Wilderness.
Photo by Roger Jenkins.*

TN, drive north about 4.45 miles on TN 68. When a railroad track crosses TN 68, begin looking on the left (west) for the Kimsey Highway (initially County 68 and subsequently FS 68). County 68 will turn left on the opposite side of the road from a sign for the Harbuck Trading Post. If you approach from the north on TN 68, drive 8.9 miles south from the Hiwassee River bridge; County 68 will turn right at a store. The Kimsey Highway is paved at first and then becomes gravel. Turn left at two road intersections near the top of the mountain. About 5.5 miles from TN 68, the gated FS 68A veers sharply to the left and provides a 0.75-mile walk up to the former Sassafras Knob Lookout Tower site and the Wilderness boundary. Continue west on the Kimsey Highway to 7.4 miles, where the Dry Pond Lead Trailhead is on the left. The trail is initially a gated road and is marked with a sign and bulletin board. Parking space is available for about four cars.

Topographic Map: Ducktown, TN.

TRAIL DESCRIPTIONS

Dry Pond Lead (Trail No. 76)

Length: 4.5 miles
Elevation Change: Start 1,150 feet, end 2,540 feet (high point 2,840 feet)
Trailheads: Dry Pond Lead (start) and Kimsey Highway (end)
Trail Connections: Rock Creek Trail
Type: Hiking

Comments: The Dry Pond Lead Trail forms the northwestern boundary of the Little Frog Mountain Wilderness Area. The trail ascends through a second-growth forest with a variety of flowering plants, trees, and shrubs. This trail and the Rock Creek Trail provide the shortest access to Pressley Cove and Rock Creek, an area of peaceful beauty with its emerald green moss-covered logs, swift-flowing streams, and small sparkling waterfalls. One trip into Pressley Cove will heighten the appreciation of hiking in a wilderness area. The Rock Creek Trail intersects the Dry Pond Lead Trail at 1.9 miles. From this intersection, Pressley Cove and Rock Creek are 0.8 miles east.

The Dry Pond Lead Trail is quite dry, as the only water sources are down in the valleys off the trail, with some difficulty of access. At 3.1 miles is a depression to the left of the trail which is usually dry, hence probably providing the name of the ridgecrest and trail.

Details: The Dry Pond Lead Trail starts directly across from the Ocoee No. 3 Power House and Thunder Rock Campground. The trail immediately starts uphill, with a small creek on the right. Twenty-seven paces along there is a visitor's trail registry on the left. A few paces further, the trail ascends through two switchbacks, first to the left and then to the right, 50 paces apart. From here the trail ascends through a delightful stretch, passing through a second-growth forest with groves of pine and a scattering of mountain laurel, flame azalea, and trailing arbutus. At 0.2 mile, the trail passes a small stand of hemlock on the right. Hemlocks are easily recognized by their flattened row of green needles on each side of the branch. On the underside of these needles are two whitish lines. The trail emerges from a grove of pines at 0.3 mile and passes through an open field of ferns and broom sedge. From here there is a good view through the field of Power House No. 3 and the large, light-green steel surge tank. The trail plateaus a short distance from the field and passes three holly trees standing as silent sentinels to the left of the trail at 0.5 mile. The trail continues fairly level while crossing small ridges and through gaps. At 0.6 mile it turns to the right and passes through a pine forest with ferns literally covering the ground, a bit of enchanted forest. The trail ascends at 0.9 mile, and here and there you should expect to see a few blow-downs. The trail levels out for a brief stretch and then ascends for the next 2.0 miles. At 1.9 miles, a large wooden sign marks the intersection with the Rock Creek Trail, which drops down to the right.

The Dry Pond Lead Trail continues straight, northwardly, and begins to ascend and traverses left following the west side of the ridge. At 2.3 miles there is a different valley to the left with a view of Brock Mountain across the way. At 2.35 miles, an old road cut crosses the trail. This is the first crossing of an old road that will be crossed and followed many more times. At its first appearance, the old road appears to go straight down the side of a ridge to the left. Toothwort flowers bloom along this stretch of the trail in the spring. At 2.4 miles the trail crosses the old road again. Follow the double white trail blazes painted on the trees. At 2.6 miles the trail levels out and passes a scattered outcropping of white quartz. This is a hard attractive stone with a rating of 7 on a hardness scale (with 10 being the hardest). Quartz is harder than some knife blades.

Between 2.7 miles and 3.7 miles the trail becomes hard to follow, not only crossing the old road but also following it along different parts of the trail. A fire-plow furrow is visible near the roadbed, as are some blackened trees, both resulting from a fire in 1991. Be sure to follow the two white trail blazes painted on the trees, for they identify the trail. This area also has deep leaf clutter, making walking difficult. At 3.6 miles the trail ascends through a scattered pine thicket, then tops out at 3.7 miles and becomes level as it veers east of the ridgetop.

The trail passes a wilderness boundary sign at 4.0 miles and enters an abandoned wildlife opening that is now filled with locust trees and briers. The crest of Dry Pond Lead has turned eastward at this point and will rapidly gain elevation as it continues toward Sassafras Knob. The trail crosses the opening diagonally (northeasterly) and exits from the crest at 4.1 miles. It then descends on an old roadbed and reaches the Kimsey Highway Trailhead at 4.5 miles. The last 0.5 mile or so of the trail has been relocated twice, more recently in 1987.

Rock Creek (Trail No. 125)
Length: 5.5 miles
Elevation Change: Start 1,480 feet, end 1,880 feet (high point 2,320 feet)
Trailheads: Rock Creek (start) and Dry Pond Lead Trail (end)
Type: Hiking

Comments: The Rock Creek Trail winds through the center of the Wilderness Area, bordered on the east by Little Frog Mountain and on the west by Dry Pond Lead. This trail offers the variety one would expect while hiking in the TN foothills of the southern Appalachians. The trail winds through a second-growth forest with flowering trees, plants, and shrubs along the way, leading across creeks, over ridges, and through gaps. The trail leads into a beautiful valley called Pressley Cove. While descending into the valley, the trail passes rhododendrons, holly, and hemlock, with the swift-flowing Rock Creek undulating through its center.

Details: The trail descends to the left of the Rock Creek Trail sign and crosses a small branch at 0.07 mile. Just past the branch there is a trail registry on the side of the trail. A short distance down the trail at 0.1 mile is a leaning beech tree growing to the left. It is a handsome tree with smooth gray bark and sawtooth leaves. The beech also produces small edible nuts in the fall of the year. The trail descends and passes a rhododendron thicket on the left, next to a small stream, at 0.3 mile. In late spring the rhododendron, particularly those along the stream banks, put on a spectacular display of large blossoms. Along this section of the trail the beautiful crested dwarf iris also grows. The trail crosses two more splendid creeks a few yards apart at 0.4 mile, the latter being Laurel Creek, which is the largest. The stream may be between 5 to 8 feet wide, depending on the time of the year. Try to keep your feet dry—there is a lot of trail ahead. From here the trail ascends for the next 2.3 miles with few plateaus in between before descending into Pressley Cove. Along the way while ascending at 0.44 mile there is a switchback to the left, and then the trail enters a small pine grove. The light-green steel surge tank at Ocoee Power House No. 3 is visible to the front left, west of the trail.

While hiking, expect to see a few blow-downs. The trail ascends through a switchback to the right at 1.1 miles. While you ascend at 1.4 miles, watch for an opening; the Ocoee River may be seen on the left (west), depending on the amount of leaf cover. At 1.9 miles the trail becomes rocky for awhile, and at 2.1 miles it follows the side of a ridge with a deep valley to the left of the trail. Listen for the sounds of the pileated woodpecker, the largest of the North American woodpeckers, echoing through the valley or along its ridges. Also inhabiting the Area are deer, black bear, wild hog, turkey, and various types of small game.

The trail crosses to the east side of the ridge for the final time and, at 2.7 miles it turns west through a gap and follows an old logging road for about 150 yards down a hollow. The trail then makes a 135-degree turn to the left and exits the roadbed (the road continues in an arc to the left up a knob, where it disappears; a couple of dim blazes might lead you incorrectly up the knob). Just after you leave the road there is a small spring off the trail to the left; it may be hard to find. The trail continues down and bears slightly to the right beneath the knob as it enters the upper elevations of picturesque Pressley Cove with Rock Creek flowing through its center. The trail then makes a gradual descent into Pressley Cove.

Before descending a steep switchback to the left at 3.5 miles, notice the hemlock and holly trees growing along the trail. Such moist, cool valleys are good places to find hemlocks. At 3.6 miles the trail passes a large hemlock tree to the left of the trail that escaped the logger's ax. As you descend into the valley, the cool air will rise to greet you. The trail crosses a feeder stream and then arrives at a beautiful mountain creek, Rock Creek, at 4.0 miles. This is an excellent place to have lunch. The area is an open wooded cove with a scattering of older second-growth trees and an under-story of rhododendron overhanging the swift-flowing Rock Creek. Lean back and enjoy the beauty of Pressley Cove. Crossing Rock Creek will usually require wad-ing; it is about 10 feet wide where the trail crosses and 6 to 12 inches deep, depend-ing on the amount of rainfall. The trail follows Rock Creek for a short distance. At 4.3 miles there is a perfect open vista of a quite picturesque 5-foot waterfall to the left of the trail. The trail crosses a feeder stream at 4.5 miles, and at 4.7 miles the trail ascends to leave Rock Creek. It continues to ascend until it terminates at 5.5 miles into the Dry Pond Lead Trail. To the left the Dry Pond Lead Trail leads 1.9 miles to US 64 across from the Ocoee Power House No. 3.

Rogers Branch (Trail No. 138)
Length: 2.3 miles
Elevation Change: Start 1,140 feet, end 1,480 feet (high point 1,640 feet)
Trailhead: Rogers Branch (start and dead-end)
Type: Hiking

Comments: This trail was at one time a motorcycle trail but is now restricted to hik-ing. Although not in the Little Frog Mountain Wilderness, it is nearby and provides a pleasant walk up a creek valley to the foot of Brock Mountain. The trail begins on the north side of US 64 across from the Ocoee Recreation Area/Rogers Branch Put-In. The trailhead is also marked with a large metal sign, and there is a registration box. On the south side of US 64 is the boat put-in and, to the east, upriver, a parking area. Do not park on US 64 or in the put-in area to the west. Your car may be tick-eted or towed. The area is often congested in the summer. The trail is well marked with white "dotted-i" blazes. Arson fire damaged the Trail in 1992.

Details: The trail initially proceeds up a gently sloped hollow with steep sides along Rogers Branch. Trees and large rhododendron bushes shade the trail. After about 200 yards, a side trail veers to the right to the lower of two successive small water-falls. The trail crosses the creek three times on slippery rocks. Two small switchbacks at about 0.5 mile lead up out of the hollow onto a knobby ridgecrest where the for-est alternates between pine and hardwood. Galax, trailing arbutus, and partridge berry may be seen on the ground. To the northwest two clear-cuts can sometimes be seen along much of the side of Brock Mountain. The trail continues on the ridge and passes to the left (west) of a knoll at approximately 1.0 mile. Thereafter, the trail crosses to the right of the ridgecrest and descends into the Gassaway Creek valley but does not reach the creek. Instead, it follows the west side of Gassaway Creek for a short distance, looping around a side valley, and ends at 2.3 miles. A maple tree with a single band of white tape in a grove of small hemlock trees marks the trail's end. Brock Mountain is to the left (northwest), and Dry Pond Lead is to the right (southeast).

Other Trails

A trail known as Little Frog Mountain Trail once existed along the crest of Little Frog Mountain. It started near the point where Brush Creek crosses under US 64 at a shooting range. It ran westward up a lead to the Little Frog Mountain crest, just bypassing Boyd Gap, and then proceeded northward along the ridge to Sassafras Lookout Tower. The trail was around 5.5 miles long but is now overgrown, partially as the result of intense fires that swept up the west side of the ridge at Boyd Gap in 1978 and 1983. Any attempt to follow it should be considered off-trail hiking. The fire tower has been removed. Views from the ridgeline of Little Frog Mountain are obscured except from the ridgetops just north of Boyd Gap, where the Ducktown/Copperhill devastation to the east contrasts with the Wilderness to the west.

25. BIG FROG WILDERNESS, COHUTTA WILDERNESS (TN PORTION), AND WEST BIG FROG PRIMITIVE AREA

Big Frog Wilderness, the southernmost of the wilderness areas of the CNF, is a 8,069-acre tract encompassing the slopes of Big Frog Mountain, at 4,224 feet the highest point in Polk County, TN. Eighty-three acres of this Wilderness are located in GA's Chattahoochee National Forest and 7,986 in the CNF. On the west of the Big Frog Wilderness, 1,460 additional acres are protected as a Primitive Area. Also in the CNF are 1,795 acres of GA's 37,042-acre Cohutta Wilderness, contiguous to the Big Frog Wilderness. These areas are located in the Ocoee Ranger District. The mountain dominates the view to the southeast from Parksville Lake (Ocoee Lake). Big Frog Wilderness was at first limited to the uppermost elevation of the mountain, essentially a skullcap, and was very impractical, leaving the lower stretches of many of the access trails out of the Wilderness. Additional areas were later added as Wilderness and Primitive Areas. Big Frog Mountain rated a "21" during the USFS's wil-

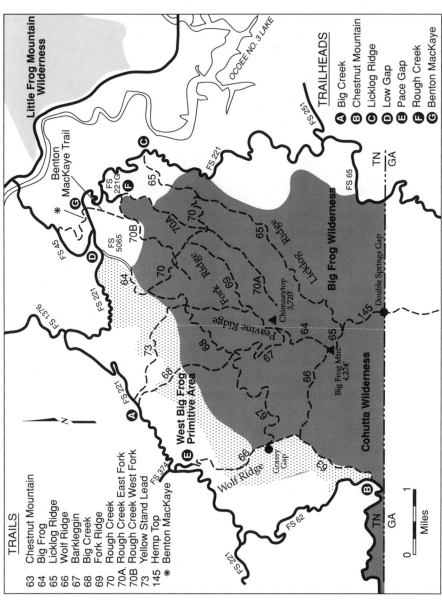

TRAILS

- 63   Chestnut Mountain
- 64   Big Frog
- 65   Licklog Ridge
- 66   Wolf Ridge
- 67   Barkleggin
- 68   Big Creek
- 69   Fork Ridge
- 70   Rough Creek
- 70A   Rough Creek East Fork
- 70B   Rough Creek West Fork
- 73   Yellow Stand Lead
- 145   Hemp Top
- *   Benton MacKaye

TRAILHEADS

- Ⓐ   Big Creek
- Ⓑ   Chestnut Mountain
- Ⓒ   Licklog Ridge
- Ⓓ   Low Gap
- Ⓔ   Pace Gap
- Ⓕ   Rough Creek
- Ⓖ   Benton MacKaye

Big Frog Wilderness,
Cohutta Wilderness
(TN Portion),
and West Big Frog
Primitive Area.

derness inventory in the late 1970s, the highest of the CNF's inventoried roadless areas. The USFS said it rated highest on "natural integrity, apparent naturalness, and opportunity for solitude." From the standpoint of hikers, it has perhaps the greatest variety of trail types of any of the CNF wilderness areas, including a 5.0-mile stretch of perfect contour trail along a 50-degree slope (Big Creek/Bark Leggin Lead), something very rare in the East. The Big Frog, Wolf Ridge, and Licklog Ridge trails all rank among the finest in the CNF.

Big Frog Wilderness and Cohutta Wilderness together form a 45,111-acre Wilderness tract, with an adjacent 1,460-acre Primitive Area. This is the largest designated wilderness tract on USNF lands in the eastern US. And surrounding the Wildernesses and Primitive Area is an unusually wide buffer of USNF land. Consequently, the Areas provide about as remote a wilderness experience as a hiker can have in the Southeast. Only the GSMNP and a few areas in Pisgah and Nantahala Forests in NC can offer as much solitude.

Several loop hikes are possible. The hiker should be aware, however, that Big Frog is considerably drier than most other wildernesses of the CNF. Bring plenty of water in the summer and expect hot temperatures even at the higher altitudes. Remember, the southern side of Big Frog is the GA state line. You may want to hike the trails in the spring or fall for more availability of water and cooler temperatures. For experienced hikers the Areas are excellent for winter hiking.

All of the Areas are within the 52,825-acre TWRA-designated Ocoee Bear Reserve. The old black-on-orange WMA signs may be seen from several of the trails. Bears were restocked in the 1970s from the GSMNP. Their sign is fairly common today in the Wilderness. The USFS restocked 10 deer in the Ocoee area in 1937; these expanded to a substantial population by 1952 when TWRA began to allow hunting. The herd is considerably smaller in the early 1990s, and only an occasional deer may be seen in the Wilderness and on USFS lands in Polk County.

Feral hogs, or domestic hogs gone wild, used to populate the Ocoee area. Woodrow Beckler, who is probably the last person who remembers living at the "Dutch Settlement" on the northwest of the Wilderness, said that everyone let their pigs run loose. When the sow had a litter, the piglets were marked so that they could be identified and released to forage in the mountains. They would stay away for periods of two or three months, and if there was a good supply of acorns the sow would return alone. Beckler said that several times local hunters killed wild hogs that bore his mark. In the 1960s European wild hogs, or Russian boar, were trapped from the GSMNP and released in Ocoee Ranger District and other areas south of the park. Today the hogs largely have the Russian characteristics, with protruding tusks and dark coloration, although occasionally one has a white strip down his side reflecting domestic interbreeding. Wild turkeys in the Areas make their presence

View from Big Frog Wilderness Area. Photo by Russ Manning.

most evident in the late winter when there is mast in the higher elevations. Pot-hole scratches in the leaves are the result of turkeys searching for acorns. Some unusually large bobcats have also been seen in the Areas. Although the Areas border the state of GA, they are still well outside the range of lower-altitude venomous snakes, like the cottonmouth or pygmy rattlesnake. Timber rattlesnakes, however, are fairly common, as are copperheads. The area around the Big Creek camping area, at the border of the Wilderness, is home to some unusually large (40-plus inches) copperheads.

Lower elevations are forested heavily with Virginia pine. Upland hardwoods include white oak, red oak, and hickory. A tree species not regularly encountered by hikers in more northern areas of the CNF is the white pine, with its extra-long, blue-green needles. There are also beech, basswood, birch, red maple, black gum, and silverbell. Some large black cherry can be seen from the Big Frog and Wolf Ridge trails. Some tulip (what many call poplar) and oak in the coves along the slopes of Big Frog have already reached impressive size.

Dr. Gene Wofford of the University of Tennessee Botany Department surveyed the Big Frog Mountain Areas in 1981 and found four rare species of plants: catchfly, purple hyssop, cow parsnip, and rattlesnake root. Paul Somers of the Tennessee Heritage Program also hiked the Areas in 1982 and observed the rare bushpea and bush honeysuckle. Zack E. Murrell completed a two-year study of plants on Big Frog Mountain under the direction of Dr. Wofford in 1987. Of the 479 species identified, only 22 were non-native or introduced, reflecting little disturbance by human activity. Three species were found to be at the southernmost point of their range. While there is no Canadian zone, the rugged topography and high rainfall maintain a more typically northern flora. The observant hiker will notice color variations in many flower species that differ from those seen in the GSMNP and the northern CNF. Trillium, iris, and azalea all display surprisingly different color variations.

HISTORY

At the turn of the century, Big Frog Mountain and the surrounding areas were virtually trackless. An old wagon road from GA reached as far as Sylco Creek watershed, to the west of Big Frog Mountain. From that road an even smaller road led up to the "Dutch Settlement," a community of German- and French-speaking settlers. The community was established in the 1840s, apparently to raise grapes and make wine. The settlement was sometimes called "Vineland," but the wine was not a commercial success. According to Roy Lilland, Polk County historian, *dutch* was a corruption of the German *deutch.* Rosine Parmentier and her sister and brother-in-law were the investors behind the settlement. She lived in New York City but visited the area in 1852 and kept an extensive journal of the trip. The Beckler family was the last to leave the Dutch Settlement, doing so in 1927. Their cabin was torn down in 1940.

The Dutch Settlement was just west of Pace Gap, within a mile or so of the present Wilderness boundary. Pace Gap itself was named for the Pace family, who lived at what is now Big Creek camping area (not a formal, developed USFS campground but an area of concentrated public use) where FS 221 crosses Big Creek. Coming into Big Creek campground from Pace Gap, FS 221 first crosses Pace Branch and then crosses Big Creek itself a few yards beyond. To the left of the road, Pace Branch and Big Creek converge. In the small triangle formed by the two creeks and the road is the foundation of the old Pace cabin, which was occupied until sometime around World War I and stood in ruin until well into the 1920s.

The trails of Big Frog are essentially the fruits of labor of many young men in the Civilian Conservation Corps (CCC) camps of the 1930s. Three trails, however, preceded the CCC: they were the Big Frog (or Peavine), Licklog Ridge, and Wolf Ridge trails. Wolf Ridge Trail is probably the oldest, dating back to 1914-15. Big Frog and Licklog Ridge were both built during the late 1910s and 1920s. For pre-CCC creations, these trails are excellent, properly graded and switchbacked, having none of the painfully steep, "straight from here to up yonder" stretches so typical of old-timer trails in Tellico and other areas of the CNF.

The CCC entered the picture in the 1930s, improving Big Frog, Licklog Ridge, and Wolf Ridge trails and adding all the other trails presently in the system. Some were works of art: the old Grassy Gap Trail, now designated as part of the Big Creek Trail and part of the Barkleggin Trail, is a perfect contour trail, laid out by surveyor's compass and string along a 50- to 60-degree slope and kept to within 200 feet of elevation all the way around the base of Big Frog. Rarely has any government agency had the manpower and time to lay out such a trail. The result was a true trail system unrivaled in the CNF.

J. Felton Stanley, retired from the USFS, and the late Ed Magnus, fisheries biologist for TWRA, were among our sources of information on the early history of Big Frog. Magnus was with the USFS and TVA during the Depression years. Stanley worked for the USFS and the CCC. In 1990 Felton Stanley was 80 years of age and had an exceedingly sharp memory, down to individual personalities of many of the CCC men and specific hikes they took in the old days.

The trails on Big Frog Mountain were the work of young men who were supposed to be 17 to 21 years of age. But "some of them fibbed on their ages," Stanley says, because money was so scarce. The government provided each CCC man with work clothes and paid all of his doctor and dentist bills. A regular worker was paid $30 per month while an assistant leader got $36 and a leader $45.

The men who built the Big Frog system were from two CCC camps, one at Sylco to the west and the other at Tumbling Creek to the east, toward Copperhill. Each camp housed 210 men. The old CCC sites are now the Sylco and Tumbling Creek Campgrounds. Until 1936 the CNF extended far into GA, including much of what is now Chattahoochee National Forest. In 1936 the GA portion of the CNF was realigned along state lines and became the Chattahoochee National Forest. Before the realignment, Felton Stanley and others of the Cherokee branch of the USFS ranged well into GA. Stanley was part of the team that walked from Sylco Camp up Wolf Ridge and down what is now Hemp Top Trail to determine where to put the Hemp Top fire tower, which for half a century provided incredible views down into the Cohutta Mountain area. Stanley made the final decision. By then it was getting dark; they had no provisions for the night. "So we just turned around and hiked back up Big Frog, down Wolf Ridge through the old Dutch Settlement clear back to Sylco Creek Camp that night," Stanley says, for a roundtrip in a single day of nearly 30 miles, much of it on a rough manway trail and all of it in the old-style leather walking boots. And they had no flashlights.

The CCC built what is now FS 221 and the Sheeds Creek Road and improved the old preexisting road in Sylco Valley. The Big Creek Road, which follows Big Creek itself from the Big Creek campground down to the Ocoee River, was built by the Conasauga River Lumber Company and the USFS in about 1947-48. Most of the other roads between Big Frog Wilderness and the Ocoee River are recent, built in the big timber-cutting period since the 1970s. The Tennessee Power Company built Ocoee Powerhouse No. 1 in 1912, creating Parksville (Ocoee) Lake. The famous flume line from the lake to Powerhouse No. 2 was completed in 1913 and was completely rebuilt in the early 1980s.

The west peak of Big Frog Mountain, the highest point of the Areas, once had a fire tower built of heavy timbers reaching treetop level. The tower was built by Frank Payne, whose grandson was the sheriff of Polk County from 1982 to 1990. The tower was in bad repair by the 1950s and was designated to be torn down, but the USFS never got around to it. Several campers from the YMCA's Camp Ocoee climbed the tower and did the job for them: the tower collapsed. It caused only moderate injuries to the campers but considerable embarrassment to all concerned; the part of the tower still standing was then hastily torn down. Frank Payne was an early USFS warden who lived near Tumbling Creek in the valley to the east side of Big Frog. He had a camp at a dry pond on Peavine Ridge south of the present day FS 221. Bud Payne, his son, was also a Polk County sheriff.

The USFS refers to the Big Frog Mountain system of trails as "one of the most extensive, and best maintained, trail systems on the CNF." However, only in recent years have the trails been significantly maintained. Old-time hikers of the 1950s and 1960s remember trailheads and junctions with no signs whatsoever. The upper stretches of Barkleggin Trail, for example, were virtually impossible to identify. The old Grassy Gap Trail (now designated as sections of Barkleggin and Big Creek trails) was only the faintest of paths, used a few times each year by the most experienced hikers. Today there are user-friendly trail signs, wilderness signs, and information "booths" at most trailheads, and the USFS refurbished most of the trails in 1978. In the early 1990s some were still left to complete, including Fork Ridge and the western (lower) part of Barkleggin.

For many years the trails of the Areas were "maintained" solely by the use of hikers from Camp Ocoee, Boy Scout Camp Cherokee, and locals from Polk County who hiked up the mountain each year for the "Ramp Tramp." For most of the 20th century, Big Frog Mountain has been a part of the fabric of experience at Camp Ocoee. The Camp, on the shores of Parksville Lake, was founded by Glen "Chick" Ellis in 1923. Mr. Ellis was still living in 1992. Generations of campers and counselors, mostly from the Chattanooga and Cleveland area, walked the Big Frog trails during the low-maintenance years of the 1940s, 1950s, and 1960s.

Two trails of the old CCC system, the Big Creek and Grassy Gap trails, were for some reason hopelessly confused by the USFS in their trail descriptions that came out after 1978. The trails, as marked on the old 1967 USGS topographical map, formed a cross. Big Creek Trail went from Big Creek campground all the way to a junction with the Big Frog Trail just to the uphill side of Chimneytop, intersecting the Grassy Gap Trail on the way. Grassy Gap Trail went from Low Gap on Peavine

Ridge (at a junction with Big Frog Trail) following the 2,300-feet contour line around the face of Big Frog, crossing Big Creek Trail at about 1.7 miles, and continuing another 3.3 miles all the way to Grassy Gap. This is the way the trails should be designated, with the Big Creek Trail perhaps renamed the Big Creek/Barkleggin Trail for clarity. As of this writing, the trails are still confused: the upper half of Big Creek Trail and the westernmost section of Grassy Gap are together called the "Barkleggin Trail," a trail that makes no logistic sense. The eastern portion of Grassy Gap Trail and the lower portion of the old Big Creek Trail are together called the "Big Creek Trail," which makes only partial sense. The USFS will probably correct this anomaly in the future.

Big Frog Mountain was for many years the goal of the annual Polk County "Ramp Tramp." From 1958 until the mid-1980s people would hike to the top of the mountain in April, when wild mountain onions, known as ramps, could be harvested. On top a meal of cornbread, meat, fried potatoes, ramps, and eggs was prepared, using a jeep road for bringing up supplies. The Ramp Tramp was started when James Passmore, Bud Payne (son of early USFS employee Frank Payne and who was also Polk County sheriff at that time), John DeWeese, and Jimmie Passmore took Fred Colby, a state 4-H Club leader from Knoxville, to the top of Big Frog Mountain to look for ramps. The idea was originally conceived by Mrs. Dennis Blevins, former Polk County home economics agent. When the area was designated as a wilderness, several methods were used to get the supplies to the mountain top, including a helicopter. However, because of a heart-attack fatality on the hike in 1978, the difficulty of moving supplies to the mountaintop, and frequent rains on the mountain, the Ramp Tramp was converted to a festival and held at a campground. It is now held on the last Saturday in April at Camp McCroy (a former CCC camp site) on TN 30.

The Cohutta Wilderness was designated by the US Congress in 1974 and, in the same bill, 4,626 acres in the CNF were designated as a wilderness study area. The higher elevations of the Big Frog Wilderness (5,055 acres) were designated in 1984 and were followed by 3,014 additional acres in 1986. The 1,460-acre Primitive Area was designated on the western slopes of the Wilderness in 1988 in the CNF Management Plan.

TRAILHEADS AND MAPS

Most trails in the Big Frog Wilderness are reached from FS 221. There are two main access routes for FS 221 from US 64.

a. The most direct route to FS 221 is via FS 45. From Ocoee, TN, and the US 64-US 411 junction (east of Cleveland, TN), follow US 64 east past Ocoee Lake and on to Ocoee No. 3 Powerhouse at 18.6 miles, just beyond Ocoee No. 2 Dam and the area where the Ocoee whitewater trips begin. FS 45 is not marked at the junction but turns off US 64 at TVA's Ocoee No. 3 Powerhouse. A sign pointing to Thunder Rock Campground marks the junction. The gravel road crosses the river, passes the powerhouse through a wire fence, and, after taking a fork to the left, continues approximately 2.9 miles to its intersection with FS 221. Note that the trailhead distances below are given from this intersection and not the Cherokee Corners route described in paragraph *b*.

b. A longer route is as follows: take US 64 east from Cleveland, TN, to US 411. Continue past the intersection with US 411 for 2.5 miles to the Cherokee Corners store and gas station; there are also signs for the CNF, Camp Ocoee, Cookson Baptist Church, and Southeastern Expeditions near this junction. Turn right on paved Baker Creek Road (County 55). Proceed 4.1 miles on County 55, at which point it will change from a paved to a gravel road and will become FS 55. Continue on FS 55 to 4.6 miles and an intersection. A sign for FS 55 and Sylco Campground will point to the right (FS 302 and Cherokee Baptist Church will be shown as straight ahead). Turn right toward the campground but then quickly turn left (east) to stay on FS 55 and not on FS 67 which proceeds south. At 10.9 miles from US 64 reach an intersection where FS 55 makes a turn to the right (south) and the east end of FS 302 turns left (north). Continue on FS 55 past the Sylco Campground on the right at 11.3 miles, and on to an intersection with FS 221 at 11.6 miles. This is the end of FS 55; FS 221 proceeds both straight ahead (south) and to the left (east) at the junction. A sign at the intersection will point back the way you came (north) and indicate "US 64 12 miles." From the intersection take FS 221 to the left (east) to reach the Big Frog Wilderness trailheads. Going 1.8 miles on FS 221 will lead to a junction with FS 62. Turn right on FS 62 and follow it to just before the GA state line, where the Chestnut Mountain Trailhead is located on the left. Instead of turning right on FS 62, you can continue on FS 221 and reach the Pace Gap Trailhead for Wolf Ridge Trail at 4.3 miles (Pace Gap is actually up the road 0.3 mile). At 6.3 miles you will reach the Big Creek Trailhead; the Big Creek Trail starts on the right. Cross the creek and at 6.35 miles the Yellow Stand Lead Trail is on the right.

c. FS 221 may also be reached from the Conasauga area off US 411. At 6.5 miles south of the US 64-US 411 junction, an unnamed county road, which becomes FS 221, turns east. TN 313 turns west on the opposite side of US 411 at a convenience market. The curvy paved county road heads southeast. At 4.0 miles the pavement ends and FS 67 turns north. FS 221 commences at this point and continues southeast for 5.0 miles to the steel-truss Jacks River Bridge and the GA-TN state line. The 7.7-mile Jacks River Trail (No. 13) to Beech Bottoms in the Cohutta Wilderness begins at the bridge. At this point the Alaculsy Valley Road (County 16) crosses the bridge into GA; FS 221 turns northeast and at 3.0 miles reaches the intersection with FS 55 (from Cherokee Corners) described above.

d. There is another access to FS 221 from the east by TN 68 and County Highway 251 starting from the Ducktown area; however, this road may be rough in places, and maps will be necessary to follow the route. Drive on TN 68 about 2.0 miles south of US 64; County 251 will turn west at a USFS sign that reads "Tumbling Creek Campground—8 miles." The road is paved for about 4.0 miles but is quite curvy after crossing a concrete bridge over the Ocoee River. There are some confusing intersections; follow the road with the painted centerline. About 5.5 miles off TN 68, County 251 crosses Tumbling Creek at a pretty farm where FS 221 turns west at a USFS sign showing Tumbling Creek Campground to be 2.0 miles and Sylco 21.0 miles. This intersection is 7.0 miles up Tumbling Creek Road (FS 65 in TN and FS 22 in GA) from Dally Gap, the northeastern Cohutta Trailhead. The east end of FS 221 is paved for about 200 yards before turning to gravel. The Licklog Ridge Trailhead is at 5.4 miles on FS 221. The FS 45 intersection noted above is 7.0 miles on FS 221 from County 251.

The choice of access routes to FS 221 depends on your point of origin, what trailhead you plan to use, and personal preferences. Some factors to consider: although FS 221 is generally a good road, it is a dirt road and there are some eroded and muddy areas; the approach from Ocoee No. 3 Powerhouse is a more convenient access for most trails; and the area surrounding Big Frog Wilderness is an intensive timber management area, so watch for logging trucks.

The following distances to specific trailheads are given to both the east and west from the FS 45-FS 221 intersection described in paragraph *a* above.

Low Gap, Big Creek, Pace Gap, and Chestnut Mountain Trailheads

Turn right (west) and after 0.25 miles you reach Low Gap (one of two Low Gaps in the Areas) and the start of the Big Frog Trail (sometimes called Peavine Ridge Trail). The trailhead is on the left at a gated road. Continue on FS 221 westward past a road leading off to the right (FS 1376); then turn south, still on FS 221. At 5.25 miles you will reach the Big Creek Trailhead area, which is the trailhead for both Yellow Stand Lead Trail (on the east side of Big Creek) and Big Creek Trail (on the west side of Big Creek). You will first reach the Yellow Stand Lead Trail on the left at 5.25 miles. It begins at a gated road, FS 336701, and there is a large hiker sign at the gate. There is no parking; park across the creek at the Big Creek Trail. Continue across the creek to 5.3 miles; the Big Creek Trail parking area will be on your left. There is a bulletin board at the rear of the parking area where the Big Creek Trail begins. Overnight car camping is allowed just down the road on the right.

Continue on FS 221 to 7.0 miles and Pace Gap, where FS 374 turns right in the gap. Beyond the gap 0.3 miles, at 7.3 miles, is the Wolf Ridge Trailhead on the left.

A dirt road, marked by a Wolf Ridge Trail sign and FS 221E road sign, turns left off FS 221 and proceeds only 100 feet to the top of the ridge and a small parking area for the trail. FS 221E is gated at the parking area.

Continue on FS 221 to 9.8 miles and a junction with FS 62. FS 62 turns left while FS 221 continues straight. Turn left on FS 62, which is marked with a "Big Frog Loop Road" sign, and continue south about 5.5 miles to just before the TN-GA state line. The Chestnut Mountain Trailhead is on the left (south). You can continue on FS 62 for about 1.0 mile west of the Chestnut Mountain Trailhead to the trailhead for the 3.5-mile Beach Bottom Trail into GA's Cohutta Wilderness. The trailhead is on the left (south) side of FS 62 while a parking lot is on the other side. FS 62 may be partially closed in the future because of overuse of Beech Bottom.

FS 221 and FS 62 can also be reached from Conasauga (on US 411 near the GA state line) by following the Conasauga River Road east; it then becomes FS 221.

Rough Creek, Benton MacKaye, and Licklog Ridge Trailheads

Turn left (east) from the FS 45 intersection with FS 221 and proceed on FS 221 toward the valley. At 0.4 mile the Benton MacKaye Trail crosses FS 221, proceeding left (north) down the old FS 45 to the current FS 45 and proceeding right (south) down an old logging road to the Rough Creek West Fork Trail. Continue on FS 221 for 1.6 miles, going under a power line twice. Turn south at 1.6 miles on the first road to the right, FS 221G, where a power line crosses the road for the third time. Proceed on a rough dirt road 0.6 mile to a creek crossing. Cross in your car only if you feel comfortable doing so; automobiles with low wheel bases may have a problem, especially in high water. On the other side of the creek is the Rough Creek Trailhead. There is a large parking area and a junction that is the trailhead for both the Rough Creek, East Fork, and Rough Creek, West Fork, trails. The old Rough Creek, West Fork, Road (FS 221F) formerly turned right while the old Rough Creek, East Fork, Road (FS 221G) proceeded straight ahead. Both were closed at this point when the Big Frog Wilderness additions were designated in 1986.

Instead of turning off FS 221 onto FS 221G, the Licklog Trail Ridge Trailhead is reached by continuing on FS 221 to 3.3 miles from the FS 45-FS 221 intersection. The Licklog Ridge Trailhead is on the right on a ridge; a bulletin board should be visible 100 feet up the ridge. There is parking on the left for a few cars. The power line mentioned above crosses the road for the fourth time down the road.

Topographic Maps: Caney Creek, TN; Ducktown, TN; Epworth, TN-GA; Hemptop, TN-GA.

TRAIL DESCRIPTIONS

Big Frog (Trail No. 64)

Length: 5.6 miles
Elevation Change: Start 2,120 feet, end 4,224 feet (high point 4,224 feet)
Trailheads: Low Gap (start) and Wolf Ridge and Licklog Ridge Trail junction (end)
Trail Connections: Rough Creek, Yellow Stand Lead, Big Creek, Fork Ridge, and Barkleggin
Type: Hiking

Comments: Big Frog Trail, known by some hikers as the Peavine Ridge Trail, is the premier footpath of the entire Big Frog Mountain trail system. The character of the trail changes many times as it passes from the drier pine woods near the trailhead at FS 221 through shaded switchbacks leading to the scrub oak forests along the Chimneytop approach ridge and finally to Big Frog itself. You may see signs of bobcat, bear, coyote, or deer along the route. As with most of the trails in the Areas, this one is best hiked in the spring or fall; water can be hard to find in dry summers. The trail is marked with a short white painted and/or cut blaze on top and a larger one on the bottom.

If you approach the lower trailhead (FS 221) by car from Ocoee Powerhouse No. 3 on US 64—which most hikers do—it will take only about 20 minutes to reach FS 221 (turn right) and a couple of minutes on FS 221 to the trailhead. We suggest you take the time to drive past the trailhead for about a mile, then double back. For at least the rest of the 1990s there will be a fantastic 180-degree panoramic view to the north, including all of Little Frog Mountain, Chilhowee Mountain, and some of Tellico, along this route. The view came with a price tag: the downhill slope was all clear-cut in the late 1970s.

Details: An old clear-cut is visible at the trailhead. The trailhead has a USFS information board; 75 yards down the trail is a check-in box. The initial 0.6 mile of the trail is also a dirt road, FS 5065, that is gated. Some timber harvesting was done to the left of FS 5065 in 1992. The trail climbs steeply at first, then climbs more gradually toward Peavine Ridge. FS 5065 ends at 0.6 mile at a dirt turn-around area. On the far side of the turn-around an old jeep track descends to the left for about 0.2 mile to an overgrown deer field once maintained by TWRA. Stay on the main track to the right; the old field is soon visible below to the left. At 0.7 mile is the Big Frog Wilderness boundary sign, anchored to a post big enough to frustrate the most determined black bear. Not long after the sign, the trail will turn to the left and begin following Peavine Ridge, with easy walking all the way to Low Gap.

At 1.5 miles the old jeep track continues off to the left, but Big Frog Trail turns up to the right, at a pine tree with a "dotted i" blaze. From this point on, the trail is single track. Thirty yards down the path is the Rough Creek Trailhead to the left; the trail sign was partially burned as of the early 1990s. A campsite is on the left just beyond the junction. Continue south along the east side of Peavine Ridge. A small stream, which should flow in all but the driest seasons, crosses the trail at 1.6 miles.

The trail continues through the mixed pine-hardwood forest to 2.4 miles, where it turns westward to reach Low Gap, a small grassy spot on the ridgeline. Low Gap provides a campsite and is the junction with Yellow Stand Lead Trail and Big Creek Trail. Note that the trailhead on FS 221 is also called Low Gap. Some older maps distinguish the two gaps and call this southern one Hall Camp Gap. The battered trail sign at Low Gap was placed at a confusing angle in the early 1990s. Big Frog Trail goes to the left up the ridgecrest. Big Frog Trail is the only trail that climbs up from this junction. If you walk slightly to the right of the signs, just past a 1.5-foot diameter white pine, you will see the Big Creek Trail—which used to be called the Grassy Gap Trail—on the left (it is not obvious) beginning its almost perfectly con-toured route (along the bottom half of what is now called Barkleggin Trail) to Grassy Gap on Wolf Ridge. To the right of the signs, down the opposite side of Peavine Mountain from the way you came up, is the beginning of Yellow Stand Lead Trail, the fastest way to Big Creek Trailhead.

A spring is located east of Low Gap (or Hall Camp Gap). Some of the shrubby plants on the east side of the gap are buffalo-nuts, which have poisonous green-cased nuts in the late summer; they are about two inches long with five little protru-sions in a circular pattern around the bottom end of the nut.

Continue on Big Frog Trail as it proceeds straight up the ridge and then moves to the left side of the ridge. In its first 2.4 miles, Big Frog Trail has climbed only 350 feet. But this is about to change because the Fork Ridge Trail intersection 1.3 miles ahead is about 900 feet higher. Almost immediately upon leaving Low Gap you no-tice the steep grade. A very large (3.5-foot diameter) tulip poplar tree stands to the left of the trail at 2.7 miles. The next mile will be a series of well-graded switchbacks leading to Chimneytop Ridge. At 3.1 miles the trail passes through a dark, canopied area of many ferns. The trail will turn sharply to the right three times on ridgetops, once at 3.2 miles, again at 3.3 miles, and finally at 3.7 miles. The turns are inter-spersed with long, gradual grades up the sides of ridges. Just before the third sharp turn the trail arcs to the left, passing through a dark area carpeted with May apples and—if they're blooming—some of the most deeply colored purple trillium you will see.

At 3.7 miles the trail intersects with Fork Ridge Trail at the very crest of the ridge; the junction is marked by a wooden sign. Straight ahead is the very steep Rough Creek (East Fork) watershed and, in the distance, Licklog Ridge. Both of these features will be on your left for most of the remainder of the trail. Big Frog Trail turns sharply to the right—it has to—and begins a dramatically different segment as it ascends and begins following the narrow crest of Chimneytop Ridge. Fork Ridge Trail turns back to the left at the junction.

The Big Frog Trail follows a knife-edge crest beginning at 3.9 miles, where the ridgetop is only a few feet wide. The escarpment drops several hundred feet on each side. Trees are stunted, and the canopy is thin. This is one of two areas on Chimneytop that could almost be classified as mountain balds. Grasses and herbaceous material cover the ground, but there are also saw briars, blackberry vines, and hawthorn bushes to impede your travel. Some of the 10-foot-high shrubs are Carolina buckthorn, which are sometimes covered with bright red berries for a short while in the late summer before they darken. The easternmost peak of Big Frog is visible to the south. A few yards down the trail an excellent view to the left (southeast) opens up, and on a good day you can see over the crest of Licklog Ridge far into the distance to Brasstown Bald, the highest point in GA. Up over the ridgecrest, to the north, is Chilhowee Mountain. The trail climbs to the very crest of the knife-edge ridge.

At 4.0 miles, the trail turns to the right off the east side of the crest to pass 75 yards below and to the right of the peak of Chimneytop. There are many trillium and sweet white violets here. Be careful of a sloped rocky spot that is usually wet and slick or icy. After going to the west side of the ridge, you come out on a second knife-edge at 4.3 miles in the "saddle" between Chimneytop and the north peak of Big Frog Mountain, which is straight ahead. If you are looking for the Barkleggin Lead Trailhead, be on the immediate alert. At 4.3 miles the Barkleggin Trailhead is on the right side of the ridge. It is very small compared to Big Frog Trail. In the early 1990s the trail sign was down, probably chewed up by a black bear. If the sign is still down, look for a small oak tree with a distinct fork 2 feet above ground on the left, just opposite the beginning of Barkleggin Trail. The trail cuts through a pile of rocks at 4.4 miles. If you were looking for Barkleggin Trail, you've gone too far.

Just beyond 4.4 miles the trail cuts along slabs of rock on the ridgecrest. The finest views from Big Frog Trail are seen from this point, a good spot for lunch. The towns of Copperhill, TN, and McCaysville, GA, are to the east. Over the top of Licklog Ridge, to the southeast, is Brasstown Bald. At 4.5 miles the trail splits, one branch following the ridgecrest, the other slanting down to the right. You may go either way; it rejoins in just a few yards. Immediately after the rejoining, at 4.6 miles, the trail cuts sharply to the right of the crest, angling along a steep shaded slope. Do not take the steep bypass up the crest.

From the slope you can see the rhododendron "tunnel" ahead, reached at 4.7 miles. When you exit the rhododendron tunnel, look back hard to the right (northeast) to see the mountains of the Tellico area. At 4.8 miles a series of small, tight switchbacks leads to the northern peak of "The Frog." In the winter, through the trees, there is a 180-degree view from northwest to southeast. The trail immediately drops to the left of the peak. There are good views of Little Frog Mountain to the north-northeast.

The north peak of Big Frog Mountain is reached at 4.9 miles. The next 0.5 mile or so is incredibly level, following the shelf between the "tentpoles" of Big Frog, which from the distant west (the Ocoee Lake and Cleveland area) looks exactly like a giant pup tent, with the "entrance flap" (Chimneytop) facing north. Some also feel it looks more like a huge frog. At 5.4 miles the trail enters a rhododendron thicket and drops slightly to the left of the ridge. A huge black cherry tree is some 30 yards down off the ridge to the right at 5.5 miles.

At 5.6 miles the Big Frog Trail ends at the junction with the Licklog Ridge and Wolf Ridge trails. Note that this point is just below the crest and can easily become overgrown and thereby not obvious. The Big Frog Trail ends here, and two other trails begin. Wolf Ridge Trail heads south and then turns west, but its start is offset about 10 feet west of the end of the Big Frog Trail. As of the early 1990s a wooden USFS sign for "Big Frog Mtn." was lashed about 8 feet up a tree beside the Wolf Ridge Trail. Licklog Ridge Trail heads east (90 degrees to the left from the end of the Big Frog Trail). Ninety degrees to the right from the end of the Big Frog Trail is a side trail leading about 60 yards to the highest point of Big Frog Mountain at 4,224 feet. There was once an old fire tower on the peak. Look to the west; contemplate that the next mountain anywhere near the size of the Big Frog/Cohutta system—in the entire US from this point west—is somewhere in the foothills of the Rockies or the mountains of Big Bend in Texas. Big Frog Mountain and its GA sisters, Cowpen, Bald, and Grassy Mountains, are the westernmost 4,000-foot peaks of the Appalachians.

Hemp Top (Trail No. 145)
Length: 0.8 mile
Elevation Change: Start 4,100 feet, end 3,180 feet (high point 4,100 feet)
Trailheads: Licklog Ridge Trail (start) and Double Spring Gap (end)
Type: Horse

Comments: Only a short portion of the Hemp Top Trail is within the CNF, the limits of this guidebook. Hemp Top is at present the only Big Frog Wilderness trail that connects to the trails of Cohutta Wilderness to the south. In the "old days," the 1970s and before, the trail ended in Georgia at the Hemp Top fire tower, now demolished. From there a road led to Dally Gap. The road has now been closed to vehicles and seeded over. Our description of Hemp Top Trail ends at Double Springs Gap, where the GA-TN border intersects Hemp Top Ridge. Double Springs Gap is a very dependable source of water, even in the driest seasons. The trail climbs straight up or down Big Frog Mountain, depending on your direction of travel.

Details: The Hemp Top Trail intersects the Licklog Ridge Trail about 0.6 mile east of the Big Frog, Wolf Ridge, and Licklog Ridge intersection. The junction is about 0.4 mile past a spring that trickles down the Licklog Ridge Trail for about 100 yards. The junction is on top of a knob that is only a little lower than the Big Frog Mountain summit back at the western end of the Licklog Ridge Trail. In the early 1990s the junction was poorly marked by an old deep rectangular blaze about chest-high on a 12-inch hickory tree where the Hemp Top Trail veers to the right (southeast). If you are hiking from the south, another blaze is located on a large oak tree straight across from the end of the Hemp Top Trail. At that particular point the Hemp Top Trail is less defined than the Licklog Ridge Trail; it is hard to believe such a trail is the major connector to Cohutta. If you are hiking south from Big Frog Mountain, the Hemp Top Trail turns off to the right.

Hemp Top Trail begins to descend the ridge almost immediately after it leaves Licklog Ridge Trail. The trail drops and drops with little relief, losing 500 to 600 feet of elevation about as fast as if you had bushwhacked down the mountain. The trail will gradually angle to the left, or due south. By then the dark green of the conifers of Double Springs Gap will begin to show. One more steep drop down a section with a broken shale surface will bring you to the gap. A wooden sign facing GA welcomes hikers to TN and the CNF. To the left is one spring, to the right another. From this point it is about 1.2 miles on the Benton MacKaye Trail to an old fire tower site and, from there, about another 4.25 miles to Dally Gap on Tumbling Creek Road. In the summer this route will have no additional water sources.

If you continue on, two trails will intersect the trail you are on before you reach Dally Gap. At 1.75 miles past the old fire tower site, the Penitentiary Branch Trail will be on the right, and at 3.25 miles past the site the Benton MacKaye Trail will exit to the right. The only confusing point headed southward is about 1.1 miles from Double Springs Gap. At this point you follow an old logging road that is about 200 yards to the west of the ridge line. However, you must take another logging road that veers up the ridge to the left to the old fire-tower site. The old road enters the north end of the clearing about 50 feet to the west of the crest. Painted Benton MacKaye diamond blazes should mark the correct route.

Barkleggin (Grassy Gap) (Trail No. 67)

Length: 5.1 miles
Elevation Change: Start 3,640 feet, end 2,480 feet (high point 3,640 feet)
Trailheads: Big Frog Trail (start) and Wolf Ridge Trail (end)
Trail Connections: Big Creek
Type: Hiking

Comments: This trail is described as a descent rather than an ascent, as it makes better sense to do the upper section of it as an alternate route back to Low Gap from Big Frog or down to Big Creek campground from Big Frog. In the History section above we discuss the confusion wrought by blending two trails, Barkleggin and Big Creek, together. Note that the USFS may in the future correct the misdesignation of the initial 1.8 miles of this trail heading northwest from the Big Frog Trail. As of the early 1990s, that section is known as the Barkleggin Trail (No. 67), but the name may be changed to the Big Creek Trail (No. 68). Some maps show Barkleggin spelled "Barklegging." Barkleggin is also known as Grassy Gap Trail.

Details: For a precise description of the turnoff for Barkleggin Trail from Big Frog Trail, see Big Frog Trail description. Barkleggin Trail starts off as an extremely narrow, almost-manway path, but it is usually maintained all the way. Within a few yards of the trailhead, the path slices along the steep, 60-plus-degree uppermost slopes of the Big Creek watershed. There are many wildflowers along this dark section. The trail crosses a small stream at 0.3 mile and then angles right to reach Barkleggin Lead Ridge. At 0.4 mile Chimneytop Ridge can be seen, back hard to the right. The trail is much better defined from this point on to the junction with Big Creek Trail. Enter a rhododendron thicket. At 0.6 mile views to the north and northeast open up all the way to Chilhowee Mountain. This is a classic mountain ridge trail here and very remote. At 0.8 mile the trail crosses over the top of the lead to the left and then follows the other side of the lead through more rhododendron. At a big hollow maple the trail angles to the right (east).

At 1.1 miles the trail crosses the main branch of Big Creek. It cuts right to left across the ridge opposite the stream, beneath rock outcrops. Look for a 3-foot-diameter tulip tree down in the streambed. At 1.2 miles the first real indication that this is a CCC trail appears: a reinforced rockbed beneath the trail, plus grading along the uphill side. At 1.6 miles is a sharp switchback to the left (west), followed in a few yards by a large (3-foot-diameter) oak tree next to the trail. The oak sports one of the rare white blazes of this trail. Not far beyond, the trail switches back hard to the right, near a big tree with a hollow base. The trail angles down to the junction with Big Creek Trail and the Low Gap branch of Big Creek, reached at 1.8 miles.

We want to distinguish this junction so as not to encourage you to follow the rest of "Barkleggin Trail" as described by the USFS unless you intend to do so. Barkleggin—as described here—makes no sense unless you have come up Wolf Ridge, crossed the top of Big Frog, come down Big Frog Trail, and turned down Barkleggin to return via Grassy Gap back to the Wolf Ridge Trailhead. Or unless you have hiked up Yellow Stand Lead and/or Big Creek trails to the junction with Barkleggin and intend to do a roundtrip over to Grassy Gap and back to Big Creek campground via Wolf Ridge and FS 221. In any case, the lower half of Barkleggin (which we prefer to call part of "Grassy Gap Trail," that is, the contour trail to Grassy Gap) should be made as a part of a sensibly planned loop hike involving either Wolf Ridge or Big Frog Trail. Tally up the mileage for these loops in advance and allow yourself plenty of time.

As of the early 1990s, the USFS had not begun work to restore the old stretch of Grassy Gap Trail to Grassy Gap, or what we now describe as the rest of "Barkleggin." Consequently, at the trail junction it looked as if only three paths left the intersection instead of four. The beginning of the upper half (actually one-third) of Barkleggin Trail showed clearly on the slope above the junction. The section of the old Grassy Gap Trail to Low Gap (now part of Big Creek Trail) was very distinct to the northeast, having been refurbished in recent years. Big Creek Trail down the hillside was also distinct with plainly visible blazes, but the other part of Barkleggin to the southwest was nowhere to be seen except for one ancient blaze chopped in a tree a few yards to the west of the trail sign. Stand below the trail sign. Look to the right (west) and you will see the old blaze and the very, very faint path below the last few yards of upper Barkleggin Trail. Just beyond the old blaze the trail improves and from that point on is recognizable.

If you are not reasonably good at following manway or faint trails, do not try this stretch until the USFS improves it. There are many, many creek crossings on this trail, but they can be crossed with no difficulty. For the sake of brevity and to avoid virtually identical descriptions, some of the crossings and accompanying ridges will not be mentioned here. After each stream crossing, the trail follows the next ridge out away from the base of the mountain. Look for the vegetation to change dramatically just as you cross the ridgecrests. Going east to west, toward Grassy Gap, you will leave pine forest and enter oak forest as you cross the crest of each succeeding ridge. This old contour trail is the only higher-altitude trail of the Big Frog system with abundant water. Remember, distances are measured from the top of Barkleggin (at Chimneytop). So the trail sign at the junction is at 1.8 miles.

At 1.9 miles the trail crosses the main branch of Big Creek. There will be many crossings similar to this one; at the approach of each crossing look to the far ridge for the trail angling back to the right. This trail was built as a nearly perfect contour trail, a very rare thing in CNF, or in the eastern US for that matter. So the trail exiting each of these little watersheds will always be at the level of the section of trail entering it. Despite the extreme slope, you will walk the next 3.0 miles never climbing higher than 2,400 feet or lower than 2,200 feet.

At 2.3 miles the trail crosses the roots of a 2.5-feet-diameter oak on the right side of the path. Shortly afterward, a big blow-down obscures the trail. Cross a streambed, continue to the right at the same contour level on the opposite ridge, as always. At 2.6 miles the trail passes through some larger oaks. Back hard to the right is Peavine Mountain. At 3.0 miles Wolf Ridge comes into view to the northwest, looking deceptively close. A very large log is across the trail at 3.2 miles. At this point Chilhowee Mountain can be seen to the northwest.

At 3.4 miles the trail turns left into another of the seemingly endless watersheds, but this one is Penitentiary Branch, the main feeder of Peter Camp Branch, which drains the northwest side of Big Frog Mountain. Wolf Ridge fills the entire view to the right (south and west). The trail then cuts back harder left into the mountain to the southeast, and a fine view of the upper stretches of Wolf Ridge, nearly to the top of Big Frog, opens up. At 3.5 miles Penitentiary Branch is down to the right in a beautiful little gorge. The trail then crosses the branch and angles back on the opposite ridge, passing a really impressive oak, 3.0 to 3.5 feet in diameter, at 3.7 miles. Next in line is another stream, spilling over a rock base ledge. At 4.1 miles another, smaller stream crosses the trail after it cascades down a steep rock face.

At 4.2 miles the trail comes to a large streambed, which always seems to be mysteriously dry for its size. At 4.4 to 4.5 miles the trail encounters the most dramatic of the sudden pine forest-to-oak forest shifts when it crosses over another ridgecrest. At 4.7 miles, the trail climbs above 2,400 feet for the first time since Big Creek, but just barely. At 4.8 miles the *last* stream is reached, this one well worth the hike. Some very large tulip poplar and oak—up to 4 feet in diameter—adorn this little watershed. In 75 to 100 years hikers will truly appreciate the creation of Big Frog Wilderness when they view Joyce Kilmer Memorial-size trees here.

The trail begins the final approach to Grassy Gap on Wolf Ridge. There are good views to the right over Penitentiary Branch watershed all the way to Barkleggin Lead. At 5.1 miles the trail ends at Grassy Gap, amid scrub oak forest that looks considerably different from the vegetation of Barkleggin Trail. In the early 1990s the trail sign had been mutilated by bears. To the right it is about 2.0 miles down to the Wolf Ridge Trailhead at FS 221.

Big Creek (Trail No. 68)

Length: 4.0 miles
Elevation Change: Start 1,400 feet, end 2,450 feet (high point 2,450 feet)
Trailheads: Big Creek (start) and Big Frog Trail (end)
Trail Connections: Barkleggin and Yellow Stand Lead
Type: Hiking

Comments: Big Creek Trail follows the creek upstream for a couple of miles, then turns north, and continues the contour of the Barkleggin Trail to Low Gap. The contour portion is part of the old Grassy Gap Trail. The trail is marked occasionally but not well constructed—it is more of a manway in places. The USFS may in the future correct the misdesignation of the last 1.7 miles of this trail from Big Creek to Low Gap. As of the early 1990s, that section is known as the Big Creek Trail (No. 68), but the name may be changed to Barkleggin Trail (No. 67). The trail begins on the south side of FS 221 at Big Creek Trailhead. There is ample parking, as well as several shady camping spots. The Trail has ample water sources, especially in the spring.

Details: The trail meanders upstream between the creek and a ridge on the right for the first 0.8 mile, often taking you along a narrow path 100 feet above the creek. The woods here are primarily large hemlocks and rhododendron. Mountain laurel is also abundant along this stretch of the trail, blooming in mid-May. At 0.5 mile the trail crosses a wet-weather spring. Here the resourceful backpacker can find a campsite along the creek. At 0.8 mile, the path descends to creek level and intersects an abandoned road. The path is marked but could easily be missed on the return trip. Follow the trail along this road for 300 feet to the wildnerness boundary sign and Peter Camp Branch, which can be easily forded with a little rock-hopping. Here again is some level ground for camping. After the creek crossing, the Trail turns right on an old roadbed. In about 100 yards, turn left on a fork of the roadbed. In about 150 more yards, turn right on a less defined road leading southward into hardwoods and hemlocks. Shortly thereafter take a footpath to the right at a tree with carved initials "M" over "C". The next mile offers some old-growth timber, a few trees about 3 feet in diameter, and an abundance of wildflowers in spring, such as violets, crested iris, anemones, and nodding trillium.

At 2.0 miles the trail crosses Big Creek and soon turns northeast. A side trail continues straight up the creek but the turn in the main trail is marked by three blazes. At 2.3 miles is the junction with Barkleggin Trail; bear left to stay on Big Creek Trail. The view along the hillside is lovely in spring but may be obscured by foliage in summer. At 3.0 miles, cross another stream with a waterfall. At 4.0 miles, the trail ends at Low Gap, intersecting with Yellow Stand Lead and Big Frog trails. If you continue down Yellow Stand Lead, you will return to your starting point, 2.3 miles away.

Yellow Stand Lead (Trail No. 73)

Length: 2.3 miles
Elevation Change: Start 1,400 feet, end 2,450 feet (high point 2,450 feet)
Trailheads: Big Creek (start) and Big Frog Trail (end)
Trail Connections: Big Creek
Type: Hiking

Comments: Much of Yellow Stand Lead Trail lies outside the Wilderness, and its lower reaches have been turned into a logging road. It is the only trail that provides views of Big Frog Mountain as you hike up the mountain. The trailhead is off a gated logging road that turns off FS 221 at a point 5.25 miles west of the intersection of FS 221 and FS 45. The trail sign and road are on the south side of FS 221 just on the east side of Big Creek. Around 0.7 mile from FS 221 on the logging road, Yellow Stand Lead Trail veers to the left. The road curves sharply to the right at this point.

Details: After following the logging road for 0.7 mile, look for the trail on the left as the road curves to the right. The trail then follows an abandoned roadbed for 0.75 mile before becoming an excellent footpath. It gradually climbs, revealing nice views of the mountains to the south. At 1.8 miles, you will cross two branches, at least in wet weather. The trail then proceeds up to Low Gap and the Big Frog and Big Creek trails at 2.3 miles. If you prefer not to backtrack, take the Big Creek Trail back to your starting point (4.0 miles).

Chestnut Mountain (Trail No. 63)

Length: 1.9 miles
Elevation Change: Start 2,160 feet, end 3,000 feet (high point 3,000 feet)
Trailheads: Chestnut Mountain(start) and Wolf Ridge Trail (end)
Type: Horse

Comments: The Chestnut Mountain Trail begins on an old road in a heavily forested area. Numerous wildflowers may be encountered in season. The Chestnut Mountain and Wolf Ridge trails route is the shortest to the top of Big Frog Mountain, about 3.75 miles. Chestnut Mountain Trail is the northwest boundary for GA's Cohutta Wilderness.

The trail begins from FS 62 (Big Frog Loop Road). FS 62 turns off FS 221 9.8 miles west of the junction of FS 221 and FS 45. After turning onto FS 62, it is about 5.5 miles to the trailhead, on the left, which is marked by a small sign. The trailhead is at the old Van Arthur place, acquired by the USFS in 1946, and is a short distance from the TN-GA line. There is a small parking area, which will accommodate several cars.

Details: A register box is a short distance from the parking area. The trail heads northeast and begins a moderate climb, which is steep in places. At 0.9 mile, the trail has climbed to a ridge that affords scenic views in the winter. The trail heads uphill at 1.2 miles and switches back at 1.5 miles. Shortly thereafter, the trail begins a steep climb to its end at an intersection with Wolf Ridge Trail at 1.9 miles.

Wolf Ridge (Trail No. 66)
Length: 4.5 miles
Elevation Change: Start 1,680 feet, end 4,224 feet (high point 4,224 feet)
Trailheads: Pace Gap (start) and Big Frog and Licklog Ridge trails junction (end)
Trail Connections: Barkleggin and Chestnut Mountain
Type: Hiking (horse trail from Chestnut Mountain Trail to top of Big Frog Mountain)

Comments: The Wolf Ridge Trail begins on gated 221E, which turns off FS 221 0.3 mile south of Pace Gap. Drive only 100 feet on 221E to a parking area. The trail is blazed in white and sometimes in red. The trailhead is 7.3 miles west of the junction of FS 221 and FS 45. It is marked by a large brown sign reading "Wolf Ridge Trail No. 66." There is a USFS bulletin board and trail register.

The vegetation on the upper elevations of the Wolf Ridge Trail consists of two-foot-diameter stubby oaks that provide only a moderate canopy. This allows a prolific understory of wild flowers and grasses probably very similar to Rosine Parmentier's description of Big Frog Mountain in her journal when she hiked to the summit on October 13, 1852. The exception is that the Chestnut trees are, of course, gone.

A small stone monument commemorating John Curbow was formerly located on the Wolf Ridge Trail on a level spot about 1.0 mile above the Chestnut Mountain Trail intersection. Curbow was an organizer of the annual Ramp Tramp, a walk to the top of Big Frog Mountain. He died in a farming accident after returning home from the Ramp Tramp in 1968. The stone was installed in the mid-1970s but disappeared in 1980.

Details: A register box is a short distance from the trailhead. The trail goes southward on gated FS 221E for 0.3 mile, where it exits to the right at a wood sign. It makes a gradual uphill climb for around 0.5 mile, then switchbacks through a heavily wooded area that leads to a ridgetop at 0.9 mile. The trail levels and widens on the ridgetop. The forest is composed of oaks, maples, and pines, with undergrowth on the trail in places. At 1.8 miles the wilderness boundary is approached at a ridgetop, which provides panoramic views through the trees. The Wilderness is to the left, and the Primitive Area is to the right. At 2.0 miles, the Barkleggin Trail exits to the left at Grassy Gap. The slope steepens at 2.5 miles. The trail curves to the right at 2.6 miles as it enters the Primitive Area and a zone that is completely overgrown. Chestnut Mountain Trail intersects from the right at 2.7 miles. Wolf Ridge Trail continues uphill to the left. For the next 1.0 mile, the trail is mostly a rocky, uphill climb and winds to the left and right.

The trail makes a switchback onto the ridgetop at 3.6 miles. The underbrush is thick with grass, and the trail soon levels out, only to begin a gradual uphill climb to another ridge. As the trail nears the top of the mountain, it again becomes steep, rocky, and somewhat overgrown. At 4.5 miles, the trail reaches a marker at the top of Big Frog Mountain for connections to Big Frog and Licklog Ridge trails.

Rough Creek (Trail No. 70)
Length: 2.9 miles
Elevation Change: Start 2,480 feet, end 2,480 feet (high point 2,480 feet)
Trailheads: Licklog Ridge Trail (start) and Big Frog Trail (end)
Trail Connections: East Fork Rough Creek, Fork Ridge, and West Fork Rough Creek
Type: Hiking

Comments: Although it is relatively short, the Rough Creek Trail provides an opportunity to see major ridge systems and cross two major streams. The vegetation is varied, with oak and pine growing on the drier ridgetops and hemlock, rhododendron, and other moist-area species in the creek drainages. Either direction the trail is hiked involves descending a high ridge, crossing a stream, ascending and descending another ridge, crossing a second stream, and climbing a ridge to the trail's end. The trail is blazed with white paint. Rough Creek Trail begins at an intersection with Licklog Ridge Trail, 1.5 miles from its beginning on FS 221. A wooden sign marks the spot in a small gap.

Details: Rough Creek Trail descends steadily down the west side of Licklog Ridge through pine, mountain laurel, oak, and galax, switchbacking to the left at 0.1 mile. At 0.2 mile, an old road enters the trail from the right. After passing through several small streams, the trail enters a stand of white pine. At 0.8 mile, the East Fork of Rough Creek is crossed and usually can be rock-hopped. Beyond the creek, the trail ascends a bank, then turns right on an old road (Rough Creek, East Fork, Trail No 70A). A small pile of stones marks the junction. After following the road downstream, the trail leaves it and ascends steeply to the left at 0.9 mile. A destroyed sign and a pile of stones mark this point. The trail soon ascends more gradually through a mixed forest of pine, oak, and hemlock, reaching the Fork Ridge Trail (no sign) on a ridgetop at 1.4 miles. Fork Ridge Trail goes left up the ridge to the Big Frog Trail, at a white oak with three old blazes.

The trail continues downhill, crossing two small branches in a forest of hemlock and white pine. The trail makes a U-turn at the first creek and descends into a dense hemlock forest. A large beech tree with "1935" carved on its trunk announces your approach to Rough Creek. Just before crossing a larger branch, the trail drops down a bank and descends steeply to the right to a stream crossing. A few yards after crossing the stream, the trail comes very close to the larger stream but veers to the right. After descending to the left, a small campsite is passed on the right, and the trail crosses the West Fork of Rough Creek at 2.0 miles. After climbing a steep bank, at a pile of stones the trail intersects an old roadbed that is now a trail (Rough Creek, West Fork, Trail No. 70B). To the left the old road leads to a washed-out culvert; the old road continues on the other side. Rough Creek Trail turns right for 100 feet, exits Trail No. 70B at a second stone pile and climbs a steep bank to the left. The trail ascends more moderately through pine and mountain laurel. After crossing a very small stream and ascending to the left, the trail turns right on a ridgetop and enters an old clear-cut at 2.5 miles. The trail goes through, along the border of, and back through the old clear-cut as it climbs up the ridge. Near the top of the clear-cut, the trail turns left onto an old logging road through young pines and oaks. The trail soon passes a small pond to the left that was constructed in the late 1970s as a helicopter water-loading source for fire fighting. The trail then reenters uncut timber and intersects the Big Frog Trail at 2.9 miles. Note that this junction may be confusing. After you reenter the mature timber, the trail junction sign is directly ahead, but a roadbed turning right is the more obvious route. The Big Frog Trail may also be joined by following the roadbed to the right.

Fork Ridge (Trail No. 69)
Length: 1.8 miles
Elevation Change: Start 2,280 feet, end 3,360 feet (high point 3,360 feet)
Trailheads: Rough Creek Trail (start) and Big Frog Trail (end)
Type: Hiking

Comments: This trail cannot be reached by car at either end. Throughout its length, it stays on or near the crest of Fork Ridge. It is somewhat rough and narrow in places, but the grade is moderate. The tree species present are predominantly oak and pine. No water was found when this trail was hiked.

Fork Ridge Trail begins at an intersection with Rough Creek Trail on top of a ridge 1.4 miles from the start of Rough Creek Trail on Licklog Ridge Trail. The junction is on a ridgecrest, and an oak with old white blazes marks the spot.

Details: The trail ascends slightly up the ridgetop, then swings to the left side of Fork Ridge at 0.3 mile. The tread is rough in this area; the trail continues up the left side of the ridge. The trail is narrow and slopes to the side, sometimes making walking difficult. At 0.6 mile the trail passes below an obvious knoll to the right. After circling around the knoll, the trail goes up to the ridgecrest and thereafter follows the ridgecrest or goes slightly to the right of the crest. The trail circles the head of a small hollow in an area of numerous off-trail blow-downs at 1.3 miles. The trail thereafter remains on the right (west) side of Fork Ridge, passes a large beech tree on the left, and begins a long climb up the ridge. After entering the head of another cove, it continues along the right side of the ridge. Finally, the trail ascends a narrow, grass-covered ridgetop and intersects Big Frog (Peavine Ridge) Trail at 1.8 miles. A junction sign is still standing but may be damaged. Big Frog Mountain is to the left, Low Gap and FS 221 to the right. The Copperhill area is visible to the east.

Licklog Ridge (Trail No. 65)
Length: 5.9 miles
Elevation Change: Start 1,760 feet, end 4,224 feet (high point 4,224 feet)
Trailheads: Licklog Ridge (start) and Big Frog and Wolf Ridge trails junction (end)
Trail Connections: Rough Creek and Hemp Top
Type: Hiking (horse trail from top of Big Frog Mountain to Hemp Top Trail junction)

Comments: Although this trail stays on or near the crest of Licklog Ridge for much of its length, it is mostly in trees with few views. The forest is mostly oak, with mountain laurel, and galax also prominent. The trail is generally in good condition. The only reliable spring is near the trail's upper end, where a small campsite is located. Long pants may be needed due to briers in some sections.

The trailhead is in an old clear-cut on FS 221, 3.3 miles from the intersection of FS 221 and FS 45. A small parking area is on the left; look for a trail to the right, which may be obscured by vegetation. The trail is also known simply as Licklog Trail.

Details: Licklog Ridge Trail begins in an old clear-cut; in about 100 feet, a trail register is passed on the right. At the upper edge of the clear-cut (about 0.2 mile), take the left of the three logging roads at the intersection. The left road goes up a few yards and becomes a foot trail as it turns right through bigger hardwoods and then passes under a power line at 0.3 mile just below the crest of the steep ridge. After passing under the power line, the trail climbs moderately into a small saddle, then swings right and continues to climb, passing a wilderness boundary sign at 0.8 mile.

The ridgecrest is reached at 1.1 miles, with views of Ocoee No. 3 Lake to the east. At 1.5 miles, the trail passes a small log structure and reaches a junction in a gap with the Rough Creek Trail, which turns right (west). Just beyond the intersection, an old logging road turns left. This area can be a problem if you are coming down Licklog Ridge. The old logging road will start as part of the trail but will turn southeast off the ridge while the less-defined Licklog Ridge Trail will stay on the ridgeline. Licklog Ridge Trail climbs out of the gap and then continues on or near the ridgetop, passing through a pine stand at 2.2 miles. After climbing along the right side of the ridge, the trail regains the ridgetop at 2.9 miles, then traverses to the left side, passing through more pine and mountain laurel.

A possible wet-weather branch is crossed at 3.8 miles, followed by a steep switchback; the trail climbs steadily to a high point on the narrow ridgecrest at 4.4 miles, with good views of the Chimneytop and East Fork of Rough Creek to the west. This ridgecrest is almost a duplicate of the Chimneytop Ridge on the Big Frog Trail. A few yards beyond, the trail traverses left and enters the head of a hollow. At 4.8 miles the trail makes a turn to the right at Groundhog Ridge. This area can be confusing when descending the trail because an ORV track leads straight past the point where the trail turns to the left off the ridgecrest (about 0.5 mile from the Hemp Top Trail intersection). The junction is reached with Hemp Top Trail on the left at 5.3 miles. Beyond the junction, the trail widens and continues at an easy-to-moderate grade. A good spring is soon passed on the left, and the trail climbs more steeply to a small campsite and an intersection with the Big Frog (Peavine Ridge) and Wolf Ridge trails at 5.9 miles. Since the trail sign was tied up in a tree in the early 1990s, caution should be used here: Wolf Ridge drops steeply downhill to the left, Big Frog Trail goes right, and a short spur continues ahead a few yards to the high point of Big Frog Mountain.

Rough Creek, East Fork (Trail No. 70A)

Length: 4.2 miles
Elevation Change: Start 1,560 feet, end 2,600 feet (high point 2,600 feet)
Trailhead: Rough Creek (start and dead-end)
Trail Connection: Rough Creek
Type: Hiking

Comments: This trail is the remnant of a former USFS road that was closed when the area was designated a Wilderness; it is not an official trail. The trailhead is reached by following FS 45 to FS 221. Turn east (left) and proceed 1.6 miles to the first road on the right. This is FS 221G. Follow this road 0.6 mile; it crosses the west fork of Rough Creek and opens into a parking area at the trail junction. The East Fork Trail is the old road leading straight ahead; the West Fork Trail goes to the right. Both are closed to motor traffic just past the parking area. There are no blazes or trail signs.

Details: The trail is very easy walking on the old roadbed up a beautiful valley along Rough Creek. The trail proceeds deep into the Big Frog Mountain Wilderness, but there are no trail connections at the end. One must return down the East Fork or take the official Rough Creek Trail (No. 70) over to the West Fork Trail and follow it downstream to the starting point. The Rough Creek Trail junction is 2.0 miles up the trail and is marked where it joins the East Fork by a pile of stones rather than any official signs. If you stay on the East Fork Trail, you will pass a second stone pile 100 yards up the trail, indicating where Trail No. 70 exists to the left.

The East Fork Trail continues a gradual climb to a small clearing about 1.0 mile from the top of Big Frog Mountain. Total distance to the end of the old road is 4.2 miles. A poorly defined footpath continues upstream for 0.2 mile until it is no longer recognizable. However, the terrain here is so open and rocky that the adventuresome hiker could continue up to the summit. The possibility of locating a stand of large trees could reward continuing up to Big Frog Mountain.

Rough Creek, West Fork (Trail No. 70B)
Length: 2.6 miles
Elevation Change: Start 1,560 feet, end 2,000 feet (high point 2,000 feet)
Trailhead: Rough Creek (start and dead-end)
Trail Connections: Rough Creek and Benton MacKaye
Type: Hiking

Comments: This trail is the remnant of a former USFS road that was closed when the area was designated a Wilderness; it is not an official trail. The trailhead is reached from FS 45 by turning east on FS 221. Follow FS 221 for 1.6 miles and turn south on FS 221G. It is the first road to the right and is marked, although the sign is small and difficult to find in the foliage. Follow 221G for 0.6 mile. Then carefully ford the creek and park. At this point, an old road turns off to the right. It is now closed and is considered the West Fork Trail (No. 70B). It is not marked with signs or blazes except for the portion that is also the Benton MacKaye Trail.

Details: The trail follows the West Fork for the entire length of the trail. There is only one crossing, at 0.2 mile, that requires some shallow wading. The old road affords a gradual easy hike upstream along the creek. At about 0.6 mile the Benton MacKaye Trail enters from the right and continues as part of the Rough Creek West Fork Trail to the Rough Creek Trail junction at 1.9 miles.

At 1.2 miles the trail crosses the first of a series of culverts at the wilderness boundary. The concrete walls that anchor them serve as bridges. High water has washed away the dirt that previously covered the metal culverts. At 1.9 miles the junction with Rough Creek Trail is reached. This is marked by a pile of stones where it enters from the west and again where it exits to the east a few yards upstream. The Benton MacKaye Trail exits at this point and follows the Rough Creek Trail to the east. The Rough Creek, West Fork, Trail continues across Rough Creek and ends at a clearing at 2.6 miles.

Benton MacKaye (No USFS Number)

The Benton MacKaye Trail in TN is a trail in progress as the USFS and volunteer groups work to locate, design, and build it. The GA portion, approximately 80 miles from Springer Mountain to the TN-GA state line, is complete. A total of 250 miles is planned from GA to the GSMNP. The background of the trail involves the person who first proposed the AT, Benton MacKaye. He conceived the idea for a continuous Appalachian crest trail in 1921 with the original proposal having a southern terminus at Mount Mitchell in NC. In the intermediate planning stages, the route was changed to the western crest of the Appalachians through Monroe and Polk counties in the CNF. However, when the AT was built in the 1930s, it was more convenient to follow a more eastern route through NC.

The Benton MacKaye Trail has revived the proposal for a trail looping south from the AT in the GSMNP through the CNF into GA and reconnecting with the AT at Springer Mountain. A northern loop through the GSMNP to form a huge figure-8 is also being considered. The route of the southern loop would therefore roughly parallel the AT, with the AT on the east and the Benton MacKaye Trail on the west. Substantial additional long-distance hiking opportunities would be provided, thus easing pressure on the AT, and hiking access would be afforded to some scenic locations in the CNF and the Chattahoochee National Forest.

In TN the designated portion of the Benton MacKaye Trail usually follows existing trails; as of the early 1990s such trails had not all been marked with Benton MacKaye Trail logos. The first segment in TN from the GA state line to Thunder Rock Campground on US 64 was approved by the USFS in 1992. From the GA state line and Double Springs Gap, the Benton MacKaye Trail route is north on the Hemp Top Trail for 0.8 mile, west on the Licklog Ridge Trail for 0.6 mile, north on the Big Frog Trail for 1.8 miles, north on Fork Ridge Trail for 1.8 miles, west on Rough Creek Trail for 0.6 mile, and north on Rough Creek West Fork Trail for 1.2 miles. From that point, new construction will lead the trail north for 1.0 mile to a trailhead on FS 221 located 0.4 mile east of the intersection of FS 221 with FS 45. The Benton MacKaye Trail will then follow abandoned portions of old FS 45 for 1.6 miles north. An additional 1.1 miles of new construction will finally lead into Thunder Rock Campground on the Ocoee River. The route north from the Ocoee River remains to be determined, although it will probably generally follow the TN-NC state line. The USFS may solicit a volunteer task force to assist in selecting the remainder of the route for the Benton MacKaye Trail.

The Benton Mackaye Trail is generally marked by white diamond shaped trail markers.

26. CONASAUGA RIVER CORRIDOR

The Conasauga and Jacks rivers originate in the mountains of northern GA; they join together just after flowing into TN at the northern end of the Alaculsy Valley. The river continues westward as the Conasauga River through the CNF; after leaving the CNF, it curves to the south, under US 411, and back into GA. Because of its relatively unpolluted mountain source, the Conasauga is a clear, clean river as it flows through TN. The portion in TN east of US 411 is a part of TN's Scenic River System. The portion within the CNF has a protected scenic corridor and is being considered for inclusion in the National Wild and Scenic Rivers System.

The Conasauga is noted for numerous darters and chubs, and 22 species of fish not found elsewhere in TN have been recorded. The TN portion of the river is generally an easy trip for canoeists, when the water is high enough, and provides a scenic trip. The Conasauga River Trail follows the river for 2.6 miles; note there is also a Conasauga River Trail in GA's Chattahoochee National Forest.

HISTORY

The Conasauga River was involved in the earliest explorations of North America; it is likely that DeSoto and his expedition camped near the Cherokee village of Conasauga on June 1, 1540. To get to the town, DeSoto probably crossed the Conasauga River. The watersheds of the Conasauga and Jacks rivers were the site of intensive logging of virgin timber during the 1920s and 1930s; logging was then dependent on railroads for transportation. The railroad came to the town of Conasauga on US 411, where the sawmill was located just after the turn of the century. A trunk line was extended east along the Conasauga River into the mountains and to the Alaculsy site at the Jacks River and Conasauga River junction. The 1920s were spent logging the upper Conasauga from a camp known as Bray Fields; the Jacks River timber was cut in the 1930s from another camp at Beech Bottoms (in the Cohutta Wilderness). The loggers then turned to the north slopes of Big Frog Mountain, with trucks being used to haul timber to Alaculsy for loading on railroad cars. The rails along the Conasauga River were removed in 1942, leaving a railbed that the Conasauga River Trail now follows along the river.

A scenic corridor along the Conasauga River was designated as a Management

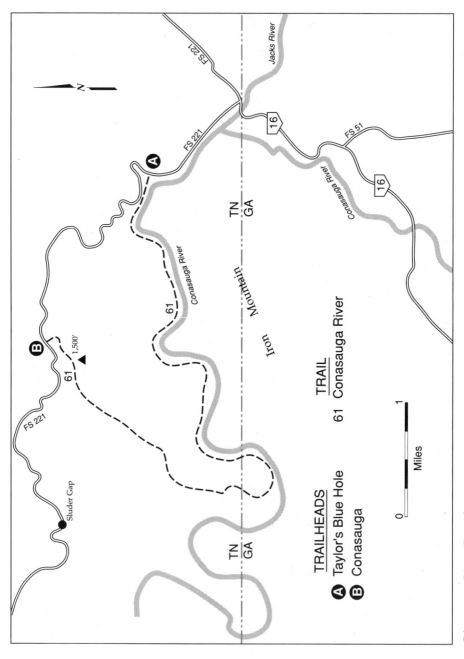

Conasauga River Corridor.

Category 5 area in the 1988 CNF Management Plan. This category protects areas with high visual sensitivity and a high degree of public interest and generally prohibits timber harvesting.

TRAILHEAD AND MAP INFORMATION

Conasauga Trailhead

Turn east off US 411 onto County 221 about 6.5 miles south of the US 411-US 64 intersection. Although County 221 may not be marked at the turn-off, TN 313 heads west from US 411 where County 221 heads east. Drive southeast on County 221 about 4.0 miles where the pavement ends and FS 67 turns north; County 221 ends at this point, but FS 221 continues as a gravel road. Proceed on FS 221 about 6.7 miles from US 411 to the Conasauga Trailhead on the right (south). This ridgeside trailhead is indicated by white trail blazes and a register box about 100 yards down the trail.

Taylor's Blue Hole Trailhead

Continue past the Conasauga Trailhead for 1.6 miles (a total of 8.3 miles from US 411) to the Taylor's Blue Hole Trailhead, which is marked by a metal sign for Trail No. 61; this will be the first time FS 221 reaches the river. This trailhead is also 0.6 mile from the bridge across the Jacks River; GA County 16 is on the other side of the bridge while FS 221 is on the north side. A parking area and information board are located about 100 yards off FS 221 at the trailhead.

Topographic Maps: Parksville, TN; and Tennga, TN-GA..

TRAIL DESCRIPTIONS

Conasauga River (Trail No. 61)
Length: 4.6 miles
Elevation Change: Start 960 feet, end 1,320 feet (high point 1,450 feet)
Trailheads: Taylor's Blue Hole (start) and Conasauga (end)

Comments: The trail follows the abandoned railroad bed along the river for 2.6 miles, where it turns to the northeast and follows a ridge to the Conasauga Trailhead. A 6.2-mile loop can be completed without a car shuttle if you walk back on FS 221 to the Taylor's Blue Hole Trailhead. However, the road is curvy and sometimes has frequent traffic.

Details: The railroad bed is gently sloped and easy walking. The adjacent Conasauga River is 50 to 125 feet wide at full flow and has some whitewater rapids. The escarpment is steep on both sides of the river at first with one hillside of large white pines on the south side. A few large hemlocks are located along the trail adjacent to the large pools and rapids, but most of the trees are small hardwoods and pines. A few trees have beaver marks. At 2.6 miles, the trail turns sharply to the right and away from the railroad bed and the river at a metal hiker insignia sign. You can proceed straight ahead on the old railbed for 0.5 miles to the former location of a railroad bridge. The trail, after turning right, goes up a ridge crest with shallow soils; the oaks and Virginia pines are often somewhat stunted. There are at least half a dozen patches of small ground pine (also called club moss) near the trail on the ridge. The trail leaves the protected corridor as it follows the ridge. The trailhead is reached at 4.6 miles.

Appendix 1

Maps

There are two principal maps available from the CNF: one of the northern CNF and one of southern CNF. They are called "Forest Visitor Maps," and each is available for $2.00 ($4.00 for both north and south) from the Cherokee National Forest, PO Box 2010, Cleveland, TN 37311. These very general maps show the Forest Service roads and developed facilities but do not show all of the boundaries of the areas in this guidebook or the details of such areas. The map "Trails of the Cherokee National Forest" is also available for $2.00 from the above address. This map shows the general locations of most trails in this guidebook. The CNF also has a combined map of the Joyce Kilmer-Slickrock Wilderness and Citico Creek Wilderness and a map of the Cohutta Wilderness, both available for $2.00 from the above address.

A book of helpful general maps, particularly for access roads, is the *Tennessee Atlas and Gazetter*, which includes all of the CNF; it is available at local bookstores or from DeLorme Mapping Company, PO Box 298, Freeport, ME 04032; telephone 207/865-4171. A similar map book is *Tennessee County Maps*, available at local bookstores or from County Maps, Puetz Place, Lyndon Station, WI 53944.

The most detailed maps available are USGS topographic maps, available from the USFS and several other sources:

The Map Store
2024 Dutch Valley Road
Knoxville, TN 37918
615/688-3608

Timley Discount Topos
9769 West 119th Drive
Broomfield, CO 80021
800/821-7609

TVA Map Files
101 Haney Building
311 Broad Street
Chattanooga, TN 37401
615/751-6277

US Geological Survey
Washington, DC 20242
(Write for index map
and price list.)

These topographic maps often do not show the boundaries of the areas in this guidebook.

Appendix 2

Forest Service Offices

The following CNF offices are open from 8:00 A.M. to 4:30 P.M., Monday through Friday, excluding holidays.

Supervisor's Office
USDA Forest Service
Cherokee National Forest
PO Box 2010
Cleveland, TN 37320
615/476-9700

Hiwassee Ranger District
USDA Forest Service
1401 S. Tennessee Avenue
Etowah, TN 37331
615/263-5486

Nolichucky Ranger District
USDA Forest Service
120 Austin Avenue
Greeneville, TN 37743
615/638-4109

Ocoee Ranger District
USDA Forest Service
Route 1, Parksville
Benton, TN 37307
615/338-5201

Tellico Ranger District
USDA Forest Service
Route 3, Tellico River Road
Tellico Plains, TN 37385
615/253-2520

Unaka Ranger District
USDA Forest Service
1205 N. Main Street
Erwin, TN 37650
615/743-4452

Watauga Ranger District
USDA Forest Service
Route 9, Box 2235
Star Route 91
Elizabethton, TN 37643
615/542-2942

Appendix 3

Outings and Issues Groups

Two clubs regularly conduct organized outings in the CNF and are active with regard to CNF issues:

Tennessee Chapter of the Sierra Club and especially its east TN groups: the Harvey Broome Group (Knoxville and Oak Ridge area), the Chattanooga Group, and the State of Franklin Group (Kingsport, Johnson City, and Bristol area). You can get any local group's current address, telephone number, and other information by calling or writing the Sierra Club at 730 Polk Street, San Francisco, CA 94109; 415/776-2211.

Smoky Mountain Hiking Club. Write for the current Outings Chair and other information at PO Box 1454, Knoxville, TN 37901.

Other groups involved in CNF issues and/or conducting outings in the CNF are:

Appalachian Trail Conference
PO Box 807
Harpers Ferry, WV 25425

Benton MacKaye Trail Association
PO Box 53271
Atlanta, GA 30355

Carolina Mountain Club
PO Box 68
Asheville, NC 28802

Cherokee Forest Voices
3200 Haggard Drive
Knoxville, TN 37917

Chota Canoe Club
PO Box 8270
University Station
Knoxville, TN 37996

Southern Appalachian
Highlands Conservancy
PO Box 2501
Johnson City, TN 37605

Tennessee Audubon Council
1725 Church Street
Nashville, TN 37203
615/321-5075

Tennessee Citizens for
Wilderness Planning
130 Tabor Road
Oak Ridge, TN 37830

Tennessee Eastman
Hiking Club
PO Box 511
Kingsport, TN 37662

Tennessee Scenic Rivers
Association
PO Box 159041
Nashville, TN 37215

Appendix 4

Outdoor Equipment Stores

Be sure to call ahead for current information.

Blue Ridge Mountain Sports
East Towne Mall, 3045-B
Mall Road North
Knoxville, TN 37924
615/544-1811

River Sports Outfitters
2918 Sutherland Avenue
Knoxville, TN 37919
615/523-0066

Mahoney's
702 Sunset Drive
Johnson City, TN 37601
615/282-5413

Mountain Sports, Ltd.
1021 Commonwealth Avenue
Bristol, VA 24201
703/466-8988

Rock Creek Outfitters
100 Tremont Street
Chattanooga, TN 37405
615/265-5969

Outdoor Adventures
2507 North Ocoee Street
Cleveland, TN 37311
615/472-4772

Appendix 5

Areas and Acreages

This list is current as of June 24, 1991.

CNF WILDERNESSES

NORTHERN CNF

Area Name	Acres	County(ies)
Big Laurel Branch Wilderness	6,251	Carter
		Johnson
Pond Mountain Wilderness	6,665	Carter
Unaka Mountain Wilderness	4,700	Unicoi
Sampson Mountain Wilderness	7,992	Unicoi
		Greene
		Washington
(Total: Northern CNF)	25,608	

SOUTHERN CNF

Area Name	Acres	County(ies)
Gee Creek Wilderness	2,493	Polk/Monroe
Joyce Kilmer-Slickrock Wilderness	3,832	Monroe
Cohutta Wilderness	1,795	Polk
Citico Creek Wilderness	16,226	Monroe
Bald River Gorge Wilderness	3,721	Monroe
Big Frog Wilderness	7,986	Polk
(plus 83 acres in Chattahoochee National Forest)		
Little Frog Mountain Wilderness	4,684	Polk
(Total: Southern CNF)	40,737	

Total Northern and Southern
CNF Wilderness Acreage   66,345

CNF SCENIC AREAS

NORTHERN CNF

Area Name	Acres	County(ies)
Bald Mountain Ridge	8,644	Greene
Doe River Gorge	1,783	Carter
Rogers Ridge	3,865	Johnson
Flint Mill	3,920	Sullivan
		Carter
Unaka Mountain	910	Unicoi
(Total: Northern CNF)	19,122	

SOUTHERN CNF

Area Name	Acres	County(ies)
Rock Creek Gorge	220	Polk
Coker Creek	375	Polk
(Total: Southern CNF)	595	
Total Northern and Southern CNF Scenic Area Acreage	19,717	

CNF PRIMITIVE AREAS

NORTHERN CNF

Area Name	Acres	County(ies)
Flint Mill	2,620	Sullivan
		Carter
Nolichucky	1,970	Unicoi
Rogers Ridge (North of Scenic Area)	1,390	Johnson
Beaverdam (Managed)	1,145	Johnson
Iron Mountain (Managed)	2,550	Johnson
Devil's Backbone	6,660	Cocke
Sampson Mountain (Motorized)	6,308	Unicoi
		Washington
Coldspring Mountain (South of Sampson Mountain Wilderness)*	380	Greene

Flint Mountain (South of Sampson Mountain Wilderness)*	480	Unicoi
Unaka Mountain (South of Unaka Mountain Wilderness)	1,248	Unicoi
(Total: Northern CNF)	24,751	

SOUTHERN CNF

Area Name	Acres	County
West Big Frog	1,460	Polk
Rough Ridge	2,970	Monroe
Upper Bald River		
a. Waucheesi	2,630	Monroe
b. Brookshire Creek	2,560	Monroe
c. Brookshire Creek (Managed)	2,420	Monroe
d. North of Bald River (Managed)	2,850	Monroe
Brushy Ridge (Managed)	4,220	Monroe
Gee Creek (Motorized and Managed)	1,400	Polk
Haw Knob (North of Kilmer-Slickrock Wilderness)	1,060	Monroe
(Total: Southern CNF)	22,570	
Total Northern and Southern CNF Primitive Area Acreage	46,321	

Not included in Guidebook.

MISCELLANEOUS PROTECTED CNF AREAS

Name	Acres	County(ies)
Nationally Designated Trails	25,122	
John Muir Trail (19 miles)		Polk
Appalachian Trail (169 miles)		Cocke
		Greene
		Unicoi
		Carter
		Johnson
		Sullivan

Warrior's Passage Trail (8 miles)		Monroe
Overmountain Victory Trail (0.5 mile)		Carter
Botanical Areas		
Bullett Creek*	150	McMinn
Moffett Laurel*	107	Carter
Highlands of Roan	2,867	Carter
Consauga River Scenic Corridor		Polk

Not included in Guidebook.

SUMMARY

There are 626,417 total acres in CNF as of October 1, 1990 (327,470 in the northern and 298,997 in the southern CNF). The above wilderness areas constitute 10.59 percent of the total CNF acreage while the scenic and semiprimitive areas constitute 10.54 percent of the total.

Wildernesses are designated by Congress pursuant to the Wilderness Act of 1964 and provide the best permanent protection for the natural resources of an area from development, road building, and clear-cutting; however, most recreational uses such as hunting (in national forests but not national parks), fishing, horseback riding, hiking, and camping are allowed.

Scenic Areas are protected only by the current CNF Management Plan; pending any change, however, the management is only slightly less protective than wilderness designation.

Primitive Areas are likewise protected only by the current CNF Management Plan; except as noted below, pending any change these areas will not have timber harvesting, road construction/reconstruction or ORV use. Note, however, that under the current Management Plan, two of these areas will have ORV or other vehicular use (indicated as "Motorized" above) and six of these areas (indicated as "Managed" above) may be managed to allow some timber harvesting; such management will generally allow cuts of 20 acres or less and new roads must be seeded and allowed to grow up after harvesting is completed.

August 4, 1988, is the date on which the current CNF Management Plan was implemented. Wilderness bills were signed into law on October 30, 1984 (southern CNF), and October 16, 1986 (northern CNF).

Appendix 6

Endangered and Threatened Species in the CNF

The categories in this list are federal designations.

PLANTS

Common Name	Scientific Name	Status
Spreading Avens	*Geum radiatum*	Endangered
Roan Mountain Bluet	*Hedyotis purpurea var. montana*	Endangered
Ruth's Golden Aster	*Pityopsis ruthii*	Endangered
Blue Ridge Goldenrod	*Solidago spithamaea*	Threatened
Virginia Spiraea	*Spiraea virginiana*	Threatened
Fraser fir	*Abies fraseri*	Candidate (Threatened)
False goat's-beard	*Astilbe crenatiloba*	Candidate (Endangered)
Piratebush	*Buckleya distichophylla*	Candidate (Threatened)
Mountain bitter cress	*Cardamine clematitis*	Candidate (Threatened)
Roan Mountain Sedge	*Careex roanensis*	Candidate (Endangered)
Bent avens	*Geam geniculatum*	Candidate (Endangered)
Gray's lily	*Lilium grayi*	Candidate (Endangered) USFS
Freser's Loosetrife	*Lysimachia fraseri*	Candidate (Endangered)
White fringeless orchid	*Platanthera integrilabia*	Candidate (Endangered)
Carolina saxifrage	*Saxifraga caroliniana*	Candidate (Endangered)
Nevius' stonecrop	*Sedum nevii*	Candidate (Endangered)
Catchfly	*Silene ovata*	Candidate (Threatened)

WILDLIFE

Common Name	Scientific Name	Status
Chub, Spotfin	*Hybopsis monacha*	Threatened
Darter, Amber	*Percina macrocephals*	Endangered
Logperch Conasauga	*Percina jenkinsi*	Endangered
Madtom, Smoky	*Noturus beileyi*	Endangered
Madtom, Yellowfin	*Noturus flavipinnis*	Threatened
Mussel, Tan Rifleshell	*Epioblasma walkeri*	Endangered
Mussel, Yellow-Blossom Pearly	*Epioblasma f. florentina*	Endangered
Red-Cockaded Woodpecker	*Picoides borealis*	Endangered
Bald Eagle	*Haliaeetus leucocephalus*	Endangered
Northern Flying Squirrel	*Glaucomys sabrinus cororatus*	Endangered

Contributors

LAMAR ALEXANDER, Washington, D.C., is the United States Secretary of Education. He was President of the University of Tennessee from 1988 to 1991 and Governor of Tennessee from 1979 to 1987.

JAMES BLACKSTOCK, Communications Technician, Knoxville, TN, contributed the "Warrior's Passage National Recreation Trail" part of Section C. His interests include the Sierra Club, development of greenways, hiking, backpacking, and bicycling.

DENNIS R. AND MARTY L. E. DANILCHUK, Outdoor Enthusiasts, Knoxville, TN, coauthored the "Little Frog Mountain Wilderness" part of Section C. Their activities include volunteer work for a marine science center, coastal cleanup, backpacking, fishing, hiking, photography, and painting.

DANIEL P. DILLON, Geographer, Church Hill, TN, contributed the "Iron Mountain Primitive Area and Trail" part of Section B. He has served as the Sierra Club's State of Franklin Group Cochairperson, and his interests include hiking, camping, canoeing, and skiing.

DANA EGLINTON, Carpenter, Bristol, TN, contributed the "Flint Mill Scenic Area and Primitive Area" part of Section B. His activities include Habitat for Humanity construction projects, the Presbyterian Church in Bristol, the Sierra Club, and building energy-efficient solar buildings.

EMILY ELLIS, University Counselor and Administrator, Knoxville, TN, contributed the "Rock Creek Gorge Scenic Area and Clear Creek Trail" part of Section C. Her interests include music, hiking, and the development of greenways.

JOHN R. FINGER, University History Professor, Knoxville, TN, contributed the "Human History" part of Section A and coauthored the "Brushy Ridge Primitive Area" part of Section C. His interests include hiking, backpacking, and trout fishing.

WILL FONTANEZ, Cartographic Coordinator, Geography Department, University of Tennessee, prepared the maps with assistance from David McElhannon, graduate student, and Brian Williams, undergraduate. Will is a national-level men's gymnastics official and enjoys outdoor activities and woodworking.

Tom Gatti, Carpenter, Kingsport, TN, contributed the "Pond Mountain Wilderness" part of Section B. His interests include the Sierra Club, recycling, volunteer work for a wildlife rehabilitation center, skiing, organic gardening, and wildflower gardening.

Russ Griffith, Retired CNF Recreation Staff Officer, Cleveland, TN, assembled information on trails, trailheads, and area boundaries for the maps.

Robert Harvey, Retired Radio/TV/Audio Engineer, Florissant, MO, coauthored the "Highlands of Roan Scenic Area and Overmountain National Historic Trail" part of Section B. His interests include Southern Appalachian Highlands Conservancy, Highlands of Roan trail maintenance and bald restoration, nature photography, and school computer-education programs.

Ray Hunt, Retired Chemical Engineer, Kingsport, TN, contributed the "Appalachian National Scenic Trail" part of Section B. He has served as Chairman of the Appalachian Trail Conference. His activities include the Tennessee Eastman Hiking Club, the Watauga Audubon Society, local historical restoration projects, Preston Hills Presbyterian Church, and the Kingsport Civitan Club.

Gary Hugh Irwin, Forest Ecologist, Knoxville, TN, contributed the "Vegetation" part of Section A, the "Sampson Mountain Wilderness and Primitive Area" part of Section B, and the "Citico Creek Wilderness, Joyce Kilmer-Slickrock Wilderness, and Haw Knob Primitive Area" part of Section C. He is Coordinator of Cherokee Forest Voices, a CNF citizen watchdog organization and has been a leader in forest management issues as a Sierra Club activist. His interests include photography, nature study, and hiking.

Roger A. Jenkins, Analytical Chemist, Knoxville, TN, contributed most of the photographs as well as the "Some Warnings and Advice" part of Section A and coauthored the "Highlands of Roan Scenic Area and Overmountain National Historic Trail" part of Section B. He has served as Chairman of the Sierra Club's TN Chapter and Harvey Broome Group and has been a leader on wilderness preservation issues. His activities include hiking, backpacking, photography, and downhill skiing.

MARTHA J. KETELLE, Environmental Professional, Deputy Forest Supervisor, Six Rivers National Forest, Eureka, CA, formerly of Knoxville, TN, contributed the "Doe River Gorge Scenic Area" part of Section B and coauthored the "Rogers Ridge Scenic Area and Primitive Area" and "Unaka Mountain Wilderness, Scenic Area, and Primitive Areas" parts of Section B. She has served as President of Tennessee Citizens for Wilderness Planning. Her activities include hiking, backpacking, cross-country skiing, and canoeing.

KIRK JOHNSON, Chattanooga, TN, authored the Conasauga River Corridor part and coauthored the "Big Frog Wilderness, Cohutta Wilderness (TN Portion), and West Big Frog Primitive Area" part of Section C. He has served as president of the Trout Unlimited Tennessee State Council and has been active on the Little Tennessee River and wildlife issues. His interests include hunting and fishing.

LANCE N. MCCOLD, Environmental Engineer, Knoxville, TN, contributed photographs as well as the "Wildlife" part of Section A. He has been a leader in wildlife issues. His interests include the Sierra Club, photography, hiking, and nature study.

DAN MACDONALD, Zoologist, Knoxville, TN, contributed the "Gee Creek Wilderness and Primitive Area" part of Section C and coauthored the "Big Frog Wilderness, Cohutta Wilderness, and West Big Frog Primitive Area" part of Section C. His interests include hiking and whitewater canoeing.

NOEL P. MCJUNKIN, Law Enforcement Ranger, Yosemite National Park, CA, coauthored the "Big Frog Mountain Wilderness, Cohutta Wilderness, and West Big Frog Primitive Area" part of Section C. His activities include backpacking, hiking, and bicycling.

DAVID MCPEAK, Accountant, Bristol, TN, coauthored the "Unaka Mountain Wilderness, Scenic Area, and Primitive Areas" part of Section B. His interests include hiking and nature study.

BARBARA J. MUHLBEIER, Attorney, Knoxville, TN, coauthored the "Coker Creek Scenic Area and Unicoi Mountain Trail" part of Section C. Her interests include backpacking, hiking, photography, and gardening.

DARROL NICKELS, Retired Chemist, Kingsport, TN, coauthored the "Big Laurel Branch Wilderness" part of Section B. His activities include AT design and maintenance and the Southern Appalachian Highlands Conservancy.

RAY PAYNE, Mechanical Engineer, Knoxville, TN, contributed the "Rough Ridge Primitive Area" and "Bald River Gorge Wilderness and Upper Bald River Primitive Areas" parts of Section C. He serves as Chairman of Great Smokies Wilderness Advocates and has been President of the Great Smoky Mountain Hiking Club and Chairman of the Sierra Club's Tennessee Chapter. He has been a leader on wilderness preservations issues. His interests include hiking, backpacking, and canoeing.

GEORGE G. RITTER, Businessman, Oak Ridge, TN, contributed the "Devil's Backbone Primitive Area" part of Section B. His interests include the Smoky Mountain Hiking Club, hiking, and backpacking.

WILLIAM H. SKELTON, Attorney, Knoxville, TN, contributed the "Political History" part of Section A and coauthored the "Rogers Ridge Scenic Area and Primitive Area," "Big Laurel Branch Wilderness," and "Highlands of Roan Scenic Area and Overmountain National Historic Trail" parts of Section B as well as the "Coker Creek Scenic Area and Unicoi Mountain Trail" part of Section C. He also contributed photographs and the otherwise unattributed portions. He served as Coordinator of the Cherokee National Forest Wilderness Coalition during the CNF wilderness campaigns and has been Chairman of the Sierra Club's Tennessee Chapter and Harvey Broome Group. He has served as Vice-Chairman of Tennessee Governor Lamar Alexander's Commission on Tennesseans Outdoors and as Chairman of the Knoxville Greenways and Community Trails Commission. His interests include backpacking, canoeing, running, mountaineering, and travel.

ARTHUR S. SMITH, Chemical Engineer, Kingsport, TN, contributed the "Beaverdam Creek Primitive Area" part of Section B. He has been President of the Audubon Society's Watauga Chapter and a leader in air and water pollution regulation. His interests include gardening, hiking, studying plants, and bird-watching.

MARY A. VAVRIK, Court Reporter, Knoxville, TN, coauthored the "Brushy Ridge Primitive Area" part of Section C. Her interests include hiking and backpacking.

KENNETH S. AND HELEN SCOTT WARREN, Retired Chemist (Kenneth) and Retired Information Analyst (Helen), Oak Ridge, TN, coauthored the "Nolichucky Primitive Area" part of Section B. Kenneth's activities include the Sierra Club's Harvey Broome Group and the Smoky Mountains Hiking Club. He has served for 25 years as Handbook Editor for the Smoky Mountains Hiking Club. Helen's activities include AT trail maintenance.

JAMES E. WEDEKIND, Geologist, Knoxville, TN, contributed the "Geology" part of Section A and the "Bald Ridge Mountain Scenic Area" part of Section B. His interests include the Sierra Club, hiking and backpacking, scuba diving, and brewing homemade beer.

JACYNE WOODCOX, Bank Trust Officer, Friendsville, TN, contributed the "John Muir National Recreation Trail" part of Section C. Her interests include hiking, recycling, Fort Loudon Lake cleanup, and photography.

OTHER CONTRIBUTORS. Although the individuals above were the principal contributors, others provided help with portions of Sections B and C, usually by hiking tails. These include Karen Young (Big Frog Wilderness), Kirk Johnson (Little Frog Wilderness), Arthur S. Smith (Rogers Ridge Scenic Area), Patricia Horton (Big Frog Wilderness), Rebecca Dotson (Coker Creek Scenic Area), Janice Irwin (Citico Creek Wilderness), Carolyn Hahs (Warrior's Passage Trail), Samantha and Kevin Pack (Rogers Ridge Scenic Area), Jacyne Woodcox (Coker Creek Scenic Area), and John Denton (Rogers Ridge Scenic Area).

Bibliography

Appalachian Trail Guide to Tennessee-North Carolina. 9th ed. Harpers Ferry, WV: Appalachian Trail Conference, 1989.

Brandt, Robert S. *Tennessee Hiking Guide.* Knoxville: Univ. of Tennessee Press, 1982.

Braun, E. Lucy. *Deciduous Forests of Eastern North America.* Philadelphia: Blakiston Co., 1950.

Brewer, Carson. *Just Over the Next Ridge.* Knoxville: Knoxville News-Sentinel Co., Inc., 1987.

Brown, Fred, and Nell Jones. *The Georgia Conservancy's Guide to the North Georgia Mountains.* 2nd ed. Rev. by Nel Jones and Thomas Perrie. Atlanta: Georgia Conservancy, 1991.

Bull, John, and John F. Farrand, Jr. *The Audubon Society Field Guide to North American Birds, Eastern Region.* New York: Alfred A. Knopf, 1977.

Cain, S. A. "The Tertiary Character of the Cove Hardwood Forests of the Great Smoky Mountains National Park." *Torrey Botanical Club Bulletin* 70: 213-35.

Campbell, Carlos, William F. Hutson, and Aaron J. Sharp. *Great Smoky Mountains Wildflowers.* 4th ed. Knoxville: Univ. of Tennessee Press, 1979.

Chew, V. Collins. *Underfoot: A Geologic Guide to the Appalachian Trail.* Washington, DC: Potomac Appalachian Trail Club, 1988.

Climbing Committee of the Mountaineers. *Mountaineering: the Freedom of the Hills.* 4th ed. Seattle: Mountaineers, 1982.

Collins, Henry Hill, Jr. *Harper & Row's Complete Field Guide to North American Wildlife, Eastern Edition.* New York: Harper & Row, 1981.

Cooper, John, et al. *Endangered and Threatened Plants and Animals of North Carolina.* Raleigh: North Carolina State Museum of Natural History, 1977.

Davis, M. B. "Pleistocene Biogeography of Temperate Deciduous Forests." *Geoscience and Man* 13 (1976): 13-26.

Davis, M. B. "Quaternary History of Deciduous Forests of Eastern North America and Europe." *Missouri Botanical Garden Annals* 70 (1983): 550-63.

de Hart, Allen. *North Carolina Hiking Trails*. 2nd ed. Boston: Appalachian Mountain Club Books, 1988.

Fletcher, Colin. *The Complete Walker, III*. New York: Alfred A. Knopf, 1984.

Forgey, William W., M.D. *Wilderness Medicine*. Pittsboro: Indiana Camp Supply Books, 1979.

Foster, Stephen, and James A. Duke. *A Field Guide to Medicinal Plants*. Boston: Houghton Mifflin Co., 1990.

Graham, A. "Origin and Evolution of the Biota of Southeastern North America: Evidence from the Fossil Plant Record." *Evolution* 18 (1964): 571-85.

Hart, John. *Walking Softly in the Wilderness*. Rev. ed. San Francisco: Sierra Club, 1984.

Homan, Tim. *Hiking Trails of Joyce Kilmer-Slickrock and Citico Creek Wilderness Areas*, Atlanta: Peachtree Publishers, Ltd., 1990.

———. *The Hiking Trails of North Georgia*. Atlanta: Peachtree Publishers, Ltd., 1980.

King, P. B., and A. Stupka. "The Great Smoky Mountains—Their Geology and Natural History." *Science Monthly* 71 (1950): 31-43.

Li, H. L. "Floristic Relationships Between Eastern Asia and Eastern North America." *Transactions of the American Philosophical Society* 42 (1952): 371-429.

Malter, Jeffrey Lowell. "The Flora of Citico Creek Wilderness Study Area, Cherokee National Forest, Monroe County, Tennessee." Master's thesis, Univ. of Tennessee, Knoxville, 1977.

Manning, Harvey. *Backpacking: One Step at a Time*. New York: Vintage Books, 1975.

Means, Evan. *Tennessee Trails*. 3rd ed. Chester, CT: Pequot Press, 1989.

Muir, John. *A Thousand Mile Walk to the Gulf*. Ed. William F. Bade. Boston: Houghton Mifflin Co., 1917.

Murray, Kenneth. *Highland Trails of Upper East Tennessee and Southwest Virginia*. Jonesborough: Upper East Tennessee Tourism Council, 1986.

Murrell, Zack Ernest. "The Vascular Flora of Big Frog Mountain, Polk County, Tennessee." Master's thesis, Univ. of Tennessee, Knoxville, 1985.

Niering, William H., and Nancy C. Olmstead. *The Audubon Society Field Guide to North American Wildflowers, Eastern Region.* New York: Alfred A. Knopf, 1979.

Peterson, Lee. *A Field Guide to Edible Wild Plants of Eastern and Central North America.* Boston: Houghton Mifflin Co., 1978.

Peterson, Roger Tory. *A Field Guide to the Birds.* 4th ed. Boston: Houghton Mifflin Co., 1980.

Price, Steve. *Wild Places of the South.* Charlotte, NC: East Woods Press, 1980.

Roberts, Harry. *Movin' On: Equipment and Techniques for Winter Hikers.* Boston: Stone Wall Press, Inc., 1977.

Stupka, Arthur. *Wildflowers in Color.* New York: Harper & Row, 1965.

Sulzer, Elmer G. *Ghost Railroads of Tennessee.* Indianapolis, IN: Vane A. Jones Co., 1975.

Sutton, Ann, and Myron Sutton. *Eastern Forests.* New York: Alfred A. Knopf, 1985.

Whitaker, John O., Jr. *The Audubon Society Field Guide to North American Mammals.* New York: Alfred A. Knopf, 1980.

Whittaker, R. H. "Vegetation of the Great Smoky Mountains." *Ecological Monographs* 26 (1956): 1-80.

Wilkerson, James A., M.D., ed. *Medicine for Mountaineering.* 3rd ed. Seattle: Mountaineers, 1985.

Wilson, Jennifer Bauer. *Roan Mountain: A Passage of Time.* Winston-Salem, NC, John F. Blair, 1991.

Wofford, Eugene B. *Sensitive Plants of the Cherokee National Forest.* US Dept. of Agriculture, Forest Service Southern Region, 1981.

―――. *Guide to the Vascular Plants of the Blue Ridge.* Athens: Univ. of Georgia Press, 1989.

Woods, Frank W., and R. E. Shanks. "Natural Replacement of Chestnut by Other Species in the Great Smoky Mountains National Park." *Ecology* 40 (1959): 349-61.

Index to Areas, Trailheads, and Trails

Trails

Wilderness Trails of Tennessee's Cherokee National Forest was designed by Kay Jursik and composed by Cynthia Wallace at the University of Tennessee Press on the Apple MacIntosh using Microsoft Word® and Aldus PageMaker®. Maps were created by the University of Tennessee Cartographic Laboratory under the supervision of Will Fontanez, using Aldus Freehand®. Linotronic camera pages were generated by AM/PM, Inc. The book is set in Palatino with Helvetica used for display and is printed on recycled 60-lb. Thor White. Manufactured in the United States of America by Braun-Brumfield, Inc.